★ MARINADES ★ RUBS ★ BRINES ★ CURES & GLAZES ★

MARINADES

RUBS, BRINES CURES & GLAZES

JIM TARANTINO

TEN SPEED PRESS
Berkeley | Toronto

Ten Speed Press
Box 7123
Berkeley, California 94707
www.tenspeed.com

Distributed in Australia by Simon and Schuster Australia, in Canada by Ten Speed Press Canada, in New Zealand by Southern Publishers Group, in South Africa by Real Books, and in the United Kingdom and Europe by Airlift Book Company.

Cover and text design by Ed Anderson / Skout

Library of Congress Cataloging-in-Publication Data
Tarantino, Jim.
  Marinades, brines, rubs, cures, and glazes / by Jim Tarantino.— Rev. and expanded.
      p. cm.
  Rev. ed. of: Marinades. Freedom, CA : Crossing Press, c1992.
  Includes bibliographical references and index.
  ISBN-13: 978-1-58008-614-1
  ISBN-10: 1-58008-614-4
 1. Marinades. I. Tarantino, Jim. Marinades. II. Title.
  TX819.M26T37 2006
  641.7—dc22

Printed in the United States of America
First printing this edition, 2006

1 2 3 4 5 6 7 8 9 10 — 10 09 08 07 06

CONTENTS

ACKNOWLEDGMENTS

To the folks mentioned below I'd like to say, "Well gang, we did it." I was far from playing solo with this work; I had the help of a great back up band.

First, I'd like to thank some very good friends of this book. The person I could throw a test recipe to over my shoulder and have him catch it every time is Peter Cravath. Peter is a well-seasoned serial griller who is detailed and relentless when it comes to cooking food over smoldering wood and coals. His recipe testing help was immense. Running the book's Ministry of Science was fellow eGulletier Jared Solomon. Jared was my first science source to bounce ideas and theories off of, and he'd return them to me in clean, clear layman's terms with a sense of humor. I'd also like to thank Diedre Watters, who did the first pass proofreading of the book. Diedre really helped to clean up Dodge and clear out some of the deadwood.

Every cookbook needs honest tasters, folks who won't simply say, "Well, it's different!" but will tell you why. My tasting crew this time around was Andy Haakenson, Carol Ann Brady, and Richard Newman. I'd also like to thank recipe contributors Barbara Boswell and Carl Doebley. And thank you to Graydon Wood for my catalog shot.

At Ten Speed Press I'd first like to thank Dennis Hayes, who's been around for both editions of this book and has never stopped supporting it. Next, I'd like to thank Aaron Wehner, who helped get the revision rolling. In acoustic jam sessions, we have a saying, "Tune it or die!" and the folks who fine-tuned the book were designer Ed Anderson, copyeditors Karen Levy and Andrea Chesman, proofreader Beverly McGuire, and indexer Ken DellaPenta. But most of all I'd like to thank my project editor, Brie Mazurek, for helping me pull the book together. She was an unflappable air traffic controller who brought the book down to earth and then corralled stray copy before the words stampeded out of control.

Last but not least, I'd like to thank my wonderful wife, Ellen, to whom this book is dedicated. Living with a cookbook author really means living with spillovers and late-night mood swings. It means eating four variations of glazed chicken (sometimes for breakfast) and living in partial isolation while the writing is going full blast. She worked as hard as I did on this project.

PREFACE TO THE NEW EDITION

In the last edition of *Marinades,* I took some mild pains to organize the recipes around food groups, but that's not the way I really cook. I don't do a month of fish, or a week of chicken wings. What mostly happens is that my wife or I spot something fresh in the market, haul it back to the house, and pull ingredients from the pantry to finish it off. Other times, I'll be out with my cronies for a Saturday lunch, and we'll be plotting and planning that night's dinner based on our cuisine mood swings, the fresh ingredients that we need to scramble for, and, most of all, what we have in our pantries.

The revised edition of *Marinades* is ingredient- and pantry-driven. Think of ingredients as flavor colors and the pantry as a palette. By stocking up on a series of ingredients you'll be able to rack up some great flavors no matter what comes in from the market that day. These pantry items range from the basics to signature ethnic ingredients from some of the world's greatest food pockets: the New World, the Mediterranean, and Asia. You'll see some overlap of spices and condiments, as well as similar recipe versions from across continents.

But reorganizing a book doesn't just revive or revise it. New recipes and techniques do. I've included new ideas, brines, cures, and glazes, plus a dusting of kitchen theory.

The musician in me likes to improvise, and I'm no different in the kitchen. There are times when I follow the recipe as a classical score, and other times I treat it as an old standard on which to improvise. What help my sense of improv are a little bit of music theory, some imagination, and lots of practice. The theory part calls on technique and knowledge as to how things fit together, the practice over time makes it intuitive, and the ingredient of imagination adds personality to make the piece unique. I know, and I have played with, some great musicians who couldn't read a quarter note if they tried. The same holds true for cooks without recipes. Some of the flavors that have blown me away have come from street food, barbecue pits, crawfish houses, clam bars, ethnic cafes, *taquerias,* neighborhood bars, and just plain old joints.

Knowing about food theory or kitchen science helps you understand how things work. Once you get a sense of the chemistry, you'll be able to intuitively substitute or scale up ingredients, troubleshoot recipes, and improvise.

Speaking of improvisation, I'm the last person in the world who would come to your door to confiscate this cookbook and cite you for recipe violations if you substitute an ingredient. In fact, I'm more likely to be guilty of aiding and abetting by wholeheartedly encouraging it. This book is really about ingredient ideas and encouraging you to have lots of imagination on your own.

Cooking with modern tastes for modern times is a combination of traditions and creative improvisations. A single dinner can have many complementary flavors and courses that cross oceans and timelines. Take a cut of fish or chicken or beef and either cure it, rub it, soak it in brine, or marinate it; add the ingredient of smoke; and you are linked to other centuries and cuisines.

INTRO

Marinades, brines, rubs, and cures started out as survival food. The majority of these began as food preservation techniques to keep populations alive, and then the flavorings came in.

The composition of early marinades was mostly determined by a country's climate. The farther north of the equator you go, the fattier the meat and the oilier the seafood, due to cold winters and cooler waters. In these regions, marinades have a higher ratio of acid in order to cut the richness of the meat or fish. The closer to the equator you go, the leaner the meat, and the marinade's ingredient ratio is reversed. Marinades and rubs in the tropical regions tend to be spicier. But there are exceptions. Anyone familiar with Korean cuisine will tell you that some of their recipes are among the "hottest."

Weather is probably the real reason that salting and smoking foods developed. Seasonal harvests and hunted migratory animals had to last through long winter months. On the other hand, countries closer to the equator could simply leave fish, meat, and vegetables out in the sun with a sprinkle of salt and let nature finish the preservation process.

In the British Isles, meat and fish were hung from rafters in "black" houses, so named for the black patina of smoke on the sides of the walls. The Scottish and Irish then settled into the mountains of the American South, bringing their music and their technique of curing, which evolved into hanging pork from the rafters and smoking it with hickory laced with a little old-time fiddle music and ballads. Native Americans devised drying sheds and racks to hold salmon over low, smoldering coals to transform it into a type of jerky that some settlers called squaw candy and, of course, their own form of jerky called pemmican.

Prerefrigeration recipes invaded Europe from every conceivable source. As populations migrated, they carried their food along with them. And that food had to be cured, brined, or marinated in order for it to travel well. The Mongol hordes gave northern and central Europeans their first taste of Chinese take-out food when they traveled with packed crocks of marinated cabbage. This spicy pickled cabbage soon evolved into sauerkraut. The Vikings, as they toured North America, noticed that herring traveled and smelled better when pickled. They adapted the Mongolian cabbage technique and applied it to herring.

Spicy brines arrived via the trade routes of the Middle East. Citrus marinades (known as escabèche) came up from the Moors in North Africa and entered Spanish cuisine. Those marinades later traveled with the Spanish to the Caribbean and were used by African slaves to create a dish known as escovitch fish.

When Christopher Columbus started his transatlantic cruises, eating was changed forever on both sides of the ocean. Spain got some chiles and, in turn, left the New World with citrus. Spanish missionaries planted citrus groves in Florida, California, and Mexico. We now have citrus juices and hot chiles in Spanish-themed marinated tapas and seviche in the Yucatán Peninsula.

In Asia, each country has its own distinctly flavored marinades and spice mixtures. Garam masala and curry powders are flavoring elements in Indian and Malaysian cuisines. Thai marinades and spices play off the sour flavors of lemongrass and lime, the heat of chiles, and the sweet, balancing action of coconut and molasses. The Chinese use spicy condiments in the south and milder marinades in the north, though there are pockets of spice in the northern provinces of Hunan and Szechuan, and subtle spice blends appear in some southern regions. The Japanese have a style of flavoring all their own, using simple ingredients with a Zenlike balance.

Today's brines, cures, marinades, rubs, and glazes combine cultures and cuisines in a culinary cross-pollination of flavors and seasonings. East-West marinades of Asian spices are combined with American chiles, Mediterranean olive oils, and Middle Eastern spice blends in a new wave that redefines how we create and think about flavor.

This new edition is a composite of traditional techniques, international ingredient blends, and playful improvisation, guaranteed to make full-flavored music for your palate.

TOOLS
& TECHNIQUES

In this section, we'll be looking at recipe techniques that will be used throughout the book to create marinades, brines, rubs, cures, and glazes. I'll identify how each technique works and provide tips on how to use it to get the most flavor. Since food is often cured or brined first and then glazed, rubbed, or marinated, cures and brines seem like a logical place to start. And since both have salt-driven chemistry, it makes sense to discuss them together.

CURES AND BRINES

Saltwater currents. That's what brines and cures are really all about: the movement of water into meat and seafood by way of a brine, and the drawing out of water by way of a cure. Which came first? I'm betting the farm on cures.

Cures are prerefrigerated food preparation at its earliest. The technique has remained almost unchanged since the dawn of food preservation. Simply put, salt draws out moisture from food that would support bacteria, and air-drying keeps meat or fish from deteriorating. The ancient Egyptians were among the first to use salt to preserve meat, fish, and some of their relatives (by way of mummification).

The Chinese were using cures to preserve fish as earlier 2000 B.C.E. Somewhere down the line, the Celts developed a specialization in curing and trading hams. They introduced salt-cured meats to the Romans, who then developed a taste for cured meats and sausages. No doubt those recipes were keepers. All you need to do is visit an Italian market for soppressata, prosciutto, and pancetta and taste the recipes that have stood the test of time.

Gravlax first appeared in Scandinavia during the Middle Ages. I would like to think that Hamlet may have eaten it, and I can just imagine him holding a lox-laden bagel in lieu of that skull. If there were any fish recipe that has galvanized more nations, it would have to be salt cod. It brought settlers to the New World, it is used in the Mediterranean, and it still shows up in Caribbean and Latin recipes.

Salt containing nitrates was used back in Homer's time (850 B.C.E.) to preserve meat. Nitrate was present originally as a natural impurity in the salts used in curing and, unknown to users at the time, was a key ingredient in the curing process. The Romans were the first to note the reddening effect. Mined sodium nitrate contains nitrite, and the reduction of nitrite to nitric oxide reacts with myoglobin (muscle pigment) to give the cured flavor and reddish-pink color of cured ham. There is also an antiseptic upside: nitrite directly inhibits the growth of *Clostridium botulinum,* a deadly microorganism that produces toxins resulting in botulism.

Duck meat has a higher content of myoglobin; it is often considered a "dark meat" rather than a "white meat." Duck can take advantage of nitrate or nitrite during the curing process to improve its color. I did not use nitrates in the Orange Duck Pastrami (page 107), and the duck ended up turning a rosy color when first sliced and then went to "cooked" gray. But it tasted phenomenal.

The main difference between curing and brining is that a cure will draw moisture out at the start. With brine, water goes both ways. The leftover mixture of water and salt after the curing process with fish is actually referred to as brine. In fact, I've heard brines referred to as "wet" cures.

CURES! REMEDIES! RECIPES!

Outrageous claims? Well, not exactly. When the word *recipe* first appeared in the English language during the fifteenth century, it referred to making medicines and prescriptions. It wasn't until the eighteenth century that it was also used to describe instructions for food preparation. Before that, the operative food word was "receipt," from the Latin *recipere.* Its abbreviation we've now come to know as Rx.

The basic chemistry behind salt-curing meat for long-term preservation is very similar to that of making jam or pickles. What you are trying to do is lock in or remove the water in meat using salt or sugar. Any time you reduce the amount of water that isn't dissolving something, you reduce the amount of bacteria that can live in it. Salt, when dissolved, does this well, but it can overpower the flavor of the food. Sugar (sucrose) in cured meat adds flavor, and it balances the taste of salt. It also creates the surface color of aged ham if caramelized sugar is used.

Using "designer" salts in curing and brining is an expensive waste of money. Sprinkling sea salt and specialty salts on food so that their texture makes a difference is a good thing. But putting them into a dish where the crystal structure dissolves is useless.

Another component entering the curing fray is smoke. Native Americans preserved meat by hanging it at the top of a tepee to maximize its contact with campfire smoke. In Europe and Britain during the Middle Ages, smoked and salted foods held people through the lean times of late winter and early spring. Without refrigeration, freshly caught fish couldn't be carried any distance unless it was preserved with salt and, in some cases, smoke.

Smoking food really comes down to two different methods: smoking for preserving and smoking for flavor. Smoking for preserving is still done today in Third World countries lacking refrigeration. The results of smoking for flavor can be found in any deli, butcher shop, or barbecue pit. The prime ingredient, wood smoke, is made up of millions of microscopic particles that rise like a fog, and vapors. The fog is mostly water, carbon, and trace solids. The vapor contains ash and volatile oils that are released from the wood to give its characteristic flavors and preservative qualities. The ash is loaded with potassium and sodium nitrates.

Unlike curing, which pulls water out of food, the water traffic in the brining process flows two ways—into the meat and eventually out of it, taking some more moisture along. As the osmotic action begins, water follows the salt into the meat. The principle is this: when two different solutions of dissolved substances are separated by a porous cell membrane, the water travels toward the solution that is denser (i.e., contains more dissolved substances). Even though a brine can have concentrated levels of salt and sugar, it's less concentrated than the water within a cell wall. Therefore, water from the brine flows into the cells within the meat.

A typical brine can have 3 to 5 percent salt and sometimes 3 to 4 percent sugar. Throw in some spices and flavorings, some of which are insoluble (such as hard spices and peppercorns), and you may have roughly 8 to 9 percent density. Meat is made up of about 60 to 70 percent water, along with protein and fat. After soaking meat in brine for a while, the water solutions reach a point of equilibrium; at that point, water tends to reverse its direction and is pulled out of the meat, as in the koshering process, thus equalizing the water concentration on both sides of the cell membranes. This usually happens over a three- or four-day period, or with brines that have such a high salt content that they are actually wet cures.

The juiciness created with brines has less to do with unraveling the collagen (or muscle fibers) or trapping water in the cells, and more to do with denaturing the proteins in the meat. The brining process turns collagen soluble or juicy, rather than coagulating the collagen while cooking.

Heat also denatures protein. When you're cooking meat, muscle does not become soluble in the same way that long cooking times or moderate-high temperatures turn collagen into gelatin. A grilled steak or a long-cooked brisket will hold its general shape with the muscle fibers still intact as you slice across the grain. However, if you increase the salt content, you can get some of the actomyosin (the proteins in muscle tissue) to dissolve when you apply heat. The texture changes are more obvious when the meat cools. A brined turkey breast that has been roasted and cooled can be put on a meat slicer and yield clean, even slices, while an unbrined turkey breast may be more fibrous and may splinter in sections. The collagen stays moist during cooking; when cooled, it congeals around a now spongy actomyosin and forms a dense, springy piece of meat. It's the difference between a deli-turkey slice and the day-after-Thanksgiving snack from an unbrined bird.

Why do certain cuts of meat that weigh the same take longer to brine than others? For brining times, there are a few things one needs to consider. The first is thickness and size. It will take longer to brine a 3- to 4-pound whole turkey breast than it to brine 3 to 4 pounds of turkey meat cut into small, 1-inch pieces for kabobs. Also, the direction of the grain has some bearing. Think of it in the context of wood. A pork tenderloin's grain runs along its length, with the exposed grain on the ends, a lot a like a log of wood. A center-cut pork chop is like a cross section of a tree trunk, with greater areas of grain exposed. With wood, exposed grain absorbs more stain because the direction of the wood fibers makes it more porous. The same principle holds true for the direction of muscle fibers of meat when absorbing anything from a brine to a marinade.

Muscle tissue is shot through with various kinds of vascular passages, or fluid transport systems. If you have whole muscle, especially with skin, such as a turkey drumstick, you have a lot less access to this network, which carries the brine through the tissue. Therefore, a skinless chicken breast, though larger than a drumstick with skin, will brine or marinade much faster.

Brining is more of a white meat's pastime. Most red meats with a high fatty content, such as beef, lamb, and duck, do not lend themselves to a long, slow soak at the brining spa. Brisket is one of the exceptions when it is brined for corned beef or pastrami, but I wouldn't recommend brining it and then flipping it into the smoker. My favorite bird and animal parts for brining include chicken breasts, turkey breasts, Cornish hens, pork tenderloin, pork chops, and baby back or spare ribs.

BRINING CONTAINERS

The containers you use for brining need to be clean, food-friendly, and nonreactive, such as turkey roasting bags, 1- or 2-quart resealable plastic bags, or stainless steel stockpots. Restaurant supply houses are great sources for cooks who need even larger brining containers.

Any food-grade HDPE (high-density polyethylene), polypropylene, or polycarbonate container is appropriate for brining. These hard plastic materials can withstand the salts that are used in brines. Think pickles, barbecue sauce, soy sauce, chocolate syrup, puddings, pie fillings, and shortening—all these things come in food-grade plastic buckets, and you can usually get them free from restaurants, caterers, and bakeries. I especially like the glass 1-gallon deli pickle jars for brining a couple of pork loins or a batch of chicken breasts. Ice chests of various sizes can handle large turkeys.

Avoid soft porous plastic containers like plastic garbage cans or pails, mop buckets, plastic garbage bags, or any food-grade container that has been used to store nonfood items such as paint or detergent.

Now comes the problem of where to put a restaurant-size bucket holding a turkey and its brine for a Thanksgiving dinner, a tailgating party, or an outdoor festival featuring deep-fried turkey. **The Ice Cream Method: Chilling large brining containers.** I got this idea from the old-fashioned way of making ice cream using ice and rock salt. You can lower a covered brining container into a clean plastic trash can that's large enough to give you 3 to 4 inches around

the sides. Fill the trash can with ice and/or plastic "blue" cooling bricks approximate halfway up the brining container. Add some coarse-grain salt and a little bit of water and you have refrigeration. The water level should be roughly the same as that in the brining container. You need to maintain the temperature around 38° to 40°F, so a thermometer comes in very handy. If the brine becomes too cold, lose some ice and add some water, and vice versa if the temperature begins to rise.

BRINING TIPS

Cool it! Don't put a couple of gallons of off-the-stove hot brine directly into the fridge. You don't want to raise the temperature inside the refrigerator, or cause it to work too hard to stabilize the temperature to where it should be. You DO need to cool down the brine before you put it in the refrigerator.

Avoid flavor-enhanced meats. In most cases, they have been prebrined and you'll only be oversalting.

The brine and brinee (meat or bird) need to be the same temperature, and that's cold! The temperature should be between 38° and 40°F. At a lower temperature, you get less infusion and flavor. At a higher temperature, you get a saltier end result.

The brine needs to cover the meat completely. If you're brining in a 1- or 2-quart plastic resealable bag, place the bag in a mixing bowl to give it support. Bowls from electric mixers are perfect for this sort of thing. If you're brining in a solid container, the brine should cover the meat by 2 or 3 inches. Place a heavy plate or a brick wrapped in a resealable plastic bag on top to keep the food submerged, so it won't bob to the surface.

CALCULATING YOUR BRINE

This is an easy way to figure out how much brine you need for anything from 3 pounds of chicken breasts to a 24-pound Thanksgiving turkey. Place the meat into your brining container and cover it with cold water. Remove the food from the brining container and measure the remaining liquid.

The chart below will give you an idea of the ratio of salt to liquid that you will need to make the brine. Your sweeteners can be matched equally to the weight of the salt, and you can scale up your ingredients accordingly. Because the brine will be boiled to dissolve the salt and sweeteners, it will also kill any residue bacteria left behind in the liquid.

Water	Diamond Crystal kosher salt (4.8 oz per cup)	Morton kosher salt (8 oz per cup)	Table salt (10 oz per cup)	Sweeteners
2 quarts	½ cup	⅓ cup	¼ cup	½ cup
1 gallon	1 cup	¾ cup	½ cup	1 cup
2 gallons	2 cups	1½ cups	1 cup	2 cups
3 gallons	3 cups	2¼ cups	1½ cups	3 cups
5 gallons	5 cups	3¾ cups	2½ cups	5 cups

BRINING BRICKS

Waiting for a large volume of brine to cool down before adding food can take almost long as brining the food itself. Making full-volume brines ahead is fine if you happen to have a walk-in freezer or refrigerator with lots of space, but most of us don't. For those of you who need to have their brines chill out in a hurry, here is a good alternative. Make your salt/sugar solutions and flavorings in 1-quart quantities, place them in 2-quart or 1-gallon resealable plastic bags, and freeze them.

Salt and sugar in liquid act as culinary antifreeze, and you really need a temperature of 0°F to solidify 1 cup of salt in 1 quart of water. To compound that, sugar in brine will lower the freezing temperature, just as sugar syrup lowers the freezing temperature of sorbet. The result is a bag of slush. But that bag can lower the temperature of a brine in minutes.

Making brine is really about dissolving salt and sugar in water, and brewing your flavorings. Dispersion is done at the same time. You can brew first and disperse later using a large wooden spoon to stir things up. It's as simple as that, once you understand the math.

Most of the brining solutions hover around ¾ to 1 cup kosher salt and roughly the same amount of sugar, maple syrup, or honey per 1 gallon of brine. I use Diamond Crystal kosher salt in my brines, and it weights about 4.8 ounces per cup. This gives my brine 4 percent salinity per gallon. If one were to follow the math, that would be 2.4 ounces, or ½ cup, of Diamond Crystal kosher salt for a 2-quart solution.

Make your brining concentrates in 1-quart batches using 1 cup Diamond Crystal kosher salt, or ¾ cup Morton salt, plus 1 cup of sweetener and the brewing, or flavoring, ingredients. Bring the liquid to a boil, stirring to dissolve the sugar and salt, and brew the ingredients for 30 minutes to bring out the flavor. Top the brine off with cold water in the event there is some evaporation. This will give your solution about a 30 percent salinity. (You could float in this solution if you made enough.) Place the solution in a 2-quart resealable plastic bag and place the bag in an 8 by 8-inch glass baking dish. The dish, instead of the floor of your freezer, will catch any accidental runoff.

The ratios are not an even 4 to 1, that is, the concentrate may have sugar and other flavorings in it, and so I use the following concentrate-to-volume ratios:

- 2 quarts liquid volume to 1 cup brining concentrate
- 1 gallon liquid volume to 2 cups brining concentrate
- 2 gallons liquid volume to 1 quart brining concentrate
- 3 gallons liquid volume to 1½ quarts brining concentrate
- 5 gallons liquid volume to 2½ quarts brining concentrate

Start with cold water, then add the concentrate and stir. This technique comes in particularly handy for brining large cuts of meat and whole turkeys.

FLAVOR AMPLIFIERS FOR BRINES

You can get a lot of juiciness from the three "neutral" flavors of water, salt, and sugar, and it's really all you need for a simple brine. Let's think about some flavoring possibilities and see what works in the mix.

Salt substitutes: The flavor of sea or "boutique" salts, which are much more expensive than the other three salts mentioned above, gets lost in the mix. It's better to taste it on your food than in a brine. If you want to add soy, teriyaki, ponzu, or Asian fish sauce, you'll need to reduce the salt level proportionally.

Water substitutes: For water, you can substitute apple cider, which already has a sugar content, so in that case you'll need to reduce the sweetener as well. Watch the amount of citrus juice in a brine. Citrus juices have an acidic content, and you'll be kicking off a marinating reaction. You're much better off getting your citrus flavor from the zest. For additional liquid flavor, add ¼ to ⅓ cup bourbon, cognac, fruit brandy, or Calvados per ½ gallon of brine. Avoid red wine because of the color and acidic content. I've seen recipes that use buttermilk for brining whole turkeys and large cuts of lamb. Technically, that's a combination of a marinating process and a brine. It's good, though, should you want to try it. Make a concentrate of salt, sugar, and your choice of spices in about 2 cups of water, cool it down, and then add it to 2 quarts of buttermilk.

Sugar substitutes: For granulated sugar, you can substitute ½ cup maple syrup or honey; for brown sugar, you can substitute ¼ cup molasses, golden syrup, or cane (Steens) syrup.

Other ingredients: For additional flavor, you can add to 2 quarts of liquid ¼ to ⅓ cup cracked black or white peppercorns; coriander seeds; Spanish or sweet paprika; grated fresh ginger; chopped fresh herbs, such as rosemary or tarragon; minced garlic; juniper berries; mustard seeds; Old Bay or Tony Chachere's brand seasoning; or any of the rub recipes throughout the book. Additional options include 1 to 2 tablespoons curry powder, garam masala, dried oregano, garlic or onion powder, thyme, star anise, hot pepper flakes, chipotle powder, Szechuan peppercorns, vanilla extract, wasabi paste, Worcestershire sauce, or hot sauce. You can also add a chopped stalk of lemongrass or 3 to 4 bay leaves or kaffir lime leaves.

When you're adding fresh or dry ingredients to any brine, remember that the brine needs to brew for at least 30 minutes for the ingredients to meld. Certain dry ingredients, such as turmeric, will color the meat. I would not exceed ½ cup of any combination of dry or fresh ingredients per 2-quart batch if you still want the flavor integrity of the meat to come through. For added flavor, spices should be lightly toasted, and peppercorns and round seeds should be cracked, not whole.

MARINADES

Marinades are simply an emulsion of acids, oils, and aromatics. Marinating creates a chemical reaction and a flavoring process. As acid denatures and, in some cases, dries food, you get the feel of moisture by way of the oil, with a collection of aromatics tagging along for the ride.

The word *marinade* derives from the Latin or Italian *marinara,* which means "of the sea." In Spain, the word *marimar* means pickling in brine, sometimes with an additional acid, such as vinegar, citrus juice, or wine. In Roman times, salted fish was packed in barrels for long voyages. I have to think that a barrel full of salted fish, along with its runoff of water and fish oil, would start to smell rather ripe after a while. Eventually, the mix was replenished with fresh seawater and seasoned with spices and peppercorns from African and Indian ports of call. The concoction of salt water, oil, and spices laid the foundation for something we now called a marinade.

Some of those brines, with the help of salt, seawater, and sun, fermented into a pungent fish sauce called *garum,* which was used as a condiment in Roman cooking. There's a theory that the Romans exported it to India. Then, in the nineteenth century, the British brought it back to England, thinking they found something new, and called it Worcestershire sauce.

Marinades, as we know them, evolved from two traditional techniques for preserving food: brining and pickling. When the key preserving element in the solution is salt, you have the makings of a brine; when the acidic content is high, you have a pickling solution. A marinade pulls certain ingredients from both of these preservation techniques, with the added ingredient of oil.

HOW MARINADES WORK (AND HOW THEY DON'T)

Marinades do not tenderize food, but trauma does. The acidic content from citrus, wine, or vinegar in a marinade softens, or denatures, the surface tissue of food by modifying its molecular structure. The word *tender* carries the connotation of being warm, caring, and sensitive; tenderizing is anything but. Tenderizing is about controlled food damage, and it can happen in food when muscle tissue is separated, torn, or bruised—as when one pounds a chicken breast or a veal scallop with a kitchen mallet. But in spite of the beating, the chemical or molecular structure stays the same; the meat is still raw.

Denaturing does not mean that the same textural chemical change happens to all proteins. There are a number of different ways it can happen. Cooking a piece of chicken changes it from a raw food to a cooked food. It creates a molecular change, but one that is different from that created by a marinade.

The acid in a marinade attacks the collagen on the surface of meat and unravels the normally twisted braids into less convoluted shapes, and these shapes are responsible for most of the physical and chemical cell properties. Air-drying a ham or sausage with a salt cure will have a similar effect by kicking off a fermentation process. Jerky making will do it through the forced evaporation of moisture during the drying process. In all cases, the proteins have changed their textures or lost their original natures. They have been denatured. But they haven't been cooked.

Lemon juice, lime juice, vinegar, and wine aren't the only ingredients in a marinade that can create that effect. Other players include enzymes found in certain fruits and root vegetables. These include pineapple and green papaya, which contain an enzyme called papain that breaks down protein. Kiwi contains a similar enzyme, but not in as strong a concentration. Fresh ginger, when juiced, is pretty hot stuff and is another activator. Some Iranian and Indian recipes mix minced lamb meat with raw onion paste, and then leave it to "marinate" for some hours. The ratio of raw onion to meat is critical. Turkish recipes also use raw onion juice in a similar way in a marinade.

Yogurt and buttermilk are a third set of marinade activators, and they are the most powerful. It's not the lactic acid in yogurt and buttermilk that causes meat muscle to soften; it's the digestive qualities of user-friendly bacteria called lactobacillus. Lactobacillus is found in fermented milk products, the strongest being yogurt and then buttermilk. Marinades using this third group tend to make food moister when cooked.

Marinades do not penetrate deeply into muscle tissue. At best, a marinade will penetrate ⅛ to ¼ inch deep. When a marinade hits the surface of meat or poultry, the muscle tissue unravels and expands; in some cases, this stops penetration. Meat can also be made too soft on the exposed surface, with less effect in the interior.

Marinades do not have an antiseptic effect on food because they lack the acid concentration of pickling. The acid in a marinade may kill certain strands of bacteria over a long period of time—maybe several hours or up to a couple of days. But don't roll the dice on this. The acid won't kill all bacteria, including salmonella.

Oil in a marinade thickens the marinade and keeps the flavoring ingredients well distributed. Marinades have a high ratio of water (citrus juice, wine, vinegar, fruit juice, and so on) to oil. Oil and water are insoluble; they can coexist, but they can't become one. Oil, besides adding flavor, acts as a binder and a buffer. A marinade fully blended would look like an aquarium under a microscope, with small floating globules of oil attached to particles of spices, herbs, and other aromatics.

With just citrus juice, wine, or vinegar, and with some herbs and spices blended in, a marinade will actually start a seviche-like process and eventually begin drying your food (but not curing it). Oil from a marinade sits on the surface, collecting aromatics and then adhering to the meat as the acid softens it. The flavor buffer zone of oil and aromatics also slows the penetration of acid. However, you don't need to worry about the fat content from oil piling on the calories; very little actually goes along for the ride to the grill, unless you're basting with it.

Temperature is a deciding factor on how quickly a food will absorb flavors from a marinade. Cold temperatures tighten up muscle tissue a bit. This explains why marinating at room temperature is faster (but riskier) than marinating in the refrigerator. When marinating on a counter in a warm kitchen, you run the risk of food spoilage and bacteria growth, even when the food is submerged in the marinade. Take your time and marinate it in the fridge, then let it come to room temperature in the marinade before cooking.

The tighter the tissue of a food, the longer the marinating time. Fish, with its loose, soft tissue, absorbs a marinade faster than can a beef brisket, which is generally considered a tough or dense cut of meat.

Don't leave food in a marinade beyond its recommended time. Over-marinated food cooks unevenly. You can tell when food is over-marinated just by looking. Fish will become slightly opaque—salmon turns a light pink, and tuna turns a light gray—just as any fish in a seviche turns opaque. Chicken breasts or pork tenderloins will turn white, and beef will turn light gray. When that happens, pat the food dry and strain out the marinade's solids. Rub the solids lightly onto the food surface, wrap in plastic wrap, and refrigerate until you're ready to cook.

The degree to which food is covered also influences a marinade's effectiveness. The greater the coverage, the faster the marinating process, because liquid is a much more significant aromatic medium than air is. However, marinating a large cut of meat requires quite a bit of marinade. For this reason, I recommend marinating in a tightly sealed plastic bag with the air squeezed out. This also reduces the amount of marinade needed.

HOW HOT IS YOUR MARINADE? A PH SCALE OF MARINATING INGREDIENTS

To give you an idea of how hot is hot, this is a list of typical ingredients found in marinades, glazes, and brines. I've listed some other items to put them in context. To understand the scale, you have to count backward to figure out the pH level. The lower the number on the scale, the higher the acidity. Many of the pH readings are separated by a few decimal points, but that's a lot. The acidity increases exponentially by a factor of 10 with each step, as you can see in the second column. Even within the groups, a few decimal points can mean a lot of acid. So if you thought that you could substitute a few tablespoons of vinegar for white wine, get out your calculator—it's not an even exchange.

	Comparative Strength	pH	Ingredients
High Acidity	10,000,000	0	Battery acid
	1,000,000	1	Stomach acid
	100,000	2	Lemons, limes, cider vinegar, hot sauce, pomegranate juice
	10,000	3	Grapefruit juice, orange juice, wine, balsamic vinegar, rice wine vinegar, fruit and herbal vinegars, pineapple, sherry, tangerines, tomatillos, blackberries, raspberries, ketchup
	1,000	4	Tomatoes, beer, honey, soy sauce, yogurt, buttermilk, chile peppers (hot), Dijon-style mustard, Worcestershire sauce, Asian fish sauce, honey, some cured sausages
	100	5	Chile peppers (mild), brown mustard, molasses, maple syrup, sweet bell peppers, red and white onions, ginger, most fresh herbs, ham
	10	6	Capers, anchovies, coconut milk, green onions, milk, mustard, mango, papaya, tamarind, fresh poultry, beef, lamb, pork
Neutral	0	7	Pure water
	–10	8	Salt water, brines
	–100	9	Baking soda
	–1,000	10	Detergent
	–10,000	11	Household ammonia
	–100,000	12	Soapy water
	–1,000,000	13	Bleach
High Alkalinity	–10,000,000	14	Liquid drain cleaner

MAKING MARINADES

Making marinades is easy; you can assemble most marinade recipes in a few minutes. But the order and the methods by which you combine ingredients are important. What you want is a stable marinade that has an equal distribution of oil, acid, and aromatics. When making a marinade, you have to deal with two elements: an oil and an acidic liquid, which can be wine, vinegar, citrus juice, or fruit juice, whose primary component is actually water. As everyone knows, oil and water do not mix—oil floats on water. If your marinade is not emulsified, patches of oil will coat your food, along with acidic and aromatic elements floating around in it. Here's how to bring the two elements together.

Whisking the oil, a little bit at a time, into the acidic liquid breaks down the oil into tiny droplets that will remain suspended, or emulsified. Shaking a marinade will produce a similar effect, because the agitation between the two liquids also works to emulsify the marinade. A blender is preferable over a food processor because a food processor tends to throw ingredients outward to the sides. A blender has gravity working for it, because the ingredients are propelled upward and then fall back down onto the blades.

An emulsified marinade will not be thick like mayonnaise; it will be a cloudy, not clear, liquid. The emulsion of a marinade is temporary. When the oil content of the marinade is less than 20 percent, the emulsion can break down in a matter of hours. Should you make a marinade for use the following day, store it in a glass jar that you can shake. Because the exteriors of meat and poultry contain some fat and surface oils, which act as emulsifying agents, and because a refrigerator's cold temperature can increase an oil's viscosity, there's really not much risk of a marinade breaking down while it is soaking flavor into your next meal.

EQUIPMENT

When it comes to equipment, I can count on a single hand the number of necessary pieces you need to start marinating. What is imperative is that every surface a marinade comes into contact with must be clean and made from a nonreactive material. That is, no aluminum foil, pots, utensils, or containers. Aluminum baking dishes will interact with the marinade's acid, and you'll have acid interaction instead of flavor penetration.

The single appliance that I would have a hard time parting with is a blender. A blender can grind spices; chop shallots, garlic, and ginger; and emulsify the oil in marinades in just one pass. You also need an inexpensive grater or a rasper for grating citrus zest and ginger, a glass or wooden reamer for juicing citrus, and measuring spoons and cups. Rummage through your cabinets and see what's around.

CONTAINERS

Traditionally, marinating containers were earthen crocks that would sit covered in a root cellar. Today, we have to rely on our refrigerators and other forms of containers. Think glass or ceramics as marinating containers. Pyrex baking dishes are perfect for marinating cuts of food that are no more than 1 inch thick. Deep ceramic bakeware and mixing bowls work as well, but with a note of caution. Handmade painted ceramics, be they from your local potter or from your last trip to Mexico, may contain lead-based paints or glazes. As pretty as they are, I wouldn't recommend serving acid-based food in them, let alone marinating something in one for several hours. The plain old garden-variety ceramic mixing bowls found at your local hardware store will work just fine. Terracotta containers are too porous to be used for marinating. Earthy as they look, they absorb flavors, odors, and food colors like a sponge. Above all, make sure that the containers you use are free of cracks and chips, because these are breeding spots for bacteria.

Overall, my first preference for marinating containers is a 1-gallon resealable plastic bag, which can hold up to 1 pound of food and 2 to 3 cups of marinade. You can recycle the bags by washing them in warm water and detergent. For bigger cuts of meat, such as briskets, roasts, and whole turkey breasts, my containers of choice are large plastic oven-roasting bags. Marinating overnight in a plastic roasting bag is fine, but because citric acid can interact with plastic during longer stays in the fridge, stick with glass or non-aluminum containers.

SAFETY ISSUES

My best advice is keep it clean. Every area or surface that comes into contact with your marinade must be kept clean. Remember, you're wrapping food with these ingredients. Every cutting surface, knife, blender, jar, container, basting brush—everything—needs to be washed between tasks. Citric acid or vinegar won't kill all bacteria; cleaning will. It also makes sense on more than one level to keep your grill clean. On that surface you have charred food material sometimes hiding a bit of rust. A grill surface should be as clean as a good set of pots. Would you eat at a restaurant that washed its pots only on a weekly basis?

Another important safety issue concerns reusing marinades. When marinating raw meat, especially chicken or turkey, some blood will naturally seep into the marinade, so there is a risk of salmonella bacteria getting into the marinade. Another reason not to reuse a marinade is that herbs and spices will usually adhere to meat en route to the grill or skillet, thus thinning out a good deal of the marinade's aromatic content. Finally, the alkalis present in some ingredients, such as peppercorns, will break down the acids found in wine, vinegar, and citrus juice, and will cause them to lose some of their bite.

BASTES, MOPS, AND SOPS

Okay, so you're ready to grill, but look at all that leftover marinade! It would be a shame to let it go to waste. Well, before you go for the brushes and mini mops, there are a few things to keep in mind.

First, heat the marinade. Cook it for about 5 minutes in a microwave on high or bring it to a rolling boil for 3 minutes on the stove. You want it hot enough to kill off any remaining bacteria and avoid a fire-hose effect; that is, a cold liquid on a hot surface. If you want to baste with your leftover marinade, remember that oil is fuel. In the case of a hot grill, where there's fuel there's smoke, and where there's smoke there's flare-up. I brush grilling food judiciously by hitting only one surface at a time. Allow some time for the marinade to evaporate before you flip and baste again. But there are other ways to work around this, if you plan ahead.

Converting a marinade recipe into a mop or a sop is easy, and it's more about knowing what to leave out than what to put in. The first ingredient to eliminate should be oil. Aside from the flare-up issue, a mop needs to be thinner than an emulsified marinade. After you blend your ingredients, strain the marinade so that what you have left is only liquid without the solids. Next, you may want to cut the marinade with water, fruit juice, beer, wine, or vinegar. What works for me is a two-to-one ratio of additional liquid to marinade. A mop isn't just another type of baste; it's a thin, watery solution that drips over meat, adding moisture to combat the drying effect of an open fire.

Another approach to making a mop is to hit on a rub. Adding a few tablespoons of a rub to a liquid, such as beer, wine, Worcestershire sauce, fruit juice, or a combination of these, is quick and easy. Mops can be based on a number of primary ingredients. Apply a mop three or four times at regular intervals during the cooking process.

DIPPING SAUCES

Dipping sauces are a marinade's encore. Here's where you can spotlight some of the flavors you've used in your marinade by serving them as an accompaniment. With a couple of ramekins of dipping sauces centered on serving plates and surrounded by skewers of grilled meat, seafood, and vegetables, you can combine cuisines and achieve a potpourri of flavors.

Dipping sauces can be anything from Thai peanut sauce to your own barbecue sauce. I often use leftover marinade ingredients as the basis for a sauce. The sauce need not be as intense as the marinade you've used. Chances are, you may come across a marinade recipe that you feel would make a marvelous dipping sauce. Go right ahead and use it—with one note of caution: don't use a leftover marinade as a dipping sauce after it has been in contact with raw food. In all likelihood, bacteria will be present. Reserve a little marinade for a dipping sauce before you begin marinating the food.

RUBS

A dry rub is any combination of spices and dried or fresh herbs that is thoroughly rubbed into the meat. Practically every cuisine uses them, from Morocco's ras al hanout and harissa, to India's garam masala and curry powders, to China's five-spice powder, to France's quatre épices.

Chemically speaking, rubs lack the denaturing properties that acids in a marinade contain. They keep the food pretty much intact, unless the rub contains a large amount of salt; in that case, I would use the rub as a cure.

Rubs bind with meat by pulling some of the meat's juices toward the surface. When food hits grilling heat, a searing effect creates a crust that most folks associate with the taste of grilled food. Add a dry rub, and that flavor becomes more intense and complex as the flames react with the spices. Rubs have a stronger flavor than marinades, and they also adhere better to the surface of meat.

There is a wide range of "wet" flavors from marinades that simply don't translate into rubs. Wet rubs or pastes such as pestos and some Mexican recados and Latin adobos are part dry rub and part thick marinade. They pick up moist flavorings from fresh herbs, citrus juices, oils, or spirits. It's best to apply them under the skin of poultry or after the final flip on the grill. They do not adhere as well as dry rubs do, but they can be just as delicious.

Applying a rub couldn't be easier. Just rub it over the entire surface of the food using a little

MAXING OUT MARINADES

Here are some ways to bring out just a little more flavor from your marinades.

Purée, purée, and purée some more. A typical marinade is an emulsion of an acidic liquid, oil, and suspended solids. The fewer solids you have in a marinade, the more even the flavor. By juicing or puréeing garlic, ginger, or onions, you intensify their flavors and, in some cases, even speed up the marinating process by capitalizing on their enzymatic assets. I've put my juicer and blender on overdrive.

Let your flavors meld. Typically, when you finish making a marinade, you immediately add it to food in a resealable plastic bag and place it in the fridge for a few hours. By the time the food is out of the bag and hits the grill, the marinade's aromatics are just beginning to meld. If you have a chance to make a marinade the day before, do it, but add the acidic liquid at the last minute. This also works for make-ahead marinades that you have stocked in the freezer. Defrost the marinade and add the acidic liquid. The melding process can be sped up on the countertop. But for safety's sake, make sure the marinade comes down to the refrigerated temperature of the food you're using it with.

Turn your food while it's marinating. It may seem obvious, but food lying flat against a resealable plastic bag or a glass baking dish is not exposed to a marinade.

Let your marinated food come to room temperature in the marinade. A good bet is to leave it out for about 45 minutes but no longer than 1 hour before you grill or cook. This way, the food will cook evenly and you'll avoid cold spots.

pressure to form a crust. This can be done several hours in advance or 5 minutes before cooking. When smoking meat low and slow, lightly apply a rub at least 8 to 12 hours in advance to form a wonderful crust that pit bosses call the bark. You don't want to pack it on because it can stop smoke penetration. Although rubs can climb the highest on the flavor pop charts, their flavor intensity is not right for all foods.

GLAZES

When you think of glazes, think of last-minute flavors that are easy to prepare. Glazes are the icing on the cake, and a sneaky way of having dessert first. They can bail you out of those spur-of-the-moment potluck parties when you don't have time to marinate something. Glistening glazes are a perfect way to finish off both fish and fowl; they add shining color and create sweet flavors that offset the smokiness of wood chips.

Glazes differ from marinades and rubs in a number of ways. Obviously, they're sweeter. A glaze can pick up some of its sweetness from honey, maple syrup, fruit, or liqueur. Whereas a marinade uses an acidic liquid and an oil to bind some of the aromatics to the food, a glaze uses its sugar content. A barbecue sauce is the most familiar example of a glaze. Because of the sugar content, a glaze needs to be added at the end of the cooking process instead of before, as you would with a marinade. The sugar content will caramelize over high heat and burn, much like those dreaded barbecued chicken legs from Labor Day picnics of yesteryear.

The word *sugar* may set off dietary alarms and press the wrong button on some of your taste buds, but it's not really as sweet as all that. The actual amount of glaze that coats your food is really a thin sheen, and the proportion of sugar is pretty low in relation to the rest of the ingredients. See the chart on pages 20 and 21 for ideas on substituting sugars.

Although glazes tend to be shiny, they still need to be brightened. Citrus juice, fruit, or flavored vinegar will do the trick. Citrus juice should be added to a glaze the day of grilling or cooking if you're making the glaze ahead of time.

Glazes can be made several days ahead and refrigerated. Bring the glaze to room temperature before you begin to brush and grill the food. This will open up the glaze's flavors and enable you to apply it more easily and more evenly across your food. Think of trying to brush a tablespoon of honey or molasses after your jar has been sitting in a cold kitchen cabinet. It needs heat to thin it out.

From a technique standpoint, timing is essential when you're cooking with a glaze. If you're grilling, you need to apply the glaze only after the final flip to the top side of your food. As heat rises, the glaze's viscosity becomes thinner. Move your food off the flame, if possible, to avoid having the glaze drip over the coals or heating unit. Then cover your grill. If I had to quantify the timing for applying a glaze, I would say it takes as long as melting a slice of cheese on a hamburger.

Even though smoking food low and slow avoids the caramelization problem, a glaze, if applied too early in the cooking process, will block smoke penetration. Remember, a glaze sits on the surface of the food. If you're smoking ribs or poultry, apply the glaze during the last 30 minutes of cooking time.

Finish meat and poultry dishes with a glaze by mixing it with a reduced stock or demi-glace. A good ratio is three to four parts stock to one part glaze. Start light with the glaze and adjust it accordingly. To finish shellfish and seafood dishes, you can drizzle or streak glazes from squirt bottles across the plate to add some color.

SAVORY CARAMELS

Savory caramels take a different spin on a recipe that typically has an address in the dessert section. Sounds trendy, one may think, but actually it's quite traditional in Vietnam. Nuoc mau (page 306), a caramel, is a staple in Vietnamese kitchens and is used as a savory ingredient to balance flavors. I use caramel as a first step in making maple sugar, which you can flavor with other liquors. These maxed-out sugars can be used in cures and rubs calling for brown sugar.

Savory caramels are a great way to tweak brines and glazes as well. With brines, you can substitute an equal amount of caramel for sugar, maple syrup, or honey, giving your dish added depth. With glazes, they can be the starting foundation that supports puréed fruit, citrus juice, or flavored vinegar. Caramels can handle aromatic spices, liquors, and even Asian condiments. Another advantage is that caramels, like glazes, can be made in advance and gently reheated before adding other ingredients.

CARAMEL EQUIPMENT LIST
. . . .

If you're going to get involved with savory caramels, you'll need the right equipment. I'm not suggesting that you add to your kitchen's "only-used-once" gadget collection, but you will need certain equipment for safety reasons. Sugar caramelizes at around 330°F. That's hot, and it's not made for tasting with your fingers.

Get the heaviest stainless steel saucepan you can find. I have one devoted only to caramels. It's heavy, and it won't tip over. Although copper pots give you spin-on-a-dime heat control, they're not the best for reading caramel's color stages.

Long wooden spoons and a pastry brush are necessary. When hot molten sugar caramelizes, it seems to lose its temper when you add liquid to it. You need to keep your distance, and wood won't conduct heat like a metal spoon will. A wet pastry brush will help you brush down the sugar that crystallizes on the side of the pot. There are silicon versions that I like because they can withstand high heat. Have a heat-resistant measuring cup or an ovenproof bowl of water at the ready to wash off any crystals clinging to the spoon or brush.

Another functional tool is a silicon mat. These are sold in cookware stores and are really handy for making Maple Bourbon Sugar (page 71).

If you're adding liquid off heat, they will provide counter protection.

FLAVOR MANAGEMENT

Taste involves only one of the five senses, while flavor is a combination of multiple sensations in the mouth and nose at the same time. In other words, flavor is a cocktail of taste and smell. The sensation of taste—like all sensations—resides in the brain. So you can say that your taste preferences are truly all in your head.

There are barbecue fanatics who swear they love the flavor of smoke. Actually, they don't, unless the smoke is in good company. Try this experiment: take an unseasoned hamburger patty and put it in a smoker or a covered grill with presoaked wood chips. Cook it on low and slow smoke for an hour or two until the internal temperature is around 160°F. Take a forkful and pinch your nostrils. Almost immediately you will be looking for something to balance the bitter taste of acrid smoke. It could be sweet ketchup, sour salsa, or even a couple shakes of salt or a few turns of the peppermill. Even with your nostrils open, the burger still needs something. Why? Because smoke is acrid, and it hits the bitterness receptors on the tongue.

With brines and cures, the main taste sensation, as you can probably guess, is salt. Brining is an infusion process. Because the main ingredient is salt, you need to balance brines with something sweet. By increasing the sweetness, you decrease the feel or taste of salt in cures and brines.

A marinade contains sour notes from citrus juice, wine, or vinegar, along with some sweet notes from root vegetables such as onions and shallots. There's also some salt that sits in and plays a few licks, and finally there can be a little bitterness from some of the herbs and ground black pepper.

Rubs, spice mixes, pestos, and pastes (recados) add concentrated flavor to the food's surface. The trio of tastes that plays the loudest in a dry rub or spice mix is salty, sweet, and bitter. But there is a need to counterbalance it with a little acidity. In a barbecue pit, where the taste and flavor of smoke are holding court, rubs are used to caramelize the meat's surface. Most pit bosses also brush the meat with a thin, vinegary mop. In fact, you need only look as far as the Carolinas to see vinegar used as a barbecue sauce. Some of the wet pastes may also include a little acidity from vinegar or citrus juice, and these are really a cross between a marinade and a dry rub.

A glaze's main taste component is sweet, and it usually calls for something sour or citrusy to balance it out. If you find that one of your glazes is a little too sweet, you can brighten it on the back end with freshly squeezed citrus juice and grated zest, or flavored vinegar. A pinch of salt added to a glaze rounds out its flavor. Although glazes like to pal around with something sour, it doesn't have to be in the glaze itself; it could be a side dish, such as Lime-Cilantro Jicama Slaw (page 213) or Sweet Corn Salsa (page 166).

WHOLLY SMOKE

Every year, right around the time the flies come out, hard-core serial grillers begin relentlessly grilling or smoking just about anything they can get their hands on. You would think that the flavor chase is about grilled seafood or poultry or meat on the hoof. Or maybe it's the marinades, rubs, or salsas that go along for the ride. What it's really about is that single ingredient that's in almost anything that's cooked outdoors—the ingredient of smoke.

The ingredient of smoke is a balancing act of equipment, wood moisture, atmospheric conditions, and heat of the fire, all of which contribute to the final flavor. Talk about traditional food and getting back to basics—grilling and smoking food are dawn-of-time cuisine.

Grills are high-heat cooking in the fast lane and are best suited for tender food that can cook quickly. High-heat grilling makes it tough for food

to hang out on the grill for any long period of time without being scorched to a flaky black crust. Outdoor gas grills may have the advantage of an instant, albeit limited, heat source, but unless you add presoaked wood chips or chunks, they are more neutral in imparting flavor than their charcoal-powered cousins. Charcoal grills give you more smoke flavor and burn hotter than most gas grills do, reaching surface temperatures of up to 700°F, if you are using lump hardwood charcoal, and up to 900°F if you are using mesquite wood chunks.

Two types of smokers, water smokers and offset fuel smokers, are available to the home pit boss through specialty hardware stores and by mail order. Water smokers are about 3½ feet high and 1½ feet wide, with a dome lid that usually has a temperature gauge. It uses a "wet" smoking process by combining steam from a water pan over burning wood chips or chunks. For added flavor, you can fill the water pan with anything but water. Try orange juice for poultry, white wine for fish, red wine for meat, apple juice or cider for pork tenderloin or turkey breasts, or even leftover marinades for any of the above.

You can improvise a water smoker with a kettle grill and a wok (with metal handles). Place the wok on the bottom charcoal grate of your Weber. Line the outside with coals and smoking chips (a charcoal chimney starter is ideal for adding coals). Add the liquid to the wok, replace the top grill, and place your food in the center of the grill. Close the lid and you're ready to smoke.

Offset fuel smokers are the equivalent of graduate school for pit bosses. They're called "offset" because smoking wood and coals are placed in an offset fuel box, which feeds smoke into the smoker. This is a "dry" low heat or "cold" smoking process that is as close as it gets to real pit barbecue. I've seen some models locally and they range from $200 to $275. Some Texas mail-order models can cost over $3,000 and come with their own trailer hitch, which makes it convenient should you just happen to run across some fresh venison unexpectedly.

My jury still hasn't returned a verdict on wood chips verses wood chunks or logs, but I'll tell you what my nose thinks. I get more flavor from the chunks and logs than I do from packaged wood chips. Because certain woods impart bitterness, regardless of the amount of smoke, those wood chips are often cut with another, more neutral wood. Typical combinations are hickory and oak, and mesquite and oak. There is no way of knowing whether a bag of chips is all mesquite or hickory or whether it has a little filler added. Think of the surge of popularity of wood chips in the past few years and then think of the last time you drove past a mesquite or hickory farm. I found that an equal amount of mesquite wood chunks packs a lot more flavor and lasts longer than the same amount of commercial wood chips. And yes, wood chunks can be soaked. One thing to note, however, is that placing a piece of chicken or beef over a hot grill with smoking wood chips for just 10 minutes or so will only give you hints of a smoked flavor. For a more seasoned smoke flavor, indirect cooking or cold smoking is the way to go.

Even though I use smoke as an ingredient, I can't really measure a specific amount by traditional means. It would be nice to have a few balloons filled with hickory smoke floating around the grill, like a spice rack ready to disperse flavor at a moment's notice. However, the better pit masters seem to be able to "read" their wood, and then play with the quantity and heat to get pretty consistent results with regard to flavor. It's not unusual to see the wood separated into two piles by degree of dryness, one pile for the wood that's ready now, and the other for wood that's a bit green, or wet. These pit masters know that one type will give more smoke than another, with a resulting difference in flavor.

You can use moisture to control the amount of smoke flavor. If you use wet chips or chunks that have been soaking in water for at least 20 minutes, the smoke level will be much higher. Wet (marinated) foods pick up less smoke than dry foods do, and oiled or glazed foods pick up even less smoke than marinated foods do.

A dry smoke (that is, a dry hardwood as the only heat source) will make a "clean" fire, one that puts out no noticeable smoke. With a clean fire, the smoke is less intense, but it will give you a subtle, sweet, smoky taste. However, a wet smoke, or "heavy" fire, puts out noticeable smoke, and the smoky taste can be more intense in the food.

Sometimes getting a good stash of local fruit wood is all about timing. The end of the season is the best time to hit the groves for local woods such as peach, apple, cherry, and pear. Some orchards sell their fruit wood as firewood. Your best bet is to ask at the orchard when you're buying cider to see what they have lying around. Grilling season may be over by then, but with woods like these I can smoke right through the winter.

Because of their density, hickory, mesquite, and oak, which are aromatic hardwoods, will burn hotter and smoke longer than most woods, and they will also throw off more aroma than charcoal briquettes and lump hardwood charcoal. They take longer to come up to their heat peaks, but they do hang in a lot longer once they get there. So, when timing dinner for your guests, double your fire-up time when cooking with hardwoods.

Of the seasoned hardwoods, mesquite burns the hottest, reaching up to 900°F, but its scent can vary wildly from a sweet to a slightly bitter aroma. Each batch can be different, so try a little first, and then stand downwind, sniff, and test. Oak has a smoother and more neutral flavor. Perhaps because of a flavor-memory I associate with bacon or ham, hickory seems to have the most pronounced flavor of the three hardwoods.

Sugar provides balance to the bitterness of smoke. I have a recipe that calls for tuna to cure in a brine of salt, ancho chile powder, brown sugar, and maple syrup for 1 hour. It sounds eccentric, but the end result is a smoky-sweet, somewhat-spicy smoke flavor that just melts in your mouth!

It's a real pleasure experimenting with seasoned smoke as an added flavor ingredient, but ultimately you have to taste the food first, and the smoke second.

SUGAR ALTERNATIVES

The word *sugar* can press a lot of the wrong buttons for some folks with flavor preferences and dietary issues. If you're preparing food for people who have to check their sugar intake for medical reasons, don't assume that because it's not white refined sugar you're out of the woods. Some of these items can raise blood sugar levels even higher. Check first, and when in doubt, leave it out.

Sweetener	Description	How to Use
Barley Malt Syrup	This is dark brown, thick, and sticky; it has a strong, distinctive flavor, like molasses, and is half as sweet as white sugar.	Use this sparingly in brines and glazes. Substitute 1⅓ cups barley malt syrup for every 1 cup white sugar.
Blackstrap Molasses	This is 70 percent sucrose, and it marginally qualifies as a natural sweetener. This is "leftovers" from the sugar-refining process and has a very strong flavor.	Blackstrap molasses can overpower other flavors in a glaze or brine where sugars are one of the dominant ingredients, but it can give some depth to barbecue sauces or any other strong-flavored recipes. It's not for delicate or subtle recipes. You can substitute 1 cup blackstrap molasses for 1½ cups dark brown sugar, caramelized.
Brown Rice Syrup	This amber-colored syrup has a mild butterscotch flavor and is half as sweet as white sugar.	Substitute 1⅓ cups brown rice syrup for every 1 cup white sugar. It works fine in brines, glazes, and some marinades.
Dark Corn Syrup	Corn syrup has a mild molasses flavor.	Dark corn syrup is slightly sweeter than light. It can be used as an equal substitute for molasses in barbecue sauces.
Date Sugar	This ground sugar has moist, coarse granules, with a mahogany color. It is not as sweet as white sugar.	This is a good substitute for light and dark brown sugars, and you can substitute equal amounts. It has a high caramelization point, which may not make the cut for certain rubs, but it can be used in brines, cures, and marinades. Refrigerate after opening.
Evaporated Whole Cane Juice	This product has amber-colored, coarse granules, with a mild molasses-like taste. Evaporated whole cane juice is a term used loosely on labels like turbinado, and raw sugar definitely does not qualify. It's a good substitute if it's 100 percent organic for light and brown sugar.	You can substitute equal amounts of evaporated whole cane juice in recipes calling for white and brown sugars.
Golden Syrup	This is popular among British, Caribbean, and Creole cooks. It really doesn't qualify as a sugar substitute because it's made by evaporating sugar cane juice.	This can be used in brines, marinades, and glazes in place of maple syrup or honey.

SUGAR ALTERNATIVES

Sweetener	Description	How to Use
Honey	Honey, like maple syrup, has its own flavor stamp. It's a combination of fructose, glucose, and sucrose. The color and taste depend on the flower and how it was produced. Buy only pure, raw honey from a reputable source.	Honey can be anywhere from 20 to 60 percent sweeter than white sugar, so adapt it to glazes and brines accordingly. Substitute anywhere from ½ cup to ⅔ cup for 1 cup white sugar.
Pure Maple Syrup	Pure maple syrup comes from the sap of maple trees and is not the imposters found in grocery stores, which are usually based on corn syrup and flavored with either artificial flavoring or real maple syrup. It takes close to 40 gallons of sap to produce 1 gallon of syrup. Maple syrup is graded by flavor and by color. Grade B, sometimes called Cooking or Table Syrup, is made late in the season and is very dark, with a very strong maple flavor and some caramel flavor. As long as it's pure, it's fine for any of the recipes in the book that call for it.	Use pure maple syrup in brines, glazes, and marinades. Substitute anywhere from ½ cup to ⅔ cup for 1 cup white sugar.
Maple Sugar	This dehydrated maple syrup is essentially made by cooking it to 45°F above the boiling point, producing light brown granules with a maple flavor. It's hard to find and somewhat expensive when you do find it. You can make your own (see page 71)	Maple sugar is one of my favorite all-around sugar substitutes. I use it mostly in cures and in some rubs, where the flavor can really stand out. It can get lost in a brine or a glaze, and you may as well use maple syrup. Substitute equal amounts for white and brown sugars.
Fruit Juice Concentrates	Peach, pear, grape, and pineapple juices are most commonly used as sugar substitutes. They contain sucrose and some natural fructose. They are generally amber colored and fruity tasting.	Some fruit juice concentrates are more acidic than others and can give a boost to fruit-based marinades and glazes or brines. They can replace equal amounts of honey or maple syrups.
Stevia	A perennial shrub of the aster family, stevia is available in whole or broken leaves, coarse ground powder, powder extract, or liquid extract. It is 8 to 300 times sweeter than white sugar but with 0 calories.	Essentially, stevia is a highly concentrated taste and flavor substitute for sugar. I don't use it in glazes or anywhere I need a sweetener in bulk as a binding component. It can work in brines to offset the taste of salt, and it can be a nice flavor enhancer and a good dietary substitute in rubs and cures. Use 1 teaspoon dried or concentrated stevia for 1 cup white sugar. You'll need to experiment in converting recipes, to make up for the lack of volume.

SMOKING TIPS AND TIMES

Preferred smoking temperatures for meat is 200° to 250°F, and 180° to 190°F for fish. Allow meat to come room temperature for 1 hour (but no longer than that), and fish for about 30 minutes before smoking; this keeps the food from having a cold center that can foster bacteria. (One of the best smoking tools you can own is a pocket thermometer for testing internal temperatures.) You can get the best of both worlds by smoking tender meat and fish for half the suggested time and then finishing it on the grill.

According to chef Lynn Buono, of Miss Amelia's Barbecue of Northern Liberties in Philadelphia, most smoked meat can be frozen, especially spareribs. Wrap the meat in aluminum foil for freezing. Defrost the meat overnight in your refrigerator and then reheat in the oven at 250°F for 30 to 40 minutes prior to serving. Note that smoke will give fully cooked chicken a tinge of pink, but not to worry—it's not undercooked.

THE FOOD GROUPS

Up to now we've investigated marinades, brines, rubs, cures, and glazes. As much as I like them on their own, they taste so much better with accomplices like fish, poultry, and other meat. I'm going to round up the usual suspects—fish and shellfish, poultry, pork, beef, lamb, veal, and game meat—and grill them for some tasty cooking information.

FISH AND SHELLFISH

The real reason you should marinate is not to repair bad food, but to heighten good food. This is especially true for seafood. A good marinade is like a setting for a jewel. If the seafood is fresh, the recipe will sparkle. All the seasoning in the pantry is not going to make old fish taste fresh. Old fish will still have that fishy odor along with the marinade's flavors.

Unless you live on the coast, most "fresh" saltwater fish (which could be FAS, or frozen at sea) has an 8- to 12-day trek from the net to your dinner plate. Aquaculture speeds the processing and distribution system a bit. Fresh is when you catch it yourself. Fresh, when applied to store-bought fish, simply means unfrozen. However, some fish are fresher than others. Here's how to check.

With fillets and steaks, the skin should be shiny, with an almost metallic glisten, and it should look smooth, not puckered in areas. The flesh should be clean of spots, translucent (no matter what the color), and have a sheen. Once the shine goes from fish, so goes the freshness. The flesh should feel firm and bounce back. With old fish, your finger may make a lasting impression. The flesh shouldn't separate into large flakes. When touching the skin, the surface shouldn't slide away from the flesh. It should be tight.

Fresh fish will have a clean smell, without a fishy odor, a little like seaweed. Avoid buying fish with off odors, such as sulfur or ammonia. Avoid buying shrimp or shellfish with a medicinal odor. A fishy odor indicates old fish. A marinade won't hide that.

SEAFOOD PORTION CONTROL

If everything checks out to this point, the question is how much seafood to buy. Depending on the number of other courses and accompaniments, and the dietary company you keep, here are some basic guidelines. Fillets should weigh in at around 6 to 8 ounces per serving, with about 1 cup of marinade per 1 pound of fish. With whole fish, allow 12 to 16 ounces per serving with 1½ cups of marinade per pound. Shrimp should weigh in at about ½ to ¾ pound per serving, but the truth is that the more shrimp you put out, the more everyone will eat. Figure 1 cup of marinade per pound of shrimp.

Most store-bought shrimp will have been prefrozen. Should you be lucky enough to find fresh shrimp with the heads on, please don't marinate them. Cook them as is. It's a rare treat. For portions, go for large (16 to 20 count per pound) unpeeled shrimp, and allow 4 to 5 per serving. The smaller sizes aren't as tasty, and you'll likely get bored peeling them. Some shrimp aficionados will tell you that when you peel shrimp, you also peel away flavor. Perhaps, but a marinade won't penetrate the shell. And when you ultimately peel the shell away from cooked shrimp, so goes your marinade.

KEEPING SEAFOOD FRESH

After you've landed the right catch, how do you keep it fresh, especially if you're not going to start marinating it until the next day? The first step is to unwrap it. Seafood wrapped in paper or plastic has no air circulating around it. Because wrapping acts as insulation, the fish is not evenly chilled. Pack a deep baking dish with crushed ice cubes or plastic blue ice packs, lay the fish on top of the ice (skin side down if there is skin), and cover with plastic wrap, leaving about ½ inch of headroom. Place the fish on the bottom part of your refrigerator (where it's coldest). Your fish will stay fresh a little longer this way.

When preparing fish for marinades, rinse the fish lightly under cold water. Remove any bones from fillets with a set of tweezers or needle-nose pliers. Also, if you are marinating salmon fillets, remove the dark gray fat area if necessary. With tuna, marlin, or swordfish steaks, the skin carries the oil and fat, and it can be removed before marinating. Go for thick cuts, as these fish tend to dry out quickly over high-heat grilling or broiling.

COOKING TIMES

Generally, some fish take about 8 to 10 minutes of cooking time per inch. But on the grill, cooking times vary with the cut and texture of the fish, how long it has been marinating, and how hot the fire

is. If you are sautéing indoors, the heat of the skillet affects timing. You want to hold some of that wonderful moisture in the center of the cooked fish for flavor. It should be steamy opaque, not translucent raw or dry brittle white (which may indicate that your fish is overcooked).

POULTRY

Chicken, especially breast meat, is the ultimate canvas for flavor painting with marinades. I often use chicken breasts as a test when balancing the flavors of my marinades. Once skinned and trimmed of fat, chicken breasts average about 200 calories per serving (before marinating).

Because boneless, skinless chicken breasts tend to dry out fairly quickly, if you are going to wait a day or two before you use them, buy the breasts with the bone and skin intact. Remove the skin before marinating to cut down on calories and to enhance flavor penetration. Soft as it may be, poultry skin is nature's protective covering, with a little bit of fat thrown in for insulation. For a slow oven roast, I prefer to leave the bone in for more moisture and flavor.

How long do you need to marinate chicken? Average times can be within 2 to 3 hours for light flavor, and 6 to 8 hours (but not longer than that) for stronger flavor. The longer you leave chicken in a high-acid marinade, the more shrinkage you'll have during cooking. For lengthy marinating times, go light on acids such as wine, lemon juice, or lime juice, or add them gradually during the marinating period. Too much acid will denature chicken meat while it is marinating. The surfaces will turn white and opaque, and the chicken will cook unevenly.

To speed things up, you can always tenderize a boneless chicken breast by placing it between two pieces of waxed paper and flattening it with a rolling pin or kitchen mallet. The breast will cook more quickly and evenly.

One of the nicest benefits of a marinade is the amount of flavor it can add to frozen chicken. Frozen chicken will, however, lose its moisture more quickly during the cooking process, so I suggest quick sautés rather than slow roasts.

PREPARING CHICKEN WINGS

To trim and separate chicken wings, lay the wing "elbow" (the joint between the drumstick and the wing section) on a chopping block. With a sharp knife, cut away and discard the weblike skin between the drumstick and the wing section. Grasp both the wing and the drumstick section and force them apart at the joint by bending them backward. Cutting between the two sections will give you two separate pieces: a drumstick and a wing section.

One of my favorite types of poultry to marinate is turkey breast. Because turkey is grown all year round (and frozen for the Thanksgiving rush), fresh young and tender turkeys are more readily available during the summer months. They are great for large outdoor (and indoor) potluck dinners, and turkey is one of the few types of poultry that tastes just as good cold as it does hot. Depending on the number of guests you are feeding, you can marinate several whole turkey breasts with different marinades or rubs, smoke with different woods, and serve with regional condiments. Turkey breast with the skin and bone intact is extremely succulent and can handle high-acid marinades and slow roasting times, much like a beef brisket does.

Duck and goose are festive and formal. Because the fat content of these birds is naturally high, the moisture (oil) content of the marinade should be lower, and in some cases nonexistent. If you are marinating breasts, remove the bird's skin and fat. To counteract their natural richness, don't add more acid, but do add more sweetener in the form of a dessert liqueur.

Nowadays, most hunting for game birds such as quail, wild duck, and pheasant seems to take place in specialty food stores rather than in the wild. With game farms producing domesticated fowl for the American table, we have the opportunity to try an entire group of range-free poultry. Farm-raised game is free of the hormones, steroids, and antibiotics used in mass-produced, water-filled chicken. Game fowl is different from domestic poultry and must be handled differently when marinating. Game fowl, such as quail, wild duck, and wild turkey, whether commercial or wild, tend to be dry (especially if they have been frozen). The birds require marinades low in acid and high in moisture, and they should be left with the skin and bone intact.

Wild birds' gamy and fishy flavor can be tempered by a marinade, and soaking it overnight in whole milk or buttermilk will wash away unpleasant flavors. Discard the milk bath and then use your favorite marinade.

SAFETY CONCERNS

Assume that poultry is guilty of food bacteria contamination until proven innocent. If you are using frozen poultry, begin defrosting it in the refrigerator (never at room temperature) and rinse it under cold water before marinating. Bacteria (such as salmonella or campylobacter) that can cause food poisoning usually exist between 45° and 140°F. Therefore, marinate poultry in the refrigerator, not on a warm kitchen countertop. Marinated poultry should remain out of the refrigerator no longer than 1 hour before you begin to cook it. If you are taking marinated poultry to be grilled at a cookout or an outdoor picnic, pack it in ice.

Although the acid content in marinades may kill off some of the salmonella in the marinade, it can take anywhere from several hours to several days to kill them all. Never reuse a marinade after you remove poultry from it. Aside from the fact that the flavor will have diminished, particles of chicken and blood that can carry bacteria will be present in the uncooked marinade.

When using your marinade to baste poultry on the grill, bring the marinade to a low boil in a nonreactive saucepan, or microwave the marinade for 3 minutes on high. This will kill off any bacteria that may be present, and you will also avoid the fire-hose effect of lowering your cooking temperature by pouring cold liquid on hot food. Needless to say, smart cooks will make sure that their basting brushes are thoroughly clean before each use.

Finally, if you cooked too much marinated poultry and figure that the leftovers will make a great chicken salad, refrigerate it. Don't leave it out at room temperature.

PORK

Pork is raised much leaner than it was twenty years ago; in fact, pork tenderloin is almost one-third leaner than beef tenderloin. Not only is pork leaner, but it's also considered to be safer than it once was. Trichinosis is almost unheard of these days, but to be safe, cook chops, ribs, and tenderloin to an internal temperature of 150° to 160°F. You can also deep-freeze them at 0°F for about 3 weeks, then defrost them and marinate some flavor and moisture back into the meat.

There are two cuts of pork that lend themselves particularly well to brines, marinades, rubs, and glazes: the loin and spareribs. The loin area, I feel, is the most versatile. It's the leanest and sweetest area, and it gives us tenderloin, pork chops, and cutlets. Loin meat should be whitish pink when purchased.

Slow cooked or braised, rubbed or marinated, smoked, grilled, or glazed—ribs tie it all together for me when I think of outdoor cooking. This is an area where serial grillers play outdoors for hours. Part of the deal with smoking ribs is the nose action that you get when the ribs and smoke hit their point of aromatic equilibrium. It's like hickory-scented incense. Ribs demand patience; cooking them is an all-day affair. Like beef brisket, the longer they cook over low heat, the more tender they become. High-heat grilling or broiling

HOW TO SUBSTITUTE A GOBBLE FOR AN OINK

As much as I like pork loin, pork chops, and pork kabobs, there are times when substitutions are necessary. Turkey is the seamless substitute. In most cases, both turkey and pork are interchangeable with the same brines, marinades, rubs, and glazes. Here are some replacement ideas.

For pork chops: Turkey chops are carved-out, bone-in turkey breasts. They weigh about 6 to 7 ounces each. They are about 1 inch to 1½ inches thick and are actually cross-section cuts of whole turkey breasts. The breast is frozen and table-sawed across the grain by the butcher.

For pork tenderloin: The small inner lobe of turkey breast called the tenderloin is about 7 to 8 ounces. Two of them are about two thirds the weight of a small pork tenderloin. If you want to go thicker, there's always the lower half of a skinless turkey breast.

For pork spareribs: Some ambitious poultry butchers are leaving about 1 inch of meat on the breastbone and are sawing them into rib-size strips. Although they are not the rack of spareribs or baby back ribs we know and love, they take to rubs and barbecue sauces like the best of them.

For pulled pork barbecue: You can replace pork shoulder with an equal weight of bone-in turkey breast, and place a rub beneath the skin. Cooked turkey meat is fibrous enough to work in place of pulled pork. Place pieces of your finished smoked turkey and a couple cups of unsalted chicken broth in a slow cooker for 8 hours and you'll end up with a good, fork-pulled pork texture.

FREEZER BURN! MARINATING IN THE ICE AGE

One of the things that came up in my post-book conversations is the idea of freezing food in marinades and then defrosting them in the refrigerator.

In general, freezing a marinade can have some traumatic effects. The first to be hit is the acidity, if you're using fresh citrus. It definitely drops off over time due to evaporation and condensation, which you can see on the interior of the bags. Next, freezing breaks the marinade's emulsion. When oil is frozen, it solidifies with suspended aromatics within fat globules. When defrosting, oil and water separate into their own corners. I'd suggest that you make your marinades ahead without citrus and add it after the meat has been completely defrosted. Although the marinade won't be emulsified, the citrus juice will brighten it.

After a marinade has been frozen for longer than 3 months, the flavors tend to flatten and meld together, leaving little or no distinction around some of the principal ingredients. Typically, freezing throws a marinade out of balance.

When you freeze food, you are not placing it in an endless time lock. Freezing merely slows the process of decay and can inflict its own kind of trauma on food. The deeper the freeze, the slower the decaying process, but food and ingredients do indeed change.

Bear in mind that freezing can cause some drying in the process. When meat freezes, the soft membranes expand as the liquid in the tissue solidifies into ice crystals that can puncture the tissue walls. When meat defrosts, the fluid is lost from the damaged membranes, making the meat dry and mushy. Mushy is not tender. As the liquid flows out, so do some of the nutrients and the flavor. To prove this, take two pork loins of identical weights. Freeze one for 48 hours and refrigerate the other. When you weigh them again before cooking, the frozen one will be lighter. And there will be a definite difference in texture and flavor.

Prebrining poultry and pork before freezing creates a different textural effect. Turkey or chicken, when defrosted and cooked, has the texture of a deli slice.

You can minimize some of the texture and flavor loss by freezing meat as quickly as you can while keeping as much air circulation in the freezer as possible. Speed is of the essence when it comes to freezing. The colder your food as it starts to freeze, the faster the temperature drop. If you load your freezer with room-temperature food all in one shot, you'll raise the temperature of the freezer. Refrigerate food for a few hours before freezing to give it a running start. And, because of the salt and some sugar content, brined food will take longer to freeze.

Defrosting pork and poultry in a marinade is almost a 24-hour process and the flavor return is no great shakes compared to marinating fresh meat. Food with a frozen solid surface will take longer to bind with a marinade's flavors.

Putting any poultry into a brine to defrost is even more problematic for the simple fact that a brine can't penetrate a solid object like a frozen piece of food. When the food finally defrosts, some parts of the meat will be saltier than others because of the uneven brine penetration.

makes them tough. I've seen recipes that suggest parboiling ribs and then browning them on the grill. Forget it. You simply can't get the same flavor that you would get by taking your time. Boiling ribs only hardens the fat, which is part of the flavor; it doesn't render the fat.

The anchor cut of ribs is St. Louis–style spareribs. These are spareribs with the breastbone trimmed out. They have a rectangular shape and come with about 2 inches of meat on them. Personally, I think they have a lot more finger meat (that is, meat between the ribs) than baby backs do. You can figure two to three portions per slab of ribs.

I did a marketing survey on baby back ribs at a farmers' market and a couple of supermarkets. I priced out individual slabs of baby backs and equal lengths of pork tenderloin and found that the sum of the parts is more expensive than the whole by almost 40 percent. Bone-in pork loins were far cheaper by the pound. Bear in mind that this is the same cut of meat undivided. It makes better sense to buy the ribs with the loin attached and then trim them out yourself or have your butcher do it.

Brining ribs, even if you are going to marinate them, gives an added burst of juiciness. You can start the recipe with most of the brines in the book, and then go for either a rub or a marinade. Then you can finish the ribs with a glaze or a sauce.

Marinate ribs in the refrigerator and bring them to room temperature for about 45 minutes before cooking. Barbecue sauces should not be used as marinades for ribs. Their sugar content (if they are ketchup-based) will caramelize and burn. Serve barbecue sauce on the side or add it at the very last minute. Allow about ½ to 1 pound of ribs per person, but always cook some extra. Leftover ribs (if there are any) can be reheated the next day.

Pork shoulder takes to barbecue as though it were invented for it. Its natural fat content makes it self-basting. When the meat is done, most of the fat will have been rendered off, leaving wonderfully tender, juicy pork. A whole pork shoulder can weigh in at 12 to 18 pounds. Usually, a pork shoulder is cut into two pieces, which are also called picnic, from the bonier part of the shoulder, and Boston butt, from the upper part of the shoulder (not from where the name implies).

I don't recommend brining pork shoulder. Brining will make it juicy, but it will also tighten the meat in a "hammy" kind of way. You want the pork to splinter with a fork.

Smoking a pork shoulder can be an all-day love affair. But why smoke just one, when in the same amount of time (depending on the size of your cooker) you can smoke two? You can freeze the second one.

Smoked meat freezes well, and the process seems to turn its flavor amp up to 11! Thaw the pork shoulder overnight in the refrigerator. The day of serving, preheat the oven to 225°F. Place the shoulder in an 8-quart Dutch oven, add a can of low-salt chicken broth, and braise the pork for 2 to 3 hours. The pork should easily fall apart. This also works well with a slow cooker by setting it on high for the first hour and then on low for 5 to 6 additional hours.

BEEF, LAMB, VEAL, AND GAME MEAT

The traditional idea of "tenderizing" tough slabs of meat is still linked with marinades. By the time meat is butchered, refrigerated, and displayed in the supermarket, its tenderness is already a done deal. In general, the most expensive cuts of meat are considered to be the most tender. Well, what are we really paying for? In some cases, fat and aging—which is also ultimately true in life. When

> # TIP
>
> *Anything that is put into an airtight oven for 1 hour or more will start to dry out. Place a water pan on the floor of the oven, and fill it with orange juice, apple cider, wine, or, according to one Southern cook, root beer. The liquid will simultaneously steam, moisturize, and flavor the ribs.*

cattle are fed grains and supplements to create fat within the muscle, called marbling, some cooks and meat inspectors see this as an indication of a tender cut. But marbling is only a small part of tenderizing factors.

Marinating simply for the sake of softening meat is no longer necessary. Although marinating a cheaper cut of meat will not make it taste expensive, it can make it tasty.

Completely covering the meat with the marinade is essential. The greater the coverage, the faster the flavoring process. To speed up the flavoring process, you can always cut the meat into smaller pieces. Place beef in the freezer for 30 minutes to firm it up for easy slicing or cubing before you marinate it.

Even though a marinade can reduce meat's cooking time, it may, depending on the amount of acid used, draw off fluid from the meat and cause some dryness during cooking. To avoid this, check your meat for graying while it's marinating. That's usually an indication that the marinade is reacting with the meat much like the process of a seviche. At that point, remove the meat from the marinade and place it in a covered container in the refrigerator until you are ready to cook it.

Frozen meat can be defrosted in your marinade, but this will slow down both the defrosting time and the marinating process. To ensure even cooking, it's best to defrost first, and marinate after.

Marinades not only add extra flavor, but they also enable you to use leaner cuts of meat. That's because some of the caloric moisture found in the fat that has been trimmed away will be replaced with oil in the marinade. If the cut of meat that you are using is marbled, such as a filet, you need not add as much oil to the marinade. This will enable you to deglaze the sauté pan with the marinade and not have the oil separate out over high heat.

Not all cuts of meat require the same amount of refrigerated marinating times. Naturally soft or well-marbled beef or lamb, such as filet mignon or rack of lamb, need only a few hours. Aged meat has a slight grayness to it and requires

a shorter marinating time as well. Cuts of meat from the leg, which has a much denser muscle system, can handle 1 to 2 days. The tougher cuts of beef, such as mutton, brisket, loins, and flank steak, can marinate anywhere from 2 to 4 days. Not only do these cuts require longer marinating times, but, in some cases, they also need more acid in the marinade.

Farm-raised game sounds like an oxymoron, but game farms are putting the culinary wild right into our backyards. Through a network of specialty food stores and mail-order firms, we're getting access to cuts of venison, boar, and bison that marry well with some of the fruitier marinade recipes in this book.

Farm-raised game is meatier, fattier, and more tender than wild game is, and it has a bit less fat than beef and pork. That's because fat in game animals is concentrated on the back and under the spine, rather than marbled throughout. The percentage of fat calories in beef is anywhere between 20 and 60 percent; most game meats have only 13 to 14 percent of their calories derived from fat. Here's the best part: farm-raised game is available all year long, so you don't have to wait for hunting season. But what about that gamy taste when the real thing comes back from a hunting trip? Cookbook author Frank Davis recommends soaking game in milk overnight to remove some of the unwanted "wild" flavor. This works up to a point, but it removes a bit of the desired flavor as well. I recommend using a second marinade to put some flavor back in. Game on hoof, such as venison, tends to be dry. The muscle tissue is firmer, meaning there is less fat and leaner meat. Dairy-based marinades are especially good for adding some moisture.

At the end of some of my favorite music festivals the performers climb back on stage for one large encore. In that spirit we'll close with some notes that tap into all of the food groups playing on brines, cures, marinades, rubs, and glazes as part of their ingredient instruments. And the encore for this chapter is jerky.

DESIGNER JERKY

Jerky is hip again. It may not look pretty, but it does have its fans. There are jerky cults that include foodies, campers, and hunters, and they are as every bit as intense as competitive barbecue teams. Even the Atkins types like it for low-carb protein snacks, and it has become as popular as home-baked cookies for folks serving overseas.

Jerky is simply raw meat that's flavored and air-cured at a low temperature to the point where it loses weight and volume. Prehistoric cooks made jerky from buffalo, antelope, deer, elk, and whatever else they could catch. Jerky, or *ch'arki,* was first introduced to the Spaniards by a Peruvian native tribe (originally part of the ancient Inca empire) as early as 1550. The Spanish then laid claim to it and renamed it *charqui* (pronounced "sharky"), from which the word *jerky* is derived. Native Americans and early settlers made it primarily from deer and buffalo, using salt and whatever spices they had. The meat was then dried and cured in the sun, requiring quite a bit of salt and some understanding neighbors.

JERKY PREPARATION

Jerky making is not an exacting science. Like barbecue, a lot depends on temperature, humidity, meat, moisture, and thickness. Jerky can be made from lean cuts of meat such as venison, beef skirt steak, eye of round, sirloin tip, brisket, inside round, flank steak, and chicken or turkey breast. Trim the meat of all visible fat, gristle, and membranes. Fat does not dry and can become rancid. Slightly freezing the meat for 2 hours makes it easier to cut. Slice across the grain for tender jerky and with the grain for chewy jerky. The slices can be around 5 to 6 inches long by 2 inches wide and ¼ inch thick.

When using any of the marinades in the book, omit the oils except those used for flavor, such as sesame or chile oil. Allow roughly 1 cup of marinade or ¼ cup of rub for each pound of meat. You need as much soaking time as possible in a nonreactive container, about 8 to 12 hours. If

you notice your beef turning gray or poultry looking translucent around the edges, remove it from the marinade to avoid a seviche effect. A marinade has a penetration point of little more than ⅛ inch per side, so a ¼-inch-thick strip of jerky will get almost full saturation. What may be a subtle balance in a marinade or rub comes out full blast in jerky. As food dehydrates, the meat's real estate shrinks and the flavors intensify along the lines of a stock or sauce reduction. With jerky, glazes are sweeter, cures and brines can be saltier, and chiles are even spicier. So pull back on the habanero; you'll thank me for it later.

Salt, as you may know, retards bacteria growth. but you can counterbalance the taste of salt with a glaze. Because brining will draw water in initially, your drying time may be an hour or two longer.

JERKY SAFETY

Most people don't have bad luck with the traditional way of making jerky or barbecuing. But if you want some extra security, here are a few things you can do before you start. Make sure that anything that comes into contact with your jerky is scrupulously clean, including cutting boards, utensils, and most important, yourself.

Illnesses due to salmonella and *E. coli* are raising safety issues about drying methods for homemade beef and venison jerky. The USDA Meat and Poultry Hotline's current recommendation for making jerky safely is to heat the meat to 160°F before the dehydrating process. This is because in a dehydrator or a low-temperature oven, evaporating moisture absorbs most of the heat. The meat does not begin to rise in temperature until most of the moisture has evaporated. When the dried meat's temperature finally begins to rise, the bacteria have become more heat resistant and are more likely to survive.

Avoid postheating jerky in a microwave oven because it cooks unevenly and leaves "cold spots," where harmful bacteria can survive. Food scientist and nutritionist Dr. Pat Kendall, of Colorado State University, suggests a 10-minute premarinade vinegar dip as an alternative to preheating jerky. The vinegar needs to be at least 5 percent acetic acid. If you have any question about the source of your meat, or if you are using game, freeze the batch for at least 1 week in a 0°F freezer.

In reality, properly made jerky has a number of preservation things in its favor. First, the salt level, which is higher than in some other cooked meats, and the 145°F drying process eliminate practically 90 percent of the moisture, and most of the bacteria along with it.

DRYING JERKY

All raw meats need to be dried at a temperature of 145°F. Once the meat has been marinated or seasoned, spray your dehydrator or oven-ready racks with cooking spray for easy cleanup. Arrange the slices so they don't overlap or touch each other. Average drying times can run as long as 5 to 20 hours, depending on the wattage of the dehydrator, the temperature of the oven or grill, and the moisture content and thickness of the meat. The longer the drying time, the more shrinkage and hardness of the finished product. Finished jerky should be dry to the touch and should bend without snapping.

Oven drying: Line the bottom of the oven with either aluminum foil crimped with an edge or a wide baking pan to catch the drippings. Preheat the oven to 170°F for 30 minutes, and then reduce the heat to 140°F. Thread the meat strips onto skewers and space them so that they dangle between the openings of the oven racks. Another option is to lay the strips on a cake rack or grid. I like to use a pizza "screen," a circular mesh that fits inside a pizza pan. If you have one, place the screen on one rack with the pan directly under it on one of the bottom racks. You can also lay out the strips in rows and in a single layer on a cookie sheet lined with aluminum foil (or use a silicone

mat as a last resort). The drying process may take a bit longer due to the lack of circulating air. When the strips start to harden, rearrange and turn them. The ones along the edge of the sheet will dry faster. Think circulation; you'll need to keep the oven slightly ajar to let the moist air escape. A convection oven is ideal for making jerky if your oven has that feature.

Dehydrator drying: Dehydrators are one of the easiest and most consistent ways of making jerky. Besides the convenient "set-it-and-forget-it" factor, it enables you to do large batches and multiple recipes without tying up your oven. A dehydrator also comes in handy for making citrus and vegetable powders that are used throughout the book.

Run the dehydrator about 20 to 30 minutes to reach temperature. If you have an oven thermometer, test the setting on your dehydrator to make sure it is within calibration. Remember, the more trays of meat you pack in, the longer the drying time.

Smoker drying: I've always treated smoke as a flavor as well as a cooking process. To prepare marinated strips of jerky for smoking, let them air-dry in the refrigerator for 8 to 12 hours on a baking rack over a pan. This forms a pellicle. Smoke does not penetrate wet surfaces, but it sticks to dry ones. As with barbecue, glazes work best when applied during the last hour of drying or smoking time; otherwise, the glaze will block smoke penetration.

As for my choice of woods, I use what's available in the Northeast—hickory, maple, oak, and fruit woods. I've found that smoking jerky for 3 hours at 170°F is more than enough to infuse the meat and poultry with a smoky flavor. At that point, you can finish the jerky in either a dehydrator or an oven. Once indoors, you can glaze to your heart's content. If you can resist the snack factor, allow jerky to cure for 24 hours after drying to develop its flavor.

THE PANTRIES AND RECIPES

The recipes in the following chapters couldn't be easier to use. You'll find recipes for marinades, rubs, brines, cures, and glazes using basic ingredients and with step-by-step instructions. You'll find most of what you need in your spice rack, your pantry, and the crisper section of your refrigerator. Each chapter leads off with a basic ingredient list for a particular recipe theme, cuisine, or region, and then drills down to specialty ingredients that may be used more exclusively in that style of cooking.

Some ingredients, such as fresh ginger, allspice, olive oil, and honey, have become transcontinental. Living near an East Coast city, I have access to a wide range of ingredients and ethnic markets. But I'm realistic enough to know that getting chipotle chiles, kaffir lime leaves, or even lemongrass becomes more difficult the farther away you are from the ethnic communities that cook with them. I suggest substitutes where I can, and online sources such as Food411.com are just a click away for the ingredients that are difficult to match.

When substituting ingredients, it's always a creative judgment call. Try to get a feel for the context in which the ingredient is used. Swapping lemons for limes is easy; swapping equal amounts of vinegar for lemon juice, however, can throw a recipe out of balance because of different acidity levels. Chiles can be an issue because of the ranges of heat, so the chart on pages 136 and 137, will aid your quest for fire.

My hope is that these recipes and techniques will show you the endless possibilities of cooking with marinades, rubs, brines, cures, and glazes—enough to inspire your own indoor and outdoor cooking creations. Experiment, improvise, and enjoy.

TIMELINES AT A GLANCE

How long does it take to brine that turkey, or marinate that pork tenderloin? When should you brush on a glaze, or throw a rub on a steak? My stock answer: It depends! It actually depends on a number of factors, such as the thickness of the seafood, poultry, or meat. It could depend on the acetic level of the marinade, the salinity level of the brine, and the temperature of the food itself.

The charts on pages 32 through 35 are general guidelines to help you with your own kitchen timing. The individual recipes that follow in the next chapters will give you more precise times. These are all minimum times. With seafood, you want to stay pretty close to the given range, while poultry can be left in the marinade for the better part of a day. Large cuts of poultry can handle up to 12 hours in a marinade. You do need to check your food for a seviche effect no matter what your timing. If chicken becomes translucent around the edges and red meat begins to turn gray, remove it from the marinade.

TIMELINES AT A GLANCE			
	Brines	**Dry and Wet Cures**	**Low-Acetic Marinades**
Recipe Notes	Brines have ratios of ½ cup kosher salt/ sugar to 2 quarts liquid.	Wet cures are actually brines with a higher salinity.	Asian-style marinades use mostly shelf staple ingredients and rice wine vinegars.
SEAFOOD			
Salmon Steaks and Fillets	30 minutes to 1 hour	2 to 3 days	4 to 6 hours
Tuna Steaks		2 to 3 days	4 to 6 hours
Swordfish Steaks			3 to 4 hours
Red Snapper, Catfish, Sea Bass, Halibut			3 to 4 hours
Scallops	1 hour		3 to 4 hours
Shrimp	1 to 2 hours		3 to 4 hours
POULTRY			
Chicken Breasts and Kabobs	4 to 6 hours	12 to 24 hours	4 to 6 hours
Chicken Wings, Thighs, and Legs	8 to 12 hours		4 to 6 hours
Whole Chicken	8 to 12 hours		6 to 8 hours
Cornish Hens	6 to 8 hours		4 to 6 hours
Turkey Breast	12 to 24 hours		6 to 8 hours
Duck Breast		3 to 4 days	4 to 6 hours
Quail	4 to 6 hours		4 to 6 hours
Whole Turkey (12 to 16 pounds)	12 to 24 hours		
Whole Turkey (17+ pounds)	12 hours to 2 days		
PORK			
Tenderloin	6 to 8 hours		4 to 6 hours
Chops	6 to 8 hours		4 to 6 hours
Shoulder	8 to 12 hours		8 to 12 hours
Kabobs	6 to 8 hours		4 to 6 hours
Baby Back Ribs and Spareribs	8 to 12 hours		8 to 12 hours

TIMELINES AT A GLANCE			
Full-Strength Marinades	**Yogurt-Based Marinades**	**Rubs**	**Glazes**
Full-strength marinades include citrus juice, wine, and some vinegars.	These include marinades from the Middle East and India used with kabobs and tandoori.	Rubs can be applied right before cooking on smaller cuts of meat.	Glazes can be applied during the end of cooking. In fact, they can be warmed and streaked over the finished dish as a sauce.
SEAFOOD			
3 to 4 hours			Last 5 minutes of cooking
3 to 4 hours			Last 5 minutes of cooking
2 to 3 hours			Last 5 minutes of cooking
2 to 3 hours			Last 5 minutes of cooking
2 to 3 hours			Last 5 minutes of cooking
2 to 3 hours	3 to 4 hours		Last 5 minutes of cooking
POULTRY			
3 to 5 hours	6 to 8 hours	1 hour	Last 5 minutes of cooking
8 to 12 hours	8 to 12 hours	1 hour	Last 5 minutes of cooking
4 to 6 hours		1 hour	Last 5 minutes of cooking
4 to 6 hours		1 hour	Last 5 minutes of cooking
6 to 8 hours	12 to 24 hours	1 hour	Last 5 minutes of cooking
4 to 6 hours		1 hour	Last 5 minutes of cooking
4 to 6 hours		1 hour	Last 5 minutes of cooking
		1 hour	Last 5 minutes of cooking
		1 hour	Last 5 minutes of cooking
PORK			
4 to 6 hours	8 to 12 hours	1 hour	Last 5 minutes of cooking
4 to 6 hours	8 to 12 hours	1 hour	Last 5 minutes of cooking
8 to 12 hours		8 to 12 hours	Last 5 minutes of cooking
4 to 6 hours	8 to 12 hours	1 hour	Last 5 minutes of cooking
6 to 8 hours		8 to 12 hours	Last 5 minutes of cooking

TIMELINES AT A GLANCE			
	Brines	**Dry and Wet Cures**	**Low-Acetic Marinades**
Recipe Notes	Brines have ratios of ½ cup kosher salt/sugar to 2 quarts liquid.	Wet cures are actually brines with a higher salinity.	Asian-style marinades use mostly shelf staple ingredients and rice wine vinegars.
BEEF			
Filets and Rib Eye			6 to 8 hours
Sirloin, Porterhouse, New York Strip, and Tri Tips			6 to 8 hours
London Broil, Skirt Steak, and Flank Steak		12 to 24 hours	6 to 8 hours
Brisket, Prime Rib, and Rib Roast			12 to 24 hours
Beef Kabobs			6 to 8 hours
Ground (Burgers)			1 hour
Short Ribs			12 to 24 hours
VEAL			
Loin and Paillards			6 to 8 hours
LAMB			
Rack and Rib Chops			6 to 8 hours
Leg of Lamb			6 to 8 hours
Lamb Kabobs			
Ground Lamb			
VENISON			
Steaks			8 to 12 hours
Tenderloin		2 to 3 days	8 to 12 hours
Chops			8 to 12 hours

TIMELINES AT A GLANCE			
Full-Strength Marinades	**Yogurt-Based Marinades**	**Rubs**	**Glazes**
Full-strength marinades include citrus juice, wine, and some vinegars.	These include marinades from the Middle East and India used with kabobs and tandoori.	Rubs can be applied right before cooking on smaller cuts of meat.	Glazes can be applied during the end of cooking. In fact, they can be warmed and streaked over the finished dish as a sauce.
BEEF			
6 to 8 hours		1 hour	
6 to 8 hours		1 hour	
8 to 12 hours		8 to 12 hours	
12 to 24 hours		6 to 8 hours	
6 to 8 hours	6 to 8 hours	1 hour	
1 hour		6 to 8 hours	
8 to 12 hours		8 to 12 hours	
VEAL			
6 to 8 hours			
LAMB			
3 to 4 hours	6 to 8 hours	1 hour	
6 to 8 hours	8 to 12 hours	1 hour	
	8 to 12 hours	1 hour	
		1 hour	
VENISON			
6 to 8 hours		1 hour	
6 to 8 hours		1 hour	
6 to 8 hours		1 hour	

BASIC RECIPES
& INGREDIENT THEMES

In the last chapter, we looked at how marinades, rubs, cures, brines, and glazes were wired together and how they light up seafood, poultry, pork, beef, veal, and game. Now we're going to take a closer look at ingredients themselves—how to use them and how to store them—and then we'll play with some recipe ideas to see how we can get the most flavor bang for the buck. We'll start with some basic recipes and then play out ingredient themes using citrus, fruit, fresh herbs and vegetables, and liquors—basic and accessible pantry items that can develop into some very sophisticated eating. Let's begin on a sour note, with citrus.

UNDERSTANDING CITRUS

Citrus fruit adds spark to the marinating process. It sets off the denaturing process, with aromatics fusing flavor and with oils working as a lubricant. Just the idea of throwing any citrus into a marinade is not as simple as it sounds. Try pouring an 8-ounce glass of orange juice on one chicken breast and the same amount of fresh lemon juice on another, and then marinate them in their own containers for a couple of hours. The reaction will be as different as day and night. The chicken breast that was marinated in lemon juice will have an almost chalky-white complexion. When grilled, it will taste fairly dry because of the moisture that was leached out by the lemon juice. The orange juice version won't be as dry, but it will only carry hints of flavor. You would probably say, "It needs something." It probably needs a lot.

Measuring acidity in citrus can be a bit confusing. A low pH number indicates high acidity. Each step down the pH scale, from the neutral pH value of 7 to the high-acid value of 1, increases the acidic level, so the lower the number, the more acidic the juice. Orange juice has a pH of 3.5, while lemon juice has a pH of 2.3, which is considerably more acidic. In common kitchen-speak, it comes down to this: the higher the acidity level of a citrus, the more difficult it is to drink straight. If you can swallow it easily like a glass of grapefruit or orange juice, it has a lower acidity level. Conversely, the more pucker behind the juice, as with lemon or lime, the more acidic bite to the marinade. High-acid citrus juices can denature, or soften, food faster than some wines, but the juices lose their strength during the cooking process. You can always add some fresh lemon or lime juice at the last minute to bring up the tang before serving a dish.

Room-temperature citrus will always yield more juice than cold citrus straight out of the refrigerator. Before juicing, microwave the fruit on high for 15 seconds, or immerse it in hot water for 10 minutes, then roll the fruit between your palm and the countertop for a few seconds.

Peak-season citrus fruit tends to be heavier, with a sweeter juice content. Both lemons and limes have about the same acidity content when ripe. When buying freshly squeezed citrus juices in soft plastic containers, transfer them to glass bottles or jars and refrigerate them to extend their shelf life. Lemon juice will interact with soft plastic and shouldn't be frozen in it.

The recipes that follow always call for freshly squeezed juice. Bottled lemon and lime juices are no substitutes. If you're going to add fresh citrus flavor, the freshly grated zest is really where the tang is. Each recipe in this book, when calling for a specific amount of fresh citrus juice, will likely include the grated zest of the fruit that produces it. Be careful to avoid grating into the white pith, the bitter layer between the skin and the flesh. Lemons and limes will discolor dark meat over long marinating stretches and should be avoided. Use red wine instead.

Lemons: Lemons impart a neutral flavor in a marinade. You can feel their presence, but not necessarily taste their flavor (which comes from the citrus oils in the grated zest). They're grown all year round and are at their peak in midsummer, with thin-skinned, juicy fruit. Choose lemons with smooth, brightly colored skins without tints of green, which indicate that they were picked before their time. Lemons last for about 2 weeks refrigerated. There are 4 to 5 medium lemons in 1 pound. A pound of lemons yields ⅔ to 1 cup of juice and about 3 tablespoons of grated zest. One medium lemon yields 3 to 4 tablespoons of juice and 2 teaspoons of grated zest.

Limes: Limes are used extensively in the marinades of Asia, the Southwest, and the Caribbean. Limes impart a tropical flavor, and their juice and zest have a more pronounced flavor than their yellow cousin, the lemon. Although limes are available all year round, off-season limes in late winter and early spring tend to be pulpy, juiceless, and expensive. Peak-season limes from May to August are dark green and filled with juice that can freeze well for up to 6 months. There are 6 to 8 medium limes in 1 pound. A pound of limes yields ¾ to 1 cup of juice and about 2 tablespoons of grated zest. One medium lime yields about 2 to 3 tablespoons of juice and 1 to 2 teaspoons of grated zest.

Juice oranges, tangerines, and grapefruit: These low-acid citrus fruits make up in flavor for what they lack in bite. They may need to be supplemented with either lemons or limes in order to activate a marinade. Juice oranges are the citrus of choice in the orange family; the zest is the most flavorful, and the juice is the sweetest compared to other oranges. Tangerines can be delightful in most orange- or lemon-based marinades, and the tropical combination of grapefruit and orange juice can give a marinade a savory sourness. There are 3 medium oranges in 1 pound. A pound of oranges yields 1 to 1½ cups of juice and ¼ to ⅜ cup of grated zest. One medium juice orange yields ⅓ cup of juice and 1 tablespoon of grated zest.

THE FRUIT FACTOR

Fruit-based brines, marinades, and glazes have always been part of my cooking repertoire. Working with fruit in a savory recipe is part reinforcement and part innovation. Fruit reinforces memory flavors that have been around us since childhood. We have a pretty clear idea of what an apple or a strawberry will taste like. But the innovation begins when we start using fruit outside of its traditional garden of eating. If you want to assemble a simple pantry list that includes fruit, I suggest you get a few different jars of seedless berry jams, a couple of bags of assorted frozen berries, and a calendar to keep track of the seasonal changes. You don't need a lot to get this part of your pantry up and running, and the recipes are probably the most accessible and flavorful you can make on the spur of the moment.

When my glazing recipes went out for testing, I asked my friends for their opinions. Apparently, the kids couldn't get enough of the fruit glazes. But it wasn't just the kids who were clamoring for more. Fruit-based marinades and glazes perk up the taste buds and make a simple recipe such as grilled chicken more appealing.

Fruit can also give a dish a flush of color, with balanced sweetness and a little touch of pucker. Fruit flavors are recalled in certain wines, so why not pair them in a marinade or a glaze? Unlike most ingredients, fruit can always enter the pantry from a number of different directions. First, there are the seasonal transients and their frozen versions, which I've found can be just as tasty and have the advantage of being around all year long. Canned and jarred fruits have the added syrup that can be incorporated into a glaze. If it wasn't for canned fruit, I would spend hours peeling lychees.

When my wife and I go to the Southern Appalachians, we're always hauling back jars of mountain honey, homemade jams, and jellies for glazes. They are simple flavors in a jar that can be combined with mustard, grated citrus zest and juice, and salt and pepper, and then brushed on a side of salmon. Closer to home are the upscale jams and jellies popping up at food boutiques and the wonderful tropical jams of guava, passion fruit, and mango in Latin markets and the Spanish sections of local supermarkets.

USING HERBS AND VEGETABLES

Up to this point, fresh herbs and root vegetables were part of the marinating aromatic backup band. Herbs were used to freshen and brighten the acids and oils, and root vegetables would give the blend some depth and sweetness. In this chapter, we'll be bringing them up to play more solos.

It would be great if greengrocers sold fresh herbs in tablespoon or quarter-cup portions, but a reality check in produce aisle 2 says otherwise. The sturdier the stem, the longer the shelf life; a sturdy stem also indicates that the herb has been freshly cut. Leftover leaves do become an issue. You can store leftover or even freshly bought herbs in the refrigerator wrapped in a damp paper towel and placed in a plastic bag. Some store-bought herbs come bedded down in well-insulated plastic containers. After you've finished your recipe, recycle the containers for garden-grown herbs or herbs bought in bunches. Storage units don't get any better than this.

With leftover herbs you can make extracts that will add flavor to brines, marinades, and glazes. Heat the herbs in a small amount of champagne or rice wine vinegar, then strain the liquid. Store in clean, sterile jars, just as you would with any flavored vinegar. When stored in a cool, dark place, the extracts have a shelf life of 6 months to 1 year.

Vegetables such as red and yellow peppers and tomatoes can hold smoke like a sponge. I incorporate smoked sweet peppers and tomatoes into salsas and condiments. Smoke them for 30 minutes to 1 hour at 220°F. You don't want to cook them, and you do want to keep an eye on their color. You're looking for a slight smoke bronzing. A mesquite-smoked yellow pepper sauce or hickory-smoked tomato ketchup can provide nice hints of smoke that you can store in the refrigerator.

Root vegetables such as green onions, onions, garlic, and shallots are not really vegetables at all but subterranean bulbs. Ginger, a rhizome, is actually a stem. Carrots and beets are the real roots of the vegetable family. Vegetables grown underground have staying power. One of their jobs is to act as starch storage centers to nourish the rest of the plant. Let's talk about storing them out of the ground.

Garlic, onions, and shallots like locales similar to dungeons in cheap English horror movies: dim, dark places away from sunlight. They're good unrefrigerated for several months or until they sprout. Ginger packs the most moisture of the underground roots and has the least staying power. Carrots will last for several months refrigerated. The first thing you should do is lose the green tops, though. A carrot with greens attached is a work in progress. The tops will drain the root of its nutrients, moisture, and flavor. The same thing applies to beets, but their mortality rate is only a couple of weeks. One of my favorite uses for underground ingredients is turning them into savory powders to amp up brines, cures, and rubs.

If you've ever cooked or grilled for large gatherings, you'll know that there is a fair amount of individual food preferences that demand creativity. There is a series of grilled veggie and tofu recipes at the end of this chapter that fill the vegetarian bill nicely. Although they're portioned as main course recipes, they can be converted to sides as well. Make a lot; I've seen carnivores snatch them up as well.

WORKING WITH DRY INGREDIENTS

One of the best things you can do to improve flavor in your spice rack is to ditch your old ground spices and replace them with fresh whole spices. Whole spices have four times the flavor power of ground spices, and they only get better when you toast them. When ground spices begin to fade in a spice mix, they will throw the recipe out of balance. If you make the switch to whole spices, you'll need a spice grinder or an inexpensive coffee mill in which to grind them. A blender or a food processor will grind them unevenly because they chop coarsely and spray the spices upward and outward.

Age accounts for flavor, so check the dates on your spice jars. When you buy a new jar, put at least a purchase date on it in permanent marker. Ground spices and pepper have a shelf life of only 6 months to 1 year. Whole spices have a shelf life of up to 2 years when stored properly. Spices should be stored away from sunlight or heated appliances, and below 70°F to maintain their potency.

Avoid putting your spices near or over the stove; it's the quickest route to flavored sawdust. If you like to sprinkle spices when you're cooking (and I like to do it, too), put what you need in small bowls or ramekins on the counter where they will be handy.

Untoasted spices in recipes are like dancing with your shoes tied together. It's just going through the motions before the ultimate loss of balance. Toasting whole spices simply amplifies their flavor. Some of that can happen during the actual cooking process, but it happens unevenly. Whole spices work best for toasting because ground spices burn easily. Whole spices have four times the shelf life of ground spices because their seed coatings and barks actually protect their flavor, which isn't released until the spices are ground or heated.

To toast spices, in a small frying pan, place the spices and heat them over medium heat, shaking the pan or stirring the spices with a wooden spoon, for about 5 minutes, until they become fragrant. Remove them from the pan quickly because they will continue to cook and you do not want them to burn.

Let the spices cool and then place them in a spice mill or a blender and grind to a coarse powder. You can use an inexpensive coffee mill, but it should be dedicated to spices only, unless you enjoy cumin-flavored espresso.

Toast only what you need for a recipe. The flavor will last for a couple of weeks, but it will fade faster than whole, untoasted spices.

Technically, garlic and onion powders are not really spices, but they do find their way onto the spice rack, and their flavor is among the first to fade when exposed to air. Many folks tend to hold on to their spices way past their expiration date.

Aged onion and garlic powders, like an elderly batch of ground pepper, are a notch above flavored sawdust. They should have some concentrated flavor when you taste them. Why add them to a recipe if they don't? One of the solutions is to dry your own.

Drying is easy with or without a dehydrator. The trick to remember when drying is that the thinner the cut, the faster the drying process. Depending on the vegetable, I get about a 4-to-1 ratio of whole fresh fruit or vegetable to the same thing dried. When drying vegetables, you want the texture of a wooden matchstick. In other words, you should be able to bend and snap it. The freezer is the shelf-life extender of these powders, so save your glass medicine jars.

Although the recipes call for a powdering process, there's no reason why you can't use dried fruits and vegetables as chips for added texture in your dishes. Even in their powdered form, they add a colorful dusting to your dinner plate. Once you've tasted fresh grinds you'll never second-guess your spice rack again.

THE WELL-STOCKED LIQUOR PANTRY

Most cooks think that once they've lit a match to a saucepan and lit up the kitchen in a blue flame of bourbon, they've cooked off all the alcohol. Testing shows that they may be burning off only around 15 percent of the alcohol before the flame goes out.

To keep the flame, there needs to be a percentage of alcohol present in the vapors. Once the alcohol is burned down to below that point, out goes the flame, leaving almost 80 to 85 percent of the alcohol behind. This doesn't apply to beer and wine because of their low alcoholic content. So you couldn't light them with a butane torch even if you wanted to. (Note: The acids in wine are "nonvolatile," so they don't boil off; rather, they get more and more concentrated. The more you boil wine, the more sour it will taste.)

You should inform your guests when you are cooking with alcohol in case they have allergies or health issues. With marinades, the majority of the alcohol will be left behind in the bag or container. There is a fair amount burned off when you reduce liquids to concentrate flavors in a glaze. When you divide a typical glaze over a few portions, the

amount of glaze that actually adheres to food is a few tablespoons at most, and the alcohol is even less so.

BEER

Beer gives marinades a certain bitterness because of the hops. And the more the beer is cooked and reduced, the stronger and sweeter its flavor will be. Which kinds of beer are best to cook with? I'm partial to these three types.

Porters and stouts: These beers have a much stronger flavor than the lighter Pilsners. They can have aromas of chocolate, toffee, and caramel. Black or chocolate malt gives the porter its deep-brown color. Porters are a heavily malted, medium-bodied beer and can also be sweet. Porters are often confused with stouts. The classic dry stout, normally associated with Guinness, is black opaque, with a medium body and a medium to high hop bitterness. Stouts get their flavor from unroasted barley, as opposed to the roasted barley used in porters. Sweet stout, or cream stout, one of my favorite cooking beers, is similar in color to a dry stout, but it is much sweeter. Some stouts also have a coffee flavor.

Nut browns and ambers: These beers have a color range from reddish-brown to dark brown, and they are lower in alcohol content than porters. With a medium- to full-body flavor, these beers are great with food, and are particularly good for braising ribs.

Pale ales: Ales are light in color, ranging from a golden to a light copper hue. The style of this beer is defined by the hops used to make it. American hops are typically high in bitterness and aroma.

WINE

Wines, with their acetic content, will touch on the sour taste bud as well as the sweet. Is it really necessary to use the wine that you'll be serving in the glass as part of the marinade? No, but it's essential that the wine be drinkable on its own. Don't use opened wine that has been sitting in your refrigerator for a couple of weeks or commercial cooking wines. If you're not willing to serve it in a glass, don't soak good food in it.

Red wines: Young, full-bodied red wines, such as Zinfandels, Cabernets, Riojas, and Chiantis, make great marinades. They don't have to be expensive, just young. Light-bodied red wine, such as Beaujolais, brings berrylike flavors to marinades and is soft enough to make an excellent red wine marinade for fish.

White wines: Dry white wines like Sauvignon Blancs from South Africa or New Zealand and inexpensive Vinho Verdes from Portugal work best in savory marinades. In lieu of rice wine vinegar in Asian-style marinades, a light wine like a dry Riesling works particularly well. Unless the marinade features Chardonnay as a principal flavor, this wine gets lost in the shuffle of aromatics and oil. Avoid blush wines and white Zinfandels; they can give your marinade and glazes a soda pop flavor. Champagne is all but useless in marinades and glazes. The effervescent qualities fizzle out way before the cooking process even starts. Champagne that has a quality flavor also commands a quality price. Save it for that special occasion, or create one by just popping the cork.

Surprising enough, along with Rieslings, one of the white wines that I've found packs the most acidity is Sauternes. A good Sauternes needs a good acidic balance to offset its sweetness. For an interesting twist on Asian-style marinades, substitute Sauternes for rice wine vinegar. You'll discover that Sauternes pairs wonderfully with freshly grated ginger.

Fortified wines: Sherry, whose nutty flavor pairs nicely with nut and sesame oils, is one of the more flexible fortified wines in marinades and glazes. It knows no continent when it comes to flavor, and it's at home in both Asian- and Mediterranean-style marinades. Port brings a bit more fruit to marinades and glazes than sherry does. Madeira and Marsala play more of an aromatic role in marinades. Their strength tends to be domineering, so use them judiciously in marinades for meat.

LIQUEURS AND LIQUORS

Whiskeys, cassis, and rum will caramelize over high heat and form some of the sweetest-tasting binders for glazes. Food just loves to cling to it. Sunlit liqueur decanters are pretty to look at, but the heat causes the flavor to fade. Keep them cool in a cool dark place. If a recipe calls for a small amount of specialty spirits and you don't want to shell out the money for a full fifth, you can buy mini bottles similar to those served on airplanes. They're perfect portion control.

THE **BASIC PANTRY**

CITRUS: Lemons, limes, oranges.

DAIRY: Yogurt.

FRUIT: Fresh or frozen raspberries, cranberries.

VEGETABLES: Chives, garlic, fresh ginger, green onions, red onions, sweet onions (Vidalia or Maui), shallots, tomatoes.

FRESH HERBS: Basil, cilantro, dill, flat-leaf parsley, mint, oregano, rosemary, sage, tarragon, thyme.

CHILES (FRESH AND DRIED): Jalapeños, serranos, red pepper flakes, sweet paprika, cayenne pepper.

SPICES: Allspice, bay leaves, whole black and white peppercorns, cardamom, 3-inch-long cinnamon sticks, cloves, coriander seeds, cumin, dry mustard powder, garlic powder, ground ginger, juniper berries, mace, mustard seeds, dried oregano, nutmeg, kosher salt, coarse-grain salt.

OILS, VINEGARS, AND CONDIMENTS: Canola oil, extra virgin olive oil, grapeseed oil, peanut oil; balsamic vinegar, apple cider vinegar, fruit-flavored vinegars, red and white wine vinegar; capers, soy or tamari sauce, Tabasco or other hot sauces, vanilla extract; coarse-grain mustard, Dijon-style mustard, fruit mustards.

SWEETENERS: Granulated sugar, light and dark brown sugar, honey, maple syrup, fruit syrup. *Special ingredients:* Syrups.

WINES AND LIQUORS: Red wines such as Zinfandels, Cabernets, Riojas, Beaujolais, and Chianti Reservas; acidic white wines such as Sauvignon Blancs and inexpensive Vinho Verdes; fortified wines such as sherries, Madeira, and Marsala; spirits such as bourbon, gin, sour mash whiskey, crème de cassis, brandy, cognac, rum, vermouth, and vodka; extra credit for orange or pear liqueurs.

DRIED, CANNED, OR BOTTLED INGREDIENTS: Apple cider. *Special ingredients:* Fruit juices, basic jams and jellies, tropical jams and jellies.

SPECIAL INGREDIENTS

BASIC JAMS AND JELLIES: Apricot jelly; seedless raspberry, black raspberry, or blackberry preserves; black or red current jelly.

TROPICAL JAMS AND JELLIES: Passion-fruit, mango, pineapple, papaya, guava jams and jellies (available in Latin American grocery stores).

FRUIT JUICES: Bottled pomegranate juice (off-season substitute), tropical fruit nectars, pineapple juice.

SYRUPS: Look for Al Wadi or Cortas brand pomegranate molasses in Middle Eastern markets and gourmet stores. Store it in the refrigerator, where it will keep almost indefinitely. You can reduce 2 cups of pomegranate juice to ¼ cup and add 1 tablespoon of molasses to substitute for pomegranate molasses.

BASIC DRY CURE FOR SMOKED POULTRY
MAKES 2¼ CUPS

Although the recipe title sounds like a turn-of-the-nineteenth-century remedy, you can combine this cure with the Maple-Pomegranate Glaze (page 87) for the excellent Smoked Chicken Breasts (page 105).

1 cup kosher salt
⅔ cup firmly packed dark brown sugar
1 tablespoon freshly ground black pepper
1 tablespoon freshly ground white pepper
1 tablespoon garlic powder
1 tablespoon grated nutmeg
1 tablespoon ground coriander
1½ teaspoons ground cloves
1 teaspoon ground allspice
½ teaspoon cayenne pepper

Combine the salt, brown sugar, black pepper, white pepper, garlic powder, nutmeg, coriander, cloves, allspice, and cayenne in a nonreactive mixing bowl. The cure can be stored in a clean, airtight container in the refrigerator for at least 6 months.

ORANGE AND JUNIPER CURE MAKES 2 CUPS

This recipe is from Philadelphia food consultant Aliza Green. It's used with Juniper and Orange Cured Venison with Herb Salad (page 126). Use this cure on venison loin, whole fillet of beef, and pork tenderloin.

¼ cup juniper berries
¼ cup grated orange zest (3 or 4 oranges)
2 tablespoons kosher salt
2 tablespoons freshly crushed black peppercorns
2 tablespoons chopped fresh thyme leaves
2 tablespoons chopped fresh summer savory leaves
1 tablespoon crushed coriander seeds
1 tablespoon crumbled bay leaves

Combine the juniper berries, orange zest, salt, pepper, thyme, savory, coriander, and bay leaves in a blender or a food processor. Process to a fine paste.

JUNIPER-GIN CURE MAKES 3 CUPS

This is my base recipe cure for Juniper-Gin Cured Gravlax (page 98). The recipe will yield enough to cure 3 pounds of fish.

¼ cup gin
1 cup firmly packed light brown sugar
1 cup kosher salt
3 tablespoons crushed white peppercorns
6 to 8 coarsely crushed juniper berries
2 tablespoons freshly grated lemon zest
1½ bunches fresh dill, roughly chopped (about 3 cups)

Reserve the gin to sprinkle over the fish fillets. Combine the sugar, salt, peppercorns, juniper berries, lemon zest, and dill in a small bowl and mix.

BASIC LEMON CURE. Omit the gin and the juniper berries and increase the lemon zest to ¼ cup. Proceed with the recipe as described above.

LEMON-MINT CURE. Omit the juniper berries. Replace the gin with lemon juice and the dill with fresh mint. Proceed with the recipe as described above.

TIP: When curing salmon fillets, distribute the cure according to the thickness of the fish. Apply more cure toward the head and less cure toward the tail, so that both sections will cure evenly.

CITRUS SEAFOOD CURE MAKES ABOUT 4 CUPS

This is a cure for all seasons and seasonings. The added liquors are optional, but they give the citrus in the recipe a nice, bright flavor push.

¼ cup cognac, Grand Mariner, or limoncello (optional)
1 cup firmly packed dark brown sugar or Maple Sugar (page 71)
1 cup kosher salt
1 cup coarsely ground black pepper
½ cup coarsely ground juniper berries
Grated zest of 2 large pink grapefruits (about ⅓ cup)
Grated zest of 2 oranges (about ¼ cup)
Grated zest of 1 lime (about 1 teaspoon)
Grated zest of 1 lemon (about 2 teaspoons)

Reserve the liquor to sprinkle over the fish fillets. Combine the sugar, salt, pepper, juniper, grapefruit zest, orange zest, lime zest, and lemon zest in a medium bowl. Stir to mix thoroughly.

**TIMETABLE
(FOR BOTH RECIPES):**

Chicken breasts, kabobs, or quail: 6 hours

Chicken wings, thighs, legs, or whole chicken: 8 to 12 hours

Cornish hens: 6 to 8 hours

Turkey breast: 12 to 24 hours

Whole turkey, 12 to 16 pounds: 12 to 24 hours

Whole turkey, 17 pounds and over: 12 to 48 hours

Pork tenderloin, chops, or kabobs: 6 to 8 hours

Pork shoulder, baby back ribs, or spareribs: 8 to 12 hours

ALL-PURPOSE BASIC BRINE MAKES 8 CUPS

You can get a lot of mileage from these three "neutral" flavored ingredients. If you simply want the texture of a juicy pork chop or chicken breast, this is the jumping-off point. It only gets better from here. The recipe can be easily scaled up for larger cuts of food.

**2 quarts water
½ cup kosher salt or other coarse-grain salt
⅓ to ½ cup firmly packed light or dark brown sugar**

In a large saucepan over medium-high heat, combine the water, salt, and brown sugar. Bring to a boil, stirring to dissolve the salt and sugar. Remove from the heat and let the mixture cool to room temperature, then refrigerate to 40°F before adding meat or poultry.

BASIC CITRUS BRINE MAKES 6 QUARTS

This brine will give chicken, turkey breasts, and pork tenderloin and chops a simple citrus undertone. It's not overpowering, and it will brighten just about any "white" meat.

**Julienned zest and juice of 3 oranges (about 1 cup)
Julienned zest and juice of 3 lemons (about ⅔ cup)
Julienned zest and juice of 3 limes (about ⅓ cup)
5 quarts water
1 cup kosher salt
¾ cup firmly packed light brown sugar**

Combine the orange, lemon, and lime zest and juices in a small nonreactive saucepan. Bring to a boil and decrease the heat. Simmer and reduce to 1 cup. The zest should sink to the bottom.

Bring 1 quart of the water to a boil in a 6-quart saucepan and add the citrus reduction, salt, and sugar, stirring to dissolve. Remove from the heat, add the remaining 4 quarts water, and let the mixture cool to room temperature, then refrigerate to 40°F before adding the food.

BASIC BRINE FOR PORK AND POULTRY

MAKES 8¼ CUPS

• •

This brine is my first stop for pork and poultry. It can be scaled up for whole turkeys, or multiple racks of ribs or chops. The seasoning is not overbearing, and the juices just run with flavor.

2 quarts water
1 cup chopped Vidalia or other sweet onion
   (substitute red onion, if needed)
4 to 6 cloves garlic, chopped
½ cup kosher salt
½ cup firmly packed dark brown sugar
1 tablespoon fresh thyme
1 tablespoon fresh rosemary, finely chopped
¼ cup coarsely ground black pepper
1 teaspoon hot paprika
1 teaspoon cumin seeds
3 or 4 bay leaves

To open up the flavor of the onions and garlic, place 1 cup of the water, the onions, and the garlic in a blender or a food processor. Process until all the ingredients are blended.

In a large saucepan or stockpot over medium-high heat, combine the remaining 7 cups water, onion-garlic mixture, salt, brown sugar, thyme, rosemary, pepper, paprika, cumin seeds, and bay leaves and bring to a boil for 10 minutes, stirring to dissolve the salt and sugar. Decrease the heat and simmer for 30 minutes to brew the ingredients.

Remove from the heat and let the mixture cool to room temperature, then refrigerate to 40°F before adding the food.

TIMETABLE:

Chicken breasts, kabobs, or quail: 6 hours

Chicken wings, thighs, legs, or whole chicken: 8 to 12 hours

Cornish hens: 6 to 8 hours

Turkey breast: 12 to 24 hours

Whole turkey, 12 to 16 pounds: 12 to 24 hours

Whole turkey, 17 pounds and over: 12 to 48 hours

Pork tenderloin, chops, or kabobs: 6 to 8 hours

Pork shoulder, baby back ribs, or spareribs: 8 to 12 hours

Chicken breasts, kabobs,
Cornish hens, or quail:
6 hours

Chicken wings, thighs,
legs, or whole chicken:
8 to 12 hours

Turkey breast:
12 to 24 hours

Whole turkey, 12 to 16
pounds: 12 to 24 hours

Whole turkey, 17 pounds
and over: 12 to 48 hours

BASIC BRINE FOR WHOLE ROAST CHICKEN
MAKES 4 QUARTS

Roast chicken is pure comfort food. One of the problems is that sometimes it gets too dry. A flavorful brining solution can be the perfect solution. This brine can be scaled up to handle any size chicken.

4 quarts water
1 cup kosher salt
¾ cup firmly packed dark brown sugar
4 bay leaves
1 tablespoon fennel seeds
1 tablespoon coriander seeds, cracked
1 tablespoon black or white peppercorns, cracked
1 tablespoon mustard seeds, cracked
1 3-inch cinnamon stick

In a large saucepan over medium-high heat, combine the water, salt, and sugar. Bring to a boil, stirring to dissolve the salt and sugar. Add the bay leaves, fennel seeds, coriander seeds, peppercorns, mustard seeds, and cinnamon. Decrease the heat and simmer for 30 minutes to brew the ingredients.

Remove from heat and let the brine cool to room temperature, then refrigerate to 40°F before adding the food.

TIMETABLE:
Chicken breasts, kabobs,
Cornish hens, or quail:
6 hours

Chicken wings, thighs, legs,
whole chicken, or rabbit:
8 to 12 hours

Turkey breast:
12 to 24 hours

Whole turkey, 12 to 16
pounds: 12 to 24 hours

Whole turkey, 17 pounds
and over: 12 to 48 hours

APPLE CIDER BRINE MAKES 9 CUPS

Depending on how much you like apple cider you can tag team this brine with the Apple Cider Marinade (page 56) for the grill or for a formal fall sit-down dinner. Brining a turkey breast and smoking it over apple wood are true autumn bliss. This recipe can be scaled up.

8 cups apple cider
½ cup finely chopped onion
3 cloves garlic, pressed
2 tablespoons black peppercorns, ground
2 tablespoons fresh rosemary
1 tablespoon ground mustard seed
1 bay leaf
¼ teaspoon ground nutmeg
½ cup honey
¼ cup firmly packed dark brown sugar
½ cup kosher salt

Combine 1 cup of the cider, the onion, and the garlic in a blender or a food processor and process until blended. Combine the cider purée, the remaining 7 cups cider, peppercorns, rosemary, ground mustard, bay leaf, and nutmeg in a saucepan and bring to a boil. Decrease the heat and simmer for 30 minutes to infuse the ingredients. Stir in the honey, brown sugar, and salt to dissolve. Simmer for an additional 15 minutes.

Remove from the heat, allow the brine to cool completely, remove the bay leaf, and then refrigerate to 40°F before adding the meat or fish.

MAPLE-BOURBON BRINE MAKES 6¼ QUARTS

Brining baby back ribs or spareribs in this recipe is worthy of competition barbecue circuits. It's a winner around your grill as well.

6 quarts water
1 cup kosher salt
1½ cups maple syrup
1 cup bourbon
2 tablespoons ground mustard
2 bay leaves
1½ teaspoons hot red pepper flakes
2 tablespoons chopped rosemary

In a large saucepan over medium-high heat, add the water, salt, maple syrup, bourbon, ground mustard, bay leaves, red pepper flakes, and rosemary. Bring to a boil, and stir to dissolve. Decrease the heat and simmer for 30 minutes to brew the ingredients. Remove from the heat and let the brine cool to room temperature, then refrigerate to 40°F before adding the food.

HONEY-COGNAC BRINE. This is great with grilled chicken breasts. Substitute honey for the maple syrup and cognac for the bourbon.

TIMETABLE, *continued:*
Pork tenderloin, chops, or kabobs: 6 to 8 hours

Pork shoulder, baby back ribs, or spareribs: 8 to 12 hours

TIMETABLE:
Chicken breasts, kabobs, Cornish hens, or quail: 6 hours

Chicken wings, thighs, legs, or whole chicken: 8 to 12 hours

Turkey breast: 12 to 24 hours

Whole turkey, 12 to 16 pounds: 12 to 24 hours

Whole turkey, 17 pounds and over: 12 to 48 hours

Pork tenderloin, chops, or kabobs: 6 to 8 hours

Pork shoulder, baby back ribs, or spareribs: 8 to 12 hours

BASIC MARINADE FOR SEAFOOD MAKES 2½ CUPS

This is the recipe I recommend for folks who need an easy marinade for seafood. It is simple and good. You really can't go wrong with white wine, citrus, olive oil, and fresh herbs. Note that this marinade packs a fair amount of acid, so don't overmarinate the seafood.

3 cloves garlic, pressed
3 to 4 tablespoons chopped fresh parsley, mint, cilantro leaves, or basil
1 teaspoon dried oregano
1 teaspoon chopped fresh rosemary
1½ teaspoons capers (optional)
1 teaspoon coarse-grain salt
1 tablespoon freshly ground black pepper
1½ cups dry white wine, or 1 cup dry vermouth
Grated zest and juice of 2 lemons (about ⅓ cup)
¼ to ½ teaspoon Tabasco sauce
½ cup extra virgin olive oil

Combine the garlic, parsley, oregano, rosemary, capers, salt, pepper, wine, lemon zest and juice, and Tabasco sauce in a blender or a food processor. Cover and process for about 20 to 30 seconds, until all the ingredients are blended. While the motor is running, drizzle in the oil a little at a time. Use the marinade within 24 hours.

LIME-CILANTRO MARINADE. Replace the lemons with 4 or 5 limes, and replace the herbs with cilantro leaves only.

BASIC MARINADE FOR POULTRY MAKES 1½ CUPS

Don't be put off by the word basic. This is my stock chicken breast marinade that reeks of citrus, mustard, and herbs. All of the ingredients are available throughout the year. The prep is easy, and the flavors just hang in there. Even though the recipe title says poultry, you can also use it with shrimp.

Grated zest and juice of 2 juice oranges (about ⅔ cup)
Grated zest and juice of 2 lemons (about ⅓ cup)
2 or 3 cloves garlic, chopped
¼ cup chopped fresh parsley
1 tablespoon Dijon-style mustard
1 teaspoon Worcestershire sauce
1 teaspoon coarse-grain or sea salt
1 tablespoon cracked black peppercorns
1 teaspoon dried oregano
¼ cup canola oil

Combine the orange zest and juice, lemon zest and juice, garlic, parsley, mustard, Worcestershire sauce, salt, pepper, and oregano in a blender or a food processor. Process until all the ingredients are blended. While the motor is running, drizzle in the oil a little at a time. This marinade freezes well with food for up to 3 months.

LEMON MARINADE MAKES 1½ CUPS
. . . .

Simply lemon, this is a marinade with pucker and attitude that begs for seafood.

Grated zest and juice of 3 lemons (about ⅔ cup)
¼ cup chopped red onion
¼ cup chopped fresh flat-leaf parsley
3 tablespoons coarsely ground mixed peppercorns
     (black, white, green, pink, etc.)
¼ teaspoon cayenne pepper
½ teaspoon coarse-grain salt
½ cup light extra virgin olive oil

Combine the lemon zest and juice, onion, parsley, peppercorns, cayenne, and salt in a blender or a food processor and process until all the ingredients are blended. While the motor is running, drizzle in the oil a little at a time. Use the marinade within 3 days.

LEMON-DILL MARINADE. Replace the parsley with dill. Omit the cayenne, and add 1 tablespoon Dijon-style mustard.

LEMON-SORREL MARINADE. Reduce the amount of lemon zest and juice to ⅓ cup. Add ¼ cup sherry or balsamic vinegar and 1 tablespoon Dijon-style mustard. Replace the parsley with ½ cup chopped fresh sorrel leaves and 1 teaspoon fresh thyme. Omit the cayenne.

LAUREL AND LEMON MARINADE. Add ¼ cup dry vermouth and 3 bay laurel leaves.

LIME MARINADE. Replace the lemons with 4 or 5 limes (about ½ cup juice).

TIMETABLE:
Salmon steaks or fillets, red snapper, catfish, sea bass, halibut, or scallops: 1 to 2 hours

Red snapper, catfish, sea
bass, halibut, or swordfish
steaks: 2 to 3 hours

Chicken breasts or
kabobs, Cornish hens, pork
tenderloin, or pork chops:
3 to 4 hours

LEMON-SOY MARINADE MAKES ½ CUP

It's simple and easy, but oh so effective. This marinade by Jon Jividen defies ethnic pantry categories by pairing soy and Asian peanut oil with Dijon-style mustard.

⅓ cup soy or tamari sauce
Grated zest and juice of 1 lemon (about 3 tablespoons)
2 teaspoons Dijon-style mustard
1 clove garlic, minced or pressed
¼ cup Asian or domestic cold-pressed peanut oil or canola oil

Combine the soy sauce, lemon zest and juice, mustard, and garlic in a food processor or a blender. Process until all the ingredients are blended. Whisk in the oil a little at a time. This marinade freezes well with food for up to 3 months.

TIMETABLE:

Baste throughout your
cooking time over
salmon steaks or fillets,
swordfish steaks, red
snapper, catfish, sea
bass, halibut, scallops,
shrimp, chicken breasts or
kabobs, chicken wings or
legs, turkey breast, pork
tenderloin, pork chops,
pork kabobs, baby back
ribs, or spareribs

HOT CHILE–LIME BASTE MAKES 1½ CUPS

I developed this baste with Peter Cravath to replace the Lime Marinade for the Zesty Lime Grilled Chicken Wings (page 106). Because of the rules of the New England Snowshoe Challenge, the wings had to be prepared on the spot and grilled with no time to marinate. The alternative was this lime-flavored wing wash with just a hint of heat. The trick is to liquefy the jalapeños, garlic, and onions in a blender to maintain a loose consistency.

2 or 3 jalapeño chiles, seeded and deveined
2 or 3 cloves garlic, minced
½ cup diced sweet onion
1 teaspoon ground cumin
1 tablespoon coarse-grain salt
1 tablespoon freshly ground black pepper
Grated zest and juice of 6 medium limes (about ¾ cup)

Combine the jalapeños, garlic, onion, cumin, salt, pepper, and lime zest and juice in a blender or a food processor and process until all the ingredients are liquefied. Stored in a clean, airtight container, this will keep in the refrigerator for 1 week.

ORANGE MARINADE MAKES 1½ CUPS

This marinade has orange written all over it, from its bright orange color to its intense orange flavor. It is great for marinating chicken wings or breasts, as well as for basting pork chops or spareribs.

Grated zest and juice of 2 juice oranges (about ⅔ cup)
Grated zest and juice of 1 lemon (about 3 tablespoons)
½ cup Cointreau or other orange liqueur (optional)
2 tablespoons Dijon-style mustard
2 tablespoons Madeira
2 cloves garlic, chopped
1 tablespoon cracked black peppercorns
1 teaspoon coarse-grain salt
¼ cup chopped fresh herbs (sage, rosemary, thyme, parsley, etc.)
¼ cup light extra virgin olive oil

Combine the orange zest and juice, lemon zest and juice, Cointreau, mustard, Madeira, garlic, pepper, salt, and chopped herbs in a blender or a food processor and process until all the ingredients are blended. While the motor is running, drizzle in the oil a little at a time. The marinade will keep for up to 1 week in a tightly covered jar in the refrigerator.

ORANGE-CINNAMON MARINADE. Replace the Cointreau and the Madeira with 1½ cups dry white wine; delete the mustard; and add ½ teaspoon ground coriander, 1 bay leaf, and 1 tablespoon cinnamon.

ORANGE-SAFFRON MARINADE. Add ⅛ teaspoon saffron threads, crushed and dissolved in 2 tablespoons boiling water. Replace the Cointreau and the Madeira with ⅔ cup Sauternes or Essina Orange Muscat wine. Replace the garlic with 2 to 3 tablespoons chopped shallots. Reduce the Dijon-style mustard to 1 teaspoon.

TIMETABLE:
Salmon steaks or fillets, or tuna steaks: 2 to 3 hours

Chicken breasts or quail: 3 to 4 hours

Cornish hens, turkey breast, duck breast, goose breast, pork tenderloin, pork chops, or pork kabobs: 4 to 6 hours

Baby back ribs, spareribs, venison steaks, or venison chops: 6 to 8 hours

ORANGE-TARRAGON MARINADE MAKES 2½ CUPS

The bittersweet flavor of Seville oranges in the marmalade pairs nicely with the tarragon in this recipe. Use the marinade on roast chicken or Cornish hens, and then glaze carrots with the pan juices and remaining marinade.

Grated zest and juice of 3 juice oranges (about 1 cup)
½ cup Seville orange marmalade
⅓ cup tarragon vinegar
2 tablespoons chopped shallots
1 tablespoon chopped fresh tarragon
1 teaspoon cracked white peppercorns
1 teaspoon cracked black peppercorns
1 teaspoon coarse-grain or sea salt
½ cup canola oil

In a small nonreactive saucepan, bring the orange zest and juice to a low simmer and stir in the marmalade until dissolved. Remove the saucepan from the heat and cool to room temperature.

Combine the marmalade mixture, vinegar, shallots, fresh tarragon, white and black peppercorns, and salt in a blender or a food processor and process until all the ingredients are blended. While the motor is running, drizzle in the canola oil a little at a time. This marinade will keep for up to 1 week refrigerated in a clean, airtight container. It freezes well with food for 3 to 4 months.

TIMETABLE:
Cornish hens or quail:
3 to 4 hours

Pork tenderloin, pork chops, or pork kabobs:
4 to 6 hours

Whole chicken:
6 to 8 hours

ORANGE-GINGER MARINADE MAKES 1½ CUPS

I like the type of marinade that you can make before you go to the market. Whatever you return with, be it chicken, ribs, or tuna steaks, this make-ahead marinade will always come through with flying colors. By combining the Mediterranean flavors of orange, extra virgin olive oil, and balsamic vinegar with the Asian tang of ginger, the marinade's flavor is constantly unraveling, bite after bite.

Grated zest and juice of 2 juice oranges (about ⅔ cup)
2 tablespoons balsamic vinegar
2 tablespoons soy or tamari sauce
2 tablespoons minced fresh ginger
1 teaspoon dry mustard
1 teaspoon coarse-grain or sea salt
1 tablespoon cracked black peppercorns
¼ cup light extra virgin olive oil

TIMETABLE:
Tuna or salmon steaks:
2 to 4 hours

Chicken breasts:
3 to 4 hours

Pork chops or tenderloins:
4 to 6 hours

Chicken wings:
6 to 8 hours

Baby back ribs or spareribs:
6 hours or overnight

Combine the orange zest and juice, balsamic vinegar, soy sauce, ginger, dry mustard, salt, and pepper in a blender or a food processor and process until all the ingredients are blended. While the motor is running, drizzle in the olive oil a little at a time. This marinade will keep in a clean, airtight container in the refrigerator for at least 1 week and freezes well.

ORANGE-GINGER GLAZE. To use this marinade as a glaze for chicken wings or pork ribs, omit the oil and add ½ cup orange marmalade or ginger preserves. In a small nonreactive saucepan, combine the orange zest and juice with either the orange marmalade or the ginger preserves. Simmer to dissolve, remove from the heat, and let cool. Complete the recipe as above. If you are grilling or roasting seafood, meat, or poultry, turn and baste with the glaze during the last 5 minutes of cooking.

TANGERINE–PINK PEPPERCORN MARINADE
MAKES 1⅓ CUPS

TIMETABLE:
Smoked salmon or smoked trout: 2 hours

Scallops or shrimp:
3 to 4 hours

This actually started as a marinade-style dressing for the recipe Smoked Salmon with Tangerine–Pink Peppercorn Marinade (page 94). I thought this was a perfectly good, light marinade that could play with other food toys like shrimp and scallops. And it does play well with others, especially if the playground is your grill.

Juice of 6 tangerines (about 1 cup)
1 teaspoon grated tangerine zest
Juice of 1 lemon (about 3 tablespoons)
1½ teaspoons honey
1 teaspoon coarsely crushed coriander seeds
2 teaspoons coarsely crushed pink peppercorns
1 teaspoon freshly ground black pepper
1 tablespoon chopped fresh dill

Combine the tangerine juice and zest, lemon juice, honey, coriander seeds, pink peppercorns, black pepper, and dill in a nonreactive mixing bowl. Stored in a clean, airtight container, this will keep in the refrigerator for 1 week.

GINGER AND LIME MARINADE. Replace the tangerine zest and juice with grated zest and juice of 2 limes. Add 1 to 2 inches fresh gingerroot, peeled and grated, and 1 tablespoon light soy sauce to the ingredients above and whisk in 4 tablespoons extra virgin olive oil a little at a time.

TIMETABLE:
Salmon steaks or fillets:
2 to 3 hours

Chicken breasts or
kabobs: 3 to 4 hours

Pork tenderloin, pork
chops, pork kabobs, or
rabbit: 4 to 6 hours

Chicken wings, thighs,
or legs; Cornish hens; or
turkey breast: 6 to 8 hours

APPLE CIDER MARINADE MAKES 2 CUPS

I think of apple cider as autumn's reward for getting through August's heat. This marinade has a slight pitch of sweetness with a savory undertow that gives any pork or poultry dish a fall flavor.

4 cups apple cider
¼ cup cider vinegar
1 tablespoon Dijon-style mustard
1 tablespoon chopped fresh tarragon
1 tablespoon apple butter or honey
1 teaspoon coarsely ground black pepper
1 teaspoon coarsely ground mustard seeds
2 shallots, diced (about 1½ tablespoons)
1 teaspoon coarse-grain salt
¼ cup grapeseed or light olive oil

Bring the apple cider to a boil in a nonreactive saucepan and reduce to about 1½ cups. Remove from the heat and cool to room temperature.

Combine the reduced cider, cider vinegar, mustard, tarragon, apple butter, pepper, mustard seeds, shallots, and salt in a blender or a food processor, and process until all the ingredients are blended. While the motor is running, drizzle in the oil a little at a time. This marinade freezes well with food for up to 3 months.

CIDER-CALVADOS MARINADE: Replace the cider vinegar with dry white wine. Add 2 tablespoons Calvados and 1 tablespoon herbes de Provence (page 228).

TIMETABLE:
Quail: 3 to 4 hours

Chicken breasts:
4 to 6 hours

Turkey, duck, or goose
breasts: 6 to 8 hours

BASIC BERRY MARINADE MAKES 2 CUPS

Basic, yes; boring, no. You can easily swap out the raspberries for blackberries, strawberries, or even cooked cranberries. This marinade complements Muscovy duck breasts and fruitwood smoke.

1½ cups fresh or frozen raspberries
½ cup raspberry vinegar (or balsamic vinegar, if you're using strawberries)
Grated zest and juice of 1 lemon (about 3 tablespoons)
1 to 2 tablespoons chopped shallots
1 tablespoon maple syrup
1 clove garlic, chopped
1 tablespoon coarsely ground black pepper
1 teaspoon coarse-grain salt
3 or 4 fresh herb sprigs, such as tarragon or rosemary
⅓ cup canola or grapeseed oil

Process the raspberries in a food processor fitted with a plastic dough blade. (A steel blade will crush the seeds, which will lend a bitter taste to the food.) Strain and return the purée to the food processor. Add the vinegar, lemon zest and juice, shallots, syrup, garlic, pepper, salt, and herbs. Process until all the ingredients are blended. While the motor is running, drizzle in the oil a little at a time. This marinade freezes well with food.

RASPBERRY-BEAUJOLAIS MARINADE

MAKES 3¾ CUPS

This marinade is fruitier than the typical red wine marinade. The berrylike flavor of the Beaujolais complements the raspberries, and the aromatics give the marinade a savory contrast, which can hold up to game birds or venison. I've used this marinade on wild duck, quail, grouse, and other wild things, and the domesticated chicken breast takes to it just as well.

1 (12-ounce) bag frozen unsweetened raspberries, defrosted
1 cup Beaujolais (or other light, fruity red wine)
Grated zest and juice of 1 juice orange (about ⅓ cup)
2 tablespoons soy or tamari sauce
2 or 3 cloves garlic, chopped
¼ cup chopped green onions, white part only
1 bay leaf, crumbled
2 or 3 whole cloves, crumbled
1 teaspoon coarsely ground black pepper
1 teaspoon coarse-grain or sea salt
½ teaspoon ground coriander
½ teaspoon ground nutmeg
¼ cup light extra virgin olive oil or canola oil

Process the raspberries in a food processor fitted with a plastic dough blade. (The steel blade will crush the seeds and lend a bitter taste to the food.) Strain the purée, return it to the processor, and add the wine, orange zest and juice, soy sauce, garlic, green onions, bay leaf, cloves, pepper, salt, coriander, and nutmeg. Process until all the ingredients are blended. While the motor is running, drizzle in the oil a little at a time. This marinade freezes well with food.

STRAWBERRY-BEAUJOLAIS MARINADE. Replace the raspberries with an equal amount of strawberries.

RASPBERRY-BEAUJOLAIS GLAZE. Omit the oil and place the finished recipe in a saucepan. Simmer to reduce to 1 cup.

TIMETABLE:
Chicken breasts or quail:
3 to 4 hours

Game birds, such as
wild duck and grouse:
4 to 6 hours

Venison loin: 8 to 12 hours

TIMETABLE:
Chicken breasts, chicken
kabobs, or quail:
3 to 4 hours

Chicken wings, thighs, or
legs; or pork tenderloin,
chops, or kabobs:
4 to 6 hours

Turkey breast, duck breast,
or venison steaks or chops:
6 to 8 hours

CRANBERRY MARINADE MAKES 3 CUPS

I love the tart flavor of cranberries so much that I've often substituted them for fresh currants with some awesome results. Although I often pair this recipe with turkey breasts, this marinade can fly to greater heights with roast pork tenderloin, roast chicken, and, especially, chicken wings. Since cranberries freeze so well, stock up on extra bags for the summer grilling months.

1 (12-ounce) bag fresh or frozen cranberries (about 3 cups)
Juice of 3 oranges (about 1 cup)
1 tablespoon freshly grated orange zest
⅓ cup black currant or raspberry vinegar
2 tablespoons unsulphured molasses
2 tablespoons Chambord or crème de cassis
2 tablespoons chopped shallots
1 teaspoon coarse-grain or sea salt
1 tablespoon cracked black peppercorns
⅓ cup canola oil

Combine the cranberries and orange juice in a heavy-bottom nonreactive saucepan. Bring to a low boil. Simmer for 10 to 20 minutes, until the berries burst. Remove the berries from the heat, cool to room temperature, and process in a food processor. Strain the cranberry purée through a fine sieve or a food mill with a fine grate.

Combine the cranberry purée, grated orange zest, vinegar, molasses, Chambord, shallots, salt, and pepper in a food processor and process until all the ingredients are blended. While the motor is running, drizzle in the oil a little at a time. The marinade will keep in a clean, airtight container for 1 week in the refrigerator, and it freezes well with food.

RED CURRANT MARINADE. Substitute 1½ cups fresh red currants and proceed with the recipe above.

TIMETABLE:
Salmon steaks or fillets,
salmon trout, or fresh brook
trout: 3 to 4 hours

YOGURT-DILL MARINADE MAKES 1½ CUPS

This marinade seems to scream for salmon, and it's no wonder. Mustard and dill, with hints of horseradish in a wrapper of yogurt, will cover salmon steaks or whole salmon trout with a blanket of flavor. I've even had a request from a friend to use this marinade as a sauce for smoked brook trout at brunch, and I happily obliged.

¼ cup chopped fresh dill
1 cup whole-milk yogurt
2 tablespoons grated horseradish
1 tablespoon coarse-grain mustard
2 tablespoons sherry vinegar
1 teaspoon coarsely ground black pepper
¼ teaspoon coarse-grain or sea salt
3 tablespoons olive oil

Combine the dill, yogurt, horseradish, mustard, vinegar, pepper, and salt in a blender or a food processor and process until all the ingredients are blended. While the motor is running, drizzle in the oil a little at a time. Stored in a clean, airtight container, this will keep in the refrigerator for 1 week.

SMOKED PEPPER MARINADE FOR SEAFOOD
MAKES 2 CUPS

TIMETABLE:
Salmon steaks or fillets, swordfish steaks, or shrimp: 3 to 4 hours

Secret smoke! This marinade imports a subtle smoked flavor without grilling by using an offset heat or water smoker, or a covered kettle grill, to start this recipe. Use this marinade with grilled or broiled fish.

2 to 3 yellow or red bell peppers (about ½ pound)
Grated zest and juice of 2 limes (about ¼ cup)
1 jalapeño chile, seeded, stemmed, veins removed, and diced
¼ cup white wine vinegar or white balsamic vinegar
¼ cup chopped chives
¼ cup chopped fresh cilantro
1 teaspoon coarse-grain or sea salt
1 tablespoon cracked black peppercorns
¼ cup extra virgin olive oil

Smoke the peppers for no longer than 2 hours in a water smoker with presoaked smoking chips such as mesquite or hickory. If you are using a covered kettle grill instead, smoke the peppers as above over low, indirect heat with a water pan. Note that a high heat will result in blistered skins that will impart a burned taste. The peppers will darken slightly and become soft. Remove the peppers from the smoker, place in a resealable plastic bag, and refrigerate for about ½ hour. The steam will have loosened the skin to make the peppers easier to peel.

TIP: If you don't want to crank up the smoker, you can substitute jarred pimentos, thoroughly rinsed, and ½ teaspoon Liquid Smoke for your pepper batch.

Peel the peppers, and remove the stem, seeds, and membranes. Place in a food processor or a blender with the lime zest and juice, jalapeño, vinegar, chives, cilantro, salt, and pepper. Process until blended. While the motor is running, drizzle in the olive oil a little at a time. Stored in a clean, airtight container, this will keep in the refrigerator for 1 week.

Swordfish steaks, red snapper, catfish, sea bass, halibut, scallops, shrimp, or soft-shell crab: 2 to 3 hours

SAGE-VERMOUTH MARINADE MAKES 2½ CUPS

There is nothing delicate about the in-your-face flavors of this recipe. The classic flavors of citrus and herbs pick up some heat from the hot sauce in this assertive seafood marinade.

1 cup dry vermouth
Grated zest and juice of 1 lemon (about 3 tablespoons)
1 to 2 tablespoons Louisiana red pepper or Tabasco sauce
⅔ cup fresh chopped sage
3 tablespoons chopped chives
2 cloves garlic, chopped
2 teaspoons coarse-grain or sea salt
1 tablespoon freshly ground black pepper
¼ teaspoon dried marjoram or oregano
¼ teaspoon dried thyme
½ cup extra virgin olive oil

Combine the vermouth, lemon zest and juice, hot sauce, sage, chives, garlic, salt, pepper, marjoram, and thyme in a blender or a food processor and process until all the ingredients are blended. While the motor is running, drizzle in the oil a little at a time. Stored in a clean, airtight container, this will keep in the refrigerator for 1 week.

Beef filets, rib eye, sirloin, porterhouse, New York strip, tri tips, or beef kabobs: 4 to 6 hours

London broil, skirt steak, flank steak, beef brisket, prime rib, rib roast, veal chops, or venison steaks or chops: 8 to 12 hours

SPICY BEER MARINADE MAKES 3 CUPS

Chef Kevin von Klaus of Philadelphia combines the flavor of garden-fresh tomatoes with a spice and a surprise guest ingredient: beer. This tomato-based, Tabasco-tinged marinade reminds me of a Bloody Mary with a beer kick. A low-oil marinade, this is especially good for a hot grill.

1 cup lager beer
1 cup beef broth
1 teaspoon fresh thyme leaves
3 tomatoes, peeled, seeded, and diced
2 teaspoons Worcestershire sauce
1 teaspoon Tabasco sauce
2 bay leaves, crumbled
1 teaspoon freshly cracked black peppercorns
¼ cup chopped fresh parsley

Combine the beer, beef broth, thyme, tomatoes, Worcestershire, Tabasco sauce, bay leaves, peppercorns, and parsley in a blender or a food processor and process until all the ingredients are blended. Stored in a clean, airtight container, this will keep in the refrigerator for 1 week.

GUINNESS STOUT MARINADE MAKES 2 CUPS

The inspiration for this marinade came from one of my sorbets. I've always liked the relationship of stout and lime. The lime zest cuts the bitterness of the beer, and people rave about the flavor that they somehow can't place.

1 (12-ounce) bottle Guinness Stout or any stout or porter
Grated zest and juice of 2 limes (about ¼ cup)
¼ cup finely chopped fresh basil
2 tablespoons finely chopped fresh tarragon
1 tablespoon finely chopped fresh thyme
¼ cup chopped shallots
3 cloves garlic, pressed
1 tablespoon coarsely ground black pepper
1 teaspoon coarse-grain salt
⅓ cup extra virgin olive oil

Combine the beer, lime zest and juice, basil, tarragon, thyme, shallots, garlic, pepper, and salt in a blender or a food processor and process until all the ingredients are blended. While the motor is running, drizzle in the oil a little at a time. Stored in a clean, airtight container, this will keep in the refrigerator for 1 week.

TIMETABLE:
Beef filets, rib eye, beef kabobs, sirloin, porterhouse, New York strip, or tri tips: 6 to 8 hours

London broil, skirt steak, flank steak, beef brisket, prime rib, or rib roast: 8 to 12 hours

TIP: If you are using the marinade for the Stout-Braised Beef Short Ribs (page 121), reduce the extra virgin olive oil to 2 tablespoons to avoid excess skimming, because the oil will float to the top during the cooking process.

CHARDONNAY MARINADE MAKES 1½ CUPS

This marinade combines the buttery vanilla taste of chardonnay and lemon with a little heat. You can substitute other dry white wines in this marinade. But whatever you choose, keep an extra bottle around for serving at the table. This prime-time seafood marinade is excellent with pompano, yellow fin tuna, and red snapper.

Grated zest and juice of 2 lemons (about ⅓ cup)
1 cup chardonnay
1 teaspoon vanilla extract
¼ teaspoon coarse-grain salt
1 teaspoon freshly ground black pepper
1 teaspoon diced jalapeño chile, deveined and seeded
2 cloves garlic, chopped
¼ cup grapeseed oil

Combine the lemon zest and juice, chardonnay, vanilla, salt, pepper, jalapeño, and garlic in a blender or a food processor and process until all the ingredients are blended. While the motor is running, drizzle in the oil a little at a time. Stored in a clean, airtight container, this marinade will keep in the refrigerator for 1 week.

TIMETABLE:
Salmon steaks or fillets, tuna steaks, swordfish steaks, red snapper, catfish, sea bass, halibut, or scallops: 2 to 3 hours

Sirloin, porterhouse, New York strip, tri tips, beef kabobs, buffalo, or venison: 6 to 8 hours

London broil, skirt steak, flank steak, roast, or beef short ribs: 8 to 12 hours

BASIC RED WINE MARINADE FOR BEEF
MAKES 2½ CUPS

This all-around basic marinade works great with round steak, flank steak, and London broil. Marinate thick cuts of beef for at least 12 hours but no longer than 48 hours, or the marinade will overpower the meat and leave it with a mushy texture. You can intensify the flavor of this marinade by bringing it to a simmer for about an hour, cooling it, and then adding it to the beef.

2 cloves garlic, chopped
1 teaspoon coarse-grain salt
1 tablespoon freshly ground black pepper
2 tablespoons chopped fresh parsley
2 tablespoons chopped fresh herbs (rosemary, tarragon, thyme, etc.)
¼ cup sherry vinegar or red wine vinegar
1 cup dry red wine
2 tablespoons soy or tamari sauce
1 tablespoon Worcestershire sauce
1 teaspoon sugar
¼ cup extra virgin olive oil

Combine the garlic, salt, pepper, parsley, herbs, vinegar, wine, soy sauce, Worcestershire, and sugar in a blender or a food processor. Process until all the ingredients are blended. While the motor is running, drizzle in the oil a little at a time. Stored in a clean, airtight container, this will keep in the refrigerator for 1 week.

SAGE–PORT WINE MARINADE. Substitute 1½ cups ruby port for the red wine, ¼ cup fresh sage for the mixed herb, ⅓ cup raspberry or balsamic vinegar for the sherry or red wine vinegar, and ¼ cup walnut oil for the olve oil.

Salmon steaks or fillets, tuna steaks, swordfish steaks, red snapper, catfish, sea bass, halibut, or scallops: 2 to 3 hours

VODKA-DILL MARINADE MAKES 1½ CUPS

A martini for salmon! Vodka provides a savory complement to dill, which is highlighted by the freshness of lemon zest. This cocktail adds fuel to the ongoing and sometimes delightfully heated relationship of salmon and dill.

¼ cup vodka
Juice and grated zest of 2 lemons (about ⅓ cup)
¼ cup chopped fresh dill
¼ cup chopped green onions, white part only
½ teaspoon sugar
1 teaspoon coarse-grain or sea salt
1 tablespoon cracked black peppercorns
¼ cup canola oil

Combine the vodka, lemon zest and juice, dill, green onions, sugar, salt, and pepper in a blender or a food processor and process until all the ingredients are blended. While the motor is running, drizzle in the canola oil a little at a time. This marinade freezes well.

JUNIPER-LIME MARINADE. Add 1 tablespoon crushed juniper berries. Substitute grated zest and juice of 4 limes (about ½ cup) for the lemons, ¼ cup gin for the vodka, and ¼ cup flat-leaf parsley for the dill. Add 1 teaspoon thyme.

RUM-ROSEMARY MARINADE MAKES 1½ CUPS

This flavor-layered marinade pairs fresh and dried herbs with the three-way acidity of tarragon vinegar, vermouth, and lemon. Although this marinade could work well without it, dark rum gives it an unexpected sweet twist. I've always felt that the combination of rum and rosemary pairs nicely with shellfish and poultry. This type of marinade can be an all-around shelf staple all year long.

⅓ cup dark rum (preferably Myers's)
¼ cup dry vermouth
3 tablespoons tarragon vinegar
Grated zest and juice of 2 lemons (about ⅓ cup)
1 tablespoon herbes de Provence (page 228)
2 tablespoons fresh rosemary, chopped
1 teaspoon coarse-grain or sea salt
1 tablespoon cracked black peppercorns
⅓ cup grapeseed oil or extra virgin olive oil

Combine the rum, vermouth, vinegar, lemon zest and juice, herbes de Provence, rosemary, salt, and peppercorns in a blender or a food processor and process until all the ingredients are blended. While the motor is running, drizzle in the oil a little at a time. This marinade freezes well with chicken breasts. Stored in a clean, airtight container, the marinade will keep in the refrigerator for 1 week. It freezes well with food for up to 3 months.

TIMETABLE:
Scallops, shrimp, chicken breasts, or quail:
2 to 4 hours

Lamb rack or rib chops, lamb kabobs, veal loin, or veal paillards: 6 to 8 hours

Lamb shoulder or leg:
8 to 12 hours

TIMETABLE:
Chicken breasts:
3 to 4 hours

Pork tenderloin or pork
chops: 4 to 6 hours

Turkey, duck, or goose
breasts: 8 to 10 hours

Venison steaks or chops:
8 to 12 hours

CASSIS MARINADE MAKES 2¼ CUPS

You can use this sweet marinade on duck or goose breast, but don't stop there. The marinade plays nicely against a hickory-smoked turkey breast and works as a light baste for grilled pork chops. The dried currant gives the marinade a bit of texture when you reduce it for a sauce. This is a multilevel soak. You can use this as a marinade, reheat for baste, or reduce to 1 cup for a glaze.

½ cup dried currants
1 bay leaf
½ cup dry red wine
1 cup crème de cassis
3 tablespoons chopped shallots
1 teaspoon cracked black peppercorns
1 teaspoon herbes de Provence (page 228)
Grated zest and juice of 1 lemon (about 3 tablespoons)

Soften the currants by combining them with the bay leaf and red wine in a nonreactive saucepan. Bring to a low boil, decrease the heat, and simmer for 10 minutes. Or microwave for 4 to 5 minutes on high. Cool to room temperature. Remove and discard the bay leaf.

Combine the currants and wine mixture, cassis, shallots, peppercorns, herbes de Provence, and lemon zest and juice in a blender or a food processor and process until all the ingredients are blended. The marinade will keep in the refrigerator in a clean, airtight container for up to 1 week. It freezes well with or without food.

TIMETABLE:
Swordfish steaks, red snapper, catfish, sea bass, halibut, scallops, or shrimp:
3 to 4 hours

HAZELNUT-GALLIANO MARINADE MAKES 1¼ CUPS

Sweet vanilla-flavored Galliano balances the nutty flavor of the hazelnuts and the tart lemon zest in this seafood marinade. The marinade works particularly well with scallops or firm-textured fish, such as tuna, swordfish, or mackerel.

¼ cup Galliano
Grated zest and juice of 1 lemon (about 3 tablespoons)
¼ cup chopped fresh parsley
2 to 3 tablespoons chopped shallots
¼ cup hazelnut oil
¼ cup chopped toasted hazelnuts, skins removed (optional)

Combine the Galliano, lemon zest and juice, parsley, and shallots in a food processor and process until all the ingredients are blended. While the motor is running, drizzle in the oil a little at a time. Add the hazelnuts and pulse to mix lightly.

BASIC RUB FOR MEAT AND POULTRY MAKES ½ CUP

One of my working definitions of basic is easy and flexible, and this rub defines exactly that. This recipe packs a bit of a heated punch, so feel free to pull back on the cayenne.

2 tablespoons hot paprika
1 tablespoon cayenne pepper
1 teaspoon dried thyme
1 teaspoon dried oregano
1 teaspoon freshly ground black pepper
1 teaspoon freshly ground white peppercorns
1 tablespoon coarse-grain salt
1 tablespoon garlic powder
1 tablespoon onion powder or Red Onion Powder (page 67)

Combine the paprika, cayenne, thyme, oregano, black and white pepper, salt, garlic powder, and onion powder in a small bowl. The rub can be stored in a clean, airtight container in the freezer for up to 3 months.

TIMETABLE:

Chicken wings, pork tenderloin, pork chops, or pork kabobs: 6 to 8 hours

Beef filets or rib eye: 3 to 4 hours

Brisket: 8 to 12 hours

BASIC MIXED PEPPERCORN RUB FOR BEEF

MAKES ½ CUP

I have a pretty simple attitude when it comes to grilling steaks, namely that less is more. In this case, the ingredients of the rub complement the steak, instead of competing with its flavor. When grilling over or broiling under high heat, the peppercorns caramelize and sear into the crust, thus locking the flavor of a good filet inside a thin, savory, crisp shell.

2 tablespoons black peppercorns
2 tablespoons white peppercorns
1 tablespoon pink peppercorns
1 tablespoon mustard seeds
1 teaspoon garlic powder
1 teaspoon coarse-grain salt

Combine black, white, and pink peppercorns; mustard seeds; garlic powder; and salt in a spice grinder or a blender and grind to a coarse meal.

TIMETABLE:

Beef filets, rib eye, sirloin, porterhouse, New York strip, tri tips, or burgers: 1 to 2 hours

TIMETABLE:

Salmon steaks or fillets, tuna steaks, scallops, shrimp, chicken breasts or kabobs, or turkey breast: 1 to 2 hours

LEMON-CINNAMON POWDER MAKES 2¹/₂ TABLESPOONS

This recipe is a great starting point for a number of citrus powder spin-offs, listed below as variations. I've always thought that the real flavor appeal of citrus lives in the rind. When the peel is dried, it amplifies the flavor by concentrating the oils. You can add a couple of tablespoons of the powder to any cure, brine, marinade, rub, or glaze recipe. By itself, the powder is a simple rub with a clear citrus focus that you can dust on salmon steaks or fillets, scallops, or shrimp. The recipe can also be easily scaled up.

Dried peel of 6 to 8 lemons
1 (3-inch) stick cinnamon

Scrape and discard the white pith from inside the peel and cut the peel into strips. Spread the peel on trays without overlapping and dry in an oven at its lowest setting for 10 to 12 hours or in a dehydrator for 8 to 10 hours at 120°F until crisp. Combine the dried peel and cinnamon in a blender or a food grinder and grate to a fine powder. The powder can be stored in a clean, airtight container in the freezer for 1 to 2 months.

LEMON-SAGE POWDER. Replace the cinnamon with 1 teaspoon dried sage.

LIME-CHILI POWDER. Replace the cinnamon with 1 tablespoon dried pequín chiles or dried Asian chiles.

ORANGE-CUMIN POWDER. Replace the lemon peel with the dried peel of 3 to 4 juice oranges and the cinnamon with 1 teaspoon whole cumin seeds.

TANGERINE-CORIANDER POWDER. Replace the lemon peel with the dried peel of 5 to 6 tangerines and the cinnamon with 1 tablespoon toasted coriander seeds.

GRAPEFRUIT–BROWN SUGAR POWDER. This combination actually tastes like a sweet spice and is wonderful on grilled papaya or mango, splashed with a little rum. Replace the lemon peel with the dried peel of 1 pink grapefruit and the cinnamon with 1 tablespoon dark brown sugar.

LEMON-GARLIC POWDER MAKES ¼ TO ½ CUP

While technically garlic and onion powders are not really spices but do find their way onto the spice rack, their flavor is among the first to fade when exposed to air. One way to get a great-tasting vegetable powder is to dry your own. This recipe can also be easily scaled up.

**2 to 3 garlic bulbs, peeled, separated into cloves,
    and thinly sliced (about 2 cups)
Sliced peel of 2 lemons**

Spread the garlic and lemon peel on trays with no overlaps and dry in an oven at its lowest setting for 10 to 12 hours or in a dehydrator for 8 to 10 hours at 120°F until crisp. Combine the ingredients in a blender or a food grinder and grind to a fine powder. The powder can be stored in a clean, airtight container in the freezer for 1 to 2 months.

RED ONION POWDER. Substitute 1 pound red onions, peeled and thinly sliced, for the garlic and lemon.

CARROT CURRY POWDER. Substitute 2 cups shredded carrots and 2 teaspoons curry powder, garam masala, star anise pods, or five-spice powder for the garlic and lemon.

TIP: Depending on the vegetable, you'll get about a 4 to 1 ratio of fresh vegetable to dry. When drying any of the following vegetables, you want to shoot for the texture of a wooden matchstick. In other words, you should be able to bend and snap it. The freezer is the shelf-life extender of these powders, so save your glass jars.

ORANGE PASTRAMI SPICE MIX MAKES 1 CUP

Lacking salt, this can be used as a spice rub rather than a cure. Yet, combined with a dry cure it will form a savory, pastrami-style crust for salmon, turkey breast, or duck breast.

**1 tablespoon coriander seeds
2 teaspoons whole cloves
2 tablespoons black peppercorns
1 tablespoon white peppercorns
1 tablespoon dried thyme
3 bay leaves, crumbled
3 cloves garlic, minced
2 tablespoons grated orange zest**

Combine the coriander seeds, cloves, and black and white peppercorns in a spice mill or a blender and coarsely chop. In a small mixing bowl, combine the peppercorn mixture, thyme, bay leaves, garlic, and orange zest. Stored in a clean, airtight container, this will keep in the refrigerator for 1 week.

Chicken breasts or kabobs,
Cornish hens, turkey breast,
duck breast, quail, veal
loin, paillards, lamb rack
or rib chops, lamb kabobs,
lamb shoulder or leg, pork
tenderloin, pork chops, or
pork shoulder: 1 to 2 hours

TIP: High heat will result
in blistered skins that will
impart a burned taste.
The peppers will darken
slightly and become soft.
Remove the peppers from
the smoker and place them
in a resealable plastic bag
and place in the freezer for
about ½ hour. The steam
will loosen the skin to make
the peppers easier to peel.

Swordfish, chicken breasts,
lamb chops, or rack of
lamb: 1 to 2 hours

SMOKED PEPPER POWDER MAKES ¼ CUP

Smoked pepper powder is my instant smoke. There's a concentration of
sweetness from the dried peppers that complements the wood smoke. This
single-ingredient rub is outstanding on scallops and swordfish. Just a little
goes a long way. The recipe also scales up well.

3 or 4 red or yellow bell peppers (about 1 pound)

Smoke the bell peppers for no longer than 2 hours in a water smoker with
presoaked smoking chips like mesquite or hickory. If you are using a covered
kettle grill instead, smoke the peppers as directed above over low indirect
heat with a water pan.

Peel the peppers, and remove the stem, seeds, and membranes. Julienne
the peppers into ¼-inch slices. Spread the slices on trays without
overlapping and dry in an oven on the lowest setting for 10 to 12 hours or in a
dehydrator for 8 to 10 hours at 140°F until crisp and brittle. Place the peppers
in a blender or a food grinder and grind to a fine powder. The powder can be
stored in a clean, airtight container in the freezer for up to 1 month.

ROSEMARY SEASONING RUB MAKES ½ CUP

I began using this rub on grilled chicken, and I liked the combination of
rosemary and cracked peppercorns so much that it seemed like a natural
for lamb dishes. Now, it's been finding its way onto grilled swordfish. This is
a great all-purpose rub. Coat your fish or meat with a tablespoon of olive oil
and this rub, and marinate for the times suggested.

¼ **cup fresh chopped rosemary**
2 teaspoons coarse-grain or sea salt
1 tablespoon freshly ground black pepper
1 tablespoon freshly ground white peppercorns
¼ **teaspoon cayenne**
1 teaspoon dry mustard powder
1 teaspoon dried oregano
1 teaspoon garlic powder or Lemon-Garlic Powder (page 67)

Combine the rosemary, salt, black and white pepper, cayenne, mustard
powder, oregano, and garlic powder in a spice mill or a blender and grind
to a coarse powder. Stored in a clean, airtight container, this will keep in the
freezer for 3 to 4 months.

FINES HERBES PESTO RUB MAKES 2 CUPS

Fish fillets: 3 to 4 hours

Chicken breasts or lamb chops: 4 to 6 hours

Leg of lamb: 8 to 12 hours

Fines herbes mix is a staple of Provençal pantries. A couple of spoonfuls of this rub, created by Chef Jon Jividen, placed under the skin of chicken breasts or coating a leg of lamb make a dish truly sublime. You can convert this to a rub for beef by substituting ¼ cup Madeira for ¼ cup of the olive oil.

¼ cup fresh thyme
¼ cup fresh rosemary
½ cup fresh oregano
1 cup fresh flat-leaf parsley
1 tablespoon coarse-grain salt
1 teaspoon freshly ground black pepper
½ cup extra virgin olive oil

Strip the thyme and rosemary leaves from the stems and remove the leafy parts from the oregano and parsley (you should have approximately 3 cups of loose herbs after cleaning). Place the herbs, salt, and pepper in a blender or a food processor. With the motor running, slowly add the olive oil and process until the pesto is blended. The mix will keep for 1 week, refrigerated.

ROSEMARY-MINT PESTO. Substitute ½ cup fresh mint for the parsley and ¼ cup rosemary for the oregano.

ROASTED GARLIC AND JALAPEÑO PASTE
MAKES 2½ CUPS

Sometimes the simple ingredients pack the most flavor. Chef Bruce Cooper, of Jake's in the Manyunk section of Philadelphia, roasts garlic and jalapeño together, then adds extra virgin olive oil for a taste that is far more complex than it seems. You can walk away from this easily made recipe and come back an hour later with a paste that performs culinary marvels on grilled tuna and swordfish.

1 pound jalapeño chiles, stemmed, seeded, and deveined
2 pounds peeled cloves garlic
½ cup water
1 cup extra virgin olive oil

Preheat the oven to 350°F. Place the jalapeños and garlic in a roasting pan, then add the water and olive oil. Roast for 1 hour. Remove the roasted garlic, jalapeños, and pan liquid, and cool to room temperature. Place the garlic, jalapeños, and pan liquid in a blender or a food processor and process until all the ingredients are blended.

SOUR MASH–PINK PEPPERCORN RUB MAKES ½ CUP

The sour mash in this rub is none other than Jack Daniels, and there's no stopping the flavor. I like foundation recipes with interchangeable parts. You can swap out the mash and replace it with Scotch, cognac, or Armagnac. Use this elegant rub to dress salmon fillets bound for the grill or the broiler. This recipe will make enough rub for 2 to 4 servings.

3 tablespoons pink peppercorns
2 tablespoons black peppercorns
2 tablespoons white peppercorns
1 teaspoon whole yellow mustard seeds
1 teaspoon whole coriander seeds
2 tablespoons finely diced shallots
1 tablespoon chopped fresh dill, or 1 teaspoon dried dill, crumbled
3 tablespoons Jack Daniels or bourbon
1 tablespoon honey

Combine the peppercorns, mustard seeds, and coriander seeds in a spice mill or a blender and grind to a coarse powder (about 3 or 4 pulses). Place in a nonreactive bowl and add the shallots and dill.

To use as a rub, combine the Jack Daniels and honey. Brush onto ⅔ to 1 pound of fish fillets, flesh side up. Press the spice mix into the surface of the fish and marinate in the refrigerator for 2 to 3 hours. Grill or broil the fillets.

MAPLE SUGAR MAKES ¾ CUP

Maple sugar is my all-time favorite sugar substitute in marinades, rubs, brines, cures, and glazes. It's extremely simple to make. Because the yield is about one-quarter to one-third of the original volume, it's easy to see why it's expensive when buying it retail. The maple grade to use is grade B; the pricier grade A will just get lost in the shuffle. Granulated maple sugar is made by heating maple syrup to a temperature 40° to 45°F above the boiling temperature of pure water (212°F at sea level).

2 cups grade B maple syrup

In a heavy stainless-steel saucepan, heat the syrup and begin stirring until the syrup reaches about 265°F on a candy thermometer or until granulation is achieved and all apparent moisture is gone. Lightly butter a baking sheet or use a silicon mat. Immediately remove the pan from the heat and pour the mixture onto the prepared baking sheet. Let cool completely. When the syrup has cooled and hardened, use a kitchen mallet or a rolling pin to crack the caramel. Place the broken pieces in the bowl of a food processor and pulse to get a granulated consistency. Store in a clean, airtight container and refrigerate until ready to use.

MAPLE-BOURBON SUGAR. Replace 1 cup maple syrup with 1 cup bourbon (or Southern Comfort, whiskey, or cognac). The addition of bourbon or any liqueur adds an entirely different dimension to a dry ingredient. It's best used where its flavor will bloom and not be overpowered by any other ingredients, such as in a cure. If it's used in a rub that's heavily spiced, the bourbon in the sugar will lose its focus. In that case, the flavor is stronger from the bottle.

Both the maple syrup and the bourbon will need to cook a little longer to evaporate the additional liquid. As good as this is, you'll need to use it within a month because the bourbon flavor is fleeting after the first or second week.

TIMETABLE:
Salmon steaks or fillets, shrimp, chicken breasts or wings, Cornish hens, quail, pork tenderloin, pork chops, or pork kabobs: baste during the last 5 minutes of cooking

LEMON GLAZE MAKES 2 CUPS

My friend Barbara Boswell makes a lemon glaze that picks up an additional allure of citrus by way of some orange juice. The glaze pulls the lemon three different ways for three levels of flavor. The first level is from the marmalade, which forms the basis of the glaze; the second is from the zest, which gives a fresh lemon flavor; and the third is from the juice, which gives the glaze a nice tang and tempers the sweetness of the marmalade.

½ cup lemon marmalade
2 tablespoons water
Grated zest and juice of 1 juice orange (about ⅓ cup)
Grated zest and juice of 2 lemons (about ½ cup)
1½ tablespoons diced fresh ginger
3 cloves garlic, chopped
½ teaspoon dried basil
½ teaspoon cracked black peppercorns
1 tablespoon fresh sage, chopped

In a small nonreactive saucepan, combine the marmalade, water, and orange zest and juice, and simmer over medium heat until the marmalade dissolves. Cool to room temperature. Combine the marmalade mixture with the lemon zest and juice, ginger, garlic, basil, pepper, and sage in a blender or a food processor and process until all the ingredients are blended. Store in a clean, airtight container and refrigerate until ready to use. The glaze can be made ahead and will keep in the refrigerator for 3 weeks.

Rewarm over medium heat, whisking occasionally, before basting the food.

SAVORY LIME GLAZE. Replace the lemon marmalade with lime marmalade and the lemons with 3 to 4 limes.

SAVORY ORANGE GLAZE. Replace the lemon marmalade with orange marmalade.

CANDIED JALAPEÑO LICORICE (GLAZED JALAPEÑOS) MAKES ¼ CUP

Peter Cravath and I were fooling with recipes for the New England Barbecue Society Snowshoe Grilling Challenge. We wanted some "heat full" candy-flavored crunch to flick into a glaze for chicken wings. There are two ways for you to use the jalapeño licorice; you can candy it in julienned strips or dice it into confetti. Peter and his crew rolled the diced version into the Zesty Jalapeño Lime Glaze (page 74) for their grilled wings entry, and the wings really took off and flew (page 106). This recipe can be scaled up.

1 cup sugar
1 cup water
1 tablespoon light corn syrup
1 teaspoon ground ginger
1 teaspoon ground cumin
1 cup thinly sliced jalapeño or serrano chiles,
    stemmed, seeded, and deveined

In a 2-quart heavy bottom saucepan, combine the sugar, water, and corn syrup and bring to a boil. Decrease the heat and add the ginger, cumin, and chiles. Simmer for 20 minutes. Remove from the heat and strain, reserving the jalapeño syrup for a later use (see Tangerine-Serrano Glaze on page 74). Line a baking pan with parchment, coat with cooking-oil spray to reduce sticking, and arrange the chile strips. Dry in an oven at its lowest setting for 12 to 24 hours or in a food dehydrator at 120°F to the desired texture. The longer the drying time, the more brittle the chiles. After 24 hours you'll get a green "licorice" effect.

HEAT-SEEKING CANDIED DISKS. By slicing the jalapeños into ¼-inch round slices, you pick up additional heat from the seeds and the ribs.

ZESTY JALAPEÑO LIME GLAZE MAKES 1½ CUPS

This gives chicken wings or breasts a beautiful emerald sheen. The heat from the jelly doesn't come off blistering strong, but it has a nice zing to it.

1 cup jalapeño jelly
Julienned zest and juice of 3 limes (about ½ cup)
2 cloves garlic, minced
⅓ cup diced sweet onions
½ teaspoon ground cumin
1 teaspoon coarse-grain or sea salt
1 teaspoon freshly cracked black peppercorns
¼ cup Candied Jalapeño Licorice (page 73)

Dissolve the jelly in a microwave at 50 percent power for 3 minutes, or bring it to a low simmer in a heavy-bottom enamel saucepan. Combine the hot jelly and the lime zest, stirring fully to coat the zest. Stir in the garlic, onions, cumin, salt, and pepper, and simmer for 5 minutes. Remove the glaze from the heat and cool to room temperature. It should be thick like ketchup, but not solid. Stir in the lime juice and the Candied Jalapeño Licorice to brighten the glaze. Refrigerate until ready to use. The glaze can be made ahead and will keep in the refrigerator for 3 weeks. To use the glaze after refrigerating, warm it over medium heat, whisking occasionally. Refresh the glaze with an additional tablespoon of fresh lime juice before basting.

TIMETABLE:
Salmon steaks or fillets, shrimp, chicken breasts or kabobs, chicken wings, chicken thighs, chicken legs, baby back ribs, or spareribs: baste during the last 5 minutes of cooking

TANGERINE-SERRANO GLAZE MAKES ¾ CUP

Tangerine season in this neck of the woods lasts from late November until mid-April, which can be a real problem if you like to grill all year-round. I was thinking about something heat-seeking with a citrus tang to aim at the grill. Asian ingredients are always hanging around the pantry. But I needed tangerines, and then they came to me in the frozen juice aisle, and does it ever work. If you can't find tangerine concentrate, you can substitute orange or any other concentrate that tickles your fancy, including the punch mixes.

½ cup water
½ cup sugar
¼ cup soy or tamari sauce
1 (6-ounce) can frozen tangerine concentrate, thawed
1 tablespoon peeled and grated fresh ginger
½ teaspoon ground star anise
1 teaspoon Szechuan peppercorns
3 serrano chiles, stemmed, seeded, and deveined

TIMETABLE:
Salmon steaks or fillets, shrimp, chicken breasts or kabobs, chicken wings, chicken thighs, chicken legs, Cornish hens, quail, pork tenderloin, pork chops, baby back ribs, or spareribs: baste during the last 5 minutes of cooking

Combine the water, sugar, soy sauce, tangerine concentrate, ginger, star anise, Szechuan peppercorns, and serrano chiles in a blender or a food processor and process until all the ingredients are blended.

In a heavy, nonreactive saucepan, bring the tangerine mixture to a simmer, and reduce the mixture by half, to about ¾ cup. Remove the glaze from the heat and cool to room temperature. Refrigerate until ready to use. The glaze can be made ahead and will keep in the refrigerator for 3 weeks. To use the glaze after refrigerating, warm it over medium heat, stirring occasionally. For an added garnish, use the recipe for Candied Jalapeño Licorice (page 73), but replace the jalapeños with serrano chiles.

SAVORY CITRUS CARAMEL MAKES 1 CUP

This is one foundation recipe I'm always reaching for. You can add it to glazes and brines. Nearly every type of citrus can work with it, including lemons, oranges, tangerines, and grapefruit. It's also sturdy enough to take anything you want to roll into it, such as Candied Jalapeño Licorice (page 73), toasted shredded coconut, mixed cracked peppercorns, or even preserved ginger. Welcome to Citrus Caramel base camp. It will take you to new heights.

1 cup sugar
1 tablespoon water
Grated zest and juice of 4 limes, or 3 lemons, or 2 oranges,
    or 1 pink grapefruit (½ to ⅝ cup)
1 teaspoon coarse-grain or sea salt
1 teaspoon freshly ground black pepper

Combine the sugar and water in 2-quart heavy-bottom saucepan and bring to a boil. Do not stir until all the sugar has dissolved and it begins to color around the edges. Cook for about 10 minutes, until a medium amber color. When the caramel reaches the desired color, remove it from the heat and carefully stir in the citrus zest and juice, salt, and pepper, then let the caramel cool to room temperature. Pour into a clean, airtight container and refrigerate until ready to use. The glaze can be made ahead and will keep in the refrigerator for 3 weeks. To use the glaze after refrigerating, warm it over medium heat, stirring occasionally.

TIMETABLE:
Salmon steaks or fillets, shrimp, chicken breasts or kabobs, chicken wings, chicken thighs, chicken legs, Cornish hens, quail, pork tenderloin, pork chops, baby back ribs, or spareribs: baste during the last 5 minutes of cooking

CARAMELS

The color cues in making caramel are a lot like the color cues for making roux in Paul Prudhomme's *Louisiana Kitchen*. Like roux, caramel making is a visual, high-heat cooking process that changes moment to moment, and it really requires some eye-nose coordination. If you're not used to making caramel, I suggest you make the basic recipe a few times to get the feel of it, and then move on to the other recipes.

Start with 1 cup sugar, ¼ cup water, and 1 teaspoon light corn syrup. Place the sugar, water, and corn syrup in a heavy skillet over high heat and stir constantly. Timing is everything. Any stirring will kick up sugar syrup onto the sides of the pan and form sugar crystals. Keep a pastry brush close by in a heat-resistant bowl full of water, and use it to wash down the sides. Remember, the more water you add during this process, the longer the caramelization will take.

After about 10 minutes, the sugar will begin to caramelize and turn color. You'll see it change from the color of white wine to tea and then to something close to cola. Once the sugar begins to boil, stop stirring.

Watch the sugar closely, because it will turn darker by the second; a reddish amber cast will set in as the bubbles become a burned orange. Pay attention to the color of the caramel underneath the bubbles. At this point, remove the pan from the heat. If you happen to scorch the caramel, you'll know by the dark color and the burned smell. As with a burned roux, you'll need to start over from scratch. The syrup will still continue to cook after it's removed from the heat. Plunging the bottom of the pan into an ice water bath will stop the cooking process. Have this set up in advance because you'll need to spin at a moment's notice once the caramel color comes up. Chill the pan for only a few seconds. If you chill it too long, the caramel will thicken.

Added liquids such as liqueurs or citrus juices will cool the caramel and stop the cooking process. Add the liquids gradually and at arm's length, because the caramel will sputter and bubble.

In the event of a cooking accident—that is, scorching the caramel—do not pour the hot caramel into the sink, especially if you have a garbage disposal with hard rubber flanges. Hot caramel will solidify, and only hot boiling water will dissolve it. To dissolve caramel from the sides of the pot or wooden spoon, fill the pan with water and bring it to a boil. The caramel will melt and you'll be able to stir off the sugar crystals that cling to the cooking utensils.

FRESH RASPBERRY GASTRIQUE MAKES 1½ CUPS

Gastriques are fruit syrups with an acidic edge that happen to make great glazes. Because of their simplicity, the recipes that follow are really templates for a series of quick fruit glazes.

2½ cups fresh or frozen raspberries or blackberries
1 cup sugar
½ cup raspberry or rice wine vinegar
Pinch of salt

Process the berries in a food processor fitted with a plastic dough blade. (The steel blade will crush the seeds and lend a bitter taste to the food.) Strain the purée through a fine sieve and pour into a nonreactive, heavy-bottom saucepan. Add the sugar, vinegar, and salt. Bring the liquid to a boil and reduce to a simmer. Cook the mixture for 25 to 30 minutes, until the mixture becomes thick and syrupy. Remove from the heat and strain. Cool to room temperature, pour into a clean, airtight container, and refrigerate until ready to use. The recipe can be made ahead and will keep in the refrigerator for 3 weeks.

STRAWBERRY-BALSAMIC GASTRIQUE. Replace the raspberries with strawberries, and the raspberry vinegar with balsamic vinegar. Add 1 tablespoon freshly cracked black peppercorns.

BLACKBERRY GASTRIQUE. You can use this recipe variation for any preserve that comes in a jar, including chile jellies. Replace the raspberries with 1 cup seedless blackberry preserves; replace the rice wine vinegar with red wine vinegar; and decrease the sugar to ¼ cup.

TANGERINE GASTRIQUE. Replace the raspberries with 1½ cups freshly squeezed tangerine juice or ¼ cup frozen tangerine concentrate, thawed. Replace the raspberry vinegar with 1 cup white wine vinegar.

TIMETABLE:
Salmon steaks or fillets, scallops, shrimp, chicken breasts or kabobs, chicken wings, chicken thighs, chicken legs, Cornish hens, quail, pork tenderloin, pork chops, baby back ribs, or spareribs: baste during the last 5 minutes of cooking

GASTRIQUES

You can have a lot of food fun with gastriques. Part sauce and part glaze, gastriques are sweet acidic reductions that can be infused with fresh fruit purées or jams, as well as fresh herbs. They have a thinner viscosity than glazes but are just as versatile. A great taste balancer, they give you a chance to play with flavored vinegars and give your dishes a particular tartness that hangs in there during the entire cooking process.

TIMETABLE:
Salmon steaks or fillets, shrimp, chicken breasts or kabobs, turkey breast, duck breast, quail, pork tenderloin, pork chops, baby back ribs, or spareribs: baste during the last 5 minutes of cooking

CRANBERRY-CASSIS GLAZE MAKES 1¼ CUPS

Instead of adding sugar directly to this recipe, we're pulling it out of the caramelized shallots, which offset the sourness of the cranberries. Whether you use this on grilled pork chops, barbecued spareribs, or smoked pork tenderloin, the flavor is sublime. The yield for this glaze is just right for a whole turkey.

1 tablespoon canola oil, for cooking
¼ cup finely chopped shallots
2 fresh sage leaves
1 teaspoon whole juniper berries
1 cup fresh or frozen and thawed cranberries
⅔ cup maple syrup
⅔ cup crème de cassis
½ cup red-currant jelly
1 teaspoon coarse-grain salt
1 teaspoon freshly ground black pepper
    (about 4 or 5 turns on a peppermill)
1 teaspoon apple cider or cider vinegar, if needed

In a nonreactive saucepan, heat the oil over medium heat. Add the shallots and cook, stirring occasionally, for about 2 minutes, until translucent. Add the sage leaves and juniper berries, and cook, stirring, for 1 minute. Add the cranberries, maple syrup, cassis, jelly, salt, and pepper. Simmer until the cranberries are soft and starting to burst, 20 to 30 minutes. Cool the cranberry mixture to room temperature.

Place the mixture in a food processor. Process until smooth. Strain the purée through a fine sieve and return the glaze to the saucepan. Simmer gently over medium heat until it has thickened, 10 to 15 minutes; you should have about 1¼ cups. If the glaze seems too thick, thin it with a little apple cider or cider vinegar. Cool the glaze, store it in a clean, airtight container, and refrigerate until ready to use. The glaze can be made ahead and will keep in the refrigerator or freezer for 3 weeks. To use the glaze after refrigerating, warm it over medium heat, stirring occasionally.

BING CHERRY GLAZE MAKES 2 CUPS

After painting grilled quail, this glaze becomes a savory cherry lollipop for adults. I've set the recipe for summer's sweet Bing cherries, but this glaze has an interesting twist when using sour cherries as well. The basil is the surprise savory contrast in this glaze. This is a "double-decker" recipe; see the recipe variation below to convert it to a marinade.

3 cups red wine
½ pound fresh Bing cherries, pitted
½ cup crème de cassis
2 tablespoons finely chopped fresh basil
1 teaspoon allspice
¼ teaspoon mace
¼ teaspoon ground ginger
1 teaspoon coarse-grain or sea salt
1 tablespoon cracked black peppercorns

In a nonreactive saucepan, simmer together the wine, cherries, cassis, basil, allspice, mace, ginger, salt, and peppercorns for about 30 minutes, until reduced by half. Remove from the heat and cool to room temperature. Pour the mix into a blender or a food processor and process. Strain the liquid through a food mill or fine-mesh strainer. Cool the glaze, store in a clean, airtight container, and refrigerate until ready to use. The glaze can be made ahead and will keep in the refrigerator for 3 weeks. To use the glaze after refrigerating, warm it over medium heat, stirring occasionally.

CHERRY-BASIL MARINADE. To use the glaze as a marinade, follow the recipe up to the point of blending, then add the juice of 2 fresh lemons, 1 teaspoon chopped garlic, and 2 tablespoons chopped red onion. Process in a blender or a food processor. With the motor running, drizzle in ¼ cup canola oil a little at a time.

TIMETABLE:
Chicken breasts, chicken wings, quail, Cornish hens, pork tenderloin, pork chops, baby back ribs: baste during the last 5 minutes of cooking

RASPBERRY-PORT GLAZE MAKES 1¹/₂ CUPS

This glaze has so much depth it needs a diving board. The raspberry flavor is heightened by port wine, which gives the glaze its hint of sweetness.

1 (12-ounce) bag frozen unsweetened raspberries, defrosted
1 cup ruby port
⅓ cup raspberry or other fruit vinegar
Grated zest and juice of 1 juice orange (about ⅓ cup)
1 tablespoon chopped shallots
½ teaspoon herbes de Provence (page 228) (optional)
¼ teaspoon ground coriander
1 teaspoon coarsely ground black pepper
1 teaspoon coarse-grain salt

Process the berries in a food processor fitted with a plastic dough blade. (The steel blade will crush the seeds and lend a bitter taste to the food.) Strain the purée through a fine sieve and pour into a nonreactive, heavy-bottom saucepan. Add the port and simmer for 20 minutes. Remove from the heat and cool to room temperature.

In a food processor or a blender, add the vinegar, orange zest and juice, shallots, herbes de Provence, coriander, pepper, and salt, and process until all the ingredients are blended. Store in a clean, airtight container and refrigerate until ready to use. The glaze can be made ahead and will keep in the refrigerator for 3 weeks. To use the glaze after refrigerating, warm it over medium heat, stirring occasionally.

TIMETABLE:
Chicken breasts, Cornish hens, guinea hens, or quail: baste during the last 5 minutes of cooking

MORELLO CHERRY GLAZE MAKES 2 CUPS

Canned fruit in their own syrup make great candidates for glazes. Their color and flavor are set at the time of canning, so you can enjoy fruit glazes all year-round. Although this recipe calls for canned or jarred Morello cherries, any canned fruit can be used in its place.

2 tablespoons olive oil
½ cup chopped shallots
2½ cups Morello cherries (canned cherries in syrup)
2 tablespoons soy or tamari sauce
¼ cup balsamic vinegar
1 tablespoon spicy brown mustard
1 tablespoon diced fresh gingerroot
1 teaspoon Worcestershire sauce
1 teaspoon coarse-grain or sea salt
1 tablespoon freshly ground black pepper

TIMETABLE:
Chicken breasts or kabobs, chicken wings, chicken thighs, chicken legs, Cornish hens, quail, pork tenderloin, pork chops, baby back ribs, or spareribs: baste during the last 5 minutes of cooking

In a 1-quart nonreactive saucepan, heat the oil and sauté the shallots over medium heat or until translucent. Place the cherries with the syrup in a blender or a food processor and process. Add the cherry purée, soy sauce, vinegar, mustard, ginger, Worcestershire sauce, salt, and pepper to the saucepan with the shallots. Bring to a boil and decrease the heat. Simmer for about 20 minutes, until reduced to 2 cups. Cool the glaze, store in a clean, airtight container, and refrigerate until ready to use. The glaze can be made ahead and will keep in the refrigerator for 3 weeks. To use the glaze after refrigerating, warm it over medium heat, stirring occasionally.

APRICOT GLAZE MAKES 1½ CUPS

TIMETABLE:
Shrimp; chicken breasts, kabobs, wings, thighs, or legs; Cornish hens; pork ribs, chops, or tenderloins: baste during the last 5 minutes of cooking

On the surface, this glaze appears to be one sweet shellac. Sweet, yes, but there's enough tang from the wine, vinegar, and mustard to anchor and balance the flavor. Not only does this apricot lacquer work wonderful glazing magic on chicken wings and spareribs, but it's also one of my favorite glazes for Cornish hens.

½ cup diced dried apricots
1 cup dry white wine or fresh orange juice
½ cup apricot preserves
½ cup white wine vinegar
3 tablespoons fruit mustard or Dijon-style mustard
1 tablespoon soy or tamari sauce
½ teaspoon coarse-grain salt
1 teaspoon coarsely ground black pepper

In a nonreactive saucepan, simmer the apricots in the wine for about 20 minutes to soften. (Alternatively, to save time, microwave the apricots and wine on high for 8 minutes, then add them to the saucepan.) Add the preserves and vinegar; simmer until the preserves are dissolved. Remove from the heat and cool to room temperature.

In a blender or a food processor, process the apricot mix, mustard, soy sauce, salt, and pepper. Cool the glaze, store in a clean, airtight container, and refrigerate until ready to use. The glaze can be made ahead and will keep in the refrigerator for 3 weeks. To use the glaze after refrigerating, warm it over medium heat, stirring occasionally.

APRICOT-CHIPOTLE GLAZE. Replace the mustard with 2 tablespoons puréed chipotle adobo.

APRICOT-BRANDY GLAZE. Replace the wine with ¼ cup apricot or regular brandy.

Shrimp; scallops; chicken breasts, kabobs, wings, thighs, or legs; Cornish hens; pork ribs, chops, or tenderloins: baste during the last 5 minutes of cooking

CARROT-CURRY CARAMEL MAKES ¾ CUP

Just a little dab of this savory caramel on a grilled scallop will have your guests diving into their plates. You can add it to a squirt bottle to streak across platters. I've also added this in brines for a robust citrusy-carrot flavor.

1 cup sugar
¼ cup water
1 teaspoon light corn syrup
2 cups carrot juice
1 teaspoon curry
1 teaspoon vanilla
2 tablespoons soy or tamari sauce

Combine the sugar, water, and corn syrup in a 2-quart heavy-bottom saucepan and bring to a boil. Do not stir until all the sugar has dissolved and it begins to color around the edges. Cook for about 10 minutes, until a medium amber color. When the caramel reaches the desired color, remove it from the heat and carefully stir the carrot juice, curry, vanilla, and soy sauce. Return the saucepan to the heat, bring to a simmer, and simmer for about 20 minutes, until reduced to ¾ cup. Let the caramel cool to room temperature. Pour the caramel into a clean glass jar and refrigerate until ready to use. The glaze will keep in the refrigerator for up to 3 weeks. To use the glaze after refrigerating, warm it over medium heat, stirring occasionally.

TIMETABLE:

Chicken wings, chicken thighs, chicken legs, beef kabobs, burgers, pork kabobs, baby back ribs, or spareribs: baste during the last 5 minutes of cooking

SWEET-AND-SPICY PEPPER GLAZE MAKES 2 CUPS

This thick, savory glaze could almost be used as ketchup or a barbecue sauce. You can change the color by using yellow bell peppers and replacing the maple syrup with honey. Different flavor, but just as good.

2 tablespoon unsalted butter
2 red bell peppers, seeded, deveined, and diced (about 1½ cups)
2 cloves garlic, minced or pressed
½ cup cider vinegar
¼ cup maple syrup
¼ cup firmly packed light brown sugar
1 teaspoon Worcestershire sauce
1 teaspoon coarse-grain salt
1 tablespoon freshly ground black pepper
1 teaspoon crushed red pepper flakes

Melt the butter in a heavy-bottomed saucepan. Add the bell peppers and garlic and sauté until tender, 8 to 10 minutes. Add the vinegar, maple syrup, sugar, Worcestershire sauce, salt, black pepper, and red pepper flakes, and simmer for about 15 minutes longer. Remove the pepper mixture from the heat and cool to room temperature. Transfer the pepper mixture to a food processor and process until smooth. Store in a clean, airtight container and refrigerate until ready to use. The glaze can be made ahead and will keep in the refrigerator for 3 weeks. To use the glaze after refrigerating, warm it over medium heat, stirring occasionally.

APPLE-BEET GLAZE MAKES ⅔ CUP

My friend Barbara Boswell uses beet sugar as part of a glaze, which plays a lot of fun taste games. The Sephardic sweetness from the beets, apple, and honey toys with the spicier pulls of the mustard and horseradish. The dill is just hanging around for a nice piece of salmon to happen upon.

1 cup beet juice
¼ cup freshly juiced or bottled apple juice
¼ cup minced shallots
2 whole cloves
1 tablespoon cider vinegar
2 tablespoons stone-ground mustard
1 tablespoon prepared horseradish
2 tablespoons honey
1 tablespoon fresh dill, chopped
1 tablespoon cracked black peppercorns
1 teaspoon coarse-grain or sea salt

If using a juicer, scrub the beets, leaving the skin on, and cut into small pieces. Feed the tops through the juicer first, followed by the remaining pieces. One pound of beets (about 2 beets) will yield about 1 cup of juice, depending on the juicer; some juicers are more effective with hard roots like carrots and beets than others are.

Combine the beet juice, apple juice, shallots, and cloves in a small saucepan over medium heat and reduce to 1 cup, 10 to 15 minutes. Remove from the heat and cool to room temperature. Add the vinegar, mustard, horseradish, honey, dill, pepper, and salt in a blender or a food processor and process until all the ingredients are blended. Stored in a clean, airtight container, this will keep in the refrigerator for 1 week.

ORANGE-BEET GLAZE. If you can possibly find golden (yellow) beets for this recipe, the color and flavor will be dramatic. Replace the apple juice with the grated zest and juice of 3 juice oranges (about 1 cup). Omit the cloves. Replace the horseradish with 2 tablespoons Dijon-style mustard. Replace the dill with 1 tablespoon chopped fresh thyme and 1 tablespoon chopped fresh rosemary.

TIMETABLE:
Salmon steaks or fillets, chicken breasts or kabobs, or turkey breast: baste during the last 5 minutes of cooking

TIP: This recipe calls for beet juice, and you do need a juicer or a friend who has one. The next best thing is a health food store with a good produce selection and a juice bar. They may be willing to do the juicing for you. When juicing whole beets, don't trim the tops or the stringy roots. They're rich in vitamin A.

Salmon steaks or fillets, chicken breasts or kabobs, turkey breast, quail, pork tenderloin, pork chops, pork kabobs, baby back ribs, or spareribs: baste during the last 5 minutes of cooking

CASSIS–RED ONION GLAZE MAKES 1½ CUPS

Sweet, sassy, and savory, Cassis–Red Onion Glaze is truly an elegant knockout on just about anything—from tuna, shrimp, and salmon to chicken breasts, pork tenderloin, pork chops, and baby back ribs. The sweetness of the caramelized red onions is balanced by the acidity of the vinegar. The sun-dried fruit gives this glaze an added tasty texture.

6 red onions (about 2½ pounds)
2 to 3 tablespoons unsalted butter
2 cups red wine vinegar or cassis vinegar
¼ cup sun-dried cherries or cranberries
½ cup crème de cassis, or ¼ cup Torani black currant syrup
    (available at specialty grocery stores and coffee outlets)
1 cup red wine or port
1 teaspoon coarse-grain or sea salt
1 tablespoon freshly ground black pepper

Peel and slice the onions into ¼-inch-thick rings. In a large saucepan over medium heat, melt the butter, add the onions, and sauté for 15 to 20 minutes, until they're soft and translucent. They should not brown. Add the vinegar, sun-dried cherries, cassis, and wine to the saucepan, and decrease the heat. Simmer until the liquid is thick and coats the onions like a syrupy glaze. Remove from the heat and season with salt and pepper. Stored in a clean, airtight container, this will keep in the refrigerator for 2 to 3 weeks, and frozen for 6 to 8 months in 1-cup containers.

SAVORY RASPBERRY GLAZE. Substitute raspberry vinegar for the red wine vinegar, substitute raspberry liqueur for the cassis, and add ½ cup seedless raspberry jelly.

RED ONION–MARMALADE GLAZE. Substitute 1 cup grenadine for the cassis.

POIRE WILLIAM GLAZE MAKES 2 CUPS

In my previous book, I offered a Poire William marinade, but I thought these ingredients might be more playful as a glaze. I tweaked the recipe by caramelizing the shallots in Sauternes, making a pear liqueur reduction. Still not wanting to leave well enough alone, I converted the recipe again to a finishing sauce in a variation. And to bring it all back home, the original marinade is included as well.

2 to 3 tablespoons butter
¼ cup chopped shallots
1½ cups Sauternes or late-harvest dessert wine
¼ cup Poire William (or pear brandy)
2 ripe Bartlett pears, peeled, cored, and chopped,
    or 1 cup good-quality pear pie filling
¼ cup fresh lemon juice
1 tablespoon coarsely ground black pepper

In a large saucepan over medium heat, melt the butter and sauté the shallots for about 5 minutes, until they're translucent. Caramelize the shallots by adding the Sauternes and pear liqueur, bring it to a simmer, and simmer for about 30 minutes, until reduced to ½ cup. Remove from the heat and cool to room temperature.

In a blender or a food processor, combine the caramelized shallots, pears, lemon juice, and pepper, and process until all the ingredients are blended. Store in a clean, airtight container and refrigerate until ready to use. The glaze can be made ahead and will keep in the refrigerator for 3 weeks. To use the glaze after refrigerating, warm it over medium heat, stirring occasionally.

POIRE WILLIAM MARINADE. Omit the butter and reduce the Sauternes quantity to 1 cup.

POIRE WILLIAM SAUCE. After the shallots have been reduced to 1 cup, purée the pears in a food processor with 1 cup of chicken stock. Combine the purée with the caramelized shallots, maintain a simmer, and reduce the sauce 1½ cups. The sauce is made ahead at this point. Before serving, gently warm the sauce and add the fresh lemon juice and pepper.

TIMETABLE:
Salmon steaks or fillets, chicken breasts or kabobs, turkey breast, quail, pork tenderloin, pork chops, pork kabobs, baby back ribs, or spareribs: baste during the last 5 minutes of cooking

TIMETABLE:
Whole chicken, Cornish
hen, turkey breast, duck
breast, pork chops, pork
tenderloin, or spareribs:
baste during the last
5 minutes of cooking

PLUM-CASSIS GLAZE OR BASTE MAKES 3 CUPS

The combination of plum and cassis when paired with hickory smoke is a flavor onto itself. A turkey breast would be proud to wear it. This glaze can also double as a basting sauce for barbecued ribs or an oven-roasted turkey breast. It can also handle a reduction should you want to increase its density and make a thicker glaze.

The yield for this glaze is just right for a whole turkey breast. Since this recipe freezes well, use half the recipe on ribs and pork chops and save the rest in your freezer for when plums are out of season.

6 plums (about 1 pound), pitted and coarsely chopped
¼ cup crème de cassis
⅓ cup cider vinegar
¼ cup Madeira
2 cloves garlic, minced or pressed
1 teaspoon dry mustard
1 tablespoon dark brown sugar
¼ teaspoon freshly grated nutmeg
½ teaspoon salt or 1 teaspoon soy sauce

Combine the plums and the cassis in a nonreactive saucepan. Bring to a boil, decrease the heat, and simmer for about 20 minutes. Remove the plum mixture from the heat and let cool to room temperature.

Combine the plum mixture with the vinegar, Madeira, garlic, dry mustard, brown sugar, nutmeg, and salt in a blender or a food processor and process.

Cool the glaze, store in a clean, airtight container, and refrigerate until ready to use. The glaze can be made ahead and will keep in the refrigerator for 4 weeks. To use the glaze after refrigerating, warm it over medium heat, stirring occasionally.

TIMETABLE:
Salmon steaks or fillets;
shrimp; scallops; chicken
breasts, kabobs, wings,
thighs, or legs; Cornish
hen; turkey or duck breast;
quail; pork tenderloin or
chops; baby back ribs; or
spareribs: baste during the
last 5 minutes of cooking

POMEGRANATE-COGNAC GLAZE MAKES ¾ CUP

This recipe started out as a marinade for grilled duck breast in the last edition of this book, but in its heart it was pure glaze. It blends caramelized shallots, pomegranate, cognac, and cardamom for a multilevel set of flavors for the grill and the broiler.

1 tablespoon canola oil
¼ cup finely chopped shallots (about 3 to 4)
2 cups bottled pomegranate juice
¼ cup pomegranate molasses (available at
   Greek or Middle Eastern grocery stores)
¼ cup cognac
¼ teaspoon ground cardamom
1 teaspoon coarsely ground black pepper
½ teaspoon coarse-grain or sea salt

In a saucepan over medium heat, combine the oil and shallots and sauté the shallots for 5 minutes, or until they become translucent. Add the pomegranate juice and simmer for about 30 to 40 minutes, until reduced to 1 cup. Add the molasses, cognac, cardamom, pepper, and salt and simmer on low for 15 minutes, or until the glaze is reduced to ¾ cup. Cool to room temperature.

In a blender or a food processor, process until all the ingredients are blended. Store in a clean, airtight container and refrigerate until ready to use. The glaze can be made ahead and will keep in the refrigerator for 3 weeks. To use the glaze after refrigerating, warm it over medium heat, stirring occasionally.

MAPLE-POMEGRANATE GLAZE MAKES ABOUT 1 CUP

Instant flavor! This is a three-ingredient wonder that's easy, fast, and versatile.

½ cup maple syrup
¼ cup pomegranate molasses (available at
   Greek or Middle Eastern grocery stores)
⅓ cup light olive oil

Combine the maple syrup, pomegranate molasses, and olive oil in a blender or a food processor and process until the ingredients are blended. Store in a clean, airtight container and refrigerate until ready to use. The glaze can be made ahead and will keep in the refrigerator for 3 weeks. To use the glaze after refrigerating, warm it over medium heat, stirring occasionally.

TIMETABLE:
Chicken breasts, kabobs, wings, thighs, or legs; Cornish hens; turkey breast; pork tenderloin or chops; baby back ribs; or spareribs: baste during the last 5 minutes of cooking

TIMETABLE:
Salmon steaks, chicken
breasts, chicken wings,
pork chops, or spareribs:
baste during the last
5 minutes of cooking

BASIC MUSTARD GLAZE MAKES 1 CUP

This is one of my favorite glazes when a side of salmon just happens to wash ashore after swimming upstream from my favorite fishmonger. Something as effortless and tasty as this basting glaze takes as much time to put together as it does to light a grill or warm a sauté pan.

½ cup coarse-grained brown mustard
¼ cup white wine vinegar
2 tablespoons soy or tamari sauce
1 teaspoon Tabasco sauce
2 tablespoons honey
2 tablespoons dark brown sugar

Combine the mustard, vinegar, soy sauce, Tabasco, honey, and brown sugar in a blender or a food processor and process until all the ingredients are blended. Store in a clean, airtight container and refrigerate until ready to use. The glaze can be made ahead and will keep in the refrigerator for 3 weeks. To use the glaze after refrigerating, warm it over medium heat, stirring occasionally.

DIJON MUSTARD–SHERRY GLAZE. Substitute Dijon-style mustard for the brown mustard and dry sherry for the white wine vinegar.

TIMETABLE:
Shrimp, chicken wings, pork
chops or cutlets, baby back
ribs, or spareribs: baste
during the last 5 minutes
of cooking

MAPLE-BOURBON GLAZE MAKES 1 CUP

You can customize this glaze to your palate's content. The sweet flavors of maple syrup and bourbon are gently tempered by orange so that the glaze doesn't taste overly sweet, but instead deep and savory.

½ cup maple syrup
½ cup bourbon or sour mash whiskey
½ cup cider vinegar
Grated zest and juice of 2 juice oranges (about ½ cup)
1 tablespoon dark brown sugar
¼ cup brown or full-flavored yellow mustard
¼ teaspoon cayenne
¼ cup soy or tamari sauce

In a heavy nonreactive saucepan, add the maple syrup, bourbon, vinegar, orange zest and juice, brown sugar, mustard, cayenne, and soy sauce. Bring to a simmer and simmer for about 30 minutes, until reduced to 1 cup. Cool the glaze, store in a clean, airtight container, and refrigerate until ready to use. The glaze can be made ahead and will keep in the refrigerator for 3 weeks. To use the glaze after refrigerating, warm it over medium heat, stirring occasionally.

COGNAC–DIJON MUSTARD GLAZE. Substitute honey for the maple syrup, cognac for the bourbon, and Dijon-style mustard for the brown mustard.

SCOTCH AND MUSTARD GLAZE. Substitute Scotch whisky for the bourbon and a dark grainy English mustard for the brown mustard.

SOUTHERN COMFORT–HONEY MUSTARD GLAZE. Substitute Southern Comfort for the bourbon, honey mustard for the brown mustard, and ¼ teaspoon freshly ground nutmeg for the cayenne.

GRAND MARNIER GLAZE. Substitute Grand Marnier (or another orange liqueur) for the bourbon and a fruit mustard for the brown mustard.

CALVADOS-CIDER GLAZE. Substitute Calvados for the bourbon and apple cider for the orange juice. Omit the orange zest.

TEQUILA-JALAPEÑO GLAZE. Substitute tequila for the bourbon, ¼ cup fresh lime juice for the orange juice, lime zest for the orange zest, Ancho chile powder for the cayenne, and jalapeño jelly (melted in a microwave or over low heat until liquid) for the honey. Omit the mustard.

SAVORY BOURBON CARAMEL MAKES 1 CUP

This is a recipe rocket. Making a batch of this in advance can just launch any last-minute glaze with some added orange juice and mustard. The caramel can be used for the sugar portion of brines.

1 cup sugar or maple sugar
1 cup bourbon
1 teaspoon dry mustard
1 teaspoon coarse-grain or sea salt
1 teaspoon freshly ground black pepper

Combine the sugar and 1 tablespoon of the bourbon in a 2-quart heavy-bottom saucepan over a boil. Do not stir until all the sugar has dissolved and it begins to color around the edges. Cook for about 10 minutes, until a medium amber color. When the caramel reaches the desired color, remove the pan from the heat and carefully stir in the remaining bourbon, dry mustard, salt, and pepper. Return the caramel to the heat and simmer for about 20 minutes, until reduced to 1 cup. Remove the caramel from the heat and let the caramel cool to room temperature.

Pour the caramel into a clean, airtight container and refrigerate until ready to use. The glaze can be made ahead and will keep in the refrigerator for 3 weeks. To use the glaze after refrigerating, warm it over medium heat, stirring occasionally.

TIMETABLE:
Salmon steaks or fillets; shrimp; chicken breasts, kabobs, wings, thighs, or legs; Cornish hen; turkey breast; or pork tenderloin or chops: baste during the last 5 minutes of cooking

Salmon steaks or fillets, scallops, or shrimp: baste during the last 5 minutes of cooking

COGNAC-BALSAMIC GLAZE MAKES ½ CUP

Once I was working with a recipe that called for a fifty-year-old balsamic vinegar, and not having one available, I thought I'd substitute an alternative. I combined a ten-year-old balsamic sibling along with cognac and a little bit of vanilla to simulate oak and reduced the mixture by half. Well, the aging process didn't happen that quickly, but what did happen was a rich balsamic glaze that found its way onto grilled seafood.

1 cup good-quality balsamic vinegar
¼ cup cognac
1 teaspoon vanilla extract

In a nonreactive heavy-bottom saucepan, combine the vinegar, cognac, and vanilla. Bring the liquid to a boil, reduce to a simmer, and simmer for 25 to 30 minutes, until the mixture is reduced to ½ cup. It should look thick and syrupy. Store in a clean, airtight container and refrigerate until ready to use. The glaze can be made ahead and will keep in the refrigerator for 3 weeks. To use the glaze after refrigerating, warm it over medium heat, stirring occasionally.

GRAPPA GLAZE. Replace the cognac with ¼ cup grappa.

TIMETABLE:
Chicken breasts, chicken wings, pork chops, spareribs, or pork tenderloin: baste during the last 5 minutes of cooking

HONEY-GINGER GLAZE MAKES 1 CUP

Visualize chicken breasts or double-cut pork chops with a wonderful tinge of gold. But that tinge packs quite a bit of flavor, as the zesty combination of lemon and ginger contrasts with the sweetness of honey, and the chopped mint adds a gust of coolness to the overall tang.

Grated zest and juice of 2 lemons (about ⅓ cup)
⅓ cup honey
2 tablespoons chopped fresh mint
3 tablespoons freshly grated ginger
2 cloves garlic, chopped

Combine the lemon zest and juice, honey, mint, ginger, and garlic in a blender or a food processor and process until all the ingredients are blended. Store in a clean, airtight container and refrigerate until ready to use. The glaze can be made ahead and will keep in the refrigerator for 1 week. To use the glaze after refrigerating, warm it over medium heat, stirring occasionally.

FAUX PHILLY CHEESE STEAK SANDWICH

SERVES 4

I really look forward to having vegan guests over for dinner. It gives me a chance to stretch and have some real playtime with food. I know I'm going to get a lot of "Yo, 'smatter wid you?" rants from my hometown on tampering with one of our sacraments: The Philly Cheese Steak. But this vegetarian version, using portobello mushrooms, is worth the heat.

The technique I learned for preparing the portobellos is from Eric Tucker's *The Millennium Cookbook*. His presteaming method is infallible for preparing grilled mushrooms.

4 portobello mushrooms. stemmed and brushed
1 cup Tomato-Basil Marinade (page 218)
1 cup grated Cheddar cheese or nondairy substitute
4 long Italian or long thick-crusted rolls (about 9½ inches)
Toppings of your choice: mushrooms, raw onions, fried onions,
    sautéed sweet red and green peppers, pizza (tomato) sauce

Slice the mushrooms into thin (¼ inch) slices. In a large nonreactive saucepan or a skillet, heat about ½ inch water until boiling, add the mushrooms, gills down, cover, and steam for 5 minutes. Put the mushrooms in a nonreactive mixing bowl and toss with the marinade. Let them sit for 15 minutes. Return the mushrooms and the marinade to the saucepan and sauté until the marinade has almost evaporated. Fold in the cheese and cook until the cheese is melted.

TIP: If you're using a vegan or nondairy cheese, the cheese will not melt completely, but it will soften.

To serve, slice the rolls lengthwise and open them like a book. Add the mushrooms and toppings of your choice. Serve immediately.

GRILLED PORTOBELLO BURGER. This is a vegetarian hamburger helper. Keep the portobello mushrooms whole. Replace the marinade with Balsamic-Herbal Marinade (page 217) or Provençal Red Wine Marinade (page 227). Grill the mushrooms, top with crumbled Gorgonzola, and serve in a round roll.

GRILLED SHIITAKE MUSHROOMS

SERVES 4 AS AN APPETIZER

Fresh shiitake mushrooms are the next best thing to hamburgers on a grill, and they can handle "beefy" marinades as well. They grill up crisp and meaty, the flavors of the marinade sealing inside the gills. With sprouts and pita bread, they make a great vegetarian standby at a barbecue. Go for the largest mushroom caps you can find, but if you can't find shiitakes, portobello mushrooms will be just as tasty.

SUBSTITUTIONS: Replace the marinade with Korean-Style Marinade (page 284), Madeira Marinade (page 222), or Provençal Red Wine Marinade (page 227).

¾ pound shiitake mushrooms, caps only
1 cup Lemon-Soy Marinade (page 52)

If the mushrooms are dirty, rub their surfaces gently with a cloth or paper towel. Lightly score the mushroom caps with a knife. Place the mushrooms in a nonreactive container or a 1-gallon resealable plastic bag, pour the marinade over the mushrooms, and refrigerate for 6 hours.

Remove the mushrooms from the marinade. Bring the marinade to a rolling boil and reserve for basting.

To grill: Lightly brush the grill with vegetable oil and grill the mushrooms over medium-high heat, stem side down first, then the cap, for 3 to 5 minutes, basting with the warm marinade. Grill the mushrooms until they are tender and juicy and no longer dry.

To cook indoors: Pan-fry the mushrooms, cooking both sides, in a skillet over medium-high heat for no longer than 3 minutes total. Sauté the mushrooms until they are tender and juicy and no longer dry.

Serve immediately.

COGNAC-PEPPERCORN CURED SALMON OR SALMON PASTRAMI SERVES 12 AS AN APPETIZER

Naming a recipe can be harder sometimes than developing one. To solve the dilemma, I used one side of salmon at a New Year's Eve dinner party and called it Cognac-Peppercorn Cured Salmon. The following day, while watching the Philadelphia mummer's parade on TV, it magically turned into Salmon Pastrami.

⅔ cup mixed peppercorns (black, white, and pink)
1 teaspoon whole coriander seeds, lightly toasted
1 cup dark brown sugar or Maple Sugar (page 71)
1 cup kosher salt
2½ to 3½ pounds salmon
⅓ cup cognac, bourbon, or dark rum
1 bunch dill (about 1 cup)
Capers, for garnish
Chives, for garnish
Diced red onion, for garnish

Combine the peppercorns and coriander seeds in a spice mill or a blender and pulse to crack the peppercorns. It's best to do this 1 tablespoon at a time to avoid pulverizing some of the peppercorns into ground pepper. In a small mixing bowl, combine the peppercorn-coriander mixture, sugar, and salt.

Rinse the salmon briefly under cold running water and pat dry with paper towels. With a pair of tweezers, remove any small bones that run up the center. Lay the salmon fillets on top of one another, with the skin facing out (flesh facing in), on a cutting surface and trim evenly. Lay the salmon skin side down in a large ceramic or glass baking dish.

Evenly spread each fillet with the cure. Sprinkle each fillet with the cognac. Add the dill. Lay the salmon fillets on top of one another with the skin out (flesh in). Wrap the salmon in plastic wrap, place it in a baking dish, and weight it down with a brick or heavy cans. You need to make sure that the weight is evenly distributed. Refrigerate for 2 to 3 days, turning approximately every 12 hours.

To serve, unwrap the salmon, and slice it very thin on the diagonal. Garnish with capers, chives, and diced red onion.

TIP: Sometimes getting equal cuts of center-cut salmon can work better than a side. The cuts can be sandwiched together with the cure and the dill in the middle. Plus, they tend to be an even thickness, which makes for a more controlled cure.

SMOKED SALMON WITH TANGERINE–PINK PEPPERCORN MARINADE SERVES 4 AS AN APPETIZER

This easy recipe has the prettiest presentation in the book, with rosettes of translucent orange salmon on bouquets of dill branches, and the wonderful flavor of the dish lives up to its looks. The tangerine tempers the smoke flavor and cuts the saltiness of the salmon's brine.

½ pound Maple Smoked Salmon (page 99) or good-quality smoked salmon, thinly sliced into 1-inch to 2-inch strips
1⅓ cups Tangerine–Pink Peppercorn Marinade (page 55)
1 bunch chives
1½ to 2 cups alfalfa sprouts
1 bunch fresh dill (minus the dill used in the marinade recipe)

Place the salmon in a flat glass baking dish, add the marinade, and refrigerate for 2 hours.

Arrange 3 long chives at the ten o'clock position on each salad plate. Finely dice the remaining chives and sprinkle along the outer edge of the plates. Form a nest with the sprouts in the middle of each plate. Break the remaining dill into branches and place them in the center of the sprouts to form a bouquet. Remove the salmon from the marinade and reserve the marinade. Gently roll the salmon strips into rosettes and place 3 or 4 of them in the center of the dill branches.

In a small saucepan or in the microwave, gently warm the marinade, but do not bring to a boil. You want to warm the marinade slightly to bring out the salmon's flavor. Spoon the warm marinade over the salmon and serve.

LOWER EAST SIDE BAGELS AND LOX SERVES 6

Lox recipes, like competition barbecue rubs, are closely guarded secrets. When my wife and I would travel up to New York to see her family, my father-in-law would have a batch of the Lower East Side's finest waiting for us, along with a container of whitefish salad, one of my many guilty pleasures.

Lox is cured smoked salmon that is never cooked above 90°F. This can be a weekend-plus kind of a project. Start the 24-hour brine on a Thursday evening, let the salmon sit in the brine until Friday evening, and then let it dry overnight until Saturday morning. It's in the smoker on Saturday and it cools overnight for bagels and lox for Sunday brunch.

LOX SERVES 12

4 quarts All-Purpose Basic Brine (page 46)
1 whole salmon filet (2½ to 3½ pounds)
1 cup maple syrup, dark rum, or bourbon

0 ounces (Philadelphia) cream cheese
6 bagels, sliced in half and lightly toasted
2 large vine-ripened tomatoes, cut into ¼-inch-thick slices
1 large red onion, cut into thin slices
2 tablespoons capers

To make the lox, pour the brine into a large nonporous container, place the salmon in the brine, and refrigerate for 24 hours. Remove the pieces and, under cold briskly running water, rinse off the brine.

Place the salmon on a rack over a baking sheet and refrigerate to cure for at least 12 more hours. This allows the salt to even out.

Place the salmon in a smoker with a temperature no hotter than 90°F. Smoke for about 8 hours, or until the fish has a nice glaze, basting with the maple syrup.

Remove the salmon and let cool in the refrigerator for at least 10 hours before slicing.

To assemble the bagels and lox, spread the cream cheese on both halves of each bagel. Stack one half of the bagel with lox, tomato, and onion. Gently press the capers into the remaining half (the cream cheese will hold them in place) and cover. The next step is up to you, whether you want to slice it in half or eat it as is.

CURING AND BRINING SEAFOOD

There are so many things you can do when curing or brining seafood. When there's a brine involved, add some marinating flavor notes. When there's a cure, add some melody lines from a rub. There are three basic templates to play with: curing, brining, and the option of smoking.

There are actually only two techniques for prepping seafood like salmon or trout: a dry cure or a brine. The brine, in this a particular case, is actually a wet cure. Its salinity falls between a typical brine and a dry cure, and I don't recommend brining pork or poultry in it.

Here are some techniques and options for a 2- to 3-pound center-cut salmon fillet, which yields about 12 servings.

For dry-cured salmon, we can build on the basic curing foundation. I don't suggest replacing the salt with anything, but we can have some fun with the sugar by mixing up the sweeteners. Note that the darker the sugar base, the darker the salmon tint. Maple syrup in a cure gives the fish a bright neon-copper sheen. For a basic salt cure, use 1 cup kosher salt and either 1 cup light brown sugar, dark brown sugar, maple sugar, maple syrup, honey, kecap manis, or pomegranate molasses. To flavor the cure, combine the salt and sugar with 2 to 3 tablespoons of any of the citrus powders on page 66.

Other flavor options are ¼ to ⅓ cup Lemon-Sumac Rub (page 259), Wasabi Rub (page 297), Sour Mash–Pink Peppercorn Rub (page 77), or North African Cumin Spice Rub (page 260). In lieu of fresh herbs such as dill, add 1 cup Cilantro-Ginger Pesto (page 301) or Fines Herbes Pesto Rub (page 69), omitting the oil and citrus juices. If you're using a seasoning with a little bit of heat, you may want to start with ¼ cup the first time out.

To top off the cure with a little liquor, add ¼ cup bourbon, sour mash or Scotch whiskey, cognac, Armagnac, Southern Comfort (a particularly nice flavor), limoncello, grappa, aquavit, or any flavored vodka.

Sprinkle each fillet with 1 tablespoon of the liquor of your choice. Evenly sprinkle each fillet with the cure and lay the fish fillets on top of one another with the skin facing out and the flesh in. Wrap the fish in plastic wrap, place it in a baking dish, and weight it down with a brick or heavy cans. You need to make sure that the weight is evenly distributed.

The major difference between brining salmon and curing salmon is the thickness of the end result. If you've read the curing instructions above, you know it involves weighting down the fish, which compresses and removes some of the water along with the salt. With brines, there's no such squeeze. The salmon just lays there, relaxed and soaking away.

Let's use the All-Purpose Basic Brine (page 46) as base camp and start to climb from there. The sugar portion of the brine is one of the simplest ways to add a flavor push. Not only do you have a wide choice of sweeteners, buy you can also broaden the flavor by adding a glaze or a savory caramel.

Start with 2 quarts water and 1 cup light brown sugar, dark brown sugar, maple sugar, maple syrup honey, or molasses, or a 3-to-1 ratio of honey and kecap manis or pomegranate molasses. Or you can replace the sugar with an equal amount of Savory Citrus Caramel (page 75), Carrot-Curry Caramel Glaze (page 82), Balsamic-Berry Sauce (page 124), Orange–Star Anise Glaze (page 302), East–West Indies Tamarind Glaze (page 310), or Teriyaki Glaze (page 304). For the salt content, add 1½ cups kosher salt, or ½ cup salt and ¼ cup soy or Asian fish sauce.

If you're using just the basic ingredients of water, salt, and light brown sugar, build some flavor with a citrus push: add the grated zest of 3 oranges, 3 limes, and 3 lemons (about ⅔ cup). For a barbecue push, add ½ cup Basic Southern Barbecue Rub (page 140) or Sour Mash Pink Peppercorn Rub (page 77). For an Asian-style brine, use Asian Tea Brine (page 276), Thai-Infused Brine (page 278), Sake-Mirin Brine (page 277), or Ginger-Szechuan Brine (page 276). For extra credit, try Apple Cider Brine (page 48) or Ancho Brine (page 131).

In a large saucepan over medium-high heat, add the salt, sugar, and any of the optional ingredient suggestions, bring to a boil, and stir to dissolve. Decrease the heat and simmer for 30 minutes to brew the ingredients. Remove from the heat and let the brine cool to room temperature, then refrigerate to 40°F before adding food.

Pour the brine into a large nonporous container, place the salmon in the brine, and refrigerate according to the brining chart.

Brining times will vary according to the thickness of the fish and the recipe, but between 2 and 6 hours is standard for most recipes. I know that's a wide time range, but it really depends on your personal preference. If you're curing a 5-pound salmon or trout fillets, you'll probably want to let them soak overnight. If you need a general rule of thumb, you can use the following table to estimate your brining time.

BRINING TIMELINES FOR SMOKED SALMON

It all comes down to thickness. If you're brining scraps or ends, you can cut your brining time to 1 hour no matter what the weight. Understand that a side of salmon or a trout fillet is natural and not precisely machined, so the thickness will vary from the tail to the head. If you opt for presentation over flavor, brine the fish in segments.

WEIGHT	BRINING TIME
Up to 2 pounds	2 to 3 hours
Up to 3 pounds	3 to 4 hours
Up to 4 pounds	4 to 5 hours

Now for another flavor group: smoking! For your choice of woods, consider alder, oak, maple, or any of the available fruit woods. Hickory has a pretty robust flavor in its own right and I suggest cutting it with oak for smoking salmon.

After brining or curing salmon, place the fish on a rack over a baking sheet and refrigerate for at least 12 more hours to form a pellicle. This also allows the salt to even out. Place the salmon in a smoker with a temperature no hotter than 90°F. Cold-smoke for about 8 hours, or until the fish has a nice glaze, basting with maple syrup, rum, or bourbon. Remove the salmon from the smoker and let it cool for at least 10 hours before slicing. Vacuum-sealed, the salmon can be frozen for up to 6 months.

TIP

If you're really serious about curing salmon, cut a wooden plank to fit the interior of a ceramic or glass baking dish to distribute the weight evenly.

JUNIPER-GIN CURED GRAVLAX
SERVES 12 AS AN APPETIZER

. . . .

When setting up a buffet table, I like to have a few anchor dishes, such as homemade prosciutto, a smoked turkey breast, and a side of salmon, each surrounded by a collection of condiments for folks to choose from to build their own platters. Gravlax is always one of those anchor dishes. I make it days ahead of time, and it always comes across as truly sophisticated fare.

Traditionally, gravlax calls for aquavit or perhaps vodka. I've replaced that with gin. The juniper berries pair wonderfully well with the lemon zest. The Lime-Cilantro variation of Grilled Lemon-Cured Salmon (page 100) has a Southwestern kick to it.

2 (1-pound) center-cut salmon fillets, including skin
3 cups Juniper-Gin Cure (page 45)
¼ cup gin
Capers, for garnish
Chives, for garnish
Diced red onion, for garnish

Rinse the salmon briefly under cold running water and pat dry with paper towels. With a pair of tweezers, remove any small bones that run up the center. Lay the salmon fillets on top of one another, skin facing out (flesh in), on a cutting surface and trim evenly. Lay the salmon skin side down in a large ceramic or glass baking dish.

Evenly spread each fillet with the cure. Sprinkle each fillet with the gin. and lay the salmon fillets on top of one another, with the skin out (flesh in). Wrap the salmon in plastic wrap, place it in a baking dish, and weight it down with a brick or heavy cans. You need to make sure that the weight is evenly distributed. Refrigerate for 2 to 3 days, turning approximately every 12 hours.

To serve, unwrap the salmon and slice it very thin on the diagonal. Garnish with capers, chives, and diced red onion.

LEMON-MINT CURED BROOK TROUT. Replace the Juniper-Gin Cure with Lemon-Mint Cure (page 45). Substitute 2 brook trout, boned and filleted, for the salmon (about 2 pounds). Proceed with the recipe as above.

MAPLE SMOKED SALMON SERVES 12

Do you think that Southern barbecue has the market cornered on smoked foods? Not by a long shot. This spin on smoked salmon is from the Quebec Province, most notably Montreal. One thing I have noticed about a lot of the professional kitchens in and outside of Montreal is the fact that they are equipped with offset brick smokers. Most of the chefs will smoke their own salmon and trout on the premises over maple wood, and they also use maple sugar or syrup as part of the cure. This gives the fish a nice sweet taste, and it will melt in your mouth.

3½ cups kosher salt
2 cups light brown sugar or Maple Sugar (page 71)
1 whole salmon filet (about 2½ to 3½ pounds)
1 cup maple syrup

In a mixing bowl, combine the salt and sugar. Rinse the salmon briefly under cold running water and pat dry with paper towels. With a pair of tweezers, remove any small bones that run up the center. Lay the salmon fillets on top of one another, with the skin facing out (flesh in), on a cutting surface and trim evenly. Lay the salmon skin side down in a large ceramic or glass baking dish.

Evenly spread the cure on the salmon. Wrap the salmon in plastic wrap, place it in a baking dish, and weight it down with a brick or heavy cans. You need to make sure that the weight is evenly distributed. Refrigerate for 2 to 3 days, turning approximately every 12 hours.

Remove the pieces and rinse off the cure under cold running water. Place the salmon on a rack over a baking sheet and refrigerate to cure for at least 12 more hours to form a pellicle. This allows the salt to even out.

To smoke, place the salmon in a smoker with maple or oak wood with a temperature no hotter than 90°F. Smoke for about 8 hours, or until the fish has a nice glaze, basting with the maple syrup. Remove the salmon and let cool for at least 10 hours before slicing. Vacuum-sealed, the salmon can be frozen for up to 6 months.

MAPLE-BOURBON SMOKED SALMON. Drizzle ¼ cup bourbon over the salmon after adding the cure. Add ¼ cup bourbon to the maple syrup for basting.

GRILLED LEMON-CURED SALMON SERVES 4

The salmon will be briefly cured for the grill just long enough to intensify its flavor and color. The cooking time is short because the salmon is partially cured. You can jazz up the basic cure with a tablespoon or two of your favorite rub or spice mix. Serve with Citrus Slaw (page 125), Stir-Fried Snow Peas with Balsamic-Ginger Marinade (page 337), or Marinated White Asparagus (page 233).

SUBSTITUTIONS: Replace the cure with Lime-Cilantro Cure (page 192).

2 pounds center-cut fillet of salmon
3 cups Basic Lemon Cure (page 45)
1 tablespoon extra virgin olive oil or clarified butter (if cooking indoors)

Rinse the salmon briefly under cold running water and pat dry with paper towels. With a pair of tweezers, remove any small bones that run up the center. Lay the salmon fillet on a cutting surface and trim evenly. Sprinkle half of the cure on the bottom of a glass or nonreactive baking dish (to fit). Place the salmon, skin side down, in the baking dish, and add the remaining half of the cure. Cover with plastic wrap, place another baking dish on top of the salmon, and put a weight on the dish. Refrigerate the salmon for 6 hours to cure.

After curing, remove the salmon from the cure and rinse. Pat dry with paper towels and cut the salmon into 4 portions.

To grill: Lightly brush the grill with vegetable oil and grill the salmon, flesh side down, over medium-high heat for 3 to 4 minutes. Turn the fillet skin side down and continue grilling for 2 minutes more. Salmon is done when you can almost flake it, but it's still somewhat orange in the middle.

To cook indoors: Heat the oil in a frying pan to medium-high heat. Place the salmon flesh side down and sear for 2 minutes, pressing with a spatula to keep the salmon from curling. Turn the salmon and cook for 2 minutes longer. Salmon is done when you can almost flake it, but it's still somewhat orange in the middle.

Slide a spatula between the skin and the flesh, lift, and transfer to a serving plate.

To serve, center a rounded portion of any of the recommended side dishes on a serving plate with the salmon and serve immediately.

ORANGE-SAFFRON MARINATED TILAPIA IN PARCHMENT SERVES 4

The Orange-Saffron Marinade cultivates a steamy relationship between the moist tilapia and the succulent vegetables. The orange plays off the hints of licorice from lightly sautéed fennel. But it's the saffron that gently infuses the fish, vegetables, and steam with a tinge of culinary perfume.

4 (6 to 8 ounces each) tilapia fillets or steaks, about 1 inch thick, or other firm-flesh white fish
1½ cups Orange-Saffron Marinade (page 53)
6 tablespoons canola oil
3 small leeks, white part only, julienned into 3-inch-long strips
3 carrots, julienned into 3-inch-long strips (about 1½ cups)
¾ cup diced fennel
1 juice orange, peeled, seeded, and sliced into 1-inch pieces

Place the tilapia in a nonreactive container or a 1-gallon resealable plastic bag. Pour the marinade over the fish and marinate for no longer than 2 hours in the refrigerator. Remove the fish from the marinade and reserve the marinade.

Preheat the oven to 400°F. Cut 4 sheets of parchment paper, each measuring 12 inches by 16 inches. Fold the parchment paper in half and cut each sheet into a heart shape. Brush 1 tablespoon of the oil on the inside of each sheet.

In a heavy skillet, heat the remaining 2 tablespoons canola oil over medium-high heat. Add the leeks, carrots, and fennel along with 2 to 3 tablespoons of the reserved marinade, and lightly sauté until the marinade evaporates, 3 to 5 minutes.

Divide the orange sections into 4 portions and place each portion on the middle inside crease of each sheet of parchment. Divide the sautéed vegetables into 4 portions and place on top of the oranges. Top with the fish and spoon about ¼ cup marinade over each portion.

To close the parchment, fold the edges over and crimp the edges well. Fold the paper over twice and twist the bottom part of the heart. Place the parcels on a baking sheet and bake for 20 minutes.

To serve, remove the parcels from the oven and slide them onto serving plates. At the table, cut an X in the parchment with a sharp pointed knife and peel back the leaves.

SUBSTITUTIONS: Replace the tilapia with swordfish, red snapper, pompano, mackerel, salmon, or shellfish.

Replace the marinade with Thai Coconut Marinade (page 287), Ligurian Marinade (page 220), or Tapenade Marinade (page 220).

BRAISED SHAD WITH WHITE WINE MARINADE

SERVES 4

• •

Writing cookbooks involves just as much time in front of a word processor as it does in front of a food processor. My wife, Ellen, bailed me out with this recipe for braised shad while I was busy writing the text for the last edition. The shad is marinated along with the vegetables, and then braised in the marinade. The shad is succulent and the vegetables have just the right flavor and crunch. Serve over rice or couscous.

SUBSTITUTIONS: Replace the marinade with Basic Mediterranean Marinade (page 217), Lemon-Sorrel Marinade (page 51), or Laurel and Lemon Marinade (page 51).

1½ to 2 pounds shad fillet or any firm-fleshed fish
1 cup coarsely chopped or thinly sliced celery
1 cup coarsely chopped or thinly sliced carrots
¾ cup chopped fennel bulb and stalks (save the fronds for garnishing)
¾ cup chopped sweet onion
2½ cups Basic Marinade for Seafood (page 50)

Place the shad, celery, carrots, fennel, and onion in a nonreactive container or a 1-gallon resealable plastic bag. Pour the marinade over the shad and refrigerate for 2 to 3 hours.

Preheat the oven to 350°F. Empty the contents of the resealable bag into a shallow glass baking dish, arranging the fish on top of the vegetables. Top the fish with the reserved fennel fronds, cover the dish with foil, place in the oven, and bake for 30 minutes.

Serve hot.

GRILLED LEMON-SOY MARINATED SWORDFISH STEAKS WITH PINEAPPLE-JALAPEÑO SALSA

SERVES 8 AS AN APPETIZER OR 4 AS A MAIN COURSE

The tart flavor of the Lemon-Soy Marinade is heightened by hints of Dijon-style mustard. By accompanying the steak with the Pineapple-Jalapeño Salsa, one gets a savory contrast on the palate with the sweet pineapple, earthy saffron, and spicy jalapeño. My friend chef Jon Jividen created this recipe to use in two ways: as a main course with swordfish steaks and as an appetizer with skewered kabobs of swordfish around a bowl of salsa for dipping. You can also use the marinade on shark, mahi mahi, and grouper.

4 (6 ounces each) swordfish steaks
1½ cups Lemon-Soy Marinade (page 52)
Presoaked wooden or metal skewers, for kabobs
1½ cups Pineapple-Jalapeño Salsa (page 164)

To prepare the swordfish steaks, place the swordfish in a nonreactive container or a 1-gallon resealable plastic bag. Pour the marinade over the swordfish and refrigerate for no longer than 4 hours.

Alternatively, to make kabobs, cut the swordfish into 1-inch squares and place in a nonreactive container or a 1-gallon resealable plastic bag. Pour the marinade over the swordfish and refrigerate for no longer than 1 hour.

Remove the swordfish from the marinade. Thread the fish onto skewers if making kabobs. Bring the marinade to a rolling boil in a nonreactive saucepan, or microwave the marinade on high for 3 minutes. Use for basting.

To grill: Lightly brush the grill with vegetable oil and grill the swordfish for 5 to 6 minutes, turning after 4 minutes and basting often with the warm marinade.

To cook indoors: Preheat the broiler to its hottest setting, and line a baking sheet with foil. Arrange the swordfish on the baking sheet and broil for 6 to 8 minutes on each side, basting often with the warm marinade.

Serve with the Pineapple-Jalapeño Salsa.

SUBSTITUTIONS: Replace the marinade with Basic Asian-Style Marinade (page 278), Lemongrass Marinade (page 286), or Lime-Cilantro Marinade (page 50).

TIP: Skewers can be soaked in just about anything, such as orange juice, apple cider, red or white wine, or even bourbon. You can keep them in a bag in the freezer, so you always have some on hand.

GRILLED MAHI MAHI WITH CHARDONNAY MARINADE SERVES 4

I don't think I have to suggest a wine pairing with this dish. This firm-flesh sweet-tasting fish is a nice match for a buttery chardonnay.

4 (6 ounces each) mahi mahi fillets
1½ cups Chardonnay Marinade (page 61)

Place the mahi mahi in a nonreactive container or a 1-gallon resealable plastic bag, pour the marinade over the fish, and refrigerate for 2 to 3 hours.

Remove the mahi mahi from the marinade. Bring the marinade to a rolling boil in a nonreactive saucepan, or microwave the marinade on high for 3 minutes. Use for basting.

To grill: Lightly brush the grill with vegetable oil. Grill and baste the mahi mahi for about 5 minutes. Turn the fillets and grill for an additional 3 to 4 minutes, or until the fish begins to flake when tested with a fork.

To cook indoors: Preheat the broiler, and line a baking sheet with foil. Arrange the fish, flesh side up, on the baking sheet. Broil the fish about 6 inches from the heat source for 7 to 8 minutes, or until the fish begins to flake when tested with a fork.

Serve hot.

GRILLED ORANGE-GINGER MARINATED TUNA
SERVES 4

SUBSTITUTIONS: Replace the marinade with Yucatecan Citrus Recado (page 182), Orange-Chipotle Marinade (page 174), or Bitter Orange Marinade (page 176), and replace the salsa with Pineapple-Jalapeño Salsa (page 164).

Citrus and ginger pair off to cut the smokiness of the grilled tuna. The colorful corn salsa rounds out the dish with the Southwestern flavors of corn, lime, cilantro, and a little bit of heat from serrano chiles.

4 (6 ounces each) sushi-quality tuna steaks, ¾ to 1 inch thick
1½ cups Orange-Ginger Marinade (page 54)
1 to 2 tablespoons extra virgin olive oil or peanut oil (if cooking indoors)
2 cups Sweet Corn Salsa (page 166)

Place the tuna steaks in a nonreactive container or a 1-gallon resealable plastic bag. Pour the marinade over the tuna and refrigerate for 3 to 4 hours. Remove the tuna from the marinade. Bring the marinade to a rolling boil in a nonreactive saucepan, or microwave the marinade on high for 3 minutes. Use for basting.

To grill: Lightly brush the grill with vegetable oil and grill the tuna over high heat for 3 to 4 minutes for rare or 6 to 7 minutes for medium. Turn the tuna about halfway through the grilling time, basting with the warm marinade.

To cook indoors: Using a heavy-bottom sauce pan or a seasoned cast-iron frying pan, heat the oil. Increase the heat to high. Sear the tuna for 1 minute, turn, decrease the heat to medium, and sear for 1 minute more.

To serve, transfer the tuna to a serving plate and top each portion with ½ cup of the salsa.

TIP: Do not overcook, or the tuna will become dry and lose its flavor. The tuna should be red in the center, not gray.

SMOKED CHICKEN BREASTS SERVES 4

When I find a deal on chicken breasts, it is often more chicken than the recipe calls for. So, I take the remaining breasts and finish them off while smoking the big cuts like pork shoulder or brisket. It works so well that I no longer wait for a brisket to tag along for the ride. The recipe freezes well, so you'll have some smoked chicken ready to use for a fast salad, soup, or sandwich. This recipe can be scaled up.

4 (10 to 12 ounces each) skinless, bone-in chicken breast halves
2¼ cups Basic Dry Cure for Smoked Poultry (page 44)
1 cup Maple-Pomegranate Glaze (page 87)

Coat the chicken with the dry cure and let it rest at room temperature for 35 to 45 minutes. Rinse well and air-dry overnight (12 hours) in the refrigerator to form a pellicle. Remove the chicken from the refrigerator.

Smoke the chicken in a covered grill or smoker for 1 hour. The juices should run clear when pricked with a knife. Preheat the oven to 350°F if you'll finish the chicken in the oven. Brush the chicken with the glaze and bake in the oven for 5 to 10 minutes, or finish the chicken on a medium hot grill for 5 minutes. Serve hot.

ZESTY LIME GRILLED CHICKEN WINGS

SERVES 8 AS AN APPETIZER
. . . .

You can run with just the Lime Marinade for a perfectly tart and citrusy set of grilled wings. The instructions will show you how to use the marinade as a baste. If you follow the competition-grilling track with Peter Cravath and the Cow Pies (sorry, Peter, I know that sounds like the name of a bluegrass band), the recipe will take on two additional great tasting levels.

2 to 2½ pounds chicken wings
1½ cups Lime Marinade (page 51)
1½ cups Hot Chile–Lime Baste (page 52) (optional)
1½ cups Zesty Jalapeño Lime Glaze (page 74) (optional)
¼ cup Candied Jalapeño Licorice (page 73) (optional)

Place the wings in a nonreactive container or a 1-gallon resealable plastic bag. Pour the marinade over the wings and refrigerate for at least 6 hours.

Remove the wings from the marinade. If you're using the marinade for basting instead of the Hot Chile Lime Baste, bring the marinade to a rolling boil in a nonreactive saucepan, or microwave the marinade on high for 3 minutes.

To grill: Lightly brush the grill with vegetable oil and grill the wings for about 10 minutes, turning once. Baste and grill for 5 to 10 minutes more.

To cook indoors: Preheat the broiler, and line a baking sheet with foil. Arrange the wings on the baking sheet and broil for 10 minutes, turning once and basting. Broil for 5 to 10 minutes more.

To glaze (optional): About 5 minutes before your wings are done, begin painting them with the Zesty Jalapeño Lime Glaze, giving each wing several coats of the glaze as needed. This should be done on the cooler section of your grill to prevent scorching. Just before removing the wings, give each one a light coating of Candied Jalapeño Licorice. Allow to heat through for a few moments before serving.

Serve hot.

ORANGE DUCK PASTRAMI SERVES 8 AS AN APPETIZER

This recipe was made for a New Year's Eve buffet, where I added a splash of Quick Orange Aioli. A few days later, I ate it in a sandwich between two slices of rye bread with Citrus Slaw (page 125). This is a five-day process, so a little advance planning is the necessary ingredient. The dish is made without nitrates, which gives the duck meat a pinkish color. When sliced, the meat will turn gray, but the flavor will be just as good.

This recipe can be made with an equal amount of skinless turkey breast.

2 quarts Basic Citrus Brine (page 46)
2 whole muscovy or mallard duck breasts (1½ to 2 pounds)
1 cup Orange Pastrami Spice Mix (page 67)
1 quart duck or chicken broth
1 onion, chopped
2 cloves garlic, minced
2 sprigs fresh thyme
1 bay leaf
½ cup Quick Orange Aioli (page 247)

Pour the cold brine into a large nonreactive container, add the duck breasts to the brine, and refrigerate for 4 days. Remove the breasts from the brine and pat dry with paper towels. Score the breasts on the skin side on both diagonals to create a grid. Do not cut too deeply into the red meat. Rub the cure over both sides of the duck. Smoke the duck breasts for about 6 hours at 160°F, or until the internal temperature reaches 125°F.

In a heavy-bottomed pot or a Dutch oven fitted with a vegetable steamer or a small circular rack, combine the broth, onion, garlic, thyme, and bay leaf and bring to a simmer. Put the duck breasts on the rack, cover, and steam for 2 hours. Remove the duck from the pot and cool completely.

Tightly wrapped, the duck will keep for up to 2 weeks. Vacuum-sealed and frozen, the duck will keep for 4 to 6 months.

To serve, slice the breasts thinly and serve with the aioli.

SMOKED DUCK CONFIT WITH CRANBERRY-ORANGE CHUTNEY SALAD SERVES 8 AS AN APPETIZER

When cooking duck, I like to use everything but the quack. I'll render the fat, use the bones for stock, and stockpile the legs by sealing and freezing them to make confit later.

Confit is a preservation method. It's cooking and sealing duck in its rendered fat that results in meltingly tender, moist, and extremely flavorful meat. Introducing barbecue into the equation gives you down-home haute cuisine. This recipe became part of a summer salad, but I can just imagine how it would light up flavors in a New Orleans–style red bean cassoulet with andouille sausage.

SMOKED DUCK CONFIT

SUBSTITUTION: Replace the rub with Basic Southern Barbecue Rub (page 140).

4 or 5 cloves garlic
2 tablespoons water
1 cup kosher or sea salt
¼ cup Orange-Chipotle Powder (page 181)
¼ cup brown sugar
2 tablespoon freshly cracked black peppercorns
8 duck legs (2 to 3 pounds)
8 to 10 cups duck fat or lard

SALAD

2 bunches arugula, tough stems discarded, rinsed, and spun dry
Juice of 1 lemon (about ¼ cup)
4 cups Cranberry-Orange Chutney (page 127)
¾ cup finely chopped green onions, white parts only, or 1 tablespoon
    Cassis–Red Onion Glaze (page 84), for garnish (optional)

To make the confit, in a food processor, purée the garlic and water to a soft paste, about 30 seconds. Stop the motor and add to the processor bowl the salt, powder, brown sugar, and peppercorns. Pulse until the ingredients are thoroughly mixed.

Sprinkle a couple of tablespoons of the cure to cover the bottom of an ovenproof glass or ceramic baking dish large enough to hold the duck pieces in a single layer. Arrange the duck, skin side up, over the cure. Sprinkle the remaining cure over the duck. Cover and refrigerate for 24 hours.

Remove the duck legs from the refrigerator and rinse under cold running water. Bring a smoker's temperature to 225°F. Cook the duck legs for 2 hours. Preheat the oven to 225°F.

Melt the duck fat in a saucepan. Remove the duck legs from the smoker and transfer the legs to a deep casserole or rondo. Pour the melted fat over the duck to cover. Place the duck in the oven, and cook for an additional 2 to 3 hours, depending on the size of the duck legs.

TIP: The duck fat can be strained, cooled, and reused.

Remove the duck from the oven. Let the duck cool in the fat until it can safely be transferred to a large clean, airtight container. Strain the fat through a cheesecloth, and pour enough over the duck to cover it by at least 1 inch. Cool and store the duck in the fat. The confit will keep in the refrigerator for up to 3 months. The longer it ripens, the better it tastes.

To make the salad, in a ceramic or nonreactive mixing bowl, toss the arugula and lemon juice. Line 8 medium-size plates with the salad mix and top each with a ½-cup portion of the Cranberry-Orange Chutney at the 12 o'clock position.

Remove the duck legs from the crock. Remove the skin, scraping off any remaining fat. Remove the duck meat from the bones and chop. Divide the duck meat into 8 portions and add a portion to the center of each plate. Sprinkle with the green onions and serve.

GRILLED DUCK BREAST WITH POMEGRANATE-COGNAC GLAZE SERVES 4

I have always thought of duck as the other red meat. It's a red meat that can take to sweet berry and tart citrus sauces. Serve with Citrus Slaw (page 125) or Cashew-Ginger Chutney (page 331), if grilling, or Braised Chanterelles (page 249), if cooking indoors.

SUBSTITUTIONS: Replace the glaze with Morello Cherry Glaze (page 80), Cranberry-Cassis Glaze (page 78), or Savory Orange Glaze (page 72).

2 whole muscovy or mallard duck breasts or 4 Long Island duck breasts (about 1½ to 2 pounds)
Salt and freshly ground black pepper
¾ cup Pomegranate-Cognac Glaze (page 86)
2 tablespoons clarified butter (if cooking indoors)

Split the duck breasts into halves. Trim any overlapping skin and visible fat from the breasts. Score the skin with diagonal cuts. Dust with salt and pepper.

To grill: Lightly brush the grill with vegetable oil. Place the duck breasts on the grill, skin side down, over medium-high heat on a gas grill or medium-hot charcoals. Grill until the skin becomes crisp, 6 to 7 minutes. Turn the duck and brush with the glaze. Cover the grill and cook for 3 to 4 minutes more, or until the temperatue reachs 140°F at the thickest part. Bring the remaining glaze to a boil and brush the breasts once more before serving.

To cook indoors: Heat the clarified butter over high heat in a heavy sauté pan or seasoned cast-iron frying pan. Add the duck breasts skin side down and sauté for about 5 minutes, until well browned. Turn the duck breasts over, baste with the glaze, and continue cooking for 4 to 5 minutes, or until the juices run clear when pricked with a knife. Do not overcook or the duck will become tough.

Place the duck breasts on a platter and tent with foil. Let sit for 5 to 8 minutes before cutting.

To serve, cut the duck breasts crosswise into ½-inch-thick slices. Fan the duck breast over the plate and serve immediately.

SAUTÉED BREAST OF GOOSE WITH CASSIS MARINADE SERVES 4

When most people think of goose, they think of a whole roast. But I think that goose breast is more tender and flavorful than most of the finer cuts of beef (filet mignon included). A whole breast from a 7- to 9-pound goose will easily feed 4 people. Have your butcher bone the breast, use the remaining bones and meat for stock, and render the fat for cooking. The sweet Cassis Marinade has two functions. It cuts the natural richness of the goose breast and caramelizes its surface during a high-heat sauté. This dish goes beautifully with oven-roasted new potatoes and steamed white asparagus tips.

1 whole goose breast, halved, skinned, and with all visible
    fat and gristle removed (about 1½ pounds)
2¼ cups Cassis Marinade (page 64)
1 quart goose stock or full-bodied poultry stock
2 tablespoons clarified butter or rendered goose fat

Place the goose breast in a nonreactive container or a 1-gallon resealable plastic bag. Pour the marinade over the goose breast and refrigerate for 12 hours.

Remove the goose breast from the marinade and reserve the marinade for the sauce. Let the goose breast come to room temperature before sautéing. Meanwhile, make the sauce by bringing the reserved marinade to a rolling boil in a small nonreactive saucepan. Decrease the heat and simmer for about 30 minutes, reducing the marinade to about ½ cup. In a 2-quart nonreactive saucepan, reduce the goose stock to 1½ cups, about 45 minutes. Add the reduced marinade, and keep warm.

Heat the clarified butter over high heat in a large nonstick skillet. Add the breast to the skillet and sauté for about 7 minutes, until well browned. Turn the breast over and continue cooking for 6 to 7 minutes. Do not overcook or the goose will become tough. Place the goose breast on a platter and tent with foil. Let sit for 5 to 8 minutes before slicing. Deglaze the skillet with the cassis sauce.

To serve, cut the breast crosswise into ½-inch-thick slices. Spoon about ⅓ cup of the cassis sauce onto a warm plate. Fan the goose breast over the sauce and serve immediately.

CITRUS-BRINED TURKEY SERVES 10 TO 12

There are things you can do with a whole roasted turkey that may be too over-the-top for a traditional holiday sit-down, and this recipe is one of them. It's a great excuse to use a raspberry-citrus combo. As if you ever needed one. The citrus brine will work with chicken and smoked turkey breasts, too.

Turkeys can vary in weight and size. You will need enough brine to cover the turkey completely. To calculate the amount of brine needed, place the turkey in your container of choice and cover it with cold water. Remove the turkey and measure the amount of water remaining, rounding up to a quart, and scale up the recipe accordingly. For example, if you are using a 2-quart recipe and find you have close to a gallon and a half of water, you would need to increase the recipe by a factor of three.

SUBSTITUTIONS: Replace the Raspberry-Port Glaze with Cassis–Red Onion Glaze (page 84), Pomegranate-Cognac Glaze (page 86), or Cranberry-Cassis Glaze (page 78).

1 whole turkey (19 to 20 pounds)
Enough Basic Citrus Brine (page 46) to cover your turkey (see headnote)
1 onion, peeled and quartered
1 carrot, peeled and chopped into 1-inch chunks
1 celery stalk, chopped into 1 inch-chunks
½ cup (1 stick) butter, melted
1½ cups Raspberry-Port Glaze (page 80)

Rinse the turkey and place it in a large stockpot or a large clean plastic 5-gallon container and pour the brine over the turkey. Refrigerate and brine for 8 to 12 hours.

Preheat the oven to 325°F.

Remove the turkey from the brine and thoroughly rinse it under a slow stream of cool water, rubbing gently to release salt, both inside and out. Pat the skin and interior cavity dry with paper towels. In the cavity of the turkey, place the onion, carrot, and celery. Brush the turkey with the melted butter. Roast the turkey, breast side down, for 2 hours.

TIP: A brined turkey cooks slightly faster than an unbrined turkey, so check the internal temperature frequently.

Remove the turkey from the oven, turn the turkey breast side up, return it to the oven, and continue to roast, basting with the pan drippings. Continue to roast until the internal temperature reaches 170°F in the breast and 180°F in the thigh, about 15 minutes per pound. Brush with the glaze during the last 15 minutes of roasting.

Remove the turkey from the oven and allow it to rest for 20 minutes before carving. Bring the remaining glaze to a boil and reserve for drizzling over the sliced turkey.

TIPS FOR BRINING TURKEY

When brining a whole turkey or chicken, brine with the breast side down. To brine a whole turkey, you're going to have start the night before you plan to cook. You'll need at least 10 to 12 hours (or more), a container large enough to hold your turkey, enough brine to cover it, salt, water, seasonings, and room to refrigerate it all. (If your refrigerator is packed with other holiday foods, see "The Ice Cream Method" on page 7.) You'll also need a large container such as a large stockpot or even a clean plastic 5-gallon bucket. Whatever container you choose, the turkey needs to have at least 2 to 3 inches of brine covering it and enough room to be turned, and it shouldn't touch the sides.

Avoid self-basting and kosher turkeys, which have salt added, making your brined turkey too salty. A fresh turkey works best, but a completely thawed, frozen turkey will work almost as well. Remove the wrapped innards and thaw it completely. If it has been prefrozen, check the label for salt content.

If you are injecting spices or a marinade for a deep-fried turkey, do it after it has been brined.

Brined poultry with skin on can benefit from sitting uncovered on a platter overnight in the refrigerator. This lets the poultry air-dry and ensures a nice crackly skin.

When you are ready to start cooking your turkey, remove it from the brine, and rinse it in the sink under cold running water until all traces of salt are removed from the surface.

GRILLED TURKEY BREAST WITH LEMON MARINADE SERVES 4

The marinade, full of lemon and peppercorns, makes an excellent choice for grilled turkey, but a chance thunderstorm was responsible for the tasty indoor version. It almost made me wish it would rain more often.

4 (4 to 6 ounces each) turkey breast cutlets
1½ cups Lemon Marinade (page 51)
6 tablespoons unsalted butter, chilled (if cooking indoors)
2 cups homemade poultry stock or unsalted canned chicken broth
   (if cooking indoors)

Pound the turkey cutlets thin between two sheets of waxed paper. Place the turkey paillards in a nonreactive container or a 2-gallon resealable plastic bag. Pour the marinade over the turkey and refrigerate for 4 to 6 hours.

Remove the turkey from the marinade. Bring the marinade to a rolling boil in a nonreactive saucepan or microwave the marinade on high for 5 minutes. Use for basting.

To grill: Lightly brush the grill with vegetable oil and grill the turkey for 4 to 5 minutes, turning often and basting with the warm marinade. Serve hot.

To cook indoors: Preheat the oven to 300°F. Remove the turkey from the marinade and strain the marinade, reserving the solids and about ½ cup of the liquid. Melt 4 tablespoons of the butter in a sauté pan or skillet over medium-high heat. Sauté the turkey for 4 to 5 minutes, turning often. Remove the turkey from the skillet and place in the oven. Add the reserved solids to the skillet and sauté for 3 to 4 minutes. Deglaze the skillet with the poultry stock and reserved marinade, and reduce by half. Whisk the remaining 2 tablespoons of butter into the sauce, incorporating them 1 tablespoon at a time. Spoon the sauce onto 4 dinner plates, add the turkey, and serve.

HICKORY-SMOKED TURKEY BREAST SERVES 8 TO 12

For elegant holiday buffets or large barbecues or picnics, nothing beats a smoked turkey breast. You can theme your condiments around the flavor of the smoking woods and marinades, and have your guests suit their own palates. Hickory-Smoked Turkey Breast lends itself to various fruit chutneys, fruit mustards, and relishes. There's a brining option included in the recipe, if you have the time. The citrus in the brine is a nice counterpoint to the hickory smoke and picks up the orange in the marinade.

1 (5½- to 8-pound) bone-in turkey breast
6 quarts Basic Citrus Brine (page 46) (optional)
3 cups Cranberry Marinade (page 58)
1 quart apple cider, orange juice, or wine (if smoking)

If brining, place the turkey in a large stockpot or a clean plastic 5-gallon container and pour the brine over the turkey. Refrigerate and brine for 8 to 12 hours. Remove the turkey from the brine and thoroughly rinse under a slow stream of cool water.

If marinating, wash the turkey under cold water. Place the turkey in a plastic roasting bag; pour the marinade over the turkey. Secure the bag with a couple of twist ties, place in a shallow baking pan, and refrigerate for at least 8 hours or preferably overnight. Turn the turkey periodically to coat with the marinade.

Remove the turkey from the marinade and bring the marinade to a low boil in a nonreactive saucepan, or microwave the marinade for 3 minutes on high. Use for basting.

To cook outdoors. Smoke the turkey with presoaked hickory chunks or chips (see page 20) if you have a kettle grill and an available wok, or follow the manufacturer's instructions for indirect cooking over a drip pan. Fill the drip pan with apple cider, orange juice, or wine. The turkey will take about 20 minutes per pound. The internal temperature should read 160°F. Baste with the warm marinade during the last 20 minutes of cooking.

To smoke: Preheat the oven to 325°F. Roast the turkey for 20 minutes per pound, or until the internal temperature reads 160°F. For added moisture and flavor, place a pan of apple cider, orange juice, or wine on the floor of the oven during roasting. Refill as the liquid evaporates. Baste with the warm marinade during the last 20 minutes of cooking.

To serve, let the turkey stand for 20 minutes before carving. The turkey can be served warm or cold; it's great either way.

MESQUITE-SMOKED TURKEY BREAST. This is the dry-rub, south-of-the-border cousin of the above recipe. Replace the marinade with Yucatecan Citrus Recado (page 182). Place the turkey in a shallow baking pan. Carefully peel back the skin from the base of the breast to the top, keeping it in one piece, but do not remove it. Rub the seasoning mix into the turkey meat, replace the skin, and cover with plastic wrap. Refrigerate for at least 8 hours.

Replace the hickory chunks or chips with mesquite chunks or chips and follow the cooking instructions from the recipe above. Serve this smoked turkey with warm tortillas, mango pico de gallo, black bean salsa, or Mango-Jicama Salsa (page 166).

DESIGNER JERKY INGREDIENT IDEAS

If I had to add some suggestions for brines, marinades, rubs, and glazes for jerky, I might as well copy the book's index. It would almost be easier and take up less space to tell you what to leave out. Building on the jerky information on pages 29 and 30, here are some simple setups.

For red meat jerky: Use 2 pounds of any of the following, sliced 4 to 5 inches wide and ¼ inch thick: London broil, skirt steak, flank steak, lamb shoulder or leg, venison, elk, or buffalo.

For other red meat jerky: Use 2 pounds of any of the following, sliced 4 to 5 inches wide and ¼ inch thick: muscovy duck breast, goose breast (excellent with a brandy- or raspberry-based marinade), emu, or ostrich.

For white meat jerky: Use 2 pounds of turkey or chicken breast, sliced 4 to 5 inches wide and ¼ inch thick.

For "Indian" candy, or salmon jerky: Use 2 pounds of coho or sockeye salmon, sliced ¼ inch thick and 4 to 5 inches long, and brine it for 1 hour. Think of the most intensely flavored smoked salmon you've ever had, and you may not even be close. It is truly candy for grown-ups.

Here's a quickie shortcut. If you belong to one of the discount warehouse or buying clubs that occasionally run a sale on smoked salmon in bulk, or if you can make deals at your favorite deli for ends, you can make excellent jerky in almost half the time. An especially good salmon candidate is the peppercorn-crusted type. Soak smoked salmon strips in a marinade for 1 hour, and then dehydrate the strips for 6 hours, or until they have a licorice texture.

For ground meat jerky: When going for ground meat, get the leanest cut you can find, have it trimmed, and then have it ground. You'll only need ½ cup of marinade or 2 tablespoons of rub per pound of ground meat. Although there are some handy jerky guns or extruders available, you can get good results with either of the two following methods.

Roll out the mince to at least ¼ inch thick and cut as you would pastry into 1-inch-wide by 4-inch-long strips. Spray a pizza mesh or dehydrator screens with oil, and use a fish spatula to lay them on the mesh.

What's just as easy is to use a pastry bag with an extra-large pastry tip and pipe the ground meat in even strips onto your dehydrator screens. In fact, you may be able to pick up a cookie press at a yard sale with a pastry tip coupler, which makes a great jerky gun.

Timetable: If you're going to use a brine, count on leaving the food in the brine for 6 hours. The brining time does not have to be that long because of the thin cut of meat. I tend to go for full-blown saturation and let jerky soak for 8 hours in a marinade and 4 hours in a rub. Glazes should go on during the last hour of drying time; in other words, they should be dried on.

MAPLE TURKEY JERKY MAKES ¾ POUND

Maple Turkey Jerky, if you get the chance to add some fruit-wood smoke to it, will outshine some or the best apple wood–smoked "boutique" bacon. You will not be able to make enough, once folks get a whiff of this. It's such a pleasant edible vice. The salt in the brine and the salt in the marinade serve the dual purpose of stimulating the taste buds and preserving the meat by drawing out the moisture.

3 cups Maple-Bourbon Brine (page 49), or 2 tablespoons kosher salt
    and 1½ cups South Carolina Mustard Marinade (page 134)
2 pounds fresh turkey breast, cut into 4- to 5-inch-long by
    ¼-inch-thick strips
1 cup Maple-Bourbon Glaze (page 88)

If using brine, add the turkey strips to the brine, and brine in the refrigerator for at least 8 hours. Rinse the meat under cool running water and pat dry with paper towels. If you are not using brine, add the salt to the marinade. Place the turkey strips in a resealable plastic bag or a nonreactive bowl, add the marinade, and refrigerate for up to 12 hours.

Prepare your smoker or covered grill and smoke the jerky with presoaked fruit wood or hickory chips at 140°F for about 2 hours. Add the glaze during the last ½ hour. Watch your temperature; the idea is to dry it, not overcook it.

Preheat the oven to 140°F. Transfer the jerky to an oven or a dehydrator and continue drying until the jerky is stiff and pliable, 6 to 8 hours.

SUBSTITUTIONS: Replace the brine with Apple Cider Brine (page 48).

Replace the marinade with Apple Cider Marinade (page 56), Cranberry Marinade (page 58), or Orange Ginger Marinade (page 54).

Replace the glaze with Cognac–Dijon Mustard Glaze (page 88) or Cranberry-Jalapeño Glaze (page 144).

YELLOW SPLIT PEA SOUP WITH
MAPLE TURKEY JERKY SERVES 6

When some dinner guests asked what kind of specialty ham I had in this soup, they almost fell off their chairs when I told them it was turkey jerky. Out of the backpack and into the tureen, Maple Turkey Jerky simply perfumes the soup with a sweet-smoky, designer-bacon taste. Luckily, I had made enough jerky for them to take home. Instead of ham hocks, I use smoked turkey wings, which are available in most supermarket poultry sections. The recipe is easy to scale up and freezes well.

SUBSTITUTION: Replace the jerky with Turkey Tasso Ham (page 154).

3 cups yellow split peas, picked over and rinsed
2 quarts cold water
2 tablespoons extra virgin olive oil
1 cup finely diced carrots
1 to 1½ cups finely diced onions
2 quarts chicken stock or unsalted canned chicken broth
2 large smoked turkey wings (about 1 pound)
2 or 3 fresh thyme sprigs
1 bay leaf
1 tablespoon freshly cracked black peppercorns
1 to 1½ cups diced Maple Turkey Jerky (page 117)

Place the split peas in a large heavy pot, add 6 cups of the cold water, and refrigerate for at least 6 hours or overnight. Drain well and set aside.

In a 6- to 8-quart stockpot, heat the oil and add the carrots and onions. Sauté until the vegetables are soft, not brown, 6 to 7 minutes. Add the remaining water, peas, stock, turkey wings, thyme, bay leaf, and peppercorns. Bring to a quick boil, decrease the heat, and simmer gently for 3 hours, or until the peas are almost falling apart. Stir the soup occasionally. Remove the turkey wings, thyme sprigs, and bay leaf. Discard the sprigs and reserve the turkey for future use (which I call midnight snacking). Stir in half of the turkey jerky and return to the heat for 20 minutes.

Serve hot in individual soup bowls. Garnish with the remaining jerky. This soup freezes well in a clean, airtight container for up to 3 months.

CIDER-MARINATED RABBIT

SERVES 8 AS AN APPETIZER OR 4 AS A MAIN COURSE

The combination of freshly pressed cider with hints of mustard and honey makes this fall dish perfect for an Indian summer dinner. The marinade works equally well with chicken and Cornish hen.

2½- to 4-pound rabbit, cut into 8 serving pieces
9 cups Apple Cider Brine (page 48) (optional)
2 cups Apple Cider Marinade (page 56)

If brining, place the rabbit in a large nonreactive container and pour the brine over the rabbit, and refrigerate for at least 8 hours. Remove the rabbit from the brine, rinse the meat under cool running water, and pat dry with paper towels. If marinating, place the rabbit in a 1-gallon resealable plastic bag, add the marinade, and refrigerate for 6 hours. Remove the rabbit from the marinade. Bring the marinade to a rolling boil in a nonreactive saucepan or microwave the marinade on high for 3 minutes. Use for basting.

To grill: Lightly brush the grill with vegetable oil and grill the rabbit for 15 to 20 minutes, turning often and basting with the warm marinade. To check for doneness, pierce the meat close to the bone. The juices should run clear, and the meat should be white like chicken.

To cook indoors: Preheat the oven to 375°F, and line a baking sheet with foil. Arrange the rabbit on the baking sheet and bake for 45 to 55 minutes. Baste with the warm marinade after 15 minutes. The rabbit is done when the juices run clear when the meat is pricked with a fork.

Serve hot.

PLUM-CASSIS GLAZED PORK TENDERLOIN

SERVES 6

Roast pork tenderloin can take the same flavorings that one would use on a denser white meat, such as turkey breast. I like it better in some cases because pork tenderloin is sweeter. The glaze works wonderfully well with this dish, especially against the hickory flavor from the grill. This dish can also be cooked indoors (without the hickory). Serve some red cabbage coleslaw on the side.

SUBSTITUTIONS: Replace the brine with Apple Cider Brine (page 48), Maple-Bourbon Brine (page 49), or Basic Citrus Brine (page 46).

Replace the glaze with Pomegranate-Cognac Glaze (page 86), Cassis–Red Onion Glaze (page 84), Maple-Bourbon Glaze (page 88), or Morello Cherry Glaze (page 80).

2 to 3 pounds lean boneless pork loin
4 quarts Basic Brine for Pork and Poultry (page 47)
2 to 3 tablespoons chopped fresh rosemary leaves
1 teaspoon coarse-grain or sea salt
1 tablespoon freshly cracked black peppercorns
1 quart apple cider or orange juice
1½ cups Plum-Cassis Glaze (page 86)

Place the pork in a nonreactive container and add the brine to cover the pork, and refrigerate for 8 hours. Remove the pork from the brine, rinse under cold running water, and pat dry with paper towels. Season with the rosemary, salt, and pepper.

To grill: Build a charcoal fire in a kettle grill with a water pan, and add presoaked hickory chunks to the coals. Add the apple cider to the water pan. Lightly brush the grill with vegetable oil. Place the tenderloin on the grill, cover, and smoke for 1½ to 2 hours, until the tenderloin reaches an internal temperature of 160°F. Baste with the glaze during the last 10 minutes of cooking. Remove the tenderloin from the grill and let it rest for 10 minutes before slicing.

To cook indoors: Preheat the oven to 375°F. Pour the apple cider into a nonreactive baking pan and place the pan on the floor of the oven for flavorful steam. Place the tenderloin on a rack in a roasting pan and roast in the center of the oven for 45 to 50 minutes, until the tenderloin reaches an internal temperature of 160°F. Baste with the glaze during the last 10 minutes of cooking. Remove the tenderloin from the oven and let it rest for 10 minutes before slicing.

Serve immediately.

STOUT-BRAISED BEEF SHORT RIBS

SERVES 4

. . . .

Barbecue can claim a lot of things, but it doesn't have the market cornered on low- and slow-cooked ribs. I saw braised beef ribs on the menu at Rx, a neighborhood eatery in West Philly, in the middle of a sweltering July. I immediately dived into them. Braised Beef Ribs: they're not just for wintertime comfort food anymore. The marinade can be swapped out for any of the wine-driven marinade recipes suggested. The recipe is a definite make-ahead dish that gets better by the day. Serve with Braised Chanterelles (page 249) or Asparagus with Sherry-Hazelnut Marinade (page 233).

3½ pounds beef short ribs
2 cups Guinness Stout Marinade (page 61), with the extra virgin
    olive oil reduced to 2 tablespoons
Canola oil, for sautéing
1 cup chopped sweet onions
½ pound baby or cocktail carrots
½ pound fingerling potatoes, brushed clean but unpeeled
1 or 2 sprigs of fresh thyme

SUBSTITUTIONS: Replace the marinade with Basic Red Wine Marinade for Beef (page 62), Provençal Cognac Marinade (page 228), or Provençal Red Wine Marinade (page 227).

Cut the ribs into 2-inch to 3-inch pieces, and remove all visible fat and gristle. Place the ribs in a resealable plastic bag or a glass baking pan, pour in the marinade, and marinate in the refrigerator for 8 to 12 hours. Remove the ribs from the marinade, reserving the marinade.

Heat about ¼ inch of canola oil in a large, deep-sided skillet with a lid or in a Dutch oven, add the ribs in batches, and brown on all sides. Remove the ribs from the skillet with a slotted spoon and reserve. Add the onions and sauté for 5 to 10 minutes, until translucent. Add the carrots and potatoes and sauté for about 5 minutes, until the carrots are slightly brown. Add the reserved marinade and thyme; bring to a boil, scraping the bottom of the saucepan. Decrease the heat, return the ribs to the skillet, cover, and simmer for 2 to 3 hours, until the meat falls off the bone.

To cook in a slow cooker: Complete the recipe up to and including deglazing the skillet with the reserved marinade. Pour the marinade into the slow cooker, add the ribs and vegetables, and cook on low for 6 hours, or until the meat falls off the bone.

To serve, preheat the oven to 300°F. Remove the ribs and vegetables from the skillet, place in the oven, and cook for about 20 minutes, until the marinade is reduced by half. Transfer the ribs and vegetables to serving plates, and spoon the marinade over the ribs. Serve hot.

COLD FILET OF BEEF WITH FRESH HERB PASTE

SERVES 8 TO 10 AS AN APPETIZER

This spectacular picnic dish is made by my friend Donna West, who uses a dry marinade of fresh herbs to season her roast tenderloin. The beef is then sliced thin and served with a cold mustard sauce. Donna also suggests serving the beef with a red coleslaw.

MUSTARD-HORSERADISH SAUCE MAKES 1 CUP

¼ cup Dijon-style mustard
½ cup heavy cream
2 tablespoons prepared horseradish
2 tablespoons fresh lemon juice
1 tablespoon cracked black peppercorns

BEEF FILET WITH FRESH HERB PASTE

3 to 4 pounds filet of beef, trimmed of all visible fat
12 (3-inch) sprigs of thyme or lemon thyme
12 sage leaves
6 (3-inch) sprigs of rosemary
6 cloves garlic, quartered
1 to 2 tablespoons cracked black peppercorns

To make the mustard sauce, in a nonreactive saucepan, simmer the mustard, cream, and horseradish for 8 to 10 minutes. Remove from the heat and cool to room temperature. Stir in the lemon juice and pepper. Refrigerate until ready to use. This sauce will keep refrigerated for 2 to 3 days.

To prepare the beef, on a flat surface, place enough plastic wrap or parchment paper to wrap the tenderloin tightly. Place the tenderloin on the front edge of the wrap and rub the fresh herbs, garlic, and peppercorns into the meat on all sides. Roll the meat tightly and place in the refrigerator for at least 6 hours.

Preheat the oven to 550°F. Decrease the heat to 225°F and roast the tenderloin for 1 to 1¼ hours, until a meat thermometer registers 140°F.

Remove the meat from the oven and let it come to room temperature before slicing, or refrigerate to serve the next day.

To serve, slice the meat ¼ inch thick. Serve with the mustard sauce.

MEDALLIONS OF VENISON WITH
RASPBERRY-BEAUJOLAIS MARINADE SERVES 4

Dr. Anne Pearl and I developed this recipe during a late-night phone call when she asked me what to do with a loin of venison. Now this recipe has become part of the repertoire in both kitchens. The trick behind the recipe is that when you cut the venison loin into medallions you have better surface penetration for the marinade—more of that wonderful raspberry flavor. This dish pairs well with Stir-Fried Carrots in Orange-Cinnamon Marinade (page 127).

1½ pounds loin of venison, cut into 12 medallions
3¾ cups Raspberry-Beaujolais Marinade (page 57)
1 quart veal or game stock
2 tablespoons canola oil
1 tablespoon cracked black peppercorns

Place the venison in a nonreactive container or a 2-gallon resealable plastic bag, pour the marinade over the venison, and refrigerate for 12 hours.

Remove the venison from the marinade and reserve 2 cups of the marinade for the sauce. Let the venison come to room temperature before sautéing.

Bring the reserved marinade to a boil in a small nonreactive saucepan, decrease the heat, and simmer for about 45 minutes, until the marinade is reduced to about ½ cup. In a 2-quart nonreactive saucepan, reduce the stock to 1½ cups. Combine with the reduced marinade and keep warm.

Heat the canola oil in a large nonstick skillet over high heat. Lightly season the venison medallions with the pepper, place the meat in the skillet, and sear on all sides. Decrease the heat and gently sauté for about 4 minutes on each side. The medallions should be slightly on the rare side.

Preheat the oven to 250°F. Remove the venison from the pan, and place in the oven to keep warm. Deglaze the skillet with the sauce.

To serve, spoon about ½ cup of the sauce onto each plate. Place 3 medallions on each plate and serve.

GRILLED ROSEMARY-MARINATED LAMB SALAD WITH BALSAMIC-BERRY SAUCE SERVES 4

Chef Bruce Cooper of Jake's in Philadelphia orchestrates a variety of simple seasoning themes and builds them into a composed salad that bursts with flavor. The flavors of rosemary-marinated grilled lamb with hints of apricot from the chanterelles are enhanced by a sweet sauce containing caramelized shallots, cassis, and balsamic vinegar. The salad of tossed fresh herbs and greens is the perfect breezy contrast.

ROSEMARY-MARINATED LAMB

½ cup extra virgin olive oil
1 tablespoon chopped fresh rosemary
1 clove garlic, minced
1 tablespoon freshly cracked black pepper
4 (4 ounces each) lamb tenderloins, about 1½ inches thick

SALAD

1 tablespoon white wine vinegar
1 cup extra virgin olive oil
2 tablespoons mixed fresh herbs (such as basil, chervil,
    tarragon, and chives)
Coarse-grain salt and freshly ground white pepper
2 tablespoons unsalted butter
8 chanterelles, halved
6 cups mixed greens (mizuna, arugula, red mustard,
    or any fresh salad greens)

BALSAMIC-BERRY SAUCE

1 cup balsamic vinegar
1 tablespoon minced shallots
¼ cup Mŭre (Alsatian berry liqueur) or crème de cassis

To prepare the lamb, combine the olive oil, rosemary, garlic, and pepper in a nonreactive container or a resealable plastic bag. Add the lamb, toss to coat, and refrigerate for 6 to 8 hours. Prepare the sauce and salad dressing while the lamb is marinating.

To prepare the salad dressing, whisk together the vinegar, olive oil, herbs, salt, and pepper and allow to sit for at least 4 hours.

To make the sauce, in a nonreactive saucepan, combine the vinegar and shallots, bring to a simmer, and cook for about 20 minutes, until reduced by half. Add the liqueur and reduce to the consistency of maple syrup. Decrease the heat and keep warm.

When the lamb is done marinating, remove it from the marinade and grill over high heat for approximately 5 minutes, until the lamb is medium rare. Remove the lamb from the grill and let it rest for 10 minutes before slicing each tenderloin into ½-inch-thick slices.

To make the salad, heat the butter in a saucepan, but do not allow the butter to burn. Sauté the chanterelles for 3 minutes, until they're soft but do not change color. Toss the greens with the dressing.

To serve, place some salad in the middle of 4 plates. Place 4 sautéed chanterelle halves around each plate and alternate with thin slices of lamb. Drizzle the warm berry sauce over the lamb and mushrooms, and serve immediately.

CITRUS SLAW SERVES 6

This refreshing slaw balances anything grilled or smoked. It's a simple palate cleanser that's a real spice and smoke cutter.

CITRUS DRESSING MAKES ⅔ CUP

Grated zest and juice of 1 orange (about ⅓ cup)
Grated zest and juice of 2 limes (about ¼ cup)
½ teaspoon cracked black pepper
½ teaspoon salt
⅓ teaspoon red pepper flakes (optional)
3 tablespoons extra virgin olive oil

SLAW

4 to 5 cups shredded Napa cabbage
1 cup orange sections, diced
1 cup thinly sliced red or yellow sweet bell pepper
½ cup vertically sliced red onion

To make the dressing, combine the orange zest and juice, lime zest and juice, black pepper, salt, and red pepper flakes in a blender or a food processor and process until all the ingredients are blended. While the motor is running, drizzle in the oil a little at a time. Stored in a clean, airtight container, this will keep in the refrigerator for 1 week.

To prepare the slaw, in a large bowl, toss the cabbage, orange sections, peppers, and onion with the dressing just before serving. The dressing and vegetables can be kept separately for up to 2 days in the refrigerator, but don't mix them together until you are almost ready to serve.

JUNIPER AND ORANGE CURED VENISON WITH HERB SALAD SERVES 8

Philadelphia food consultant Aliza Green uses this recipe to take advantage of the farm-raised venison that's been finding its way into specialty food markets. She combines fresh herbs and peeled citrus to make a salad that's an instant success at an elegant wintertime buffet or a sit-down dinner.

VENISON

2 pounds venison loin (preferably fresh), trimmed of fat
2 cups Orange and Juniper Cure (page 44)

HERB SALAD

¼ cup fresh lemon juice
¼ cup fresh orange juice
½ cup extra virgin extra virgin olive oil
Coarse-grain salt and freshly ground black pepper
½ cup packed Italian parsley leaves, coarsely chopped
¼ cup chervil sprigs
¼ cup tarragon sprigs

SHALLOT-BUTTERED TOASTS

4 tablespoons unsalted butter
2 or 3 slices rye bread, crusts removed
4 to 5 tablespoons chopped shallots

To prepare the venison, spread the cure on the venison, cover, and refrigerate for 3 days, turning each day so that the spices penetrate evenly. The venison should feel firm when fully cured.

To make the salad, combine the lemon and orange juices in a nonreactive mixing bowl. Whisk in the oil a little at a time. Add salt and pepper to taste. In a nonreactive bowl, combine the parsley, chervil, and tarragon. Add the dressing, and toss to coat evenly.

To make the toasts, preheat the broiler. Butter the rye bread, top with shallots, and place under the broiler for about 5 minutes, until golden brown. Remove the toasts from the broiler and dice into cubes.

To serve, slice the venison into thin slices. Sprinkle with the herb salad, and top with the toasts.

CRANBERRY-ORANGE CHUTNEY MAKES 3 CUPS

This recipe springs to life with anything cooked outdoors. For a Cranberry-Orange Glaze for turkey, delete the almonds and purée the recipe to a smooth consistency. Try this chutney with Smoked Duck Confit (page 108).

2 whole oranges
2 cups fresh or frozen and thawed cranberries (about ½ pound)
¼ cup balsamic vinegar
1 tablespoon minced fresh ginger
1 cup sugar
1 Granny Smith apple, peeled, cored, and diced (about ½ cup)
¼ cup sun-dried cherries
¼ teaspoon ground ginger
¼ teaspoon ground cinnamon
¼ cup slivered almonds, toasted

Grate both oranges. Peel and seed one of the oranges and cut into ½-inch segments. Juice the second orange. In a 2-quart nonreactive saucepan, combine the orange zest, segments, and juice along with the cranberries, balsamic vinegar, fresh ginger, sugar, apple, sun-dried cherries, ground ginger, and cinnamon.

Bring to a boil. Decrease the heat and simmer for 10 to 15 minutes, until the cranberries split. Cool to room temperature and add the slivered almonds.

STIR-FRIED CARROTS IN ORANGE-CINNAMON MARINADE SERVES 4 AS A SIDE DISH

For a pretty presentation, lightly channel the carrots by running the tip of a sharp paring knife down the sides, then slice crosswise into florets.

1 pound carrots, peeled and sliced ¼ inch thick
1½ cups Orange-Cinnamon Marinade (page 53)
¼ cup golden raisins

Place the carrots in a nonreactive container or a 1-gallon resealable plastic bag. Pour the marinade over the carrots and refrigerate for 4 hours. Remove the carrots from the marinade, reserving the marinade.

In a wok or in a deep-sided sauté pan, cook the marinade over high heat for about 10 minutes, until reduced to one-third of its original volume. Add the carrots to the pan and stir-fry for 2 to 3 minutes. Stir in the raisins and cook until heated through, 3 to 4 minutes. The carrots should be firm but not crisp.

THE AMERICAN SOUTH & SOUTHWEST

Being a roots musician, I like to eat where I play. When I'm on the road, I like to check out what local folks are eating and listening to. That will tell me more about a locale than a travel guide ever will. There are times when I'll drop the price of airfare on a high-end dinner at a restaurant to benchmark a town's top-of-the-line culinary intake. But what brings it all back home for me is the marriage of food and music. Some of my favorite locations lace the two together with seasoning for the ear as well as the palate.

When I'm in New Orleans, I taste in my ears jazzy saxes that sass rippling pianos over raw oysters and shrimp rémoulade. Out on Highway I-10, the back parishes reek with crawfish boils and steamed boudins served up with the chanky-chank percussion of scrub boards and Cajun accordions. Nothing rocks out more than a roadhouse band playing a mix of Mexican cajunto, zydeco, Texas swing, or traditional country and western with a touch of Hank, while the kitchen dishes out beef barbecue, Tex-Mex fajitas, and bowls of chili. When eating ribs, I feel an overwhelming craving for rhythm and blues with a side of John Lee Hooker. The Appalachian Mountains are the closest thing to heaven for me, and I'm not referring to their height. I love glazed smoky hams, Carolina pulled pork, and fried chicken with a topping of bluegrass and old-time fiddle tunes. And that's just for breakfast. I can't even think about cooking or eating these recipes without hearing the music that's linked with them. It simply gives me "hungry ears" if I don't.

Southern cooking is comfort food with a swagger and a wink. It's down-home haute cuisine that can be as simple and sophisticated as the South of France. It has traditional charcuterie, spice mixes, fresh and saltwater seafood, and hardy sides. I'm just as happy eating red beans and rice as I am eating cassoulet, jambalaya, or grits. Southern recipes, as well as the music, dance with those who brought them; that is, they carry the rich traditions of Europeans and Africans. Southern ingredients are pretty accessible to most domestic pantry dwellers. With the exception of Steen's cane syrup, the majority of the ingredients are easily in reach on- or offline.

Willie Nelson sings, "My Heroes Have Always Been Cowboys." Well, some of my favorite heroes have cooked like them. Back in the eighties, chefs like Robert del Grande, Dean Fearing, Amy Ferguson, Ann Lindsay Greer, Mark Miller, Donna Nordin, Stephan Pyles, Jimmy Schmidt, and John Sedlar blew the barn doors off "New American cuisine" using Southwestern flavors. Those flavors combined hints of Port Arthur cajun, Tex-Mex roadhouses, and Mexican cantinas with Native American ingredients. It's a brash tasting and colorful flavor set that plays with traditional recipes stretched by refined classical technique.

Food moods change, and what was once "in" is now old cowboy hat. Some writers referred to Southwestern cuisine as the "Great Mesquite Scare of the 1980s." Not this one. I was drawn into it in a big way then, and I'm drawn to it now. Let me tell you why.

Southwestern cuisine embodies a pioneer attitude over regional ingredients. It settles on a series of fresh and dried chiles, imports citrus up from the Yucatán, and mixes it all with a touch of Texas smoke.

Now when I spring a Southwestern recipe on some dinner guests, I get an inquisitive first-time-in-my-mouth look, and then they declare, "That was good! Where is the recipe from?" The Southwest!

If you have been playing around with the Mexican and Caribbean pantry lists in the next chapter, you'll notice an overlap of ingredients. Southwestern cuisine pulls from some areas the Spaniards explored and settled; that's because they needed to eat what was in the neighborhood. One of those local ingredients was the chile pepper, and that's how we'll start the pantry list.

The chile pepper interlocks some of the flavors of the Southwest, Mexico, the Caribbean, and all parts of Latin and South America with one another like common DNA. The chart goes from mild to hot to enable you to substitute or bring the heat down a notch or two. I've also highlighted which chapters use them to make shopping and pantry stocking easier.

THE **AMERICAN** SOUTH & SOUTHWEST **PANTRY**

CITRUS: Lemons, limes, oranges.

DAIRY: Buttermilk.

FRUIT: Fresh mangoes, pineapples.

VEGETABLES: Garlic, fresh ginger, green onions, red onions, sweet onions (Vidalia or Maui), shallots.

FRESH HERBS: Cilantro, chives, flat-leaf parsley.

CHILES (FRESH AND DRIED): Jalapeños, serranos, cayenne pepper; see the chart Hot Flashes—A Mini Guide to Chiles on pages 136 and 137. *Special ingredients:* Anchos, chiles de arbol, chipotles, habaneros, New Mexican chiles, pequíns, poblanos.

SPICES: Bay leaves, black and white peppercorns, cinnamon, cumin, garlic powder, dry or powdered mustard, onion powder, kosher or coarse-grain salt, hot paprika, dried oregano, dried sage, dried thyme.

OILS, VINEGARS, AND CONDIMENTS: Canola oil, extra virgin olive oil, peanut oil; cider vinegar, white wine vinegar; yellow or brown mustard, Worcestershire sauce, soy or tamari sauce. *Special ingredient:* Creole mustard.

SWEETENERS: Granulated sugar, light and dark brown sugar, honey, maple syrup. *Special ingredient:* Cane syrup.

WINES AND LIQUORS: Dry white wine, bourbon, tequila.

SPECIAL INGREDIENTS

CANE SYRUP: This is sometimes incorrectly called unsulphured molasses and is often used interchangeably in the South, but they are not the same thing. Cane syrup is sugar-cane juice that has been mashed from the cane, boiled, and reduced in much the same way as maple syrup is. Molasses is actually a sugar-refining by-product. It has a softer flavor than blackstrap molasses. Look for either Lye's golden syrup or Steen's pure cane syrup. You can substitute 2 parts light corn syrup to 1 part molasses.

CHILES: Ancho, chile de arbol, chipotle, habanero, New Mexican, pequín, poblano (see chart).

CREOLE MUSTARD: Creole mustard is Southern wholegrain mustard where the seeds are slightly crushed. The mustard seeds are marinated before preparation. Look for Zatarain's or Horse Shoe brand. You can substitute 3 parts Dijon-style mustard to 1 part prepared horseradish.

ANCHO-SUGAR CURE MAKES 1¼ CUPS

TIMETABLE:
Salmon steaks or fillets,
tuna steaks, or shrimp:
1 to 2 hours

This is more of a dry glaze than a cure. By coating oily fish or shrimp, it forms a savory, candied shell. The Ancho Sugar Cure lends itself to more variations than I could list. It's the perfect vehicle for swapping out ingredient parts. For example, you can substitute New Mexico chili powder or ground chipotle for the ancho chile powder. With chipotle, you may want to start with 1 teaspoon and then work your way up the heat scale. If you want a softer cure, you can substitute, or use any combination of, cumin seeds, coriander, cinnamon, or anise seeds for the ancho chile. One or 2 tablespoons of your favorite spice mix or rub will work as well.

1 cup firmly packed brown sugar
1 tablespoon kosher salt
1 tablespoon freshly ground black pepper
1 tablespoon ancho chile powder
1 tablespoon freshly grated lemon, lime, or orange zest

In a food processor, blender, or spice mill, combine the brown sugar, salt, pepper, ancho chile powder, and citrus zest; pulse until all the ingredients are blended. The cure can be stored in a clean, airtight container in the freezer for 3 to 4 months.

ANCHO BRINE. Add 4 quarts of water and increase the salt to ¾ cup. In a large saucepan over medium-high heat, add the brown sugar, ancho chile powder, and citrus zest. Bring to a boil, and stir to dissolve. Decrease the heat and simmer for 30 minutes to brew the ingredients. Remove from the heat and let the brine cool to room temperature, then refrigerate to 40°F before adding food.

LOUISIANA TASSO BRINE MAKES 3 QUARTS

TIP: This is a curing brine. The salt to water ratio is about 24 percent, and the long curing time is designed to pull moisture out and flavor the turkey at the same time. If you want to convert the brine for pork loin or poultry, reduce the salt and syrup to ⅓ cup, reduce the cayenne to ½ teaspoon, and reduce the garlic and onion powders to 1 teaspoon each.

Although this recipe was developed for brining turkey breast, it can be used with ribs or Gulf shrimp. It can also be the foundation for a crawfish or crab boil with your favorite packet of spices, gris-gris or otherwise.

3 quarts water
1⅓ cups kosher salt
1⅓ cups Steen's cane syrup or unsulphured molasses
1 to 1½ teaspoons cayenne pepper
2 tablespoons onion powder or Red Onion Powder (page 67)
2 tablespoons garlic powder

In a large saucepan or medium-size stockpot over medium-high heat, combine the water, salt, syrup, cayenne, onion powder, and garlic powder; bring to a boil, and stir to dissolve. Decrease the heat and simmer for 30 minutes to brew the ingredients. Remove from the heat and let the brine cool to room temperature, then refrigerate to 40°F before adding food.

MAMA ROSA'S PULLED PORK MARINADE

MAKES 3 CUPS

TIMETABLE:

Pork tenderloin or pork chops: 3 to 4 hours

Pork shoulder, baby back ribs, or spareribs: 6 to 8 hours

Mama Rosa's was one of the oldest running barbecue pits in North Philadelphia. This recipe is a barbeque triple crown. It can be used as a marinade or a spareribs baste or combined with ketchup to make a sauce.

¼ cup (½ stick) unsalted butter
1 cup finely chopped onion
3 cloves garlic, pressed or minced
1 cup cider vinegar
1 cup Worcestershire sauce
2 tablespoons dry mustard
2 tablespoons dark brown sugar
2 tablespoons hot paprika
2 teaspoons coarse-grain salt (optional)
2 teaspoons cayenne pepper

TIP: If you're using leftover marinade, bring it to a boil first before combining it with the ketchup.

In a nonreactive saucepan, melt the butter. Add the onion and garlic and sauté until translucent, but not browned. Stir in the vinegar, Worcestershire sauce, mustard, brown sugar, hot paprika, salt, and cayenne pepper. Bring to a boil, decrease the heat, and simmer for 15 minutes. Remove from the heat and cool to room temperature.

MAMA ROSA'S BARBEQUE SAUCE. Combine 2¼ cups of Mama Rosa's marinade and a 14-ounce bottle of ketchup in a nonreactive saucepan and simmer for at least 15 minutes.

SOUTH CAROLINA MUSTARD MARINADE

MAKES 1½ CUPS

• •

This easy-to-prepare marinade also can be used as a basting or barbecue sauce for grilled chicken or pork tenderloin. Mustard- and vinegar-based barbecue sauces are popular on chicken in South Carolina, and the taste of this mustard marinade will show you why the flavors travel so well.

½ cup cider vinegar
¼ cup yellow mustard
2 tablespoons pure maple syrup or honey
2 tablespoons bourbon or sour mash whiskey (optional)
2 teaspoons Worcestershire sauce
1 teaspoon Tabasco sauce
¼ cup chopped fresh herbs (tarragon, rosemary, thyme, etc.)
1 tablespoon diced shallot (about ½ shallot)
1 teaspoon coarse-grain or sea salt
⅓ cup safflower oil

Combine the vinegar, mustard, maple syrup, liquor, Worcestershire sauce, Tabasco sauce, herbs, shallot, and salt in a blender or a food processor and process until all the ingredients are blended. While the motor is running, drizzle in the safflower oil a little at a time. Stored in a clean, airtight container, this will keep in the refrigerator for 1 week. This marinade freezes well with food for up to 3 months.

SOUTH CAROLINA MUSTARD BASTE. Increase the cider vinegar to 1 cup and omit the safflower oil.

CREOLE MUSTARD–BOURBON MARINADE. Substitute Steen's cane vinegar for the cider vinegar, Steen's cane syrup for the maple syrup, and Zatarain's Creole mustard for the yellow mustard, and add 2 to 3 teaspoons Louisiana style hot sauce.

TIMETABLE:
Chicken breasts, turkey breast, pork tenderloin, or pork kabobs: 3 to 4 hours

Chicken wings: 6 to 8 hours

Spareribs: 8 to 12 hours

Soft-shell crabs:
6 to 8 hours

Red snapper, catfish,
sea bass, halibut, or
shrimp: 2 to 4 hours

Chicken breasts or kabobs,
Cornish hen, or turkey
breast: 4 to 6 hours

MUSTARD-BUTTERMILK MARINADE MAKES 2 CUPS

Buttermilk, mustard, and bourbon give soft-shells a real Southern crawl. If you use this marinade as a base for fried chicken, just soak and fry. The buttermilk works as an enzymatic activator, along the same lines as yogurt. The moist, flavorful poultry kabobs from this marinade are true Southern culture "on a stick."

1¼ cups buttermilk
2 tablespoons Creole or coarse-grain brown mustard
2 tablespoons bourbon
Grated zest and juice of 1 lemon (about 3 tablespoons)
¼ cup chopped fresh herbs (parsley, thyme, and rosemary)
½ teaspoon coarse-grain salt
1 teaspoon coarsely ground black pepper

Combine the buttermilk, mustard, bourbon, lemon zest and juice, herbs, salt, and pepper in a blender or a food processor and process until all the ingredients are blended. Stored in a clean, airtight container, this will keep in the refrigerator for 1 week. This marinade freezes well with food.

MUSTARD-BUTTERMILK BARBECUE SAUCE. Place the buttermilk, mustard, and bourbon in a nonreactive saucepan and simmer for 10 minutes, stirring constantly. Remove from the heat and cool to room temperature. Add the lemon zest and juice, herbs, salt, and pepper. Refrigerate until ready to use. The barbecue sauce will keep for up to 2 weeks in a clean, airtight container in the refrigerator.

Tuna steaks or swordfish
steaks: 2 to 3 hours

Chicken breasts or kabobs,
turkey breast, duck breast,
quail, pork tenderloin,
pork chops, or pork
kabobs: 4 to 6 hours

Baby back ribs or
spareribs: 8 to 12 hours

SOUTHWEST CHILE-CORN MARINADE

MAKES 2½ CUPS

If I were to try to put all of the flavors I associate with Southwestern cuisine into one marinade, it would be this one, but my friend Barbara Boswell already did it for me. Her marinade has the right amount of heat from the habanero chiles without overpowering the rest of the ingredients. The contrasting sweetness of this marinade comes from the corn and molasses.

1 cup fresh corn kernels (preferably white)
1 tablespoon tomato concentrate (from a tube)
2 tablespoons molasses
Grated zest and juice of 1 lemon (about 3 tablespoons)
1 cup corn oil
2 habanero chiles, seeded and diced
2 tablespoons chopped cilantro
2 tablespoons chopped green onions, white part only
⅓ cup chopped green bell pepper

Combine the corn kernels, tomato concentrate, molasses, and lemon zest and juice in a food processor or a blender, and process to a smooth paste. With the motor running, drizzle in the oil a little at a time. Pulse in the habanero, cilantro, green onions, and green pepper to mix. Stored in a clean, airtight container, this will keep in the refrigerator for 1 week. This marinade freezes well with food for up to 3 months.

NEW MEXICAN PINEAPPLE MARINADE

MAKES 2¹/₂ CUPS

The sweet flavor of fresh pineapple tempers the New Mexico chili powder, while the cilantro adds an herbal aroma. I've used this marinade on grilled chicken and sautéed grouper with outstanding results. The marinade is on the mild side, but by adding additional jalapeños, you can have it walk on the wild side.

To jazz up the recipe a bit, you can handle the pineapple in two different ways. The first is to place a whole fresh pineapple in a smoker, add chips, and smoke it for 2 hours at 120°F to 160°F. Peel, core, and then chop the pineapple into cubes. The other alternative is to peel, core, and slice a whole pineapple into rings. Toss the rings in a nonreactive mixing bowl with 1 tablespoon New Mexico chili powder and 1 tablespoon brown sugar. Grill on a medium-hot fire until the rings are slightly caramelized, but not charred.

3 cups cubed fresh pineapple (about 1 whole small pineapple, peeled and cored)
Grated zest and juice of 2 limes (about ¼ cup)
2 tablespoons light soy sauce
3 tablespoons New Mexico chili powder
¹/₃ cup dry white wine
2 tablespoons diced jalapeño chiles
¼ cup chopped fresh cilantro
¼ cup chopped red onion
1 teaspoon coarse-grain or sea salt
¹/₃ cup avocado or olive oil

Combine the pineapple, lime zest and juice, soy sauce, chili powder, wine, jalapeño, cilantro, onion, and salt in a food processor or a blender and process until all the ingredients are blended. While the motor is running, drizzle in the oil a little at a time. The marinade will keep in a clean, airtight container for 1 week in the refrigerator. This marinade also freezes well with meat.

TIMETABLE:
Red snapper, catfish, sea bass, or halibut: 2 to 3 hours

Shrimp: 2 to 4 hours

Chicken breasts, pork chops, or pork cutlets: 3 to 4 hours

Spareribs: 6 to 8 hours

TIP: Pineapple is a natural tenderizer like papaya. Marinate on the low side of the timetable to avoid a seviche reaction.

HOT FLASHES: A GUIDE TO CHILES

Here's a brief guide to chiles used in this book, from relatively mild to scorching hot. The heat is measured on the Scoville scale, which indicates the amount of capsaicin (the chemical that sets your taste buds on fire) present in the chile. A bell pepper has zero Scoville units, while habaneros and Scotch Bonnets are in the hundreds of thousands.

Note that powdered ancho, New Mexican, and chipotle are not the same as chili powder, which is a blend made with an assortment of chiles and seasonings and who knows what. Powdered whole chiles are what you want to use to add greater depth of flavor to sauces and other dishes. The only things standing in your way are a good source for chiles and a spice grinder.

POBLANO

Fresh (Heat range: 1,000–2,000 Scoville units)
Poblanos (dark green) are wide at the top, shiny, and heart-shaped, about the size of a bell pepper but tapered at the bottom; when dried they become known as anchos or mulatos (dark burgundy-red), with soft, wrinkled skin. Dried ancho chiles yield a good deal of fruity pulp and are well suited for sweet, rich sauces. Used in the American South and Southwest. *Substitute:* New Mexican chile.

ANCHO

Dried (Heat range: 1,000–2,000 Scoville units)
These are dried poblano peppers and very commonly used in Mexican cuisine. They're brownish black and wrinkled. Used in the American South and Southwest, and Latin America and the Caribbean. *Substitutes:* mulato chile (darker with earthier, more pungent flavor), pasilla chile, California chile, dried New Mexican chile.

NEW MEXICAN

Fresh (Heat range: 1,000–2,000 Scoville units)
New Mexican green chiles are similar in size to Anaheim chiles, but they're hotter. New Mexican green chiles peak in late summer, while the hotter New Mexican red chiles appear in the fall. Used in the American South and Southwest, and Latin America and the Caribbean. *Substitutes:* Anaheim chile (milder) or a combination of Anaheim and jalapeño chiles.

JALAPEÑO

Fresh (Heat range: 2,500–8,000 Scoville units)
Jalapeños are close to 2 inches long and may be green or red when fresh; when dried and smoked, they become known as chipotles, which are red or tan. This may just be a regional thing, but lately I've come across some strains of domesticated jalapeños that look like the real thing but lack the bite. They may as well rename it "placebo." Hmmm, if I wanted to have less heat, I would use less jalapeño. Now I find myself using serranos in their place. If you want to maintain the heat level of a recipe and then some, use serranos. When a recipe calls for jalapeños, it's not the kind of quantity that will have you running for a fire extinguisher, so the domesticated varieties are fine for the heat-sensitive. Used in the American South and Southwest, and Latin America and the Caribbean. *Substitute:* serrano chile (slightly hotter).

CHIPOTLE

Dried (Heat range: 5,000–8,000 Scoville units)
These are usually canned in adobo sauce, but you can also buy the dried chiles in cellophane bags. See the sidebar "Chipotle Chatter" (page 175). Used in the American South and Southwest, and Latin America and the Caribbean. *Substitute for chipotles in adobo sauce:* 1 tablespoon tomato paste + ½ teaspoon liquid smoke + 1 jalapeño chile.

SERRANO

Fresh (Heat range: 8,000–22,000 Scoville units)
Serrano chiles are usually green, but sometimes red, when fresh, and are about 2½ inches long; they are narrow in width with a blunt point. They may be used interchangeably with jalapeños, but serranos have a less juicy texture and are slightly hotter. Used in the American South and Southwest, and Latin America and the Caribbean. *Substitute:* jalapeño chile (not as hot).

CHILE DE ARBOL

Fresh/Dried (Heat range: 15,000–30,000 Scoville units)
Chiles de arbol are fairly hot and can be used instead of cayenne pepper. Used in the American South and Southwest. *Substitutes:* cayenne pepper, pequín chile.

CAYENNE PEPPER

Fresh/Dried (Heat range: 30,000–50,000 Scoville units)
Cayenne peppers are brittle, skinny, dried red chiles that are 2 to 3 inches long. Cayenne pepper is sold in its ground version. I'm of the opinion that cayenne should be replaced monthly, even though I don't actually practice it. Cayenne will lose its flavor, but not its heat, over time. Heat is what most folks feel when they taste it, and so they tend to avoid using it. As a result, this chile powder tends to sit in the spice rack and age ungracefully. You're much better off from a flavor standpoint by grinding dried chiles when you need them. On a scale of 1 to 10 with 10 being the hottest, it hits number 8. Used in Latin America and the Caribbean. *Substitutes:* chile de arbol, Thai chile, habanero chile, pequín chile.

PEQUÍN

Fresh/Dried (Heat range: 40,000–58,000 Scoville units)
Pequíns are sold fresh and are only ½ inch in length, but they are hot! They look like red holiday lights in both their fresh and dried forms. Used in the American South and Southwest. *Substitute:* Thai chile.

THAI

Fresh (Heat range: 50,000–100,000 Scoville units)
Thai chiles are 1½ to 2 inches in length and very hot; they come fresh and are green or red. Used in the American South and Southwest, and Latin America and the Caribbean. *Substitute:* serrano chile.

HABANERO

Fresh, occasionally dried (Heat range: 100,000–325,000 Scoville units)
Habanero chiles are green, yellow, or red in their fresh form and shaped like lanterns. Native to the Gulf of Mexico, they are said to be the world's hottest chile and are 1,000 times hotter than jalapeños. Used in the American South and Southwest, and Latin America and the Caribbean. *Substitute:* Scotch Bonnet chile.

SCOTCH BONNET

Fresh (Heat range: 150,000–325,000 Scoville units)
This Caribbean chile is almost indistinguishable from the habanero, except that it's a bit smaller and slightly hotter. Slightly hotter? At that heat level, how can anything that hot be called "slight"? On the heat scale, Scotch bonnets top the chile hit parade at a number 10. These will earn the macho mouth a red badge of courage. Used in Latin America and the Caribbean. *Substitute:* habanero chile.

TIMETABLE:
Salmon steaks or fillets, swordfish steaks, or scallops: 2 to 3 hours

Shrimp, chicken breasts or kabobs, turkey breast, or quail: 2 to 4 hours

Sirloin, porterhouse, New York strip, tri tips, beef filets, rib eye, beef kabobs, lamb rack or rib chops, lamb kabobs, pork tenderloin, pork chops, or pork kabobs: 4 to 6 hours

Beef short ribs; chicken wings, thighs, or legs; baby back ribs; or spareribs: 8 to 12 hours

TEQUILA-ALMOND MARINADE MAKES 1½ CUPS

The margarita flavors of tart lime and tequila are enhanced by the toasted almonds. When cooking indoors, use the marinade to deglaze the pan for a wonderful light sauce. Outdoors on the grill, this recipe gets raves not only with scallops but with shrimp and chicken breasts as well.

½ cup tequila
¾ cup dry white wine
Grated zest and juice of 2 limes (about ¼ cup)
¼ cup chopped fresh cilantro
¼ cup almond slivers, toasted until brown and coarsely crushed
1 teaspoon salt
1 tablespoon cracked black peppercorns
⅓ cup canola or almond oil

Pour the tequila into a nonreactive saucepan. Bring to a boil. Decrease the heat and simmer for about 20 minutes, until the tequila is reduced by one third. Remove the tequila from the heat and let cool. Combine the tequila, wine, lime zest and juice, cilantro, almonds, salt, and pepper in a blender or a food processor and process until all the ingredients are blended. While the motor is running, drizzle in the oil a little at a time. Stored in a clean, airtight container, this will keep in the refrigerator for 1 week. This marinade freezes well with food for up to 3 months.

ADOBO RED CHILE MARINADE MAKES 2½ CUPS

Traditionally, adobo is a spicy red sauce that's used as both a marinade and a sauce for pork and poultry in Mexico. The chiles in the recipe are counterbalanced by the citrus and the spices. I've used this marinade as a substitute for the glaze in the Apricot-Glazed Ribs with Dr Pepper Baste (page 156) and as a topping for the Chicken Fajitas (page 199). This is a traditional sauce with upscale flavors.

6 dried ancho chiles
3 dried New Mexico (guajillo) chiles
2 tablespoons peanut oil or lard
½ cup diced white onion
4 or 5 cloves garlic, pressed
Grated zest and juice of 2 lemons (about ⅓ cup)
Grated zest and juice of 3 or 4 limes (about ½ cup)
1 teaspoon dried oregano (preferably Mexican)
¼ teaspoon ground cumin
½ teaspoon cinnamon
1 teaspoon freshly ground black pepper
½ teaspoon coarse-grain salt
3 tablespoons dark brown sugar
¼ cup olive oil

To prepare the chiles, see the sidebar on page 143 for preparing dried chiles. Drain and discard all but 1 cup of the soaking liquid. In a food processor or a blender, process the chiles and the soaking liquid. Heat the peanut oil in a heavy-bottom frying pan, add the onion and garlic, and sauté until they are translucent. Add the chile purée and fry for about 5 minutes over medium heat. Place the mixture back in the food processor and add the lemon zest and juice, lime zest and juice, oregano, cumin, cinnamon, salt, pepper, and brown sugar. Process until all the ingredients are blended. While the motor is running, drizzle in the olive oil a little at a time.

Place the mixture in a nonreactive saucepan and simmer the marinade on low heat for about 1 hour, stirring occasionally. Remove from the heat and cool before marinating poultry or meat. To use the marinade as a sauce, bring the marinade to a low boil and simmer over low heat until ready to use. Spoon about ⅓ cup of warm sauce onto each portion.

ANCHO-HONEY MARINADE. Add ⅓ cup honey.

TIMETABLE:

Chicken breasts, pork tenderloin, pork chops, or pork cutlets: 3 to 4 hours

Beef tenderloins or filets: 4 to 6 hours

Baby back ribs, spareribs, or chicken wings: 6 to 8 hours

TIMETABLE:

Flank steak: 6 to 8 hours

Spareribs, baby back ribs,
pork shoulder, or beef
brisket: 8 to 12 hours

BASIC SOUTHERN BARBECUE RUB MAKES 1 CUP

I used to think that a lot of Southern barbecue was pure smoking sorcery
with incantations, ointments, and gris-gris powder. But I was surprised by
how much mileage you can get from a series of very basic ingredients. This
spicy rub will enable you to create ribs that would make a pit boss proud.
Rub it into a side of ribs and marinate overnight (12 hours). Then slow smoke
the ribs over indirect heat in a kettle grill, adding a couple of handfuls of
presoaked hickory chips. Serve with your favorite barbecue sauce and a side
of coleslaw.

¼ cup firmly packed dark brown sugar
2 tablespoons coarse-grain salt
¼ cup whole black peppercorns
¼ cup hot paprika
1 tablespoon dry mustard
1 tablespoon Red Onion Powder (page 67)
2 tablespoons garlic powder or Lemon-Garlic Powder (page 67)
1 to 2 teaspoons cayenne pepper

Combine the sugar, salt, peppercorns, paprika, mustard, onion powder,
garlic powder, and cayenne in a spice mill or a blender and grind to a coarse
powder. Stored in a clean, airtight container, this will keep in the freezer for
3 to 4 months.

TIMETABLE:

Chicken breasts:
4 to 6 hours

Beef flank steak:
6 to 8 hours

Spareribs or baby back
ribs: 8 to 12 hours

CAJUN RUB MAKES ABOUT 1 CUP

This Cajun rub uses peppers in three different ways. The three different
peppers—black, white, and cayenne—hit you in three different places in
your mouth. Each one caramelizes differently when seared over high heat.
This enables them to encrust chicken, pork chops, and firm-flesh fish with a
savory shell of flavor. But flame without flavor falters rather quickly. It's the
accompanying spices and dry herbs that give this rub its staying power. Try
this rub under the skin of grilled chicken breasts and on flank steak, lamb
kabobs, and spareribs. The recipe makes enough for 2 pounds of chicken or
flank steak or a side of spareribs.

2 tablespoons whole black peppercorns
2 tablespoons whole white peppercorns
1 to 2 tablespoons cayenne
3 tablespoons hot paprika
1 tablespoon brown sugar
1 tablespoon coarse-grain salt
2 teaspoons garlic powder
2 teaspoons onion powder
2 teaspoons dried oregano
1 teaspoon dried sage
1 teaspoon dried thyme

Combine the peppercorns, cayenne (start with 1 tablespoon; if you like it hotter, add the second), paprika, brown sugar, salt, garlic powder, onion powder, oregano, sage, and thyme in a blender or a spice grinder and grind to a coarse power (not fine). Stored in a clean, airtight container, this will keep in the freezer for 3 to 4 months.

TEXAS RANCHO RUB MAKES ⅔ CUP

The secret ingredient in this barbecue rub is the dried wild mushroom, which lends it a savory muskiness. The dried chipotles add hints of smoke, and where there's smoke—you have fire. Use as a dry rub for beef brisket or beef or pork ribs.

3 tablespoons coarsely cracked black peppercorns
1 tablespoon dried oregano
1 teaspoon cumin
1 teaspoon onion powder or Red Onion Powder (page 67)
1 tablespoon chipotle chile powder (or substitute ancho chile or
    New Mexico chile powder, depending on heat preference)
1 bay leaf
1 teaspoon grated orange zest
2 teaspoons coarse-grain salt
¼ cup dried mushrooms, ground

Combine the peppercorns, oregano, cumin, onion powder, chipotle, bay leaf, orange zest, salt, and mushroom powder in a spice mill or a blender, and grind to a coarse powder. Stored in a clean, airtight container, this will keep in the freezer for 3 to 4 months.

TIMETABLE:
Beef filets, rib eye, sirloin, porterhouse, New York strip, tri tips, or beef kabobs: 4 to 6 hours

Beef brisket, flank steak, or pork ribs: 8 to 12 hours

TIMETABLE:

Chicken breasts:
4 to 6 hours

Chicken wings:
6 to 8 hours

Beef brisket or spareribs:
8 to 12 hours

SOUTHWEST CHILE PASTE MAKES 2 TO 3 CUPS

This paste, created by chef Jon Jividen, is ideal for beef brisket, chicken breasts, and spareribs. You can add a couple of tablespoons of the paste to any of the basic marinades for poultry or meat, or a tablespoon or two to your favorite barbecue sauce to liven up the flavor.

4 dried ancho chile peppers, stemmed, deveined, and seeded
2 dried New Mexico (guajillo) chiles, stemmed, deveined, and seeded
2 canned chipotle chiles
½ cup chopped onion
4 cloves garlic, minced
2 teaspoons ground cumin
2 tablespoon dried oregano (preferably Mexican)
1 teaspoon coarse-grain salt

See the sidebar on page 143 for preparing dried chiles. Remove the ancho and New Mexico chiles from the water and reserve 2 cups of the soaking water. Combine the chiles, chipotle, onion, garlic, cumin, oregano, and salt in a food processor or blender and purée until all the ingredients are blended into a smooth, thick paste. Add the reserved soaking liquid as needed to moisten the mixture to form a paste. Store in a clean, airtight container in the refrigerator for 3 to 4 weeks.

ORANGE–CHILE POWDER RUB MAKES ⅓ CUP

This seasoning will definitely give some of the commercial Cajun spice mixes a run for their money. I add a tablespoon or two to Caribbean- and Southwestern-style marinades, as well as to Cajun dishes, to give the flavors a bit of punch. Three varieties of chiles give this mix its depth.

Dried zest from 2 juice oranges, or 3 tablespoons
**   freshly grated orange zest**
3 or 4 dried chipotle chiles, or 2 tablespoons chipotle chile powder
2 tablespoons ancho chile powder
2 tablespoons New Mexico chili powder
1 (3-inch) cinnamon stick
2 teaspoons cumin seeds
1 tablespoon dried Mexican oregano
1 tablespoon coarse-grain salt

Combine the orange zest, chipotle powder, ancho powder, New Mexico chili powder, cinnamon, cumin, oregano, and salt in a spice mill or a blender and grind to a coarse powder. Store in a clean, airtight container. This will keep its potency in the freezer for 3 to 4 months.

PREPARING DRIED CHILES

· ·

To prepare dried chiles, toast them on a moderately hot, dry griddle, cast-iron frying pan, or comal by pressing them against the hot metal with the back of a spoon until they become plump and begin to soften. Do not let them burn or become crisp. The process will take a few minutes. Devein and seed the chiles, place them in a deep saucepan, and cover them with a small plate or bowl. Add boiling water to cover and soak the chiles for about 1 hour, or until they become soft and pliable.

ANCHO-ESPRESSO DRY RUB MAKES ABOUT 1½ CUPS

· ·

The hard part about this recipe is deciding which region it best fits. I was thinking of an Italian version that played off dried lemon zest and crushed red pepper. But I shifted over to the land of the ancho for a bittersweet matchup. The espresso really gives the rub some added richness, and it works especially well with the Lemon-Espresso Glaze (page 220) on grilled or broiled pork tenderloin.

½ cup firmly packed brown sugar
¼ cup ancho chile powder
⅓ cup espresso-grind coffee (very fine grind)
2 tablespoons garlic powder
1 tablespoon onion powder or Red Onion Powder (page 67)
½ teaspoon cinnamon
1 tablespoon coarse-grain salt
1 tablespoon black peppercorns

Combine the sugar, chile powder, coffee, garlic powder, onion powder, cinnamon, salt, and pepper in a spice mill or a blender and grind to a coarse powder. Stored in a clean, airtight container, this will keep in the freezer for 3 to 4 months.

ANCHO-COCOA DRY RUB. Replace the espresso with cocoa powder.

LEMON-ESPRESSO RUB. Replace the ancho chile powder with 2 tablespoons grated lemon zest, and replace the cinnamon with crushed red pepper flakes.

TIMETABLE:
Chicken breasts or kabobs, beef brisket, ground beef patties, pork tenderloin, pork chops, baby back ribs, or spareribs: 4 to 6 hours

TIP: While testing the ancho and cocoa versions of these recipes, I gave the leftover rubs to a friend, who then mixed the two of them together for a Mocha-Ancho Rub.

143

CRANBERRY-JALAPEÑO GLAZE MAKES 1½ CUPS

Who would have thought that this marriage would ever take? After all, the cranberry-jalapeño couple is from two entirely different backgrounds. Cranberry, though a bit tart, picks up on the sweetness of the maple syrup. The jalapeño, combined with the fresh ginger and garlic, provides a spicy contrast in this wedding party. Binding the lovely couple together in culinary bliss is the orange. Now this flavor combo is living happily after.

1 cup cranberry sauce (preferably jellied)
¼ cup jalapeño jelly
3 to 4 tablespoons diced jalapeño chiles, stemmed, seeded, and deveined
2 tablespoons maple syrup
3 tablespoons minced fresh ginger
2 cloves garlic, minced
2 bay leaves
Grated zest and juice of 3 fresh juice oranges (about 1 cup)
1 teaspoon coarse-grain salt

TIP: You can adjust the heat up or down by adding more or less of the jalapeño and ginger. The jalapeño jelly is more of a binder and tends not to be as hot as the real thing.

Combine the cranberry and jalapeño jellies, jalapeño chiles, maple syrup, ginger, garlic, bay leaves, orange zest and juice, and salt in a small saucepan. Simmer until the jellies melt down, and then reduce the glaze by half to a syrup consistency, about 30 minutes. For grilling or roasting meat or poultry, turn and brush with the glaze during the last 10 minutes of cooking. For grilling or roasting seafood, turn and baste with the glaze during the last 5 minutes of cooking.

GRILLED HALIBUT STEAKS WITH SAGE-VERMOUTH MARINADE SERVES 4

Southern cuisine is not just about Cajun and barbecue, even though some folks have no problem just stopping there. This recipe from chef Dave Underwood of Virgil's Fish House outside of Bogalusa, Louisiana, will give seafood a citrusy swim in Southern waters. It begins as a savory soak of lemon and herbs, and then a little bit of Louisiana hot sauce gives it a gentle nudge toward a Southern flavor exposure. This halibut recipe comes right off the menu.

4 (8 ounces each) halibut steaks
2½ cups Sage-Vermouth Marinade (page 60)

Place the halibut in a nonreactive container or a 1-gallon resealable plastic bag. Pour the marinade over the halibut and refrigerate for at least 4 hours. Remove the halibut from the marinade. Bring the marinade to a rolling boil in a nonreactive saucepan and simmer for about 10 minutes or microwave the marinade on high for 3 minutes. Use for basting.

To grill: Lightly brush the grill with vegetable oil and grill the halibut for 8 to 10 minutes on each side, using the marinade as a baste. The fish flakes with a fork when done.

To cook indoors: Preheat the broiler to its hottest setting and line a baking sheet with foil. Arrange the halibut on the baking sheet and broil for 6 to 8 minutes on each side, basting with the warm marinade. The fish flakes with a fork when done.

PECAN-BREADED CATFISH WITH
MUSTARD-BUTTERMILK MARINADE SERVES 2

This recipe has all of my favorite Southern flavors: Creole mustard, bourbon, and the sweet taste of pond-raised catfish. Pecans have long enjoyed a savory relationship with catfish, and here they become part of the breading. Serve this dish with some sautéed zucchini and yellow squash.

½ to ⅔ pound catfish fillets
2 cups Mustard-Buttermilk Marinade (page 134)
½ cup coarsely ground roasted pecans
⅔ cup Zatarain's Fish Fry, or ⅔ cup finely ground yellow
    cornmeal with 1 teaspoon grated lemon zest
Peanut oil, for pan-frying

Place the catfish fillets in a nonreactive container or a 1-gallon resealable plastic bag, pour the marinade over the catfish, and refrigerate for at least 3 hours.

Combine the ground pecans with the fish fry in a plastic or brown paper bag. Remove the catfish from the marinade and add it to the breading, gently shaking the bag to coat the fish evenly.

Heat ¼ inch of peanut oil in a skillet over medium-high heat to about 365°F (a cube of bread dropped into the hot oil will brown in 60 seconds). Pan-fry the catfish for 8 to 10 minutes on each side, until the crust turns golden brown. Drain on paper towels before placing the catfish in a cast-iron or ovenproof frying pan with a little oil. Heat the oven to 500°F and bake the catfish for 8 to 10 minutes per side. The catfish will be as crisp as if it were deep-fried.

HICKORY-SMOKED CATFISH SERVES 4

The temperature range is a cross between traditional cold smoking and Southern barbecue. Too much heat will toast this fish. The brine is essential in this recipe to keep the fish from flaking. I suggest using hickory chunks or chips for smoking.

2 (8-ounce) catfish fillets, skins removed
3 cups Maple-Bourbon Brine (page 49)
1½ cups Jack's Firehouse Mustard Barbecue Sauce (page 159)
4 cups Mango-Jicama Salsa (page 166) (optional)

Place the catfish in a 1-gallon resealable bag or a nonreactive container, pour the brine over, and refrigerate overnight (about 12 hours). Bring the fish to room temperature (no longer than ½ hour). Set up the smoker for a cold smoke at 110° to 120°F. Cold smoke the catfish for 1 to 2 hours, until it has a strong smoky flavor. When the fish is almost done, warm the barbecue sauce in a small nonreactive pot over low heat. Remove the fish from the smoker.

To serve, cut each fillet in half, and brush with the warm barbecue sauce. Top with the Mango-Jicama Salsa and serve immediately. The catfish is best when served warm. If refrigerated, bring the catfish to room temperature and gently warm it in the oven at the lowest setting.

MANGO SHRIMP FROM HELL WITH SOUTHWESTERN TABBOULEH SERVES 4

The title of this recipe sounds as though it should be appearing at a drive-in movie instead of on a salad plate, but the flavor of this mango-marinated shrimp is pure heaven. Visually, the dish looks like a Navajo sandpainting, with a circled portion of Southwestern Tabbouleh and shrimp on all four sides. I've gotten great feedback on this dish at Philadelphia's Book and the Cook for four years running.

16 large shrimp (about 1 pound), peeled and deveined
2½ cups Yellow Hell Marinade (page 180)

SOUTHWESTERN TABBOULEH

¾ cup canned tamarind, mango, or guava nectar
Grated zest and juice of 2 limes (about ¼ cup)
8 ounces medium-fine bulgur (cracked wheat)
¼ cup light olive oil
1 tomato, peeled, seeded, and diced
2 serrano chiles, stemmed, seeded, deveined, and diced
1 tablespoon grated fresh ginger
½ teaspoon ancho chile powder
½ teaspoon New Mexico chili powder or ancho chile powder
¼ cup chopped fresh cilantro
¼ cup chopped fresh mint

Place the shrimp in a nonreactive container or a 1-gallon resealable plastic bag, pour the marinade over the shrimp, and refrigerate for 3 to 4 hours.

To make the tabbouleh, an hour before you are ready to serve, combine the tamarind nectar and lime juice in a nonreactive bowl. Add the bulgur and soak for about 15 minutes, or until the liquid is absorbed. Add the lime zest, olive oil, tomato, serrano, ginger, chile powders, cilantro, and mint. Refrigerate until ready to serve.

Remove the shrimp from the marinade, reserving the marinade. Run a metal or a presoaked wooden skewer through each shrimp so that it is skewered in two places. You should have 2 shrimp on each of 8 skewers. Bring the marinade to a low boil for 3 minutes in a nonreactive pan. Use for basting and as a dipping sauce.

To grill: Lightly brush the grill with vegetable oil and grill the shrimp for 3 to 4 minutes, turning often and basting with the warm marinade, until the flesh becomes opaque.

To cook indoors: Line a baking sheet with foil. Arrange the shrimp skewers on the baking sheet and broil about 6 inches from the flame for 4 to 6 minutes, turning the skewers every few minutes and basting with the warm marinade, until the flesh becomes opaque.

To serve, pack the tabbouleh into a cup or ramekin, cover with a spatula, and invert onto the center of 4 salad plates. Slide the spatula free and remove the ramekin. Spoon 1 tablespoon of the warm marinade onto the 4 corners of each salad plate and top each pool with 1 shrimp, tail facing up.

BARBECUED SALMON SERVES 4

One would think that strong-flavored barbecue sauces would overpower delicate salmon fillets. Not so. I was amazed by the flavor combination. This sweet tomato-based sauce makes a perfect marinade for salmon. Serve the salmon with a tart red cabbage slaw.

4 (½ pound each) salmon fillets
Salt and cracked black peppercorns
1½ cups Rum Barbecue Sauce (page 161)
Canola oil, for pan-frying (if cooking indoors)

Season the salmon with salt and pepper.

To grill: Lightly brush the grill with oil and grill the salmon, flesh side down, over medium-high heat for 6 to 7 minutes. Turn to skin side down, brush with the barbecue sauce, and continue grilling for 2 minutes more.

To cook indoors: Heat the oil in a frying pan to medium-high heat. Place the salmon flesh side down and sear for 6 minutes, pressing with a spatula to keep the salmon from curling. Turn the salmon, brush with the barbecue sauce, and cook for 2 minutes longer.

Salmon is done when you can almost flake it, but it's still somewhat orange in the middle. Slide a spatula between the skin and the flesh, lift, and transfer to a serving plate. Serve at once.

GRILLED SCALLOP KABOBS WITH
TEQUILA-ALMOND MARINADE SERVES 4

Dry-packed diver scallops the size of golf balls have been hitting some of the upscale seafood sections of markets lately. There is a major difference in flavor for the better. When cooking scallops on the grill, thread scallops with two skewers instead of one. This keeps the scallops from sliding around on the skewers when you turn them.

1½ pounds large sea scallops
1½ cups Tequila-Almond Marinade (page 138)
1 tablespoon butter (for cooking indoors)
1 red bell pepper, stemmed, seeded, and cut into 1-inch wedges
1 yellow bell pepper, stemmed, seeded, and cut into 1-inch wedges

Place the scallops in a nonreactive container or a 1-gallon resealable plastic bag. Pour the marinade over the scallops and refrigerate for 4 to 6 hours.

Remove the scallops from the marinade and bring the marinade to a boil for basting.

To grill: Thread the scallops and sweet peppers onto their own individual skewers. Lightly brush the grill with vegetable oil. Grill the peppers for about 10 minutes or until they soften. Grill the scallops until light brown, 2 to 3 minutes per side, turning often and basting with the warm marinade. Remove the scallops and the peppers from the skewers.

To cook indoors: Preheat the oven to 300°F. Heat the butter in a heavy skillet, add the bell peppers, and sauté until tender. Add the scallops, and cook over high heat for about 30 seconds per side, shaking the skillet. Add the remaining marinade, bring to a boil, and simmer for 2 to 3 minutes. Remove the scallops from the skillet with a slotted spoon, and place in the warm oven. Continue cooking the marinade for about 10 minutes, until reduced to a glaze. Return the scallops to the skillet and gently sauté the scallops until firm.

Serve hot.

GRILLED TUNA WITH BEAUJOLAIS MARINADE
SERVES 4

. . . .

This particular recipe combines the flavors of the Southwest of France with the flavors of our Southwest. The berry-flavored Beaujolais plays off the fresh lemon and woodsy tang of the herbes de Provence. The slight heat of the serrano chile gives the marinade added depth.

4 (6 ounces each) tuna steaks
2½ cups Raspberry-Beaujolais Marinade (page 57)
2 tablespoons vegetable oil
1½ to 2 cups Peach Salsa (page 165)

TIP: Do not overcook, or the tuna will become dry and lose its flavor. The tuna should be red in the center, not gray.

Place the tuna steaks in a nonreactive container or a 1-gallon resealable plastic bag, pour the marinade over the tuna, and refrigerate for 4 hours. Remove the tuna from the marinade and bring the marinade to a boil for basting.

To grill: Lightly brush the grill with vegetable oil and grill the tuna over high heat for 3 to 4 minutes for rare or 6 to 7 minutes for medium. Turn the tuna about halfway through the grilling time, basting with the warm marinade.

To cook indoors: Using a heavy-bottom saucepan or a seasoned cast-iron frying pan, heat the oil. Increase the heat to high. Sear the tuna for 1 minute, turn, decrease the heat to medium, and sear for 1 minute more.

To serve, transfer the tuna to serving plates and center ⅓ to ½ cup of Peach Salsa on each plate.

GRILLED SWEET ANCHO TUNA SERVES 4

. . . .

Nowadays, my cooking style seems to lean toward culinary "no-brainers," that is, food that packs a punch with little effort. When I use this recipe as a rub, people swear there's more going on than there really is. Although the cure sounds very sweet, its sweetness really balances the natural oil of the tuna against the smoke. It caramelizes the surface of the tuna when grilled, locking in its flavor and keeping it moist. Serve with Southwestern Tabbouleh (page 148), Sweet Corn Salsa (page 166), or Lime-Cilantro Jicama Slaw (page 213).

1 cup Ancho-Sugar Cure (page 131)
4 (½ pound each) tuna steaks
2 tablespoons vegetable oil

With your hands lightly oiled, pat the cure into the tuna, coating both sides well. Cover the tuna with clear plastic wrap and marinate for 1 hour in the refrigerator. Let the tuna come to room temperature for 30 minutes before grilling.

To grill: Soak 2 handfuls of cherry wood chips in water for 20 minutes. Lightly brush the grill with vegetable oil and grill the tuna over high heat for 3 to 4 minutes for rare or 6 to 7 minutes for medium. Turn the tuna about halfway through the grilling time.

To cook indoors: Using a heavy-bottom saucepan or a seasoned cast-iron frying pan, heat the oil. Increase the heat to high. Sear the tuna for 1 minute, turn, decrease the heat to medium, and sear for 1 minute more.

Serve immediately.

ROAST CHICKEN WITH CREOLE MUSTARD–BOURBON MARINADE SERVES 4

Although this recipe doesn't go anywhere close to a smoldering wood chip, for me it's pure Southern comfort food. This recipe should be started the night before to allow time to brine.

4½- to 5-pound roasting chicken
9 cups Apple Cider Brine (page 48)
2 cups Creole Mustard–Bourbon Marinade (page 133)

Place the chicken in a large nonreactive container, add the brine, and place in the refrigerator for 8 to 12 hours. Remove the chicken from the brine, rinse, and pat dry with paper towels. Place the chicken in a nonreactive container or a plastic oven-roast bag, pour the marinade over it, and refrigerate for at least 6 hours, preferably overnight.

Remove the chicken from the marinade. Bring the marinade to a low boil in a nonreactive saucepan or microwave the marinade for 3 minutes on high; reserve for basting.

Preheat the oven to 425°F. Roast the chicken for about 30 minutes. Decrease the heat to 375°F. Baste with the marinade and roast for 15 to 18 minutes per pound, or until the juices run clear when the meat is pricked with a fork. Let the chicken rest for 10 minutes before carving.

SUBSTITUTIONS: Replace the brine with Basic Brine for Whole Roast Chicken (page 48). Replace the marinade with South Carolina Mustard Marinade (page 133).

SOUTHERN COMFORT—HONEY GLAZED HAM

SERVES 8 AS A MAIN COURSE OR 10 TO 12 AS PART OF A BUFFET

Glazed ham is among the aristocracy of pork recipes. It's centerpiece cuisine for holidays and special occasions, and eating breakfast in the Blue Ridge Mountains with a side of Southern glazed ham is about as special as it gets.

The glaze can work without the Southern Comfort or with a bourbon substitute. I've included two different versions of this recipe for both uncooked and precooked or smoked ham. Adding your own glaze to a precooked or smoked ham is the quickest and most flavorful way to fill out a picnic or buffet when time is at a premium. If using a precooked ham, check that the label says, "fully cooked."

1 (about 6 pounds) uncooked or precooked ham
1 cup Southern Comfort–Honey Mustard Glaze (page 88)

If using an uncooked ham, preheat the oven to 325°F. Place the ham, fat side up, on a large piece of foil in a large roasting pan. Warm the glaze and brush about half of it over the ham. Wrap aluminum foil loosely around the ham and bake for about 3 hours, or about 30 minutes per pound.

About 30 minutes before the ham is done, remove it from the oven. Increase the heat to 400°F. Score the glazed ham in a diamond crisscross pattern, cutting about ¼ inch deep into the fat. Spoon the remaining glaze over the ham and return it to the oven. Bake, uncovered, for the last 30 minutes, basting the glazed ham several times. A meat thermometer should register 160°F and the ham should be dark brown and crusty; cook for 15 minutes more, if necessary.

If using a precooked ham, preheat the oven to 325°F. Heat the ham for 20 minutes per pound, or to an internal temperature of 140°F. Brush the glaze over the ham about 20 minutes before it is done.

To serve, remove the ham from the oven and let cool slightly. Transfer to a serving platter, and let stand for 30 minutes before carving.

PULLED PORK BARBECUE SERVES 8

As a litmus test of barbecue joints, the first thing I try is pulled pork. You can tell the real deal by a few whiffs while walking in the door. A barbecue joint needs to smell like smoking wood. But the proof is in the tasting, and in fewer than a couple of bites you'll know whether it's on 'cue or whether the porker is a piker.

Serve the pulled pork on warmed buns or white bread, with the classic accompaniments of dill pickle chips and coleslaw.

Basic Southern Barbecue Rub (page 140)
6- to 8-pound picnic or Boston butt
3 cups Dr Pepper Baste (page 156) (for smoker basting) or
     your choice of basting liquid (such as a leftover marinade,
     red wine, orange juice, or apple cider)
Mama Rosa's Barbecue Sauce (page 133) (for oven basting)
8 hard rolls

SUBSTITUTIONS: Replace the rub with Orange–Chile Powder Rub (page 142) or Cajun Rub (page 140). Replace the sauce with Jack's Firehouse Mustard Barbecue Sauce (page 159) or Rum Barbecue Sauce (page 161).

Massage the rub into the meat. Wrap tightly in a double layer of plastic wrap and refrigerate for at least 8 hours, but no longer than 72 hours. Remove the meat from the refrigerator and let it stand at room temperature for 1 hour prior to cooking.

To smoke outdoors in a kettle grill: Place a 13 by 9-inch aluminum drip pan in the center of the charcoal or lower grate of your kettle grill. Fill the pan about halfway with Dr Pepper Baste. Put the meat into your smoker directly over the pan and cook using indirect heat and a temperature of 200° to 225°F. Figure about 1 to 1½ hours per pound. Baste the meat about every hour. When done, the meat should have an internal temperature of 170° to 180°F. Remove the meat from the smoker, let it sit for 15 to 20 minutes, and then pull it apart with a fork, discarding any large bits of fat. Combine the barbecue sauce with the pan drippings and moisten the meat.

TIP: If time is of the essence, you can split your cooking time between the smoker and the oven. Follow the above smoking directions and cook the meat for 3 hours. Preheat the oven to 325°F. Remove the meat from the smoker, place it in a pan, and wrap with foil to cover completely. Place the pan in the oven and bake for about 2 hours, until the meat is fork-tender.

To cook indoors: Preheat the oven to 450°F. Place the meat in a baking pan or an ovenproof glass baking dish, and roast for 10 minutes. Decrease the heat to 350°F, and roast until the internal temperature reaches 170°F, basting every 30 minutes. A rough time estimate is 30 to 35 minutes per pound, plus an extra 35 minutes. Remove the meat from the oven, let it sit for 15 to 20 minutes, and then pull it apart with a fork. Combine the pan juices with the barbecue sauce and moisten the meat.

Serve in a hard roll with additional barbecue sauce on the side. This dish is great the next day.

TURKEY TASSO HAM MAKES 2½ TO 3 POUNDS

Tasso ham is just as much a condiment as it is a ham. It's a cured smoked ham laden with Cajun flavor that hits the gumbos, jambalayas, and red beans and rice found along Louisiana Highway I-10. Just for lagniappe, I swapped out the pork with a turkey breast. I liked it so much that it was added to turkey gravy for Thanksgiving. The Turkey Tasso Ham freezes well, so if you're smoking it during the summer, you'll have plenty for Mardi Gras. The turkey can be sliced for sandwiches or cubed for soups, gumbos, étouffées, and jambalayas. Let the good brines roll!

5- to 6-pound turkey breast, boned, halved, and skin removed
3 quarts Louisiana Tasso Brine (page 132)
1 cup Cajun Rub (page 140)
1 quart apple cider, orange juice, or wine

Place the turkey in a large nonreactive container and pour the brine over the turkey. Allow the turkey to soak in the brine for 1 week in the refrigerator. Remove the turkey from the brine, and discard the brine. Rinse the turkey and pat dry with paper towels.

Preheat an outdoor smoker for 200° to 225°F with presoaked hickory wood chunks or a log. Evenly coat the turkey breast with the rub and work it in with your fingers.

If you have a kettle grill, follow the manufacturer's instructions for indirect cooking over a drip pan. Fill the drip pan with any of the above liquids. The turkey will take about 20 minutes per pound at 200° to 225°F. The internal temperature should read 160°F on a meat thermometer. Remove the turkey from the smoker, and let it rest for 30 minutes before refrigerating. This recipe freezes well for up to 3 months.

PULLED PORK SPRING ROLLS MAKES 10 SPRING ROLLS

There are so many esoteric variations to spring rolls that I started calling them deep-fried wrap and rolls. So we might as well as jump into the mix with some good ol' American barbecue. Serve with Jack's Firehouse Mustard Barbecue Sauce (page 159), Rum Barbecue Sauce (page 161), or Southwestern Peanut Sauce (page 162) for dipping sauces.

4 Chinese dried black mushrooms or dried shitake mushrooms
1 quart vegetable oil
8 ounces Pulled Pork Barbecue (page 153) or
  Smoked Duck Confit (page 108)
2 tablespoons Basic Southern Barbecue Rub (page 140)
½ cup finely shredded Napa cabbage
1 cup mung bean sprouts
1 jalapeño chile, finely chopped
½ cup shredded carrots
1 green onion, white and green parts, finely shredded
1 (8-ounce) can bamboo shoots, drained and julienned
2 tablespoons cider vinegar
1½ tablespoons light soy sauce
¼ teaspoon ground white pepper
1 (4-ounce) package spring roll wrappers
1 tablespoon all-purpose flour

In a medium bowl, soak the mushrooms in ¼ cup cold water for 30 minutes, or until softened. Drain and squeeze dry (you can reserve the soaking liquid for use in a brine). Cut off and discard the stems and thinly slice the caps.

Heat 1 tablespoon of the vegetable oil in a large skillet over high heat until hot but not smoking. Add the pulled pork, rub, cabbage, bean sprouts, jalapeño, carrots, green onion, bamboo shoots, and sliced mushrooms, and stir-fry for 2 to 3 minutes, until the cabbage and carrots are just limp. Add the cider vinegar, soy sauce, and pepper; remove from the heat and cool to room temperature.

When the mixture has cooled, place the spring roll wrappers on a work surface and loosely cover with a dampened cloth. In a small bowl, combine the flour and 4 teaspoons cold water. Place 1 wrapper on the work surface with a corner facing you. Spread about ¼ cup of the mixture near the bottom. Fold the flap over the mixture. Roll the wrapper up once, then fold in the sides. Continue rolling the wrapper up tightly, then, before you reach the end, lightly paint the far corner with the flour-water mixture. Continue rolling to seal the roll into a tight cylinder. Set aside, seam side down, and cover with a dampened cloth. Repeat with the remaining wrappers.

In a 3-quart saucepan or a deep-fat fryer, heat the remaining vegetable oil over high heat until the temperature reaches 375°F. Add 2 or 3 spring rolls at a time and fry, turning the rolls, for about 2 minutes, until golden brown. Remove with a slotted spoon and place on a plate lined with several thicknesses of paper towels. The rolls should have a crackly crisp skin. Carefully cut in half or into thirds. Repeat with the remaining spring rolls. Set the oil aside to cool before discarding.

Serve immediately with any of the dipping sauces.

APRICOT-GLAZED RIBS WITH DR PEPPER BASTE
SERVES 4

One of my biggest surprises came when a Southern pit boss told me that his secret baste for ribs was Dr Pepper and vinegar. I thought he was pulling my leg, but I'll try anything once, and this particular recipe seems to be one I try a lot. It works.

DR PEPPER BASTE

2 cups Dr Pepper or root beer
1 cup cider vinegar
1 to 2 tablespoons coarse-grain salt

To make the baste, combine the Dr Pepper, vinegar, and salt.

RIBS

2½ pounds spareribs or baby back ribs
Coarse-grain salt and freshly cracked black peppercorns
1½ cups Apricot Glaze (page 81)

To prepare the ribs, season the ribs with salt and pepper. Pour the baste over the ribs, place in a 1-gallon resealable plastic bag, and marinate in the refrigerator for 6 to 8 hours. Remove the ribs from the bag and let stand for 20 to 30 minutes. Meanwhile, bring the baste to a boil in a nonreactive saucepan or microwave on high for 3 minutes, and use for basting.

To cook outdoors: Follow the grill's instructions for using wood chunks or chips and cook the ribs over indirect medium heat (about 220°F) for 3 hours. While the ribs are cooking, preheat the oven to 375°F. Remove the ribs from the grill/smoker and generously baste with the Dr Pepper Baste. Finish the ribs in the oven for 30 minutes. Turn and baste with the Apricot Glaze during the last 5 minutes of cooking.

To cook indoors: Preheat the oven to 450°F, and brown the ribs for 20 to 30 minutes. Baste with the Dr Pepper Baste and decrease the heat to 300°F. Roast the ribs for about 90 minutes, basting once or twice. Brush on the Apricot Glaze and return to the oven for 5 to 10 minutes more.

To serve, remove the ribs from the oven and cut the sides in half, into pairs or individual sections. Serve on a warm platter.

GRILLED PORK TENDERLOIN WITH
ADOBO RED CHILE MARINADE SERVES 6

The marinade in this recipe does double duty as a rich adobo sauce. You can also substitute tenderloin of kid, equal weights of muscovy duck breasts, or even flank steak. The marinade has a flavor that can work with practically anything. Serve with rice pilaf and Pineapple-Jalapeño Salsa (page 164).

2- to 3-pound lean boneless pork loin
2½ cups Adobo Red Chile Marinade (page 139)
3 to 4 cups fresh orange juice or poultry stock
2 tablespoons clarified butter or peanut oil (for cooking indoors)

Leave the pork whole if you are grilling or roasting, but slice ¾-inch-thick pieces if you are planning to sauté the meat. Place the tenderloin in a nonreactive container or a 1-gallon resealable plastic bag, pour the marinade over the tenderloin, and refrigerate for 6 to 8 hours for the whole tenderloin and 3 to 4 hours for the slices. Remove the tenderloin from the marinade and bring the marinade to a boil.

To grill: Thin the marinade with orange juice to use as a sauce. Build a charcoal fire in a kettle grill with a water pan, and add presoaked mesquite chunks. Add 2 to 3 cups orange juice to the water pan. Lightly brush the top grill with vegetable oil. Place the tenderloin on the grill and smoke the tenderloin for 1½ to 2 hours, until the tenderloin reaches an internal temperature of 150°F. Remove the tenderloin from the grill and let it rest for 10 minutes before slicing into ¼-inch-thick pieces.

To sauté indoors: Preheat the oven to 250°F. Heat the clarified butter in a large skillet over medium-high heat. Add the tenderloin slices and sauté for 2 to 3 minutes per side. Place the slices in the warm oven and deglaze the pan with about 1 cup orange juice. Add the marinade and bring to a simmer. Simmer for about 20 minutes, until reduced to 1½ cups for a sauce.

To roast indoors: Preheat the oven to 375°F. Place a nonreactive baking pan with 1 to 2 cups orange juice on the floor of the oven for flavorful steam. Place the tenderloin on a rack in a roasting pan and roast in the center of the oven for 45 to 50 minutes, until the tenderloin reaches an internal temperature of 150°F. Remove the tenderloin from the oven and let it rest for 10 minutes before slicing into ¼-inch-thick pieces.

To serve, spoon 3 to 4 tablespoons of the adobo sauce onto a serving plate and overlap 3 or 4 slices on top of the sauce.

TEXAS-STYLE BEEF BRISKET SERVES 10 TO 12

The trick behind a perfectly moist beef brisket is slow, even heat or smoke. If you have a water smoker and access to mesquite chips or hard wood, Texas beef brisket takes on an added depth. But you can get nice results indoors with your own oven. The Texas Rancho Rub becomes the basis of a smoky, savory paste. Serve the brisket with your favorite barbecue sauce and a side of coleslaw and garnish with slices of grilled red onion.

Texas Rancho Rub (page 141)
Juice of 1 lime (about 2 tablespoons)
1½ tablespoons Madeira
3 tablespoons olive oil
1 (4 to 5 pounds) whole beef brisket
1 quart orange juice or wine, for drip pan (if cooking outdoors)
2 cups Mama Rosa's Barbecue Sauce (page 132)
Grilled red onion rings, for garnish

Combine the rub, lime juice, Madeira, and olive oil in a blender or a food processor. Process until it becomes a smooth paste. Or combine the ingredients in a small nonreactive bowl and stir into a paste. With your hands lightly oiled, rub the paste into the brisket, coating both sides well. Cover the brisket with clear plastic wrap and marinate for a minimum of 24 hours in the refrigerator.

Remove the brisket from the refrigerator and let it sit at room temperature for about 1 hour before you begin to cook.

To cook outdoors: Use a covered kettle grill or a water smoker. In a kettle grill, indirectly cook the brisket over a water pan containing orange juice for about 2 hours per pound, refreshing the coals with damp smoking chips every couple of hours. If you are using a water smoker, follow the manufacturer's instructions.

To cook indoors: Preheat the oven to 300°F. Put the brisket in a roasting pan and place in the center of the oven. Roast for 1 hour per pound, undisturbed. If you like, combine the pan juices with some warm barbecue sauce for serving.

The brisket should have an internal temperature of 170°F on an instant-read thermometer and a dark crust when finished. Let the brisket rest for 10 minutes before slicing.

To serve, slice the brisket across the grain. Place overlapping slices on a large platter, drizzle with barbecue sauce, and garnish with grilled red onion rings.

BARBECUED LAMB RIBS SERVES 6

This recipe comes from chef Jack McDavid of Philadelphia's Down Home Diner and Jack's Firehouse. Most cooks shun inexpensive lamb ribs because of their fat content. Through a slow braise, however, the fat is melted off, leaving tender succulent ribs that are more flavorful than beef ribs.

1 cup apple cider vinegar
5 tablespoons dry mustard
1 tablespoon cracked black peppercorns
1 teaspoon coarse-grain salt
6 racks lamb ribs (about 6 pounds)

JACK'S FIREHOUSE MUSTARD BARBECUE SAUCE

MAKES 3 CUPS

1 to 2 tablespoons olive oil
1 jalapeño chile, stemmed and diced
⅓ cup chopped onion
4 or 5 cloves garlic, chopped
2 cups ketchup
½ cup yellow mustard
2 tablespoons cider vinegar
2 tablespoons molasses
1 teaspoon chopped fresh rosemary
1 teaspoon fresh thyme
3 or 4 bay leaves

To prepare the lamb, combine the vinegar, mustard, peppercorns, and salt and rub generously over the lamb racks. Place the racks in a plastic oven-roasting bag or a nonreactive covered container and marinate for 12 hours in the refrigerator.

To make the sauce, in a large saucepan, heat the oil. Add the jalapeño, onion, and garlic, and sauté for 3 to 4 minutes, or until the onion becomes translucent. Add the ketchup, mustard, cider vinegar, molasses, rosemary, thyme, and bay leaves. Simmer over moderate heat for about 1 hour.

Preheat the broiler to its hottest setting and line a baking sheet with foil. Remove the racks from the marinade, place on the baking sheet, and brown the lamb ribs on both sides under the broiler. Preheat the oven to 400°F. Place the ribs on a rack in a Dutch oven. Cover and roast in the oven for 1½ hours. Remove the lamb ribs from the oven and brush each rack with about ½ cup of the barbecue sauce. Let the ribs stand for at least 1 hour.

To serve, preheat the oven to 400°F, heat the ribs in the oven for 10 minutes, and serve hot.

GRILLED BEEF TENDERLOINS WITH ANCHO CHILE SAUCE SERVES 4

The caramelized combination of orange and smoky chipotle chile is seared into the crust of the beef tenderloin. Because of the acidic content of the marinade and the natural tenderness of the beef, this recipe has a shorter marinating time. The Orange-Chipotle Marinade makes a wonderful basting sauce for beef ribs as well as for muscovy duck breast (not Long Island duckling).

TENDERLOINS

4 (6 ounces each) beef filets, cut about 1½ inches thick
2 cups Orange-Chipotle Marinade (page 174)

ANCHO CHILE SAUCE MAKES 1¹/₂ CUPS

6 ancho chiles, stemmed, deveined, and seeded
3 cloves garlic, pressed
¼ cup chopped white onion
3 tablespoons chopped shallots
1 jalapeño chile, stemmed, deveined, and seeded
1 tablespoon peanut oil
1 (3-inch) stick cinnamon
1 tablespoon tomato concentrate
2 cups veal demi-glace
1 tablespoon honey

To prepare the beef, place the meat in a nonreactive container or a 1-gallon resealable plastic bag. Pour the marinade over the beef and refrigerate for 2 hours. Remove the container from the refrigerator and let it stand, covered, for 1 hour at room temperature. Remove the beef from the marinade.

To prepare the sauce, for the anchos, see the sidebar on page 143 for preparing dried chiles. Drain and discard all but ½ cup of the soaking liquid. Purée the chiles in a food processor or a blender with the reserved soaking liquid, and add the garlic, onion, shallots, and jalapeño.

Heat the peanut oil in a saucepan over medium-high heat, add the purée, and cook for 2 to 3 minutes. Decrease the heat and add the cinnamon, tomato concentrate, and demi-glace and simmer for about 45 minutes, until the sauce is reduced by half. Remove the sauce from the heat and let cool to room temperature. Purée in a food processor or a blender until smooth. Add the honey to taste. Keep the sauce slightly warm while you grill the steak.

To grill: Lightly brush the grill with vegetable oil and sear the beef for 1 minute on each side. Continue grilling the beef, 5 to 6 minutes for rare, 7 to 8 minutes for medium rare, turning often. Remove the beef from the heat and let stand for 10 minutes before serving.

To cook indoors: Preheat the broiler to its highest setting. Place the beef on a broiler rack about 3 inches from the heat source and sear the beef for 1 minute each side. Continue broiling the beef, 5 to 6 minutes for rare, 7 to 8 minutes for medium rare, turning often. Remove the beef from the heat and let stand for 10 minutes before serving.

To serve, nap the Ancho Chile Sauce over the surface of 4 serving plates. Place a filet on each and serve hot.

RUM BARBECUE SAUCE MAKES 3 CUPS

This is a great starter barbecue sauce. You can jazz it up to your heart's content. An additional cup of vinegar will place the sauce in South Carolina. Add more chile powder, and you're heading for Texas.

I like to make this sauce at least once a year, and I usually make at least 2 gallons per batch. I make it in a large stockpot that I place in my oven at 220°F. Then it sits there for at least 12 hours. The longer the cooking time, the better the flavor. You can get the same results by using a Crockpot set on low and letting it run for the same amount of time.

2 tablespoons peanut oil
1 sweet (Vidalia or Maui) onion, chopped
1 clove garlic, chopped
1½ cups ketchup
⅓ cup Worcestershire sauce
½ cup cider vinegar
½ cup dark rum
2 tablespoons ancho chile powder or New Mexico chili powder
2 tablespoons hot paprika
¼ to ½ teaspoon cayenne
½ teaspoon ground cumin
½ teaspoon ground coriander

Heat the oil in a saucepan over medium heat. Add the onion and garlic, and sauté until the onion is translucent. Add the ketchup, Worcestershire, vinegar, rum, chile powder, hot paprika, cayenne, cumin, and coriander, and simmer over low heat for at least 1 hour, stirring occasionally. Remove from the heat and cool to room temperature. Stored in a clean, airtight container, this will keep in the refrigerator for 3 to 4 months.

MARINATED FLANK STEAK SANDWICH WITH SOUTHWESTERN PEANUT SAUCE SERVES 6

The marinated flank steak combines two parallel yet geographically distant cuisines. The marinade seasoning is definitely Asian, but the peanut sauce is from the American Southwest, and they play off each other wonderfully. You can serve the beef stuffed in pita bread along with some lightly grilled red onion rings, or rolled in a warm tortilla topped with cilantro and diced avocado.

SOUTHWESTERN PEANUT SAUCE MAKES 1½ CUPS

½ cup peanut butter
¼ cup canned tamarind nectar
1 teaspoon ground cinnamon
½ teaspoon ground cumin
2 tablespoons New Mexico chili powder
2 tablespoons jalapeño jelly
½ cup beef stock or low-salt canned beef broth

STEAK

2½-pound flank steak
1½ to 2 cups Basic Asian-Style Marinade (page 278)
12 flour or corn tortillas, or 6 pita breads, warmed
Avocado chunks, for garnish (if using tortillas)
Chopped cilantro, for garnish (if using tortillas)
Grilled red onion rings (if using pita bread)

To make the sauce, combine the peanut butter, juice, cinnamon, cumin, chili powder, jelly, and broth in a heavy nonreactive saucepan. Bring to a boil, decrease the heat, and simmer for 20 minutes. Keep the sauce slightly warm while you grill the steak.

To reheat leftover sauce, bring to a simmer for 5 to 10 minutes and thin with additional beef broth, if necessary, to return the sauce to its original consistency.

To prepare the steak, place the meat in a nonreactive container or a 1-gallon resealable plastic bag. Pour the marinade over the steak and refrigerate for 12 to 48 hours.

Remove the steak from the marinade. Bring the marinade to a low boil in a nonreactive saucepan and simmer for 3 minutes. Reserve for basting.

To grill: Lightly brush the grill with vegetable oil and grill the steak for 6 to 7 minutes, turning often and basting with the warm marinade. Remove the steak from the grill and let the steak rest for 3 to 5 minutes before slicing.

To cook indoors: Preheat the broiler to its hottest setting and line a baking sheet with foil. Place the steak on the baking sheet and broil for 7 to 8 minutes per side, basting with the warm marinade. Remove the steak from the broiler and let the steak rest for 3 to 5 minutes before slicing.

To serve, slice the steak diagonally across the grain. Spoon the peanut sauce into the middle of the tortillas, add the steak slices, roll the tortilla, and garnish with avocado and cilantro; place 2 tortillas on each of 6 plates. Or add the steak slices and onion slices to the pita bread, then spoon in the peanut sauce; place 1 pita sandwich on each of 6 plates.

SMOKE CUTTERS

If you want a contrasting flavor or texture to accompany your grilled food, then consider using salsas and chutneys. Salsas and chutneys perform the role of smoke cutters. They can be sweet, tart, or piquant enough to pull your palate in directions other than where the grilled flavors were taking you. For me, that flavorful push-pull experience is what grilling is all about. Here are a few of my favorite zings.

PINEAPPLE-JALAPEÑO SALSA MAKES 1½ CUPS

Chef Jon Jividen's Pineapple-Jalapeño Salsa combines the sweet with the piquant. What piques my interest is the saffron, which gives the salsa a bright, neon-yellow color and a simple savory accent to match up with grilled marinated fish and shrimp. The salsa goes well with Grilled Lemon-Soy Marinated Swordfish Steaks (page 103), Grilled Mahi Mahi with Chardonnay Marinade (page 104), or Grilled Pork Tenderloin with Adobo Red Chile Marinade (page 139).

1 cup chopped fresh pineapple
2 cups unsweetened pineapple juice
½ cup white wine vinegar
½ cup firmly packed dark brown sugar
1 generous pinch saffron threads
1 fresh jalapeño chile, seeded and diced

Combine the pineapple, pineapple juice, vinegar, sugar, saffron, and jalapeño in a nonreactive saucepan and simmer for about 30 minutes, until reduced by about half. Serve the salsa warm to use as a main-course accompaniment or serve cold with grilled swordfish. The salsa will keep for up to 2 weeks in the refrigerator.

PEACH SALSA MAKES 3 TO 4 CUPS

I like salsas that accompany grilled food with flavor as well as color. This salsa does both. This, the sweetest of the salsas, is contrasted with a slight flush of heat from the chiles. Its variety of flavors makes this one of the most flexible accompaniments in the book. Match this side with Grilled Tuna with Beaujolais Marinade (page 150), Grilled Chicken Kabobs with Provençal Cognac Marinade (page 228), or Plum-Cassis Glazed Pork Tenderloin (page 120).

1½ pounds fresh peaches (5 to 6 small or 3 to 4 large peaches)
2 tablespoons dried black currants
1 tablespoon dark rum
¼ cup finely diced red bell pepper
¼ cup chopped red onion
¼ cup white wine vinegar or peach vinegar
2 tablespoons grapeseed oil
1 to 2 tablespoons diced jalapeño chile
3 to 4 tablespoons chopped fresh basil
3 cloves garlic, minced or pressed

Bring 3 quarts of water to a rolling boil and blanch the peaches for 2 to 3 minutes. Immediately plunge the peaches into a bowl of ice water to stop the cooking process. Peel and pit the peaches and coarsely chop. Soak the currants in the rum for about 1 hour.

Combine the peaches and currants with the bell pepper, red onion, vinegar, oil, jalapeño, basil, and garlic in a nonreactive bowl and refrigerate for 4 to 6 hours before serving. This will keep for up to 2 weeks in the refrigerator.

SWEET CORN SALSA MAKES 2 CUPS

One of my favorite ways to prepare this salsa is to rub shucked corn with a little corn oil and grill outdoors for a sweet, smoky flavor. Freshly picked corn is essential because you want to contrast its sweetness with the tart lime and tangy serrano. This makes a sensational accompaniment to Grilled Orange-Ginger Marinated Tuna (page 104).

3 ears fresh corn, cooked and cooled
½ cup diced red onion
1 tablespoon diced serrano chile
2 tablespoons avocado oil
2 to 3 tablespoons chopped fresh cilantro
Grated zest and juice of 2 limes (about ¼ cup)
1 tablespoon maple syrup (optional; use if corn is not freshly picked)

Cut the corn kernels from the cobs and toss the kernels with the red onion, serrano, oil, cilantro, lime zest and juice, and maple syrup in a nonreactive bowl. Refrigerate the salsa until serving. This will keep for up to 2 weeks in the refrigerator.

MANGO-JICAMA SALSA SERVES 6

I call this recipe my grilling acrobat because of the way it balances grilled and smoke dishes. It's an easy recipe to adapt, and you can add just about anything to it.

1 fresh mango, peeled and thinly sliced (about 2 cups)
½ cup peeled and thinly sliced carrots
1 pound jicama, peeled and thinly sliced (about 2 cups)
1 red bell pepper, seeded, ribs removed, and thinly sliced
1 jalapeño chile, seeded, deveined, and diced
¼ cup chopped fresh cilantro
Grated zest and juice of 3 limes (about ⅓ cup)
Salt and freshly cracked black peppercorns

In a large bowl, toss the mango, carrots, jicama, bell pepper, jalapeño, cilantro, and lime zest and juice, add salt and pepper to taste, and serve immediately. This salsa will keep, refrigerated, for about 1 day.

LATIN AMERICA
& THE CARIBBEAN

The things one hears on cooking

shows these days! I actually heard a chef say, "I have my roots in nouveau cuisine." How can one have roots in something that means "new"? Some of the "newest" trends that I like to eat seem to have been around prior to Columbus thinking he just discovered them. Take, for example, Mexican barbacoa. Trendy? You betcha. It has everything going for it—smoky tropical food, high priests, and temples. Sounds like restaurant row in most major cities.

Although grilling is full of trends, it's important to remember that it's actually as old as time. Early barbecue was a moist, ovenlike cooking process using real pits. The Mayans had what was a communal oven or an ancient cooking hole called a *pib,* fueled by charcoal that heated the big flat stones on which everything under the sun was cooked. In the Yucatán, *pibil* refers to food

that is cooked this way, and it is usually marinated with achiote spice, which turns everything a bright crimson. The meat or fish is generally wrapped in plantain or banana leaves and marinated overnight before being put into the *pib.* This was low-heat slow cookery. Pit cooking appears in as many different cuisines as do marinades. I find it pretty funny when someone points to a cast-iron cooker with a chimney and calls it a barbecue pit. The real ones really were pits.

One of the regions of Mexico where the cuisine binds with marinating is the Yucatán. The Yucatán Peninsula has flavor combinations uniquely its own. Half the region rests in the Gulf of Mexico while the other half sits in the Caribbean Sea, and its flavors taste of neither. Yucatecan cuisine isn't even close to what people think of as traditional Mexican food. It's lighter, and is filled with citrus, preblended spices (recados), and achiote paste, lending itself perfectly to the grill.

Sweet heat, the most extreme of mouth sensations, is one of the taste signatures that I associate with the Caribbean islands. My road to the tiki bar buffet is paved with flashes of rum, mangoes, coconut, and chiles. Caribbean cooking is really a cluster of several cuisines and attitudes.

The original inhabitants, the Arawaks, had an interesting cooking technique of roasting cured meat over low, slow-burning coals. The Taino, a tribe of Haitians, called a framework of sticks for sleeping on or cooking over a *barbacoa*. The word was borrowed from the Spanish, and both the word and the technique morphed into the English term *barbecue.* Where there's rum and island cooking, there are pirates. The term *buccaneer,* a seventeenth-century adventurer or pirate, comes from the technique called *boucan* (meaning "barbecue"), a process of curing meat by smoking it slowly over a fire. Its French practitioners were called *boucaniers.*

The Caribbean has been rocked by as many different nationalities and settlers as it has been by hurricanes. Besides the pirates, there were colonists; settlers; planters of Spanish, Dutch, English, and French origin; and African slaves.

These peoples also brought their respective cooking habits along with them. The islands were a pivotal port of call for the spice trade, exporting chiles to Europe and beyond and picking up in return chutneys, curries, ginger, and nutmeg from the East Indies.

My sense of Latino food runs from the southernmost tip of the Andes to southern Florida. Latino food and music bear almost no resemblance to their Caribbean and Mexican cousins. You can hear it in the beat, and you can taste it in the chew. Some of the ingredients are shared, including mangoes, ginger, and chiles, but it seems that Latino cooking still reflects part of its Old World roots in Spain and Portugal.

Some of the world's great traditional cuisines are joined at the hip with their music, and Latino food is no exception. In fact, Latinos use musical and food terms interchangeably. You either cook with or dance to a salsa, preferably during the same meal. Here is robust food with hot, steaming music. This is one of the chapters that could use a play list as well as an ingredient list.

THE **LATIN AMERICAN** & **CARIBBEAN** PANTRY

CITRUS: Lemons, limes, oranges, grapefruit.

FRUIT: Mangoes, pineapples, bananas. *Special ingredients:* Banana leaves, coconut, tamarind, tomatillos.

VEGETABLES: Avocados, garlic, red onion, sweet onion (Vidalia or Maui), green onions, fresh ginger, red, green and yellow bell peppers, jicama, tomatoes.

FRESH HERBS: Cilantro, flat-leaf parsley, oregano, mint, marjoram or oregano, thyme.

CHILES (FRESH AND DRIED): Jalapeños, serranos, dried bird chiles, red pepper flakes, chipotles (canned in adobe sauce and dried), Scotch bonnets, fresh and dried habaneros, ancho chile powder.

SPICES: Allspice, bay leaves, black and white whole peppercorns, cinnamon, cloves, coriander seeds, cumin, ground ginger, nutmeg, dried oregano, sweet paprika, coarse-grain salt. *Special ingredient:* Annatto seeds.

OILS, VINEGARS, AND CONDIMENTS: Avocado oil, canola oil, extra virgin olive oil, peanut oil, safflower oil; cider vinegar, malt vinegar, red and white wine vinegar, sherry vinegar; Dijon-style mustard, soy sauce, Jamaican hot pepper sauce or Tabasco, vanilla extract. *Special ingredients:* Hot pepper sauce, sofrito.

SWEETENERS: Light and dark brown sugar, honey, molasses. *Special ingredient:* Tropical jams.

WINES AND LIQUORS: Dry white wine, Madeira, tequila. *Special ingredient:* Dark rum.

DRIED, CANNED, OR BOTTLED INGREDIENTS: Canned tomatoes, unsweetened coconut flakes, canned coconut milk, Coco Lopez cream of coconut, ginger beer, pineapple juice.

SPECIAL INGREDIENTS

ANNATTO SEEDS: The coloring agent of Cheddar cheese, annatto seeds, also called achiote seeds, are used in the Caribbean as a bright yellow-orange substitute for saffron, to color cooking oils and rice. Add chile peppers for some heat. Achiote paste, also referred to as *recado rojo,* uses ground annatto seeds as its base along with cumin, allspice, black pepper, and coriander with either vinegar or orange juice added to form the paste.

BANANA LEAVES: One of the inedible ingredients in the cookbook, banana leaves are used as a steaming vessel and to impart flavor in Latin, Caribbean, and Asian cooking. Banana leaves are prefrozen and available in Latin American and Asian grocery stores.

continued on page 170

SPECIAL INGREDIENTS, CONTINUED

COCONUT: The trademark of the tropics, coconut has a familiar brown appearance that represents the mature, dry stage, when the flavor goes into the white meat on the inside of the shell and makes it sweeter.

DARK RUM (preferably Myers's): This is used in several recipes as a sweetener with its own distinct flavor. Light Puerto Rican rums just don't pack enough punch.

HOT PEPPER SAUCES: The Arawaks traditionally used fresh peppers (chiles), which evolved into hot pepper sauces of all kinds throughout the Caribbean. The sauces are generally based on the Scotch bonnet and bird peppers, as with jerk seasoning. The sauces can be fruitier than Tabasco or cayenne-based sauces in the United States. (See the recipes for making your own hot sauces on pages 186, 187, and 188.)

SOFRITO: In Puerto Rico, sofrito is a condiment type of sauce used much like Creole sauce, but it is varied with coriander (cilantro) and other seasonings, to which salt pork and ham are traditionally added to make a full dish. See page 173 for making your own.

TAMARIND: Tamarind is actually a legume whose pulp is used to make tamarind nectar, a fruit-drink concentrate that makes a refreshing, tart beverage and is the principal ingredient in Worcestershire sauce.

TOMATILLOS: Tomatillos look like small green tomatoes wrapped in a parchment-like husk. They're tart and are used in Latin cooking and salsas. Store fresh ones in the refrigerator for up to 1 month. You can also substitute green tomatoes with 1 tablespoon of lime juice.

TROPICAL FRUIT JAMS, PULPS, OR PURÉES: Dried passion-fruit, mango, pineapple, papaya, tamarind, and guava pulps come in 14- to 16-ounce slabs; they are found in Latin grocery stores and make a great foundation for glazes. Their sweet counterparts can be found in jams and preserves.

YUCATECAN-STYLE BRINE MAKES 5 QUARTS

This is a good foundation brine for any of the recipes in this chapter. It gives the dish a savory infusion of citrus and spicing that are the signatures of Yucatecan cuisine. The orange can be replaced with lime.

Julienned zest and juice of 3 oranges (about 1 cup)
5 quarts water
1 cup kosher salt
¾ cup firmly packed light brown sugar
5 cloves garlic, minced or pressed
⅔ cup Yucatecan Citrus Recado (page 182)

Combine the orange zest and juice in a small nonreactive saucepan. Bring to a boil and decrease the heat. Simmer for about 30 minutes, until reduced to ½ cup. The zest should sink to the bottom. Bring 1 quart of the water to a boil in a 6-quart saucepan and add the orange reduction, salt, sugar, garlic, and Yucatecan Citrus Recado. Decrease the heat and simmer for 30 minutes to brew the ingredients. Remove from the heat, add the remaining 4 quarts water, let the mixture cool to room temperature, and then refrigerate to 40°F.

TIMETABLE:
Shrimp: 1 to 2 hours

Chicken breasts or kabobs, quail, pork tenderloin, pork chops, or pork kabobs: 6 to 8 hours

Turkey breast, baby back ribs, or spareribs: 8 to 12 hours

LIME-CHILE VINEGAR MAKES 1 QUART

You can use the Lime Chile Vinegar and the Orange Chipotle Vinegar to brighten glazes and caramels as well as to amplify the flavor of marinades.

1 quart white wine vinegar
Julienned zest of 4 limes, white pith removed
8 to 10 serrano chiles, or 2 to 4 habanero chiles
8 to 10 sprigs cilantro

Sterilize 2 pint or 4 half-pint glass jars. Bring the vinegar to a gentle simmer in a nonreactive pot. Add the lime zest and chiles. Gently simmer over low heat for 8 to 10 minutes. Cool to room temperature and strain, or leave the chiles in for a more volcanic vinegar. Pour into the sterilized glass jars. Add the sprigs of cilantro for garnish and cover. Stored in a cool dark place, the vinegar will hold its strength for 3 to 4 months.

ORANGE-CHIPOTLE VINEGAR. Replace the lime zest with the julienned zest of 2 large juice oranges, white pith removed. Replace the serrano chiles with 3 or 4 dried chipotle chiles.

ORANGE-CHIPOTLE OIL MAKES 2 CUPS

Orange zest and dried chipotle chiles infuse this oil with a smoky citrus flavor that enlivens Mexican and Southwestern-style marinades. The dried orange zest gives the oil a savory intensity, but you can use fresh zest in a pinch. You'll also find that the oil is perfect for Yucatecan-style recipes or simply for drizzling onto plates.

3 or 4 dried chipotle chiles
3 tablespoons dried orange zest (see page 66 for drying zest)
2 cups canola oil

In a spice mill, grind together the chiles and orange zest. Combine the chipotle-orange mix with the canola oil in a clean glass jar and infuse for 2 to 3 days, shaking the jar occasionally. Filter the oil through a paper coffee filter into a clean glass jar. Store in the refrigerator for up to 6 months.

LIME-HABANERO OIL. Replace the dried chipotle chiles with dried habanero chiles, and the dried orange zest with dried lime zest. Use sparingly, or you may have to apply for a license to handle dangerous materials. This oil is hot!

ANNATTO OIL MAKES ½ CUP

Once you've made Annatto Oil, you'll immediately recognize that mystery spice you've always tasted in Latin food.

½ cup peanut oil
1 tablespoon annatto (achiote) seeds

In a small skillet, heat the oil on high until a smoky haze appears. Remove from the heat and add the seeds. Let the seeds steep until the oil cools to room temperature, 2 to 3 hours. Strain the oil through a fine-mesh sieve and discard the seeds. Store in the refrigerator for up to 2 weeks.

SOFRITO MARINADE MAKES 2½ CUPS

Sofrito is the spicy tomato base for many Puerto Rican and Latin recipes. Its sweet spices really develop from a nice slow simmer. As is, it's great for saucing grilled pork or beef tenderloin. With the addition of lime juice, you can have a sizzling marinade for baked pork chops in winter or a Caribbean mixed grill in summer. You can substitute canola oil for the salt pork, and slab bacon or pancetta for the smoked ham.

2 to 3 tablespoons diced salt pork or canola oil
¼ pound smoked ham, diced
½ cup chopped onion
1 tablespoon seeded and diced fresh jalapeño chile
2 cloves garlic, chopped
1 tablespoon Annatto Oil (page 172)
½ teaspoon ground cinnamon
¼ teaspoon ground ginger
¼ teaspoon ground cloves
¼ teaspoon ground cumin
½ teaspoon ground coriander seeds
1 (12-ounce) can tomatoes
Grated zest and juice of 3 or 4 limes (about ½ cup) (for marinade)
¼ cup chopped fresh cilantro leaves (for marinade)

In a large nonreactive saucepan, render the salt pork, then remove the salt pork and discard. Add the smoked ham, onion, jalapeño, garlic, and Annatto Oil, and sauté over high heat until the onion starts to brown and the ham becomes crisp, 5 to 6 minutes. Add the cinnamon, ginger, cloves, cumin, and coriander seeds. Cook for about 3 minutes more, stirring and scraping the pan well. Decrease the heat, add the tomatoes, and simmer, partially covered, for about 1 hour. Remove from the heat and cool. At this point, you have the basic recipe for sofrito.

To use as a marinade, stir in the fresh lime zest and juice and cilantro. Stored in a clean, airtight jar, it will keep in the refrigerator for 3 days. It freezes well with food for up to 3 months.

TIMETABLE:
Chicken breasts:
4 to 6 hours

Lamb kabobs, pork tenderloin, pork kabobs, or pork chops: 6 to 8 hours

Spareribs, baby back ribs, or pork shoulder: 8 to 12 hours

TIMETABLE:
Chicken breasts or
kabobs: 4 to 6 hours

PIRI-PIRI MARINADE MAKES ¾ CUP

One of the dilemmas with piri-piri sauce is deciding which side of the South Atlantic it belongs to. The recipe shows up in Brazil and along the west coast of Africa, for which you have the Portuguese to thank. When the Portugese settled Brazil, they took chile peppers from South America back to their other African colonies, which are now Angola, Mozambique, and Zimbabwe. The chiles took root and were used to make a hot sauce that eventually found its way back to tabletops in Portugal. Piri-piri is actually the name of a pepper and not the sauce itself. The sauce begins on a sour note and builds in intensity around the chiles. It's especially good as a grilled chicken marinade.

Grated zest and juice of 2 limes (about ¼ cup)
2 tablespoons cider vinegar
½ teaspoon sweet paprika
2 dried chile de Arbol, seeded, or 2 teaspoons of
    cayenne pepper (or to taste)
2 serrano chiles, seeded, stemmed, and diced
2 cloves garlic, minced
¼ cup extra virgin olive oil

Combine the lime zest and juice, vinegar, paprika, dried chiles, serranos, and garlic in a blender or a food processor and process until all the ingredients are blended. While the motor is running, drizzle in the oil a little at a time. Stored in a clean, airtight container, this will keep in the refrigerator for 1 week.

TIMETABLE:
Chicken breasts, chicken
kabobs, pork chops,
or pork tenderloin:
3 to 4 hours

Beef tenderloin or
kid (goat) tenderloin:
3 to 4 hours

Chicken wings, baby
back ribs, or spareribs:
6 to 8 hours

ORANGE-CHIPOTLE MARINADE MAKES 2 CUPS

This marinade builds on one of my favorite culinary combinations—the sweet burst of citrus against the heat of smoky chipotle chiles (which are jalapeños that are smoked and dried). You can substitute seeded jalapeños or serrano chiles, but it won't have that same smoky flavor. The smoky flavor of chipotle also adapts well to barbecued ribs, and the slow-cooked onions caramelize nicely and give the ribs a hint of sweetness. This marinade has the consistency of a loose paste, and a little goes a long way.

⅔ cup chopped white onion

4 to 6 cloves garlic, chopped

2 canned chipotle chiles

Grated zest and juice of 2 or 3 juice oranges (about ¾ cup)

Grated zest and juice of 2 or 3 limes (about ⅓ cup)

½ cup white wine vinegar

2 teaspoons oregano (preferably Mexican)

2 teaspoons ground cumin

2 tablespoons coarsely cracked black peppercorns

1 teaspoon coarse-grain salt

⅓ cup Orange-Chipotle Oil (page 172) or extra virgin olive oil

Combine the onion, garlic, chipotles, orange zest and juice, lime zest and juice, vinegar, oregano, cumin, peppercorns, and salt in a blender or a food processor and purée until all the ingredients are blended. While the motor is running, drizzle in the oil a little at a time. Stored in a clean, airtight container, this will keep in the refrigerator for 1 week.

CHIPOTLE CHATTER

I've seen recipes calling for liquid smoke, but I would rather have the aromatic spicy smoke of chipotle. Chipotles are smoked ripe red jalapeños that are produced mostly in Mexico. They are the closest thing you can get to smoke as an ingredient. If you want to smoke your own, you'll need about 5 pounds of red jalapeños (the red variety are a bit less vegetal tasting than the green), and about 3 days around the smoker. This is both a drying and a smoking process. The 3 days will be enough to stop people in their tracks, except for a hardened chile-head with time and a palate to burn. It's easier to buy chipotles online, or in Latin American grocery stores.

If you want to smoke your own, you can take some shortcuts. I got this idea from the folks at www.fieryfoods.com. Dave de Witt suggests slicing them in half and seeding them, and then drying them in a gas oven (with the pilot light on) or in a dehydrator. They should have a licorice texture when they're finished. Next, they head into the smoker for 3 hours at 120°F.

I tried Dave's technique, and I also experimented with a second batch by reversing the process—that is, smoking first and drying later. I kept the chiles, along with a batch of red and yellow bell peppers I was using for another recipe, in the smoker for 7 to 8 hours over oak wood. The chipotles seemed to have a better intensity of smoke flavor as they absorbed the smoke, and then the drying concentrated it even more. You can also take this same technique and use it to smoke poblanos (mild), serranos (slightly hotter), and habaneros (wipe-that-smile-off-your-face hot!).

TIMETABLE:

Pork tenderloin or pork
kabobs: 4 to 6 hours

Pork chops, baby back ribs,
or spareribs: 6 to 8 hours

Pork shoulder: 8 to 12 hours

TIP: Seville oranges are not
the easiest to find. Here's a
workable substitute based
on a recipe from Diana
Kennedy's *The Cuisines
of Mexico.* Combine
1 tablespoon grated
grapefruit zest, ½ cup fresh
orange juice or juice from
1 to 2 juice oranges, ½ cup
fresh grapefruit juice, and
¼ cup fresh lemon juice in
a nonreactive mixing bowl
to make 1¼ cups.

BITTER ORANGE MARINADE MAKES 1½ CUPS

This Cuban-style marinade puts its sizzling flavor signature on grilled pork by
counterbalancing the smoky grill with a burst of citrus. The allure of the flavor
comes from the sourness of the bitter orange, which really doesn't taste like
orange at all. Bitter, or Seville, oranges can sometimes be found stateside in
Spanish markets during the winter.

1 cup bitter or Seville orange juice (see Tip)
1 teaspoon ground cumin
2 teaspoons dried Mexican oregano
3 or 4 cloves garlic, minced or pressed
¼ cup finely diced white onion
½ cup Orange-Chipotle Oil (page 172) or canola oil

Combine the orange juice, cumin, oregano, garlic, and onion in a food
processor or a blender and process until all the ingredients are blended.
While the motor is running, drizzle in the oil a little at a time. Stored in a
clean, airtight container, this will keep in the refrigerator for 1 week.

TIMETABLE:

Swordfish steaks:
2 to 3 hours

Chicken breasts or kabobs,
pork tenderloin, or pork
kabobs: 4 to 6 hours

TIP: To peel the tomatoes,
cut a very shallow X on
the bottom of the tomato.
Place a pot of water on the
stove and bring to a boil.
Drop the tomatoes into the
boiling water and remove
after 30 seconds, or when
the skin begins to peel. Run
the tomatoes under cold
water to peel the skins.

SPICY TOMATO MARINADE MAKES 2½ CUPS

When the bounty of summer-ripened tomatoes hits the produce stands
in August, this salsa-style marinade is at its prime. You can alternate or
combine colors and flavors with the slightly tart yellow tomatoes and the
sweet vine-ripened red. Marinate swordfish or tuna steaks, and gently warm
the remaining marinade for a sauce.

Grated zest and juice of 3 limes (about ⅓ cup)
½ cup extra virgin olive oil
4 firm, ripe yellow or red tomatoes, peeled, seeded, and diced
½ cup finely diced white onion
4 or 5 cloves garlic, minced
½ cup chopped cilantro
3 serrano chiles, stemmed, seeded, and deveined
1 tablespoon dark brown sugar
1 tablespoon freshly cracked black peppercorns
1 teaspoon coarse-grain salt

In a food processor, combine the lime zest and juice and the oil and process for 30 seconds to emulsify. Add the tomatoes, onion, garlic, cilantro, serranos, sugar, peppercorns, and salt and pulse to a fine texture. Do not overprocess, because the marinade should have some texture. Stored in a clean, airtight container, this will keep in the refrigerator for 3 days.

TOMATILLO RECADO MAKES 2 TO 2½ CUPS

With tart tomatillos, cilantro, and lime, backed up with a little heat from some jalapeño, this marinade is thick and actually becomes part of a sauce. My favorite way of playing with this recipe is to use it with seafood packets in parchment or banana leaves for added flavor. Tomatillos are available in Hispanic grocery stores, as well as some supermarkets and green grocers.

1 pound fresh tomatillos, outer husks removed
1 tablespoon seeded and diced fresh jalapeño chile
3 or 4 cloves garlic, minced or pressed
⅓ cup chopped fresh cilantro
Grated zest and juice of 2 limes (about ¼ cup)
¼ cup dry white wine
1 teaspoon sugar
1 teaspoon coarse-grain salt
1 tablespoon cracked black peppercorns
½ cup light olive oil
¼ cup avocado oil

Coarsely chop the tomatillos, jalapeño, garlic, and cilantro in a food processor. Remove the chopped tomatillo mixture and reserve in a nonreactive bowl. Add to the food processor the lime zest and juice, wine, sugar, salt, and peppercorns and process until all the ingredients are blended. While the motor is running, drizzle in the oils a little at a time. Pour the mixture into the chopped tomatillo, mix, and let stand at room temperature for 1 hour to let the flavors meld. Refrigerate the recado until ready to use. Stored in a clean, airtight container, this will keep in the refrigerator for 1 week.

TIMETABLE:
Tuna steaks, swordfish steaks, red snapper, catfish, sea bass, halibut, scallops, or shrimp:
2 to 3 hours

TIMETABLE:

Salmon steaks or fillets, swordfish steaks, red snapper, catfish, sea bass, halibut, scallops, or shrimp: 1 to 2 hours

CILANTRO-AVOCADO MARINADE MAKES 1 CUP

I originally used this marinade with the Crab Seviche with Jicama and Avocado (page 193), but this has become my quick and easy Island marinade for seafood.

Grated zest and juice of 4 limes (about ½ cup)
¼ cup chopped fresh cilantro
1 tablespoon, seeded, stemmed, deveined, and diced serrano chile
2 cloves garlic, minced or pressed
⅓ cup avocado oil
2 tablespoons extra virgin olive oil

Combine the lime zest and juice, cilantro, serrano, and garlic in a blender or a food processor and process until all the ingredients are blended. While the motor is running, drizzle in the oils a little at a time. Stored in a clean, airtight container, this will keep in the refrigerator for 1 week.

TIMETABLE:

Beef filets, rib eye, veal rib eye, veal chops, veal loin, veal paillards, lamb rack, or lamb rib chops: 3 to 4 hours

TIP: *Cacho de cabra,* sometimes called *merquen,* looks like a long, shiny red chipotle. They show up in Spanish markets as *aji,* which is the generic word for chile in South America.

CHILEAN-STYLE MARINADE MAKES ABOUT 2 CUPS

South American marinades may look typical at a glance, but they are anything but. This marinade seems to have a spray of flavors, but they settle around red meat nicely. Try this with single lamb chops or beef medallions.

8 to 10 cloves garlic, chopped
¾ cup red wine vinegar
1 teaspoon fresh thyme
1 teaspoon fresh marjoram or oregano
¼ cup honey
½ teaspoon *aji* or *cacho de cabra* powder (see Tip)
**   or ¼ teaspoon cayenne**
1 teaspoon coarse-grain or sea salt
1 tablespoon freshly cracked black peppercorns
½ cup extra virgin olive oil

Combine the garlic and vinegar in a blender and process until all the ingredients are blended. This will "juice" the garlic. Stop the motor, and then add the thyme, marjoram, honey, *aji* powder, salt, and pepper. Process until all the ingredients are blended. While the motor is running, drizzle in the oil a little at a time. Stored in a clean, airtight container, this will keep in the refrigerator for 1 week.

SCOTCH BONNET

When it comes to cooking with chiles, the words *Scotch bonnet* can humble even the most flame-resistant palate. Yet Scotch bonnets are one of the flavor thumbprints in Caribbean cuisine. This is not heat for the sake of heat; my attitude is strictly flavor over flame. If you could isolate and kick out the capsicum in these heat-seeking missiles, you'd swear you were eating a tropical fruit.

Scotch bonnet chiles and habaneros, contrary to popular belief, are not the same. These small, brightly colored, pumpkin-shaped chiles look alike, and they can even be used interchangeably in some recipes. Scotch bonnet can be a bit fruitier, with a light smoky flavor, while habanero can be hotter and have a bit more vegetable flavor with its fruit. How hot is hot? Well, if you're one of those chile-heads that uses a Scoville heat scale rating as a flaming red badge of courage, this chile can clock in between 150,000 to 325,000 units, as compared to a jalapeño at about 2,500 to 8,000 units or a serrano at 8,000 to 22,000 units.

In the late 1980s, Scotch bonnets were flown in from Jamaica. Nowadays, there are many domestic hybrids and less incendiary versions hitting the markets as habaneros. Some of these are milder and can lack both heat and flavor. The best way to test is to take a small taste. You should taste some fruit and a whole lot of heat. If you have a good batch, a good antidote for your taste test is dairy—milk, sour cream, yogurt, or even ice cream. Water just spreads it around in your mouth, and beer and wine will magnify it. You need to coat your mouth, not fuel it.

The seeds, tip, and ribs tend to be the hottest parts of these chiles. Discard them and cook without them (I don't think you'll need the extra heat); the recipes in this chapter will taste just as good. One more thing: when using this chile, wash every surface that it comes into contact with, especially your hands. Its heat is the gift that keeps on giving.

When shopping for Scotch bonnets, go for firm, brightly colored red and orange ones. It could have been just the batch I tried, but the green ones seem to be milder and more vegetal tasting, possibly because these chiles start out green and ripen to yellow, orange, or red. If you have any doubts about the availability, source, or quality of these chiles, some of the Caribbean bottled hot sauces make great substitutes. My personal favorites are the thick, fruit-based sauces that are like yellow ketchup. They're cut with either mango or papaya, with some mustard, spices, and vinegar thrown in. One or 2 tablespoons should be a good substitute, but taste before you add that second one.

Chicken breasts:
3 to 4 hours

Beef tenderloin, pork
chops, or pork
tenderloin: 4 to 6 hours

Chicken wings, baby
back ribs, or spareribs:
6 to 8 hours

HABANERO-RUM MARINADE MAKES 1³⁄₄ CUPS

On the first pass, the tropical flavors of sweet rum and zesty lime roll off the
marinade. Then the Scotch bonnet pepper throws a hot, tangy gale wind into
the recipe. You can substitute jalapeño or serrano chiles in the recipe for a
cooler and milder breeze. The marinade provides a nice glaze for basting
chicken wings or spareribs.

**1 Scotch bonnet or habanero chile, or 1 tablespoon diced jalapeño
    or serrano chile, seeded, stemmed, and deveined
³⁄₄ cup dark rum (preferably Myers's)
Grated zest and juice of 2 limes (about ¼ cup)
¼ cup chopped fresh cilantro
3 cloves garlic, chopped
1 teaspoon coarse-grain or sea salt
1 tablespoon cracked black peppercorns
¼ cup Asian or domestic cold-pressed peanut oil**

Combine the chile, rum, lime zest and juice, cilantro, garlic, salt, and pepper
in a food processor or a blender and process until all the ingredients are
blended. While the motor is running, drizzle in the peanut oil a little at a time.
The marinade will keep in a clean, airtight container for about 1 week in the
refrigerator, and it freezes well with food.

HOT CHILE-RUM BASTE. Combine the chile and rum in a nonreactive
saucepan. Simmer for about 30 minutes to burn off the alcohol. Cool to room
temperature and add the remaining ingredients, but omit the oil.

Shrimp or salmon fillets:
2 to 4 hours

Chicken breasts, Cornish
hen, or quail: 4 to 6 hours

Pork tenderloin, pork
chops, or pork kabobs:
6 to 8 hours

Baby back ribs or
spareribs: 8 to 12 hours

YELLOW HELL MARINADE MAKES 2¹⁄₂ CUPS

This recipe flirts with the palate with the initial sweetness of mango and
coconut; then the ginger, coriander, and cumin kick in like a steel band. My
friends call this mango marinade "Yellow Hell," but they also call for seconds.
The marinade can be used as a dipping sauce for grilled shrimp.

2 mangoes, peeled, seeded, and chopped (1½ to 2 cups)
1 Scotch bonnet or habanero chile, or 2 tablespoons seeded,
    stemmed, deveined, and diced jalapeño or serrano chile
1 tablespoon dark rum (preferably Myers's)
1 teaspoon Jamaican hot sauce or any of the hot sauces on
    pages 186 to 188
2 cloves garlic, chopped
1 tablespoon chopped fresh ginger
¼ cup dry unsweetened coconut flakes
1 teaspoon ground coriander
½ teaspoon ground cumin
½ cup canned coconut milk
Grated zest and juice of 2 limes (about ¼ cup)
2 tablespoons chopped fresh cilantro

Combine the mango, chile, rum, and hot sauce in a blender or a food processor and process until all the ingredients are blended. Add the mango purée, garlic, ginger, coconut, coriander, and cumin to a heavy nonreactive saucepan and bring to a boil. Decrease the heat and simmer for about 20 minutes. Remove from the heat and cool to room temperature. Stir in the coconut milk, lime zest and juice, and cilantro. Refrigerate until ready to use. Stored in a clean, airtight jar, it will keep in the refrigerator for 1 week. It freezes well with food for up to 3 months.

ORANGE-CHIPOTLE POWDER MAKES 2 TABLESPOONS

I could have included 2 tablespoons of Orange Chipotle Powder in nearly every recipe in this chapter: it's that versatile. You can use this powder as a stand-alone rub or dust on serving plates for an added flavor note. This recipe can be easily scaled up.

1 dried chipotle chile
Dried zest of 3 or 4 juice oranges (see page 66 for drying citrus peel)

Combine the chipotle and dried zest in a spice grinder or a blender and grind to a fine powder. The rub can be stored in a clean, airtight container in the freezer for up to 4 months.

RECADOS

· ·

In Mexican cuisine, recados are marinating pestos on overdrive. While American chefs may use rows of ramekins of fresh herbs and spices for their *mise en place,* to prepare their dishes, Mexican chefs use a series of recados to finish their cocina art. Recados can be a combination of marinades and rubs bound by fresh herbs and aromatics like onions or garlic. They run the gamut of dried chile rubs to savory wet pastes. The ingredients that you'll be using are found in salsas and even in Yucatecan green moles (with some ground pumpkin seeds and almonds).

TIMETABLE:
Salmon, swordfish, scallops, or shrimp: 2 to 3 hours

Chicken breasts or kabobs, pork tenderloin, pork chops, or pork kabobs: 3 to 4 hours

YUCATECAN CITRUS RECADO MAKES 1½ CUPS
· ·

The seasoning style of the Yucatán Peninsula mixes tangy citrus with piquant spices. This recado will work with chicken breasts, tuna, swordfish, grouper, and shrimp. It can also act as a base for seafood seviche for shrimp, bay scallops, or any firm-flesh fish.

Grated zest and juice of 2 juice oranges (about ⅔ cup)
Grated zest and juice of 2 limes (about ¼ cup)
Grated zest and juice of 2 lemons (about ⅓ cup)
**2 tablespoons Orange-Chipotle Powder (page 181), or freshly
    grated zest of 1 juice orange and 1 teaspoon chile powder**
1 teaspoon dried oregano (preferably Mexican)
3 cloves garlic, chopped
**1 tablespoon seeded, stemmed, deveined, and finely
    diced jalapeño chile**
¼ cup chopped fresh cilantro
1 teaspoon coarse-grain salt
1 tablespoon cracked black peppercorns
¼ cup avocado or safflower oil

Combine the orange, lime, and lemon zests and juices; chipotle powder; oregano; garlic; jalapeño; cilantro; salt; and pepper in a blender or a food processor and process until all the ingredients are blended. While the motor is running, drizzle in the oil a little at a time. Stored in a clean, airtight container, this will keep in the refrigerator for 1 week.

YUCATECAN ACHIOTE RECADO MAKES 1½ CUPS
. . . .

This is a wetter and less incendiary version of the Achiote Chipotle Rub (page 184), with a push to the citrus side of the Yucatán. Keep your marinating time on the low side because the recado has a fair amount of acid.

4 ounces (about ½ cup), or 1 (3.5-ounce) pack, achiote paste
   (available at Hispanic food stores)
5 cloves garlic, minced or pressed
½ cup apple cider vinegar
Grated zest and juice of 2 oranges (about ⅔ cup)
Grated zest and juice of 2 limes (about ¼ cup)
3 bay leaves, crushed
½ teaspoon dried oregano (preferably Mexican)
1 teaspoon cumin seeds, toasted and ground
2 teaspoons dark brown sugar
1 tablespoon ground cinnamon
1 tablespoon freshly cracked black peppercorns
2 teaspoons coarse-grain salt

In a blender or a food processor, process the achiote paste, garlic, vinegar, orange zest and juice, lime zest and juice, bay leaves, oregano, cumin, brown sugar, cinnamon, pepper, and salt until smooth. Let the marinade stand for several hours or up to 12 hours to let its flavors develop. Stored in a clean, airtight container, this will keep in the refrigerator for 1 week.

TIMETABLE:
Fish fillets: 1 to 2 hours

Shrimp or chicken
breasts: 2 to 3 hours

Pork chops: 3 to 4 hours

Lamb kabobs: 4 to 6 hours

MADEIRA-CHILE RECADO MAKES 1 CUP
. . . .

This rub is an improvisation on a traditional recado. Think of it as an edible Latin jazz number that just doesn't let up on flavor. The Madeira and orange add a sweet-and-sour taste to the spicy kick of the Orange-Chile Powder Rub. You can use this on eye rounds for indirect cooking in a covered grill, as well as on a roast for a Sunday night dinner in winter.

¼ cup Madeira
2 tablespoons low-sodium soy sauce
1 tablespoon Worcestershire sauce
¼ cup Orange–Chile Powder Rub (page 142)
1½ tablespoons grated orange zest
4 or 5 cloves garlic, minced

Combine the Madeira, soy sauce, Worcestershire sauce, rub, orange zest, and garlic in a blender or a food processor. Process until smooth. This recado will keep in a clean, airtight container for up to 1 week in the refrigerator.

TIMETABLE:
Shrimp: 2 to 3 hours

Chicken breasts or
kabobs: 2 to 4 hours

Beef brisket, prime rib, rib roasts, beef filets, rib eye, veal loin, veal paillards, lamb kabobs, or buffalo steaks: 6 to 8 hours

TIP: Be sure to use
tamarind pulp, not the
seedless concentrate. It is
found in Asian and Spanish
grocery stores.

TAMARIND RECADO MAKES 1 CUP

What's nice about this low-acid paste is that the longer it sits on chicken
or lamb, the better the flavor. Chef Lou Sackett, formerly of Zocalo in West
Philadelphia, has isolated two basic building blocks in Mexican cuisine: sour
tamarind and smoky chipotle chile, softened by just the right amount of
honey.

1 (12-ounce) package soft tamarind pulp (see Tip)
4 cups boiling water
4 dried chipotle chiles
½ white onion, chopped
2 cloves garlic, chopped
2 tablespoons honey
2 teaspoons coarse-grain salt

Place the tamarind pulp in a small nonreactive bowl and pour 3 cups of the
boiling water over the pulp. Let stand for 20 minutes, stirring occasionally.
Add more boiling water if the mixture is too stiff to remove the seeds. Push
the tamarind mixture through a sieve, extracting and discarding the seeds
but reserving the pulp.

Place the chipotles in a small bowl and pour the remaining 1 cup boiling
water over the chiles. Let stand for 20 minutes, or until the chiles are
softened.

Place the tamarind pulp, chiles, onion, garlic, honey, and salt in a blender or
a food processor and blend to a smooth paste. Stored in a clean, airtight
container, this will keep in the refrigerator for 1 week.

ACHIOTE-CHIPOTLE RUB MAKES ½ CUP

Not just another fiery barbecue rub, Achiote Chipotle Rub uses tangy
dried chipotles to give a smoky outdoor taste to chicken, ribs, and even
hamburger. The heat of the chile is tempered with cinnamon and orange-
cumin dust, while the aromatic achiote seeds give the rub its Latin soul.

2 tablespoons achiote (annatto) seeds (see Tip)
2 (2- to 3-inch) sticks cinnamon
2 dried chipotle chiles
2 tablespoons Orange-Cumin Powder (page 66), or 1½ teaspoons
    dried orange zest and 1½ teaspoons ground cumin
2 teaspoons coarse-grain salt
2 tablespoons cracked black peppercorns

Combine the achiote seeds, cinnamon sticks, chipotle, Orange-Cumin Powder, salt, and peppercorns in a spice grinder or a blender and process until ground. The rub can be stored in a clean, airtight container in the freezer for up to 4 months.

TIP: Achiote seeds are available where Hispanic foods are sold.

CHIMICHURRI PESTO MAKES ABOUT 2 CUPS

I first had chimichurri at a Spanish farmers' market called El Mercado in North Philadelphia. "Use it on scrambled eggs," the woman at the vegetable stall suggested. Use it I did, and talk about a wake-up call. It's a Latin pesto with a hot salsa kick! The grilling possibilities are endless. The following recipe pushes the garlic envelope over the top, but you can always scale back the clove count.

And for you chile heads: if you've been eying the jalapeño ingredient line and wondering what if, and that "if" happens to be substituting chipotle or habanero, then go for it—the Scoville scale is the limit!

1 small head garlic (8 to 10 cloves), peeled and chopped
3 bay leaves, crumbled
3 jalapeño chiles, seeded and coarsely chopped
    (or keep the seeds for added heat)
1½ tablespoons salt
1 tablespoon ancho chile powder
½ cup chopped fresh cilantro
¾ cup chopped fresh flat-leaf parsley
¼ cup chopped fresh oregano leaves
4 tablespoons distilled white vinegar
⅓ cup olive oil

Combine the garlic, bay leaves, jalapeños, salt, ancho powder, cilantro, parsley, oregano, and 1 tablespoon of the vinegar in a blender or a food processor and process until a paste is formed. While the motor is running, drizzle in the remaining 3 tablespoons vinegar and the oil a little at a time. Stored in a clean, airtight jar, it will keep in the refrigerator for 1 week.

TIMETABLE:
Red snapper, catfish, sea bass, halibut, or swordfish steaks: 2 to 4 hours

Beef filets or rib eye: 3 to 4 hours

Beef short ribs, beef brisket, prime rib, rib roasts, or lamb shoulder or leg: 6 to 8 hours

TIMETABLE:

Shrimp or pork chops:
3 to 4 hours

Chicken breasts, beef
kabobs, or lamb kabobs:
4 to 6 hours

Baby back ribs or
spareribs: 8 to 12 hours

JERK RUB MAKES 1 CUP

Jerk! That one single word blows heated flavor gales across Caribbean cuisine. What it delivers in firepower it matches in flavor. Jerk marinade finds its way onto fish, chicken, and pork chops. This fiery-hot but definitive recipe is from my late friend Dunstan Harris's cookbook, *Island Cooking*. Dunstan and I had collaborated together on a number of dinners for Philadelphia's Book and the Cook events. We paired off our recipes as "fire and ice." Dunstan would light up palates with his Jerk seasoning, and I was the culinary firefighter who would extinguish the flames with my sorbets.

2 tablespoons Jamaican pimento allspice, crushed
¼ teaspoon freshly grated nutmeg
1 teaspoon ground cinnamon
12 green onions, white part only, chopped
6 whole Scotch bonnet chiles, stemmed, or 12 serrano chiles,
    halved with seeds
⅓ cup red wine vinegar
2 tablespoons canola oil
1 tablespoon coarse-grain or sea salt
1 teaspoon cracked black peppercorns
2 tablespoons soy sauce
1 teaspoon Jamaican hot pepper sauce or Tabasco (optional)

Combine the allspice, nutmeg, cinnamon, green onions, Scotch bonnet, vinegar, canola oil, salt, peppercorns, and soy sauce in a blender or food processor, adding the hot pepper sauce to taste. Process to liquefy, 1 to 2 minutes. Pour into a jar and refrigerate for at least 12 hours or more to let the flavors develop. The sauce will keep in a clean, airtight container in the refrigerator for 3 to 4 weeks.

TIMETABLE:

Shrimp, salmon filets,
chicken breasts, spareribs,
baby back ribs, and pork
tenderloins: apply when
serving

YELLOW HELL CARIBBEAN HOT SAUCE

MAKES 2 CUPS

This sauce is my secret ingredient when a recipe calls for generic hot sauce. It has the right amount of sweet heat and tropical fruit flavoring that kicks in like a steel drum no matter how you use it. This is a concentrated version of Yellow Hell Marinade (page 180). I use 1 or 2 tablespoons in lieu of fresh chiles in marinades. For a really great glaze for chicken and shrimp, combine 2 to 3 tablespoons Yellow Hell with 1 cup melted mango jam and ¼ cup malt vinegar.

3 Scotch bonnet or habanero chiles, seeded, stemmed, and diced
¼ cup chopped fresh ginger
2 cloves garlic
1 cup chopped onion
2 cups white vinegar
1¼ cups dark rum
1½ cups puréed fresh mangoes (about 2 fresh mangoes)
2 tablespoons molasses

In a heavy nonreactive pot, add the Scotch bonnet, ginger, garlic, onion, vinegar, and rum. Partially cover the pot, bring to a simmer, and simmer for about 30 minutes, until reduced to ½ cup.

Add the mango purée and molasses. Simmer over low heat for 20 to 30 minutes. Remove the pot from the heat and let cool to room temperature. Place the sauce in a food processor and purée. Strain the sauce through a fine-mesh sieve and store in the refrigerator in a clean, covered container. The sauce will keep for up to 3 months in the refrigerator.

YELLOW HELL MANGO GLAZE. In a saucepan, mix together ¼ cup Yellow Hell Caribbean Hot Sauce, 1 cup mango jam, and ¼ cup malt vinegar. Simmer for about 15 minutes, until the jam is dissolved and the ingredients are mixed together. Cool to room temperature. Stored in a clean, airtight container, this will keep in the refrigerator for 1 month.

RED RUM REVENGE MAKES 1 CUP

This sauce tastes a whole lot better than the name implies. It's sweet, it's smoky, and all you need is a tablespoon or two to add some really great depth to a barbecue sauce or marinade.

1½ cups dark rum
3 dried habanero chiles
1 tablespoon grated orange zest
1½ cups cassis vinegar or raspberry vinegar

In a heavy nonreactive saucepan, add the rum and chiles. Partially cover the saucepan, bring to a simmer and simmer for about 20 minutes, until reduced to ¾ cup. Add the orange zest and vinegar to the pot and simmer for about 30 minutes, until reduced to about 1 cup. Strain the sauce and discard the solids. Cool to room temperature. Stored in a clean, airtight jar, it will keep in the refrigerator indefinitely.

TIMETABLE:
Shrimp, salmon fillets, chicken breasts, spareribs, baby back ribs, or pork tenderloin: baste during the last 5 minutes of cooking

TIMETABLE:
Shrimp, salmon fillets,
chicken breasts, or pork
tenderloins: apply when
serving

THE DREADED RED MENACE HOT SAUCE

MAKES 1½ CUPS

For an author's dinner I was hosting at Philadelphia's Book and the Cook event one year, I wanted to do some red sauce painting to streak through pools of Yellow Hell Marinade for a dish called Mango Shrimp from Hell (page 146). Well, the paint never made it to the shrimp; it tasted so good that we glazed chicken breasts with it instead. People are initially fooled by the sweet raspberry flavor, but this glaze rocks with a fair amount of heat.

3 dried habanero chiles (available at Hispanic groceries and
    from online sources)
Grated zest and juice of 1 juice orange (about ⅓ cup)
1 cup raspberry vinegar
1½ cups fresh or frozen and thawed unsweetened raspberries

TIP: If grilling or roasting meat or poultry, turn and baste with the glaze during the last 10 minutes of cooking. If grilling or roasting seafood, turn and bast with the glaze during the last 5 minutes of cooking.

Combine the chiles, orange zest and juice, and vinegar in a heavy nonreactive pot, and bring to a boil. Cook for about 30 minutes, until the liquid is reduced to ⅓ cup. Strain and discard the solids. Return the liquid to the saucepan. Purée the raspberries in a food processor fitted with a plastic dough blade (a steel blade will crush the seeds and lend a bitter taste to the glaze). Strain the raspberry purée and add it to the saucepan. Simmer the sauce over low heat for 20 minutes. Cool to room temperature. The glaze will keep in the refrigerator in a clean, airtight container for 1 to 2 weeks.

TIMETABLE:
Salmon steaks or fillets,
scallops, shrimp, chicken
breasts or kabobs,
chicken wings, chicken
thighs, chicken legs, quail,
pork tenderloin, pork
chops, baby back ribs, or
spareribs: baste during the
last 5 minutes of cooking

ISLAND CARAMEL MAKES 1 CUP

This is my lacquer base for Caribbean-style glazes. The three ingredients in this recipe can be singled out and made into caramels in their own right. If you want to add some texture and edible confetti to the caramel, add toasted coconut, Candied Jalapeño Licorice (page 73), or dried fruit at the end of the recipe. You can also combine the caramel with 1½ cups puréed mango, pineapple, or papaya.

½ cup fresh-squeezed lime juice
3 tablespoons chopped fresh ginger
1 cup sugar
⅓ cup dark rum (preferably Myers's)
¼ teaspoon coarse-grain or sea salt
1 teaspoon freshly cracked black peppercorns
¼ cup shredded coconut, toasted (optional)
¼ cup Candied Jalapeño Licorice (page 73) (optional)
¼ cup dried papaya, mango, or pineapple, cut into thin strips and
    reconstituted in 1 cup boiling water (see Tip) (optional)

Place the lime juice and ginger in a blender or a food processor and process for about 20 seconds, until blended, then strain out the solids and set aside. Combine the sugar and rum in a 2-quart heavy-bottom saucepan and cook for about 10 minutes, until a medium amber color. Do not stir until all the sugar has dissolved and it begins to color. When the caramel reaches the desired color, remove from the heat and carefully stir in the lime juice and ginger purée, salt, and pepper. Return to the heat until all the caramel is dissolved. Cool to room temperature. Add the coconut, licorice, and papaya. Stored in a clean, airtight jar, it will keep in the refrigerator indefinitely.

SAVORY LIME CARAMEL. Substitute ¼ cup water for the rum and omit the ginger.

TIP: To reconstitute dried fruit, place the dried fruit in a heat-resistant glass container. Pour 1 cup boiling water over the fruit and let it sit until the fruit softens.

COCONUT-CARAMEL GLAZE MAKES ABOUT 1 CUP

The only thing missing from this recipe and its variation are umbrella swizzle sticks. If you should scale up the Island Caramel recipe and freeze it in 1-cup batches, you'll be able to glaze at a moment's notice.

1 cup Island Caramel (page 188)
1 (15-ounce) can Coco Lopez Cream of Coconut
¼ cup shredded coconut, toasted

Combine the caramel and cream of coconut in a 2-quart heavy-bottom saucepan. Simmer over medium heat for about 30 minutes, until reduced by half. Add the coconut to the glaze and stir with a long wooden spoon until fully mixed. Cool the glaze to room temperature and then refrigerate. Stored in a clean, airtight jar, it will keep in the refrigerator indefinitely.

BANANA DAIQUIRI–CARAMEL GLAZE. Replace the cream of coconut with 1½ cups banana purée, omit the coconut, and proceed with the recipe as written above.

TIMETABLE:
Salmon steaks or fillets, scallops, shrimp, chicken breasts or kabobs, chicken wings, chicken thighs, chicken legs, quail, pork tenderloin, pork chops, baby back ribs, or spareribs: baste during the last 5 minutes of cooking

Salmon steaks or fillets, scallops, shrimp, chicken breasts or kabobs, chicken wings, chicken thighs, chicken legs, pork tenderloin, pork kabobs, baby back ribs, or spareribs: baste during the last 5 minutes of cooking

TIP: With passion fruit, wrinkled means ripe. Look for heavily wrinkled fruit about the size of jumbo or extra-large eggs.

PASSION-FRUIT GLAZE MAKES 1½ CUPS

Passion fruit need not be relegated to the dessert side of one's menu. This cumin-scented glaze is perfect for finishing off chicken breasts or salmon. The heat in this recipe can be scaled up or down, depending on the Teflon coating of your taste buds.

12 passion fruit or 1½ cups passion-fruit purée
Grated zest and juice of 3 juice oranges (about 1 cup)
3 tablespoons dark rum or passion-fruit liqueur
2 teaspoons Jamaican hot sauce, Tabasco, or any of the
    hot sauce recipes in this chapter
2 tablespoons molasses
1 teaspoon vanilla extract
2 or 3 cloves garlic, chopped
½ teaspoon ground coriander
¼ teaspoon ground cumin
Grated zest and juice of 2 limes (about ¼ cup)

If using fresh passion fruit, cut the fruit with a serrated knife over a nonreactive saucepan, and scoop out the seeds and pulp. Combine the passion fruit with the orange zest and juice, rum, hot sauce, molasses, and vanilla. Bring to a boil, decrease the heat, and simmer for 30 minutes, until reduced to 1 cup. Strain the mixture, discard the seeds, and cool to room temperature. Combine the passion-fruit mixture, garlic, coriander, cumin, and lime zest and juice in a blender or a food processor and process until all the ingredients are blended. Stored in a clean, airtight jar, it will keep in the refrigerator for 3 weeks. It freezes well with food for up to 3 months.

TIMETABLE:

Salmon steaks or fillets, scallops, shrimp, chicken breasts or kabobs, pork tenderloin, baby back ribs, or spareribs: baste during the last 5 minutes of cooking

BERMUDA GINGER GLAZE MAKES ABOUT 1½ CUPS

Ginger beer is slightly stronger than ginger ale and tastes much more like its name. It's available in West Indian grocery stores and shows up in some urban supermarkets as well. The ginger preserves are not "preserved" ginger but a jam I found at an upscale grocery store in the "British" section. I thought it would come in handy to put into a glaze.

1 cup ginger beer
2 tablespoons butter or margarine
2 tablespoons minced fresh ginger
½ cup ginger preserves or orange marmalade
1 tablespoon soy sauce
1 teaspoon freshly cracked black peppercorns

Combine the ginger beer, butter, fresh ginger, ginger preserves, soy sauce, and peppercorns in a saucepan and simmer until the preserves dissolve. Store in a clean, airtight container and refrigerate until ready to use. The glaze will keep in the refrigerator for 4 weeks.

GUAVA GLAZE MAKES 1½ CUPS

TIMETABLE:
Shrimp, chicken breasts or kabobs, Cornish hen, quail, pork tenderloin, pork chops, baby back ribs, or spareribs: baste during the last 5 minutes of cooking

This is a recipe that is primed for jelly and jam improvisations. The guava jelly can be substituted with the same Goya brand of papaya, mango, pineapple, or passion-fruit jelly for a tropical fixation. Other fruit jams can roll into this recipe, with maybe a touch of jalapeño jelly for a little flavor peak. The pineapple juice can be traded for fresh orange juice and zest, tropical nectars, pineapple-mango juice, or even piña colada mix.

The light brown sugar can be rolled out for molasses or dark rum. You can alter the mustards with some Jamaican-based mango hot sauces or sambals for a heat streak.

We're not finished by a long shot: the ancho chile powder can be kicked up the Scoville stairs with chipotle powder or brought down to earth with cardamom, coriander, or dashes of cumin or anise seed. Did I say a dozen variations? The possibilities are jarring.

1 (10-ounce) jar guava jelly or any of the Goya tropical fruit jams or jellies
⅓ cup unsweetened pineapple juice
2 tablespoons sherry vinegar, or 1 tablespoon cider or red wine vinegar
    and 1 tablespoon dry sherry, port, or Madeira
2 tablespoons light brown sugar
1 tablespoon Dijon-style mustard, or 2 teaspoons dry mustard
1 tablespoon ancho chile powder
2 tablespoons soy sauce
Grated zest and juice of 2 limes (about ¼ cup)

In a heavy nonreactive pot, add the jelly, pineapple juice, vinegar, brown sugar, mustard, chile powder, and soy sauce. Bring to a simmer and simmer for 10 minutes, or until the jelly has dissolved. Remove the glaze from the heat and cool to room temperature. Add the grated lime zest and juice. Store in a clean, airtight container and refrigerate until ready to use. The glaze will keep in the refrigerator for 4 weeks.

TIP: The lime is added at the end to brighten the glaze, but its pucker power will begin to recede after 1 week. When reusing the glaze, brighten it with the juice of 1 lime.

LIME-CILANTRO CURED GRAVLAX SERVES 10 TO 12

This is gravlax with a bandito attitude! Serve this on mini bagels with chipotle cream cheese and Pickled Red Onions (page 211). Brunch will never be the same.

LIME-CILANTRO CURE MAKES 1¼ CUPS

⅓ cup turbinado or light brown sugar
⅓ cup coarse-grain salt
2 tablespoons grated lime zest (from 2 or 3 limes;
    save the whole limes for future use)
1 teaspoon seeded and diced serrano chile (optional)
1 tablespoon ground ancho chile powder
1 teaspoon crushed coriander seeds
½ cup chopped unpeeled fresh ginger
½ cup fresh cilantro, chopped

SALMON

2 (1 pound each) center-cut salmon fillets, including skin
2 tablespoons tequila

To make the cure, combine the sugar, salt, lime zest, serrano, chile powder, coriander, ginger, and cilantro in a nonreactive bowl and reserve. Stored in a clean, airtight jar, it will keep in the refrigerator for 1 week.

To prepare the salmon, rinse the salmon briefly under cold water and pat dry with paper towels. With a pair of tweezers, remove any small bones that run up the center. Lay the salmon fillets on top of one another on a cutting surface, skin facing out, and trim evenly. Lay the salmon skin side down in a large ceramic or glass baking dish.

Sprinkle each fillet with 1 tablespoon of the tequila. Spread the cure evenly on both salmon fillets. Lay the salmon fillets on top of one another, skin facing out. Wrap the salmon in foil, place in a baking dish, and weight it down with a brick or heavy cans. You need to make sure that the weight is evenly distributed. Refrigerate for 2 to 3 days, turning approximately every 12 hours.

To serve, unwrap the salmon and slice it very thin on the diagonal.

SEVICHE

Seviche is derived from the word *escabèche,* which originated in Spain, where it means "pickled." Escabèche followed Spanish explorers and missionaries around the world. Traditionally, the fish fillets are cooked first, then marinated as escabèche, as opposed to being only marinated, as in a seviche.

Citrus arrived in the Americas with the second Columbian voyage in 1493. From there, the plantings followed the Spanish missionaries throughout North and South America. Seviche (pronounced seh-VEE-chay) was created when the Native American cooks of Peru and Ecuador added citrus juices to their preparations of fresh, raw seafood.

A seviche is a marinade on overdrive. As a piece of seafood marinates in a seviche anywhere from a few minutes to a couple of hours, it loses its translucence and firms up. Many people refer to the marinade as "cooking" the fish, but it's not really cooked at all. The cooking analogy comes only from the fact that heat is the most familiar protein-denaturing action, and when you either cook a piece of fish or soak it in citrus juice to make a seviche, it develops a firmer texture. The only real rule to follow in making seviche is that the seafood needs to be sushi-quality fresh.

CRAB SEVICHE WITH JICAMA AND AVOCADO

SERVES 6 AS AN APPETIZER

This first-course salad could easily double as a light main course. Jicama gives the dish its texture. The flavor bounces around the sweet avocado, breezy cilantro, and lime juice, which acts as a seviche on the crabmeat.

1 pound jumbo lump crabmeat, picked over
1 Hass avocado (the larger ones do not have the same flavor),
    peeled and diced into ½-inch pieces
1 cup finely diced jicama
1 cup Cilantro-Avocado Marinade (page 178)
Radicchio leaves, for garnish
Cilantro sprigs, for garnish

Combine the crabmeat, avocado, and jicama in a glass bowl. Pour the marinade over the crab salad, toss gently to combine, cover, and refrigerate for 4 hours.

To serve, line 6 salad plates with the radicchio. Pack the marinated crab salad into coffee cups or ramekins to use as a mold, and invert onto the individual plates. Garnish with cilantro sprigs.

SWORDFISH AND PINEAPPLE SEVICHE

SERVES 6 AS AN APPETIZER

This seviche picks up a little bit of sweetness from the pineapple to complement the sour citrus. For extra credit, there is an added crunch from toasted coconut. The seviche looks good with the carnival-colored confetti of the cilantro and red and yellow bell peppers.

12 ounces swordfish, skin and dark meat removed
1 cup plus 1 tablespoon freshly squeezed lime juice (about 8 limes)
1 small red onion, diced
1 red bell pepper, stemmed, seeded, and finely chopped (about ½ cup)
1 yellow bell pepper, stemmed, seeded, and finely chopped (about ½ cup)
1 cup ½-inch diced fresh pineapple
½ cup pineapple juice
½ cup freshly squeezed orange juice
2 jalapeño chiles, stemmed, seeded, and finely chopped
½ cup fresh cilantro leaves, chopped
¼ cup shredded coconut, toasted
¼ cup extra virgin olive oil
1 teaspoon salt
1 teaspoon freshly ground black pepper
Salad greens, for garnish (optional)

Cut the swordfish into ½-inch squares. In a nonmetallic container, toss the fish with 1 cup of the lime juice. Cover with plastic wrap and refrigerate for 30 minutes. Remove the swordfish from the refrigerator, drain, and discard the lime juice. Transfer the fish to a nonmetallic mixing bowl and add the remaining 1 tablespoon lime juice, onion, bell peppers, pineapple, pineapple juice, orange juice, jalapeños, cilantro, coconut, olive oil, salt, and pepper. Toss well and chill for 2 hours prior to serving.

To serve, remove from the refrigerator, drain well, and discard the marinade. Serve on plated salad greens or in wide martini glasses.

GRAPEFRUIT SCALLOP SEVICHE

SERVES 6 TO 8 AS AN APPETIZER

Although grapefruit juice doesn't pack the same acidity as lemon or lime juice does, it has a distinct flavor even when blended with other citrus.

GRAPEFRUIT SEVICHE MARINADE MAKES 1 CUP

1 tablespoon grated pink grapefruit zest
½ cup freshly squeezed pink grapefruit juice
Grated zest and juice of 2 limes (about ¼ cup)
1 teaspoon dried oregano
1 teaspoon coarse-grain or sea salt
1 tablespoon freshly cracked black peppercorns
Crushed red pepper flakes
¼ cup extra virgin olive oil

SCALLOP SEVICHE

1 pound bay scallops
4 green onions, white part only, trimmed and sliced into ¼-inch rings
¼ cup finely chopped red onion
2 tablespoons fresh cilantro leaves, finely chopped
2 tablespoons fresh flat-leaf parsley, finely chopped
¼ cup diamond-diced red bell pepper
Salad greens, for garnish (optional)

To make the marinade, combine the grapefruit zest and juice, lime zest and juice, oregano, salt, pepper, and red pepper flakes to taste in a blender or a food processor. Cover and process until all the ingredients are blended. While the motor is running, drizzle in the oil a little at a time. Stored in a clean, airtight jar, it will keep in the refrigerator for 3 days.

To make the seviche, combine the scallops, green onions, red onion, cilantro, parsley, and bell pepper with the marinade in a nonreactive container and refrigerate for 2 hours.

To serve, remove from the refrigerator, drain well, and discard the marinade. Serve on plated salad greens or in wide martini glasses.

GRILLED TUNA ESCABÈCHE SERVES 4

This dish has Spain and the New World written all over it. Pay particular attention to the cure and watch what happens to the surface of the tuna. The cure interacts with the tuna's natural oil and creates a light glaze. It's also a great in-a-hurry marinade.

GRILLED TUNA

4 (8 ounces each) sushi-quality tuna steaks, about 1 inch thick
1¼ cups Ancho-Sugar Cure (page 131)
1 teaspoon coarse-grain or sea salt
1 tablespoon freshly cracked black peppercorns

ESCABÈCHE

1¼ cups extra virgin olive oil
1 yellow bell pepper, seeded and thinly sliced
1 red bell pepper, seeded and thinly sliced
1 green bell pepper, seeded and thinly sliced
1 red onion, sliced into rings
3 cloves garlic, minced, or 1 tablespoon roasted garlic purée
¼ cup capers, drained
¼ cup dry white wine
Grated zest and juice of 2 Key or regular limes (about ¼ cup)
1 teaspoon kosher salt
1 teaspoon seeded and diced jalapeño or habanero chile (optional)
Freshly cracked black pepper
Mixed greens, for garnish (optional)
Heavy-crusted bread (for a sandwich)

To make the grilled tuna, place the tuna in a shallow dish and coat each side with the cure. Cover with plastic wrap and refrigerate for 1 hour or let sit for no longer than ½ hour at room temperature.

Rinse the fish lightly under cold running water and pat dry with paper towels. Sprinkle with salt and pepper to taste. Sear the fish over high heat for 1 minute or more on each side, depending on your taste for doneness. The tuna should have ¼ inch of gray surrounding a red interior. Let the tuna cool and slice into ½-inch-thick strips.

To make the escabèche, heat ¼ cup of the olive oil and sauté the bell peppers, onion, and minced garlic for 2 to 3 minutes over high heat. Or, for a smokier flavor, coat the bell peppers and onion with ¼ cup of the olive oil, grill over high heat, then combine with the roasted garlic purée. Turn off the heat and stir in the remaining 1 cup olive oil, capers, white wine, lime zest and juice, salt, chile, and pepper to taste. Pour over the seared tuna steaks. Refrigerate for at least 4 hours, preferably overnight, to let the flavors blend.

To serve, line four salad plates with mixed greens. Remove the tuna slices from the vegetable mixture, fan out the tuna slices on top of the greens, and cover with the escabèche vegetable mixture. Or serve the tuna slices and vegetable mixture in heavy-crusted bread for one whale of a tuna fish sandwich.

RED SNAPPER WITH TOMATILLO RECADO
SERVES 4

The recado flavors will arrive in two different ways once it hits the snapper. The first pass is the once-over from the marinating process. Next, the recado throws off some really wonderful steam to flavor the snapper while it's cooking. If you happen to have the recado made ahead, the preparation for this dish is effortless. Although the recipe suggests grilling the fish in aluminum foil packets, I can guarantee you amazing flavors if you switch to banana leaves. Serve with Pickled Red Onions (page 211), Marinated Black Bean Salad (page 334), or Sweet Corn Salsa (page 166).

1½ to 2 pounds red snapper fillets
2 cups Tomatillo Recado (page 177)
1 or 2 limes, thinly sliced
½ cup Kalamata olives, pitted and coarsely chopped
Freshly cracked black peppercorns

If grilling, cut the fish into 4 serving pieces. If cooking indoors, leave the fillets whole.

Place the fish fillets in a nonreactive container or a 1-gallon resealable plastic bag. Pour the recado over the fish and refrigerate for 2 to 4 hours.

To grill: Remove the fish from the marinade. Drain and reserve the marinade solids. Place each fish on an 18 by 12-inch rectangle of heavy-duty foil. Top the fish with the reserved marinade solids and lime slices. Sprinkle with the chopped olives and pepper to taste. Seal the packets by folding the foil over twice, then sealing the ends. Place the packets on the grill, cover, and cook 5 to 6 inches from medium heat for about 15 minutes, or until the fish is cooked through and flakes easily with a fork. Serve hot.

To cook indoors: Preheat the oven to 400°F. Oil a long, shallow glass or enamel baking dish. Remove the fish from the marinade and reserve the marinade. Spoon a thin layer of marinade onto the bottom of the baking dish. Add the fish, top with the lime slices and olives, and cover with the remaining marinade. Sprinkle with pepper to taste. Bake for 30 minutes, or until the fish is opaque and flakes with a fork. Serve hot.

ESCOVITCHED MARLIN SERVES 6 TO 8 AS AN APPETIZER

My late friend Dunstan Harris mentions in *Island Cooking* that escovitched fish comes from the tapas-like dish Pescado en Escabèche. This method of pickling fish is very old and predates refrigeration. I've served this particular recipe at one of Philadelphia's Book and the Cook dinners and have gotten rave reviews. The recipe works as a snack, as finger food, or as a full meal, and it travels well for outdoor picnics. To make this a complete meal, serve with a vegetable salad and French bread.

**3 pounds marlin, swordfish, red snapper, or tuna steaks,
    cut into ½-inch pieces
2 limes, sliced
1 tablespoon coarse-grain salt
1 tablespoon freshly ground black pepper
¼ cup all-purpose flour
1 cup canola oil
1 bay leaf, crumbled
½ cup malt vinegar
1 teaspoon allspice berries, crushed
2 large red or white onions, sliced into thin rings
1 Scotch bonnet or habanero chile, seeded, stemmed,
    deveined, and sliced, or 1 tablespoon seeded, stemmed,
    deveined, and diced jalapeño or serrano chile**

Wash the fish thoroughly in cold water, rinse, and pat dry with paper towels. Rub the fish with the lime slices, season with the salt and pepper, and allow to stand for 30 minutes.

Dust the pieces with a thin coating of flour. Heat the oil in a large skillet and fry the fish on both sides for about 5 minutes per side, until crisp and brown. Remove to a glass or ceramic baking dish and let the fish cool to room temperature.

Combine the bay leaf, vinegar, allspice, onions, and Scotch bonnet in a saucepan and cook for about 10 minutes, until the onions are tender. Cool, then pour the mixture over the fish and cover. Refrigerate for at least 2 hours, preferably overnight.

Serve cold or at room temperature. Spoon the marinade and spices over the fish as you serve.

CHICKEN FAJITAS
SERVES 8 AS AN APPETIZER OR 4 AS A MAIN COURSE

Rolled in a warm tortilla or stuffed into pita bread, this chicken not only tastes wonderful, but it's also easy to prepare. The flavor brims with citrus and robust Yucatecan seasonings, a true summertime delight. If you like, make a little extra recado to dress the lettuce garnish or salad.

2 whole chicken breasts, boned, skinned, and cut into ½-inch-thick strips
1½ cups Yucatecan Citrus Recado (page 182)
1 tablespoon canola oil (if cooking indoors)
1 tablespoon butter, melted (if cooking indoors)
½ cup sliced radicchio
½ cup sliced red leaf lettuce
Juice of 1 lime (about 2 tablespoons)
1 tablespoon chopped fresh cilantro
12 flour tortillas, warmed, or 6 pita breads, halved and warmed

Place the chicken in a nonreactive container or a 1-gallon resealable plastic bag. Pour the recado over the chicken and refrigerate for 6 to 8 hours. Remove the chicken from the recado and bring the recado to a boil for basting; keep warm.

To grill: Lightly brush the grill with canola oil and grill the chicken for 3 to 4 minutes on each side while basting often with the warm recado.

To cook indoors: Oil a heavy, preferably cast-iron, skillet and heat over high heat. Place the chicken strips in the hot skillet and sauté for 3 to 4 minutes on each side. Combine 3 tablespoons of the recado with the melted butter and pour it over the chicken. Cook for 1 to 2 minutes more.

To serve, toss together the radicchio, lettuce, lime juice, and cilantro. Enclose the chicken in the warm tortillas and top with the radicchio-lettuce salad.

TIP: Use a perforated vegetable grilling grate to avoid dropping chicken strips into your grill's heat source.

YUCATECAN GRILLED FISH (PESCADO TIKIN XIC) OR PULLED PORK (COCHINITA PIBIL) SERVES 6

This is really two traditional Mexican recipes in one, both using the same marinade and same steaming technique. But what a difference between the two! The key ingredient is the Yucatecan cooking chamber: the banana leaf.

The flavorful steamed fish and the succulent baked pork are worth trying even without banana leaves, but the taste will not be exactly the same. Simply omit the leaves and wrap the food in parchment paper and then in aluminum foil. Serve with Roasted Tri-Colored Sweet Peppers (page 212) or Pineapple-Jalapeño Salsa (page 164).

2½ pounds red snapper or grouper, or 2½ to 3 pounds pork tenderloin
3 cups Yucatecan Achiote Recado (page 183)
6 (12 by 18-inch) banana leaves
1 cup Pickled Red Onions (page 211), for garnish
6 corn tortillas, warmed (for pulled pork)

For Yucatecan Grilled Fish: Place the fish in a nonreactive container or a 1-gallon resealable plastic bag. Pour the recado over the fish and refrigerate for 2 to 4 hours. Remove the fish from the marinade, reserving about 1½ cups of the recado.

TIP: To prepare the banana leaves, defrost them in the refrigerator overnight. Heat each whole leaf section over a flame or dry skillet until it changes texture and become more pliable. Do not overheat or it will become brittle. Trim into 12 by 18-inch sections.

Lay out each banana leaf shiny side up. Add the fish and spoon about ¼ cup recado over each portion. Fold the flaps of the banana leaves over like an envelope and secure each side with a presoaked bamboo skewer. If your banana leaves begin to split, make a foil boat under them before placing in the oven. You still get the flavor of the leaves without losing the juices.

To grill: Place the packets over medium-high heat and cover. Grill for 10 minutes per inch of thickness for each parcel, 20 to 25 minutes total.

To cook indoors: Preheat the oven to 450°F. Place the parcels on a baking sheet and bake for 20 to 25 minutes, or 10 to 12 minutes per inch of thickness.

To serve, remove the parcels from the heat and slide them onto a serving plate. At the table, cut an X in the banana leaves with a sharp pointed knife and peel back the leaves. Garnish with the onions.

For Yucatecan Pulled Pork: Line the bottom of a large baking dish with two 12 by 18-inch sheets of aluminum foil, one lengthwise and one widthwise, letting them hang over the sides of the dish. Lay 2 banana leaves over the foil following the same pattern, so that they may be folded over the pork.

Place the pork tenderloin on the leaves. Pour the recado over the pork, fold the banana leaves over all, and roll tightly with the aluminum foil. Place in the refrigerator to marinate for at least 8 hours and preferably overnight.

Preheat the oven to 350°F and bake for 1½ hours.

To serve, remove the foil and slide the roll onto a serving plate. At the table, cut an X in the banana leaves with a sharp pointed knife and peel back the leaves. Using two forks, pull the meat apart and portion into 6 individual warm tortillas. Garnish with the onions and serve warm.

JERKED CHICKEN
SERVES 8 AS AN APPETIZER OR 4 AS A MAIN COURSE

Buffalo wings have nothing on jerked chicken wings, or whole chicken breasts for that matter. Jerked chicken tastes best roasted over low charcoal heat for the flavor of the rub to really bite into the chicken. This recipe comes from *Island Cooking* by Dunstan Harris. It is equally good on fish and pork chops. Serve with Lime-Cilantro Jicama Slaw (page 213) or Mango-Jicama Salsa (page 166).

2½ pounds combination chicken breasts, thighs, legs, and wings
Freshly squeezed juice of 4 limes (about ½ cup)
1 cup Jerk Rub (page 186)

In a nonreactive container or 1-gallon resealable plastic bag, toss the chicken in the lime juice and refrigerate for 2 to 4 hours. Remove the chicken from the refrigerator, massage the rub into the chicken, and marinate in the refrigerator for 3 to 12 hours, the longer the better. Remove the chicken from the rub and bring the rub to a boil for basting; keep warm.

To grill: Slowly roast the chicken over hot, gray ash coals, or on a gas barbecue at its lowest setting, at least 6 inches from the heat source for a minimum of 1½ hours, or until the juices run clear when the chicken is pricked with a fork. Baste with the warm rub after 15 minutes, turning frequently.

To cook indoors: Preheat the oven to 325°F and line a baking sheet with foil. Arrange the chicken on the baking sheet and bake for about 1½ hours, or until the juices run clear when the chicken is pricked with a fork. Baste with the warm rub after 15 minutes, turning frequently.

To serve, transfer the chicken to serving plates.

SMOKED TROPICAL CHICKEN SALAD SERVES 8 TO 12

This salad has just about everything going for it: a mosaic of tropical flavors, crunchy textures, and great color. The recipe is really easy to assemble in stages. The Lime Marinade can be made a few days ahead of time. The chicken can be smoked or grilled up to a day before. Or if your favorite charcuterie happens to have some interesting-looking chicken breasts in the case, save time and substitute. The pasta strips are optional, or you can substitute unsalted tortilla chips.

3 whole chicken breasts, boned, halved, and skinned
2 cups Lime Marinade (page 51)

VINAIGRETTE MAKES 1 CUP

Grated zest and juice of 2 limes (about ¼ cup)
2 tablespoons balsamic vinegar
¼ cup chopped fresh cilantro
1 to 2 tablespoons chopped fresh herbs (tarragon, lavender, etc.)
¼ teaspoon ground cumin
¼ teaspoon ground cardamom
1 clove garlic, minced
6 to 8 tablespoons extra virgin olive oil

SALAD

1 red bell pepper, seeded and julienned
1 yellow or orange bell pepper, seeded and julienned
1 fresh mango, peeled and julienned
1 pound jicama, peeled and julienned
2 or 3 carrots, julienned

GARNISH

3 cups peanut oil
1 pound assorted flavors fresh angel hair pasta (tomato, spinach, garlic, hot pepper, etc.), cooked (optional)
Assorted greens (endive, arugula, radicchio, etc.)

To prepare the chicken, place the chicken in a nonreactive container or a 1-gallon resealable plastic bag, pour the marinade over the chicken, and refrigerate for 4 to 6 hours.

Grill or smoke the chicken breasts until the meat is firm. Cool the chicken to room temperature and cut into small strips.

To make the vinaigrette, combine the lime zest and juice, vinegar, cilantro, fresh herbs, cumin, cardamom, and garlic in a food processor or a blender. Process until all the ingredients are blended. While the motor is running, drizzle in the oil a little at a time. Pour into a small bowl. Set aside.

To assemble the salad, toss the bell peppers, mango, jicama, and carrots with the chicken and set aside.

To prepare the garnish, heat the peanut oil in a wok to 375°F. Add the pasta a few strands at a time and fry for 20 to 30 seconds (not too long or the pasta will lose its flavor). Remove the pasta with a slotted spoon and drain on paper towels.

To serve, toss the chicken and salad with the vinaigrette. Line the plate with the greens. Form a nest with the fried pasta strips and add the salad.

GRILLED TURKEY KABOBS WITH PINEAPPLE GLAZE

SERVES 8 AS AN APPETIZER OR 4 AS A MAIN COURSE

Picking up on the ground-meat kabobs of the Middle East and Asia, this recipe is a New World version with a couple of twists. Start with Yucatecan Citrus Recado to give it some orange and spicy overtones. Bind it with ground cashews, toasted coconut, and a little bit of olive oil, and finish it with Grilled Pineapple–Coconut Glaze. Add some Mango-Jicama Salsa for a side dish, and you have a cruise ship of flavor docking plate side.

SUBSTITUTIONS: Replace the recado with Tamarind Recado (page 184), Jerk Rub (page 186), or Lemon-Sumac Rub (page 259).

Replace the glaze with Orange–Star Anise Glaze (page 302), Yellow Hell Glaze (page 180), or Guava Glaze (page 191).

Replace the salsa with Sweet Corn Salsa (page 166), Cranberry-Orange Chutney (page 127), or Pineapple-Jalapeño Salsa (page 164).

1 pound ground lean turkey breast
½ pound ground turkey leg meat or ½ pound ground lean turkey breast
3 tablespoons Yucatecan Citrus Recado (page 182)
¼ cup roasted cashews, ground
¼ cup shredded coconut, toasted
3 tablespoons extra virgin olive oil
3 tablespoons chopped fresh cilantro
1 teaspoon salt
1 tablespoon freshly cracked black peppercorns
1 cup Grilled Pineapple–Coconut Glaze (page 309)
4 to 5 cups Mango-Jicama Salsa (page 166)

In a large nonreactive bowl, combine the ground turkey breast and leg meat, recado, cashews, coconut, olive oil, cilantro, salt, and pepper, and mix gently with your hands or a spoon. Divide the mixture into 8 equal portions and gently roll them into sausage shapes about 6 inches long. At this point you can fry a small portion and adjust the seasoning or texture. Skewer the kabobs onto 8 presoaked wooden or metal skewers, cover, and refrigerate for at least 3 hours.

Remove the kabobs from the refrigerator and let them stand for 20 minutes at room temperature prior to cooking.

TIP: For grilling ground kabobs, I've found it handy to use a perforated vegetable rack. It gives you a flatter grilling surface and enables you to roll the kabobs across the grate for easier cooking.

Brush or spray the grilling rack with oil. When the grill is ready, grill the kabobs for 3 to 4 minutes, turning gently. Brush the glaze over the kabobs, cover, and cook for an additional 4 minutes, or until the juices run clear when the kabobs are pierced.

To serve, remove the kabobs from the grill and serve with ½ cup of the salsa for appetizers or 1 full cup for main-course servings.

GRILLED ARGENTINEAN BEEF ROLL-UPS SERVES 4

I had the idea for this recipe as a lighter version of matambre, which is a traditional Argentinean recipe of rolled beef with wonderful stuffing. But instead of battling with a large roll-up on the grill, I sliced the beef into 1½-inch rolled slices, and then grilled them grain side up. The recipe calls for a butterflied flank steak. Have your butcher handle this for you, or see the Tip below. The meat likes a good red wine marinade, and the marinating time is relatively short for this cut of beef because you tenderize the meat when you flatten it. This recipe is best started the day before grilling and can be made 2 days ahead.

Serve with Marinated Black Bean Salad (page 334), Roasted Tri-Colored Sweet Peppers (page 212), or Pickled Red Onions (page 211).

1½- to 2-pound flank steak, butterflied (see Tip)
2½ cups Basic Red Wine Marinade for Beef (page 62)
2 cups Chimichurri Pesto (page 185)
½ cup shelled unsalted pistachios, coarsely crushed

SUBSTITUTIONS: Replace the marinade with Chilean-Style Marinade (page 178) or Provençal Red Wine Marinade (page 227).

Open the steak like a book, cut sides facing up, and cut one or two ¼-inch-deep crisscrosses into each of the cut surfaces. Place the steak between two large sheets of plastic wrap. Beat with a mallet to flatten the steak to a thickness of about ¼ to ½ inch.

Place the steak in a nonreactive container or a 1-gallon resealable plastic bag. Pour the marinade over the steak and refrigerate for 6 hours or overnight. Remove the steak from the marinade and discard the marinade. Lay the steak, cut sides facing up, and brush with the chimichurri sauce. Sprinkle with the ground pistachios.

TIP: To butterfly flank steak, slice it horizontally like a hamburger bun, two-thirds of the long way across.

Carefully roll up the beef, going against the grain. Wrap in a double layer of plastic wrap and refrigerate for about 4 hours to set the roll.

Remove the roll from the refrigerator and slice into 4 (1½-inch-thick) slices. Using metal or presoaked wooden skewers, skewer each meat slice through the sides so 2 skewers cross in the middle.

To grill: Lightly brush the grill with vegetable oil and sear the beef for 1 minute on each side. Continue grilling the beef 5 to 6 minutes for rare, or 7 to 8 minutes for medium rare, turning often. Remove the beef from the heat and let rest for 10 minutes before serving.

To cook indoors: Preheat the broiler to its hottest setting. Place the beef on a broiler rack about 3 inches from the heat source and sear the beef for 1 minute on each side. Continue broiling the beef 5 to 6 minutes for rare, or 7 to 8 minutes for medium rare, turning often. Remove the beef from the heat and let rest for 10 minutes before serving.

MANGO-GLAZED RIBS WITH SAVORY ONION WET RUB SERVES 4

My friend Carl Doebley's Latin-style ribs are fall-off-the-bone perfection. He starts with a savory onion undercoating on the ribs, which is part marinade and part paste. Next, there's a delicious topcoat of sweet mango glaze. Both the wet rub and the mango are complementary opposites that balance one another. Carl smokes the racks in a covered grill with hickory chips and then finishes them in the oven in a little less than 4 hours of total cooking time.

SAVORY ONION WET RUB MAKES 1 CUP

1 tablespoon fresh rosemary
1 tablespoon fresh thyme
1 tablespoon fresh flat-leaf parsley
½ cup chopped onion
6 cloves garlic
¼ cup sherry vinegar

MANGO GLAZE MAKES 1 CUP

1 ripe mango, peeled and chopped (about 1 cup)
2 tablespoons mango or apricot jelly
2 tablespoons light brown sugar

RIBS

2 racks baby back ribs (about 4 pounds)
Salt and freshly cracked black pepper

To make the rub, combine the rosemary, thyme, parsley, onion, garlic, and vinegar in a blender or a food processor, and process until all the ingredients are finely chopped. Stored in a clean, airtight container, this rub will keep in the refrigerator for 3 days.

To make the glaze, place the mango in a blender or a food processor and purée. Combine the mango purée, jelly, and sugar in a nonreactive saucepan and stir over low heat until all the ingredients are blended. Remove from the heat and cool to room temperature. Stored in a clean, airtight container, this glaze will keep in the refrigerator for 1 week.

Season the ribs with salt and pepper. Fully coat the ribs with the rub and place in a 1-gallon resealable plastic bag and marinade for 4 to 6 hours in the refrigerator.

Remove the ribs from the bag and allow to stand for 20 to 30 minutes. Follow the grill's instructions for using hickory chunks or chips soaked in water for at least 30 minutes, and cook the ribs over indirect medium heat at about 220°F for 3 hours. While the ribs are cooking, preheat your oven to 375°F and line a baking sheet with foil. Remove the ribs from the grill, transfer the ribs to the baking sheet, and generously baste with the glaze. Finish the ribs in the oven for 30 minutes.

To serve, remove the ribs from the oven and cut the sides in half, into pairs, or into individual sections. Serve on a warm platter.

TAMARIND-GLAZED BABY BACK RIBS SERVES 4

Although both the rub and the glaze play with the sour buttons on your tongue, there are a lot of sweet and spicy flavors to balance the chew. The ingredients have an East–West Indies kick to them, with a breeze from the Yucatán Peninsula in the rub. I'm a great believer in brining ribs. It keeps them from drying out, and it gives them an added level of flavor. You have the options of brining or rubbing or doing both. Serve with Mango-Jicama Salsa (page 166).

2 racks baby back pork ribs (about 3½ pounds)
4 quarts Basic Brine for Pork and Poultry (page 47)
Salt and freshly ground black pepper
3 cups Yucatecan Citrus Recado (page 182)
1½ cups East–West Indies Tamarind Glaze (page 310)

Place the ribs in a large plastic container or a small stock pot, pour the cold brine over the ribs to cover, and refrigerate for 8 to 12 hours.

Remove the ribs from the brine, and discard the brine. Season the ribs with salt and pepper, fully coat the ribs with the recado, and place in a 1-gallon resealable plastic bag. Marinate for 4 to 6 hours in the refrigerator. Remove the ribs from the bag and allow to stand for 20 to 30 minutes. Follow the grill's instructions for using wood chunks or chips, and cook the ribs over indirect medium heat at about 220°F for 3 hours. While the ribs are cooking, preheat your oven to 375°F and line a baking sheet with foil. Remove the ribs from the grill, transfer to the baking sheet, and generously baste with the glaze. Finish the ribs in the oven for 30 minutes.

To serve, remove the ribs from the oven and cut the sides in half, into pairs, or into individual sections. Serve on a warm platter.

SUBSTITUTIONS: Replace the rub with Ancho-Espresso Dry Rub (page 143) or Tamarind Recado (page 184).

Replace the salsa with Mango-Jicama Slaw (page 166), Cranberry-Orange Chutney (page 127), or Pineapple-Jalapeño Salsa (page 164).

TIP: You can also double up with separate 1-gallon resealable bags by dividing the whole racks in half if refrigeration space is an issue.

207

CUBAN-STYLE GRILLED PORK TENDERLOIN
(COSTILLITAS DE CERDO) SERVES 6

If you were to compare the following recipe to the Grilled Iberian Pork Tenderloin with Blood Orange–Sherry Sauce (page 240), you can begin to see the culinary relationship between Cuba and Spain regarding their savory use of citrus. The mojo is a triple-action citrus push with a fair amount of pucker that's balanced by garlic and red pepper flakes. Serve with Mango-Jicama Salsa (page 166), Southwestern Tabbouleh (page 146), or Marinated Black Bean Salad (page 334).

CITRUS MOJO MAKES 2 CUPS

SUBSTITUTION: Replace the mojo with Bitter Orange Marinade (page 176).

8 cloves garlic, minced
Grated zest and juice of 1 lemon (about 3 tablespoons)
Grated zest and juice of 2 limes (about ¼ cup)
Grated zest and juice of 3 juice oranges (about 1 cup)
4 bay leaves
2 teaspoons dried oregano, crumbled
1 teaspoon red pepper flakes
1 tablespoon soy sauce
2 teaspoons dark brown sugar
¼ cup extra virgin olive oil

2 to 2½ pounds lean boneless pork loin, or
   2½ pounds boned, skinned chicken breast

To make the mojo, combine the garlic; lemon, lime, and orange zests and juices; bay leaves; oregano; red pepper flakes; soy sauce; and sugar in a blender or a food processor and process until all the ingredients are blended. While the motor is running, drizzle in the oil a little at a time. Set aside about ½ cup of the mojo to be used when serving. Stored in a clean, airtight jar, it will keep in the refrigerator for 3 days.

To prepare the tenderloin, place the tenderloin in a nonreactive container or a 1-gallon resealable plastic bag, pour the mojo over the tenderloin, and refrigerate for 3 to 4 hours.

Remove the tenderloin from the mojo, and let the meat sit at room temperature for 30 minutes before cooking.

To grill: On a gas or charcoal grill, sear the tenderloin on all sides over high heat for 4 to 5 minutes total, basting with the mojo. Move the loin to an unheated part of the grill, cover, and roast for 10 to 15 minutes, until the internal temperature reaches 140° to 150°F. Remove the tenderloin from the grill and let it rest for 10 minutes before slicing.

To cook indoors: Preheat the oven to 400°F. Drain the pork, discarding the mojo, and pat dry. In a small roasting pan, roast the pork for 30 to 40 minutes, until a meat thermometer inserted into the center registers 160°F. Transfer the pork to a cutting board and let it rest for 10 minutes.

To serve, cut the pork into thin slices, and drizzle with the reserved mojo.

GRILLED CHILEAN BEEF MEDALLIONS WITH PEBRE SERVES 4

If you think that Argentina has the market cornered on South American beef, you only need to look to the Pacific side of the Andes. There's a nice runoff of flavors hitting the beef from the marinade, and the tomato-packed pebre provides an excellent contrast. The grilled medallions should be quickly seared over high heat. Pebres are spicy pestolike salsas that are traditionally served with Chilean grilled meat, seafood, and vegetables. There is a close similarity to the Argentinean chimichurri, and they can run the gamut from mild to hot. I've seen the word *pebre* also refer to a spicy hot sauce of the same name.

PEBRE MAKES 2½ CUPS

1 bunch fresh cilantro, chopped (about 1 cup)
1 bunch fresh flat-leaf parsley, chopped (about 1 cup)
¼ cup chopped fresh mint
4 green onions, white part and 1 inch of green, chopped
3 cloves garlic, peeled and chopped
Grated zest and juice of 3 or 4 lemons (about ½ cup)
1 serrano chile, seeded and finely chopped
Salt and pepper
2 tablespoons olive oil
2 or 3 ripe tomatoes, peeled, seeded, and diced (a little over 1 cup)

BEEF

8 (4 ounces each) beef filets, cut about 1 inch thick
2 cups Chilean-Style Marinade (page 178)

To make the pebre, in a food processor, add the cilantro, parsley, mint, green onions, garlic, and lemon zest and juice. Pulse until all the ingredients are just combined. In a small nonreactive bowl, add the fresh herb mix, chile, salt and pepper to taste, olive oil, and tomatoes and toss to incorporate the ingredients. Cover and marinate in the refrigerator for at least 2 hours, preferably overnight. Stored in a clean, airtight container, this will keep in the refrigerator for 1 week.

To prepare the beef, place the beef in a nonreactive container or a 1-gallon resealable plastic bag. Pour the marinade over the beef and refrigerate for 2 hours.

Remove the container from the refrigerator and let it stand, covered, for 1 hour at room temperature. Remove the beef from the marinade, discarding the marinade.

To grill: Lightly brush the grill with vegetable oil and sear the beef for 2 minutes on each side for rare or 3 minutes for medium rare. Remove the beef from the heat and let stand for 10 minutes before serving.

To cook indoors: Preheat the broiler to its hottest setting. Place the beef on a broiler rack about 3 inches from the heat source and sear the beef for 2 minutes on each side for rare or 3 minutes for medium rare, turning often. Remove the beef from the heat and let stand for 10 minutes before serving.

To serve, place two medallions on each plate with a side of pebre.

PICKLED RED ONIONS (ESCABÈCHE DE CEBOLLA)
MAKES ABOUT 2½ CUPS

This Yucatecan relish is a cuisine jump starter, and it plays well with glazes. It's a traditional Mexican condiment that can brighten almost any grilled food.

2 cups apple cider vinegar, or 1 cup Lime-Chile Vinegar (page 171)
    or Orange-Chipotle Vinegar (page 171)
3 whole allspice berries
1 teaspoon whole black peppercorns
1 teaspoon dried oregano (preferably Mexican)
5 or 6 cloves garlic, peeled and sliced
1 teaspoon cumin seeds, toasted
½ cup firmly packed light brown sugar
3 large red onions (about 1½ pounds), thinly sliced

In a large nonreactive saucepan, add the vinegar, allspice, peppercorns, oregano, garlic, cumin seeds, and sugar and bring to a rolling boil. Place the onions in a nonreactive bowl and pour the pickling liquid over them. Toss well and allow the onions to sit, stirring occasionally, until cool. Let the onions soak for 4 hours; they will wilt and turn pink. Stored in a clean, airtight container, this will keep in the refrigerator for 2 to 3 months if you can resist snacking. Bring the onions to room temperature before serving.

ROASTED TRI-COLORED SWEET PEPPERS WITH CITRUS-CILANTRO DRESSING SERVES 8 TO 10

Charcoal-grilled or roasted over a stove, these marinated sweet peppers are the closest thing to a Southwestern antipasto. The secret ingredient in the recipe is the chipotle chile, which is a smoked jalapeño chile canned in adobo sauce. The marinade, a combination of fire and smoke, is tempered by fresh lime juice and cilantro. Equally good but less incendiary is its robust Italian cousin, described in the variation that follows the recipe.

2 red bell peppers
2 yellow bell peppers
2 green bell peppers
1 cup Citrus-Cilantro Dressing (page 213)

Roast the red, yellow, and green bell peppers over a stove burner or a charcoal grill until the skin is charred or blackened. Be careful not to burn. Immediately place the peppers in a 1-gallon resealable plastic bag and put the bag in the freezer for 10 minutes to loosen the skin and stop the cooking process. Peel the peppers, but do not rinse under water because the peppers will lose flavor. Remove the stems and seeds, and cut the peppers into 1- or 2-inch-thick strips.

Place the peppers in clean jar, add the dressing, and refrigerate for at least 6 hours. Stored in a clean, airtight jar, they will keep in the refrigerator for 1 week.

MARINATED SWEET PEPPER ANTIPASTO. Stir together ¼ cup fresh lemon juice and ⅓ cup balsamic vinegar. Whisk in ½ cup extra virgin olive oil a little at a time. Add 1 tablespoon of capers and ¼ cup chopped fresh flat-leaf parsley. Set the dressing aside. Follow the same procedure for roasting the bell peppers, then toss with the reserved dressing and refrigerate for at least 6 hours.

LIME-CILANTRO JICAMA SLAW SERVES 4

This simple dish is positively habit-forming. The marinade has the flavors of lime and cilantro, with a nice gentle chile kick to it. When the jicama is julienned into french-fry slices, it's always the first vegetarian appetizer to be totally consumed at a buffet. Julienned into matchstick size, the jicama makes a nice slaw for grilled seafood. I have even served a version of this recipe with dollops of avocado sorbet at one of Philadelphia's Book and the Cook events. Always choose jicama that is firm, not mushy.

CITRUS-CILANTRO DRESSING MAKES 1 CUP

Grated zest and juice of 2 limes (about ¼ cup)
Grated zest and juice of 1 lemon (about 3 tablespoons)
Juice of 1 orange (about ⅓ cup)
½ teaspoon red pepper flakes
⅓ cup fresh cilantro leaves, chopped
3 tablespoons avocado or olive oil
1 pound jicama

SUBSTITUTION: Replace the dressing with Coconut-Chile Dressing (page 335).

To make the dressing, combine the lime zest and juice, lemon zest and juice, orange juice, red pepper flakes, and cilantro in a blender or a food processor and process until all the ingredients are blended. While the motor is running, drizzle in the avocado oil a little at a time. Stored in a clean, airtight container, this will keep in the refrigerator for 1 week.

To prepare the jicama, peel the jicama and slice into a french-fry cut if using as an appetizer, or a matchstick cut if preparing a salad or a relish. Place the jicama in a nonreactive mixing bowl or a 1-gallon resealable plastic bag, pour the dressing over, and toss to combine. Refrigerate for least 4 hours before serving. The marinated jicama will keep for 2 to 3 days in the refrigerator; after that, the flavor will stay, but the jicama will lose its crunch.

THE MEDITERRANEAN

Nowhere in the world does a

region have as many cultures and cuisines lining its perimeter as the Mediterranean. But Mediterranean cuisine is not about the sea itself; it's more about the ingredients and cooking styles flowing into it via the spice routes coming westward from South Asia, up the Nile from sub-Saharan Africa, and downward from Central Europe. Organizing this chapter around any one region or group of countries had its own set of problems. A lot of the ingredients run across borders, from the tip of Spain the long way around to the top of Morocco. Mapping ingredients by country is like trying to bracket a color spectrum, where there is no clean break where one color leaves off and the next begins. To keep things simple, I've concentrated one set of ingredients on the styles of Spain, France, Italy, and Greece.

There are more cookbooks about these countries and their ingredients than any other region of the world, and new ones keep coming

out yearly. I'm not about to tell you these cuisines along the upper Mediterranean are similar, but there are some ingredient blends that get passed around. Let's drill down to particular countries and their signature ingredients.

The pantries of Italy and Greece tend to overlap in oils and fresh ingredients, even though their cuisines can be worlds apart. Even within Italy, the cuisines are as varied as the Italian dialects. It has been said that Italy is a series of small countries surrounded by the same language. The food reflects that as well.

Spain today is blowing the gastronomic roof off the continent. The rest of us can only sit with dropped jaws in wonderment. It's truly where innovators are cutting loose. For our purposes, we'll follow the more traditional horizon lines. Because Spain leads the world in the art of fortified wines, their recipes can be laced with them.

THE **MEDITERRANEAN** PANTRY

CITRUS: Lemons, oranges.

VEGETABLES: Garlic, red onions, green onions, shallots, tomatoes, fresh and dried mushrooms, fennel.

FRESH HERBS: Basil, marjoram or oregano, sage, chives, rosemary, tarragon, mint, flat-leaf parsley, spearmint.

DRIED HERBS: Bay leaves (preferably Turkish), basil, oregano, summer savory, sage, rosemary, thyme. *Special Ingredient:* Herbes de Provence.

SPICES: Allspice, anise, cinnamon, cardamom, cloves, ground ginger, fennel seeds, juniper berries, mace, nutmeg, dried oregano, saffron, Spanish paprika, red pepper flakes. Except for ginger, purchase all spices whole, not ground, and toast right before use (see page 40).

OILS AND VINEGARS: Extra virgin olive oil (see *Special ingredients*), hazelnut oil, almond oil; balsamic vinegar, red and white wine vinegar, sherry vinegar (see *Special ingredients*).

CONDIMENTO: Dijon-style mustard, pimentos, sun-dried tomatoes, tomato paste. *Special Ingredients:* salt-packed (cured) anchovies (big flavor difference from the ones packed in olive oil), capers, cured olives.

SWEETENERS: Honey, brown sugar, turbinado sugar, golden raisins.

WINES AND LIQUORS: Calvados, cognac, sherry (dry amontillado), Madeira, Spanish brandy.

SPECIAL INGREDIENTS

ANCHOVIES: I'm a committed lobbyist for canned salt-cured anchovies over their jarred counterparts. Salt-cured anchovies need to be soaked for 15 to 20 minutes to unlock their meatier flavor, and they taste less salty than oil-packed anchovies. Once opened, transfer the anchovies to a clean, airtight container, add an additional layer of kosher salt, and store in the refrigerator. They will keep indefinitely. Salt-cured anchovies can be found in most Italian grocery stores and online.

CAPERS: Capers are really pickled flower buds. You can get them jarred in their own brine in the condiment sections of most grocery stores. My preference is the salt-cured version found in most Italian grocery stores. Rinse either version before using. Capers can be stored almost indefinitely. Substitute chopped green olives or brine-cured green peppercorns.

continued on page 216

SPECIAL INGREDIENTS, CONTINUED

EXTRA VIRGIN OLIVE OIL: This is the primary table oil for most of the Mediterranean. I have no doubt that you can build an olive oil collection based on the regional ports of call. This could almost be called a fresh ingredient because it needs to be treated like one, once opened. Cold-pressed extra virgin olive oil will make these recipes bloom, but it does have a short shelf life unless it's kept in a cool place. You can't always go by color. Greener does not mean better; it may just mean greener olives. Different types of olives produce different types and colors of oil, from gold to green. Unless you're using special oil from a single grower, most olive oils are blended from many groves, and are just fine for marinating.

HERBES DE PROVENCE: Herbes de Provence is showing up more and more in upscale supermarkets. If you notice herbes de Provence in a recipe, note that it contains a fairly accessible inventory of herbs with the addition of lavender. Lavender is the key ingredient that distinguishes this from just another herb mix. You can make it from scratch without lavender, but the blend will lack the regional imprint, which gives the South of France its warm, vibrant flavors.

OLIVES: In the Mediterranean, olive groves are as plentiful as vineyards. Green olives are actually picked when they are unripe, making them denser than black or brown olives. Like olive oil, try to match the olive or a similar type with the regional recipe. There is such a wide range of flavors and curing traditions for olives that it would be easier to tell you what to leave out than to list them all. But when selecting or purchasing olives the thing that you should leave in for better flavor is the pit. Leave the pitted olives for the martinis.

VINEGARS: Red wine vinegar is a mildly sweet vinegar with more of a pronounced flavor than white or cider vinegar, though it is less acetic. You can substitute 2 parts red wine and 1 part white vinegar. Sherry vinegars are made using the *criaderas* or *soleras* method. This is the same process used to age fine wines and sherry. The first category of sherry vinegar is aged for at least 6 months in oak casks. The second category is called reserva (reserve), and it has been aged in oak casks for at least 2 years. The oak barrels give the vinegars unique characteristics (flavor, color, and taste), which can't be duplicated.

BASIC MEDITERRANEAN MARINADE MAKES 1½ CUPS

This marinade gives you a delicious catalog of Mediterranean flavors, and you'll find variations on this style marinade on either vegetables or chicken. Cuisine-wise, the ingredients are base camp for most of the flavors in this region, which makes this recipe fun to play with. The garlic count is the minimum amount; there are days I run with the whole bulb! This also happens to be one of my favorite seafood marinades, but you may find yourself drizzling the marinade over mozzarella cheese and fresh tomatoes as well.

⅓ cup balsamic vinegar
Grated zest and juice of 2 lemons (about ⅓ cup)
5 cloves garlic, chopped
2 anchovies, salt-packed if available
3 tablespoons capers, drained
2 or 3 green onions, white part only, chopped
¼ cup chopped fresh flat-leaf parsley
1 to 2 tablespoons freshly cracked black peppercorns
Coarse-grain salt
⅔ cup extra virgin olive oil

Combine the vinegar, lemon zest and juice, garlic, anchovies, capers, green onions, parsley, pepper, and salt to taste in a blender or a food processor and process until all the ingredients are blended. While the motor is running, drizzle in the oil a little at a time. Use the marinade within 5 days of making

BASIL MARINADE. The sambucca in the recipe adds a wisp of licorice that really perks up the basil and lemon. Add 1 tablespoon sambucca (or other licorice or anise liqueur) and replace the parsley with ⅓ cup finely chopped basil leaves, tightly packed.

DIJON PROVENÇAL MARINADE. Replace the balsamic vinegar with red wine vinegar. Add 2 tablespoons Dijon-style mustard for a French Provençal shift.

BALSAMIC-HERBAL MARINADE. Use only 1 lemon and increase the balsamic vinegar to ½ cup.

TIMETABLE:
Tuna steaks, swordfish steaks, red snapper, catfish, sea bass, halibut, or scallops: 2 to 4 hours

Shrimp or chicken breasts: 3 to 4 hours

Mushrooms: 8 hours to several days

THE STICKY ON BALSIMICO

The way to tell the real McCoy from the *fugazi* is by the words *balsamico tradizionale,* and, as much as I hate to say it, the price. Genuine balsamic vinegar is as painstaking to make as a good cask of wine and, in some cases, stays in the barrel longer. A book on balsamic vinegar by Pamela Sheldon Johns shows detailed drawings on how balsamic vinegar begins in oak barrels, but then progressively moves into smaller barrels of other woods. A good bottle of wine is rare at $3 or $4, and this is true of *balsamico*. True balsamic vinegar is never sold until it is at least 12 years old. The real deal has a caramelized balance with a nice acetic tip to its flavor. The older versions, which are quite pricy, can be sipped as an aperitif.

When I was talking to some importers during the New York Fancy Food Show, they told me that there are no regulations keeping vinegar makers from putting the word *balsamic* on the bottle, even if there is as little as one drop of real balsamic in it.

Now, am I suggesting you use 25-year-old balsamic in marinades or glazes? Hardly. There are some fine-tasting over-the-counter brands that seem to work just fine. Barring that, you can punch up the flavor a bit by simmering and reducing balsamic vinegar from large producers by half. But, it won't taste like it was aged for 25 years.

TIMETABLE:
Swordfish steaks, red snapper, catfish, sea bass, halibut, sea bass, or branzino: 2 to 3 hours

TIP: To peel the tomatoes, cut a very shallow X on the bottom of the tomato. Place a pot of water on the stove and bring it to a boil. Drop the tomatoes into the boiling water and remove them after 30 seconds, or when the skin begins to peel. Run the tomatoes under cold water to peel the skins.

TOMATO-BASIL MARINADE MAKES 1½ CUPS

Garden-fresh tomatoes and sweet basil are a great summertime combination. The balsamic vinegar and extra virgin olive oil are clues to the marinade's Italian lineage, but by substituting sherry vinegar and hazelnut oil, you can create some tasty improvisations. This marinade is simple to prepare and simply delicious with red snapper, tuna, and swordfish steaks.

⅓ cup chopped fresh basil leaves
4 or 5 medium tomatoes, peeled, seeded, and coarsely chopped
¼ cup balsamic vinegar
⅓ cup chopped green onions, white part only
3 cloves garlic, chopped
1 teaspoon coarse-grain salt
1 tablespoon freshly cracked black peppercorns
⅓ cup extra virgin olive oil

Combine the basil, tomatoes, vinegar, green onions, garlic, salt, and pepper in a blender or a food processor and process until all the ingredients are blended. While the motor is running, drizzle in the olive oil a little at a time. Stored in a clean, airtight container, this will keep in the refrigerator for 1 week.

218

SUN-DRIED TOMATO MARINADE MAKES 1½ CUPS

TIMETABLE:
Scallops, shrimp, or
calamari: 2 to 3 hours

This Italian marinade and glaze is truly all-purpose. It can be used over roasted sweet peppers, marinated mushrooms, olives, or even pizza. If the sun-dried tomatoes feel brittle, refresh them by placing them in a nonreactive bowl, add 1 cup boiling water, and let them set until plump. The parsley and basil are interchangeable, so feel free to double up based on availability and preferences.

⅓ cup chopped sun-dried tomatoes
3 tablespoons brown sugar or molasses
2 cups tomato sauce
½ cup white wine
Grated zest and juice of 1 lemon (about 3 tablespoons)
1 teaspoon dried oregano
2 tablespoons chopped fresh basil
2 tablespoons chopped fresh flat-leaf Italian parsley
1 teaspoon crushed red pepper or red pepper flakes
1 teaspoon coarse-grain salt
1 tablespoon freshly cracked black peppercorns
3 or 4 cloves garlic, chopped
⅓ cup balsamic or red wine vinegar

Combine the sun-dried tomatoes, brown sugar, tomato sauce, and wine in a small nonreactive saucepan and bring to a boil over medium heat. Immediately decrease the heat so that the sauce barely bubbles, and simmer for 1 hour, until reduced to 1 cup. Remove the mixture from the pan and cool to room temperature.

Combine the tomato reduction, lemon zest and juice, oregano, basil, parsley, red pepper flakes to taste, salt, peppercorns, garlic, and vinegar in a blender or a food processor and process until all the ingredients are blended. Stored in a clean, airtight container, this will keep in the refrigerator for 2 weeks.

TIMETABLE:

Shrimp or chicken
breasts: 3 to 4 hours

Pork chops or
tenderloin: 4 to 6 hours

Chicken wings,
spareribs, or baby back
ribs: 6 to 8 hours

LEMON-ESPRESSO MARINADE MAKES 2 CUPS

This is my Italian version of the Southern breakfast specialty, red-eye gravy. You can marinate chicken breasts and pork chops in this robust marinade, then deglaze the skillet and create a wonderful sauce with it. The espresso flavor really comes through, tempered by the sweet tang of the balsamic vinegar and musky molasses. Lemon zest and espresso go naturally in a demitasse cup. They also balance one another nicely in this recipe.

1 tablespoon instant espresso
1 cup freshly brewed espresso
¼ cup balsamic vinegar
½ cup unsulphured molasses
¼ teaspoon red pepper flakes
1 tablespoon soy sauce
Julienned zest and juice of 1 lemon (about 3 tablespoons)
½ teaspoon ground cardamom

Dissolve the instant espresso in the brewed espresso and cool to room temperature. Combine the espresso, balsamic vinegar, molasses, red pepper flakes, soy sauce, lemon zest and juice, and cardamom in a food processor or a blender and process until all the ingredients are blended. Stored in a clean, airtight container, this will keep in the refrigerator for 1 week.

LEMON-ESPRESSO GLAZE. Because the recipe contains no oil, a glaze conversion is pretty easy, and you can make it ahead. Combine the espresso, balsamic vinegar, molasses, red pepper flakes, soy sauce, and cardamom in a small nonreactive saucepan. Bring to a boil and decrease the heat. Simmer and reduce to 1 cup. Cool to room temperature and stir in the lemon zest and juice. To make ahead, proceed with the recipe without adding the lemon, refrigerate, then add fresh lemon the day of serving. Stored in a clean, airtight container, this will keep in the freezer for 3 months.

TIMETABLE:

Salmon steaks or fillets,
tuna steaks, swordfish
steaks, red snapper,
catfish, sea bass, halibut,
scallops, or shrimp:
2 to 3 hours

Veal loin or veal paillards:
4 to 6 hours

LIGURIAN MARINADE MAKES 1 CUP

I've often heard someone doctoring up bottled Italian dressing to use in a pinch as a marinade. Why hit the bottle when you can have something with a lot more depth? You can use this marinade as an antipasto drizzle or as a soak for grilled seafood or sautéed veal.

6 to 8 anchovy fillets, deboned
2 tablespoons balsamic vinegar
Grated zest and juice of 2 lemons (about ⅓ cup)
⅓ cup extra virgin olive oil
¼ cup finely chopped red onion
¼ cup chopped fresh flat-leaf Italian parsley
1 tablespoon capers
1 tablespoon cracked black peppercorns
1 teaspoon coarse-grain salt

In a blender of a food processor, purée the anchovies with the balsamic vinegar and lemon zest and juice. With the motor running, drizzle in the oil a little at a time. Pour the marinade into a nonreactive bowl and stir in the onion, parsley, capers, pepper, and salt. Stored in a clean, airtight container, this will keep in the refrigerator for 1 week.

TIP: If you can, try to get salt-brined anchovies; they're far superior to the canned versions. Soak the anchovies in milk for 1 hour and proceed with the recipe.

SICILIAN MARINADE MAKES 2 CUPS

One of the first clues to the marinade's pedigree is the raisins, a typical Sicilian ingredient. You'll notice that the aromatics are cooked, thus releasing their sweetness. The acids are added on the back end for bit of tang. This follows in the same vein as escabèche in Spain and escovitch in the Caribbean. Seems that good food really does travel well.

TIMETABLE:
Salmon steaks or fillets, swordfish steaks, red snapper, catfish, sea bass, halibut, scallops, or shrimp: 2 to 3 hours

3 to 4 tablespoons extra virgin olive oil
1 small bulb fennel, sliced into thin strips
1 red bell pepper, seeded and julienned
1 green bell pepper, seeded and julienned
2 cloves garlic, minced or pressed
3 green onion tops, finely chopped
¼ cup chopped fresh flat-leaf Italian parsley
2 tablespoons golden raisins (sultanas)
2 tablespoons balsamic vinegar
1 cup dry Italian white wine
Grated zest and juice of 1 lemon (about 3 tablespoons)

Heat the oil over medium heat in a large skillet. Add the fennel and sauté until it is translucent. Add the red and green peppers and cook for 3 to 4 minutes. Add the garlic, green onions, parsley, raisins, and balsamic vinegar and simmer for 5 minutes more until the raisins become plump. Cool to room temperature. Add the wine and lemon zest and juice. Chill the marinade before adding it to seafood. Stored in a clean, airtight jar, this will keep in the refrigerator for 1 week.

Swordfish steaks or
scallops: 2 to 3 hours

Shrimp, chicken breasts or
kabobs, lamb kabobs, or
beef kabobs: 4 to 6 hours

GREEK-STYLE LEMON-MINT MARINADE
MAKES 2 CUPS
• •

Every time I use this breezy, mint-and-lemon-scented marinade, I think of
Greek restaurants and outside dinner parties. Try drizzling the marinade over
grilled chicken or lamb kabobs, and then pack them into toasted pita breads.
This is a high-acid marinade, so keep an eye on your soaking times.

½ cup dry white wine (if marinating fish) or dry red wine
    (if marinating red meat)
Grated zest and juice of 3 lemons (about ½ cup)
¼ cup chopped fresh mint
3 tablespoons chopped shallots
3 cloves garlic, minced
1 tablespoon fresh rosemary
1 tablespoon fresh oregano
1 teaspoon coarse-grain salt
1 tablespoon cracked black peppercorns
½ cup extra virgin olive oil

Combine the wine, lemon zest and juice, mint, shallots, garlic, rosemary,
oregano, salt, and pepper in a blender or a food processor and process until
all the ingredients are blended. While the motor is running, drizzle in the oil
a little at a time. Stored in a clean, airtight container, this will keep in the
refrigerator for 1 week. This marinade freezes well with food.

TIMETABLE:
Beef filets, rib eye, sirloin,
porterhouse, New York
strip, tri tips, beef or lamb
kabobs, pork tenderloin,
pork chops, or pork
kabobs: 4 to 6 hours

Lamb shoulder or leg, pork
shoulder, or venison steak
or chops: 6 to 8 hours

London broil, skirt steak,
flank steak, beef brisket,
prime rib, or rib roast:
8 to 12 hours

MADEIRA MARINADE MAKES 2½ CUPS
• •

The almonds complement the nutlike quality of sherry vinegar in this
Spanish-style marinade, but it's the Madeira that gives the marinade its
unique signature. The marinade is a delight for a cold winter dinner of
roasted eye round, as well as a summertime grilling of beef filets.

½ cup sherry vinegar
1 cup Madeira
¼ cup chopped shallots
2 or 3 cloves garlic, chopped
3 whole cloves, crushed
3 whole bay leaves, crumbled
1 tablespoon freshly cracked black peppercorns
1 tablespoon herbes de Provence (page 228)
1 tablespoon allspice berries, crushed
2 tablespoons roasted almond slivers
1 teaspoon coarse-grain salt
¼ cup almond or hazelnut oil

Combine the vinegar, Madeira, shallots, garlic, cloves, bay leaves, peppercorns, herbes de Provence, allspice, almonds, and salt in a food processor and process until all the ingredients are blended. While the motor is running, drizzle in the oil a little at a time. Stored in a clean, airtight container, this will keep in the refrigerator for 1 week.

SHERRY-HAZELNUT MARINADE MAKES 1½ CUPS

This marinade just seems to have a Spanish thumbprint on it, and even more so with the almond variation. Some dry sherries have an almost nutty flavor to them. To play on that idea, I like to roll it around those actual flavors. In the last edition of this book, the marinade was used on asparagus; since then, I've been using it on shrimp and pork tenderloin as well.

½ cup dry sherry
3 tablespoons sherry vinegar
Grated zest and juice of 2 lemons (about ⅓ cup)
2 tablespoons chopped shallots
¼ cup hazelnut oil
¼ cup sunflower or canola oil
¼ cup peeled and roasted hazelnuts, coarsely chopped
1 tablespoon cracked black peppercorns
1 teaspoon coarse-grain salt

Combine the sherry, vinegar, lemon zest and juice, and shallots in a blender or a food processor and process until all the ingredients are blended. While the motor is running, drizzle in the hazelnut and sunflower oils a little at a time. Add the hazelnuts, pepper, and salt and pulse just to mix. Stored in a clean, airtight container, this will keep in the refrigerator for 1 week.

SHERRY-ALMOND MARINADE. Replace the hazelnut oil with almond oil and the hazelnuts with blanched and toasted almond slivers (see Tip for toasting instructions).

TIMETABLE:
Salmon steaks or fillets, swordfish steaks, or shrimp: 2 to 3 hours

Chicken breasts or kabobs, turkey breast, pork tenderloin, or pork chops: 3 to 4 hours

Beef filets, rib eye, beef kabobs, lamb kabobs, pork kabobs, or lamb rack or rib chops: 4 to 6 hours

TIP: To peel hazelnuts, combine 2 tablespoons baking soda with 2 quarts water in a saucepan and bring to a rolling boil. Blanch the hazelnuts for 5 minutes and drain in a colander. Run cold water over the nuts and peel. Toast the hazelnuts to a light brown color in a dry frying pan over medium heat.

TIMETABLE:
Tuna steaks, swordfish
steaks, scallops, or
shrimp: 2 to 3 hours

SHERRY MARINADE MAKES 1½ CUPS

This Spanish-style marinade packs a fair amount of acidity, but its mouth pucker is tempered by the sherry. How you prepare the marinade depends on the job it has to do. Following the recipe below with the aromatics stirred will give you the basis of a good seviche for a number of shellfish dishes, including scallops, shrimp, and calamari. The chopped onions and parsley will give the dish some texture. As a straight-out marinade, go for the blender to liquefy the aromatics for a more balanced flavor.

¼ cup dry sherry
1 tablespoon Spanish brandy or cognac
½ cup dry white wine
Juice of 2 lemons (about ⅓ cup)
Juice of 1 lime (about 2 tablespoons)
¼ cup chopped red onion
2 or 3 cloves garlic, minced
2 tablespoons chopped fresh flat-leaf parsley
1 teaspoon dried oregano
1 teaspoon hot paprika
½ teaspoon coarse-grain salt
¼ cup light extra virgin olive oil (preferably Spanish)

Combine the sherry, brandy, wine, lemon juice, lime juice, onion, garlic, parsley, oregano, paprika, and salt in a blender or a food processor and process until all the ingredients are blended. While the motor is running, drizzle in the olive oil a little at a time. Stored in a clean, airtight container, this will keep in the refrigerator for 1 week.

TIMETABLE:
Shrimp: 2 to 3 hours

Chicken breasts or kabobs,
Cornish hen, or turkey
breast: 3 to 4 hours

Pork kabobs, pork
tenderloin, or
pork chops: 6 to 8 hours

BLOOD ORANGE–SHERRY MARINADE MAKES 2 CUPS

If ever I need to be reminded about some of the flavors of Spain, this is the marinade I single out. It has a Moorish influence from the saffron and oranges mixing with the almondlike nuttiness of the dry sherry.

Julienned zest and juice of 3 blood oranges or juice oranges
   (about 1 cup)
Juice of 1 lemon (about 3 tablespoons)
½ cup dry (amontillado) sherry
2 tablespoons soy sauce
2 tablespoons sherry vinegar or red wine vinegar
1 teaspoon sweet paprika
1 tablespoon freshly cracked black peppercorns
Pinch of saffron dissolved in 1 tablespoon boiling water
2 tablespoons extra virgin olive oil

Combine the orange zest and juice, lemon juice, sherry, soy sauce, sherry vinegar, paprika, peppercorns, and saffron in a blender or a food processor and process until all the ingredients are blended. While the motor is running, drizzle in the oil a little at a time. Stored in a clean, airtight container, this will keep in the refrigerator for 1 week.

ORANGE-BRANDY MARINADE MAKES 1½ CUPS

This marinade was used as a dressing for smoked mussels in the last edition. But the Spanish mélange of sherry, brandy, and oranges was too good not to share it with grilled shrimp or chicken breasts. This marinade benefits from letting it sit for a few hours to let the flavors meld.

¼ cup brandy
Grated zest and juice of 2 fresh oranges (about ⅔ cup)
2 tablespoons sherry or balsamic vinegar
¼ cup finely chopped flat-leaf parsley
2 tablespoons chopped pimento (marinated sweet red pepper)
1 tablespoon capers
2 tablespoons slivered almonds, toasted
2 tablespoons extra virgin olive oil

Combine the brandy, orange juice, sherry vinegar, parsley, pimento, capers, and almonds in a blender or a food processor and pulse until all the ingredients are blended. While the motor is running, drizzle in the oil a little at a time. Stored in a clean, airtight container, this will keep in the refrigerator for 1 week.

TIMETABLE:
Salmon steaks or fillets, tuna steaks, swordfish steaks, red snapper, catfish, sea bass, halibut, or scallops: 2 to 3 hours

Chicken breasts or kabobs, Cornish hen, or quail: 3 to 4 hours

HERBES DE PROVENCE MARINADE MAKES 2 CUPS

This breezy French seafood marinade pulls in the flavors of the Provence countryside and blends them with those of the Mediterranean.

Grated zest and juice of 2 lemons (about ⅓ cup)
¼ cup dry white wine (preferably French)
2 tablespoons sherry vinegar
2 tablespoons herbes de Provence (page 228)
3 cloves garlic, chopped
1 tablespoon fresh rosemary
1 tablespoon cracked black peppercorns
1 teaspoon coarse-grain salt
¼ cup grapeseed or extra virgin olive oil

Combine the lemon zest and juice, wine, vinegar, herbes de Provence, garlic, rosemary, peppercorns, and salt to taste in a blender or a food processor and process until all the ingredients are blended. While the motor is running, drizzle in the oil a little at a time. The marinade will keep in a clean, airtight container in the refrigerator for about 1 week.

TIMETABLE:
Swordfish steaks, red snapper, catfish, sea bass, halibut, or scallops:
2 to 3 hours

Shrimp: 2 to 4 hours

TAPENADE MARINADE MAKES 2½ CUPS

This marinade is an olive lover's delight. Combining Niçoise olives with fruity olive oil and capers, this marinade coats grilled tuna steaks with a thick glaze that bursts with Mediterranean flavors. It could easily work as a cold tapenade, but when the heat hits it, the flavor changes dramatically.

1 cup pitted Niçoise (black) olives
8 anchovy fillets, deboned
3 tablespoons capers
⅓ cup balsamic vinegar
Grated zest and juice of 2 lemons (about ⅓ cup)
1 tablespoon Dijon-style mustard
1 tablespoon cognac or brandy
3 cloves garlic, chopped
1 teaspoon dried oregano
¼ cup assorted fresh herbs (parsley, thyme, sage, etc.)
1 cup extra virgin olive oil

TIMETABLE:
Tuna steaks, swordfish steaks, or shrimp:
3 to 4 hours

Combine the olives, anchovies, capers, vinegar, lemon zest and juice, mustard, cognac, garlic, oregano, and herbs in a blender or a food processor and process until all the ingredients are blended. While the motor is running, drizzle in the oil a little at a time. The marinade's flavors build the longer this marinade sits. The marinade will keep in a clean, airtight container in the refrigerator for about 1 week.

PROVENÇAL RED WINE MARINADE MAKES 5 CUPS

This is the French counterpoint to the Basic Red Wine Marinade for Beef (page 62), and nothing gets lost in this translation. Packed with herbs and the earthy aroma of mushrooms, this is a red wine marinade that is *magnifique*.

3 or 4 dried cèpes or good-quality dried mushrooms
1 (750-ml) bottle dry red wine (preferably a Côte-du-Rhône)
1 tablespoon herbes de Provence (page 228)
5 cloves garlic, pressed
¼ cup chopped fresh rosemary
¼ cup chopped fresh sage
2 tablespoons cracked black peppercorns
1 teaspoon coarse-grain salt
⅓ cup extra virgin olive oil

If using whole dried mushrooms instead of powder, grind the dried mushrooms in a blender or a spice mill. Combine the mushroom powder, wine, herbes de Provence, garlic, rosemary, sage, peppercorns, and salt in a blender or a food processor and process until all the ingredients are blended. While the motor is running, drizzle in the olive oil a little at a time. Stored in a clean, airtight container, this will keep in the refrigerator for 1 week.

BEAUJOLAIS MARINADE. Replace the dry red wine with Beaujolais wine. Omit the dried mushrooms, garlic, rosemary, and sage. Add the grated zest and juice of 2 lemons (about ¼ cup), ¼ cup chopped fresh flat-leaf parsley, and 1 tablespoon diced seeded and deveined serrano chile.

TIMETABLE:
Beef filets, rib eye, sirloin, porterhouse, New York strip, tri tips, lamb rack or rib chops, veal loin, veal paillards, venison steak or chops, or buffalo steak: 6 to 8 hours

Beef short ribs, London broil, skirt steak, flank steak, beef brisket, prime rib, or rib roast: 8 to 12 hours

Salmon steaks or fillets, swordfish steaks, red snapper, catfish, sea bass, halibut, or shrimp: 2 to 3 hours

Chicken breasts or kabobs: 2 to 4 hours

Pork tenderloin, pork chops, pork kabobs, lamb rack or rib chops, or lamb kabobs: 4 to 6 hours

Pork shoulder or lamb shoulder or leg: 6 to 8 hours

PROVENÇAL COGNAC MARINADE MAKES 3½ CUPS

The meadowlike flavor of herbes de Provence, piqued by paprika and Dijon-style mustard, balances the sweetness of the cognac. The added savory depth of the marinade comes from the olives and the olive oil.

2 tablespoons Dijon-style mustard
1 cup cognac
¼ cup herbes de Provence (below)
¼ cup chopped fresh flat-leaf parsley
½ cup hot paprika
2 tablespoons red wine vinegar
1 cup extra virgin olive oil
1 celery stalk, diced (about ½ cup)
4 to 6 pitted Niçoise (black) olives, chopped
1 teaspoon coarse-grain salt
1 tablespoon freshly cracked black peppercorns

Combine the mustard, cognac, herbes de Provence, parsley, paprika, and vinegar in a blender or a food processor and process until all the ingredients are blended. While the motor is running, drizzle in the oil a little at a time. Add the celery, olives, salt, and pepper and pulse until the ingredients are mixed. Stored in a clean, airtight jar, it will keep in the refrigerator for 1 week.

HERBES DE PROVENCE MAKES 1 CUP

Herbes de Provence is my favorite wintertime seasoning. I use a pinch of it along with a dried wild mushroom to give a woodsy taste to my stocks, soups, and sauces. Sprinkle a teaspoon on chicken and add a splash of olive oil with some salt and pepper, and you have a ready-made rub that typifies the cooking of Provençal France.

4 to 5 tablespoons dried marjoram
4 to 5 tablespoons dried thyme
4 to 5 tablespoons dried summer savory
4 to 5 bay leaves, crumbled
2 tablespoons dried basil
2 tablespoons dried oregano
1 tablespoon dried rosemary
1 teaspoon crumbled sage
1 teaspoon dried lavender

Combine the marjoram, thyme, savory, bay leaves, basil, oregano, rosemary, sage, and lavender in a small bowl. Stored in a clean, airtight jar or bottle in a cool spot away from heat and direct sunlight, it will keep for about 1 year.

CARAMELIZED ONION–FIG GLAZE MAKES 1 CUP
. . . .

This is the Mediterranean counterpart to Moroccan-Style Fig Glaze (page 262). This recipe uses fresh figs, while the Moroccan version plays with dried. But there is some additional flavor action taking place on this side of the Mediterranean. The recipe tracks its sweetness from three different sources. First up are the caramelized onions, which are lightly caramelized in white balsamic vinegar. Next are the figs themselves. In the test version, I used fresh Calimyrna figs with their yellow-green hue. Should you happen on Black Mission figs in the market, shift gears to red onions and balsamic or sherry vinegar. Finally, there's the toasty sweetness from the roasted garlic, which completes the sweet trinity.

TIMETABLE:
Swordfish steaks, red snapper, catfish, sea bass, halibut, scallops, or shrimp: baste during the last 5 minutes of cooking

1 tablespoon extra virgin olive oil
1 cup finely sliced sweet onions
1 teaspoon coarse-grain salt
1 cup white balsamic or white wine vinegar
1 tablespoon sugar
1 pint fresh Calimyrna, Black Mission, Kadota, or Brown Turkey figs
¼ cup roasted garlic purée (see Tip)
2 tablespoons chopped fresh basil
Grated zest and juice of 1 lemon (about ¼ cup)
1 tablespoon balsamic vinegar
1 tablespoon freshly cracked black peppercorns

In a large saucepan over medium heat, heat the olive oil, then add the onions. Sauté the onions for 15 minutes, or until soft and translucent. They should not brown. Add the salt, white balsamic vinegar, and sugar to the saucepan, decrease the heat, and simmer until the liquid is thick and coats the onions like a thick glaze.

Pulse the figs in a food processor to a coarse consistency. Add the fig purée to the saucepan and simmer for an additional 10 minutes, stirring to combine the ingredients.

Remove the mixture from the heat. Combine the onion-fig mixture, garlic purée, basil, lemon zest and juice, balsamic vinegar, and peppercorns in a food processor and process until all the ingredients are blended.

TIP: To roast and purée a bulb of garlic, preheat your oven to 250°F. From a whole bulb of garlic, slice off the top "beak" to expose the cloves. Loosely wrap the garlic in aluminum foil and drizzle 2 tablespoons extra virgin olive oil over the exposed cloves. Close the foil, place the garlic in an ovenproof glass baking dish, and roast for 60 minutes. Remove the garlic from the oven and let cool to room temperature. Squeeze the cloves from the skins and purée or mash.

TIMETABLE:
Pork tenderloin, pork chops, pork kabobs, baby back ribs, or spareribs: 2 to 3 hours

FINES ÉPICES PÂTÉ SPICE RUB MAKES ½ CUP

Fines épices are pâté spice mixes that can be kept as secret as competition barbecue rubs. In fact, my friend Peter Cravath used this mix in a grilled duck sausage recipe while competing at the New England Barbecue Society Snowshoe Cook-off.

1 tablespoon white peppercorns
1 tablespoon black peppercorns
1 tablespoon sweet paprika
1 teaspoon hot paprika
1 teaspoon marjoram
1 teaspoon thyme
1 teaspoon basil
1 teaspoon ground nutmeg
1 teaspoon ground mace
6 to 8 bay leaves
1 teaspoon whole cloves
1 teaspoon dried ginger

Combine the white and black peppercorns, both paprikas, marjoram, thyme, basil, nutmeg, mace, bay leaves, cloves, and ginger in a spice mill or a blender and grind to a coarse powder. Stored in a clean, airtight container, this will keep in the freezer for 3 to 4 months.

EURO SMALL PLATES

Amuse-bouche, hors d'oeurves, antipasti, meze, tapas, and canapés are not about portion control but more about how people eat in the Mediterranean. It's not that small bites are something that comes before the main attraction; they are the main attraction. Alone, a Euro small plate is a tasty appetizer. But put a group of them together and you have a whole meal.

Small plates pop up everywhere, from *bocaditos* in Mexico, a variation of tapas brought over by the settling Spaniards, to lagniappe in Louisiana, to dim sum in China. The following series of recipes follows the Mediterranean shoreline of their regional pantries.

Can you make a full-blown meal out of these recipes? Absolutely. Plan on 2 to 2½ different small-plate recipes per person, which is just enough to get a taste of everything. The recipes on pages 231 through 237—Marinated Goat Cheese, Italian Marinated Mixed Vegetables, Marinated Cremini Mushrooms, Basil-Marinated Chickpeas, Asparagus with Sherry-Hazelnut Marinade, Mediterranean Marinated Olives, Marinated Calamari Tapas, Tapas-Style Marinated Mussels Montaditos or Pinxos, and Sicilian-Style Whitefish or Smelts—all make excellent European small plates fare.

MARINATED GOAT CHEESE SERVES 6 TO 8

A mild chèvre marinated in oil and herbes de Provence makes great picnic food for open-air concerts or warm-weather buffets. Marinated cheese finds its way between slices of fresh tomatoes, tossed into pasta, mixed with salad greens, or slapped onto a chunk of crusty Italian bread for a quick bruschetta.

2 cups Herbes de Provence Marinade (page 226)
10-ounce log mild goat cheese

Slice the goat cheese into ½-inch rounds. Place the cheese in a glass baking dish or a clean wide-mouth glass jar (large glass peanut butter or mayonnaise jars are ideal). Pour the marinade over the cheese and refrigerate for at least 12 hours. The cheese will keep for up to 1 week in the refrigerator.

MARINATED MOZZARELLA. Replace the marinade with 1½ cups Sun-Dried Tomato Marinade (page 219), Tomato-Basil Marinade (page 218), or Ligurian Marinade (page 220) and the goat cheese with 1 pound mozzarrella.

SUBSTITUTION: Replace the marinade with Lemon-Sorrel Marinade (page 51) or Laurel and Lemon Marinade (page 51).

BASIL-MARINATED CHICKPEAS SERVES 8 TO 10

The nutty flavor of chickpeas makes them a popular staple all over the Mediterranean and India. I've served this salad in cups of bright red radicchio leaves, garnished with whole basil leaves. It has been equally as popular tossed in a green salad with small pieces of soppressata salami, diced prosciutto, or feta cheese. It's also great served as part of an antipasto platter.

1 cup dry chickpeas
2 quarts water
1 cup Basil Marinade (page 217)

Soak the chickpeas overnight in cold water to cover by 3 to 4 inches. Discard the soaking water, put the chickpeas in a 4-quart saucepan, and cover with 2 quarts water. Cook over low heat for 3 to 4 hours, until tender. Remove the chickpeas from the heat and let them cool to room temperature. Drain and discard the cooking liquid. Toss the chickpeas with the marinade and refrigerate. This dish keeps getting better the longer it sits. It will keep, refrigerated, for up to 2 weeks.

SUBSTITUTION: Replace the marinade with Sun-Dried Tomato Marinade (page 219), Ligurian Marinade (page 220), or Basic Mediterranean Marinade (page 217).

ITALIAN MARINATED MIXED VEGETABLES

SERVES 4 TO 6

Verdura mista marinata, Italian marinated vegetables, are traditionally marinated in olive oil and vinegar. At Philadelphia's Italian Market, vats of marinated vegetables, olives, mushrooms, and sweet peppers throw wonderful aromas into the air. These marinated vegetables are an essential part of antipasto platters and make great summer picnic food.

SUBSTITUTION: Replace the marinade with Basic Mediterranean Marinade (page 217).

1 teaspoon salt
2 tablespoons fresh lemon juice or vinegar (to maintain color)
2 quarts water
1 cup ¼-inch-thick sliced carrots
1 cauliflower head, broken into florets and sliced in half
1 small bulb fennel, chopped (about ½ cup)
1 cup Ligurian Marinade (page 220)

In a pot, combine the salt, lemon juice, and water and bring to a rolling boil. Add the carrots and cauliflower and blanch for 3 to 5 minutes. Drain, and then plunge them into a bowl of ice water to stop the cooking process; the vegetables should be firm and crisp. Drain the carrots and cauliflower, and place them, along with the fennel, in a nonreactive container or a 1-gallon resealable plastic bag. Pour the marinade over the vegetables and refrigerate for at least 4 hours. The vegetables will keep for 1 week in the refrigerator.

MARINATED CREMINI MUSHROOMS SERVES 6 TO 8

My wild mushroom source at Philadelphia's Italian Market, Michael Anastasio, pointed me toward these mushrooms one afternoon. Cremini mushrooms look like small brown button mushrooms. Michael and I both remember our fathers bringing home brown paper bags of what they called "creamers" and sautéing them with veal and Madeira. Needless to say, their flavor is sublime when marinated in sweet balsamic vinegar. If you can't find creminis, button mushrooms will work in this Italian marinade.

2 pounds fresh cremini mushrooms, tough base stems
    removed and caps brushed
2 tablespoons fresh lemon juice
1 teaspoon coarse-grain salt
1 cup balsamic vinegar
½ cup extra virgin olive oil
4 or 5 cloves garlic, minced or pressed
¼ cup chopped fresh flat-leaf parsley
1 tablespoon diced pimento
1 tablespoon cracked black peppercorns
1 tablespoon capers, drained

In a nonreactive saucepan, combine the mushrooms, lemon juice, and salt
in water to cover. Simmer for 15 minutes, or until the mushrooms are tender.
Drain and put into a bowl.

In a nonreactive saucepan, combine ⅔ cup of the balsamic vinegar, the olive
oil, and the garlic and simmer for 20 minutes. Pour the warm brine over the
drained mushrooms. Cool to room tempeature and add the remaining ⅓ cup
balsamic vinegar and the parsley, pimento, peppercorn, and capers. The
mushrooms will keep for 1 week in the refrigerator, if you can resist snacking.

ASPARAGUS WITH SHERRY-HAZELNUT MARINADE SERVES 6

A marinade of toasted hazelnuts, nutty Spanish sherry, and breezy fresh
lemon is the finest way that I can think of to welcome spring asparagus. Try
this recipe as an appetizer, or serve it to accompany freshly grilled salmon.
Use pencil-thin asparagus, if possible. Although the recipe setup is grill-
less, you can flash-cook it on a hot grill and then marinate it, or steam it with
marinade in aluminum-foil packets over your favorite outdoor heat source.

TIP: To revive soft asparagus spears, trim about ¼ inch off the ends, stand them upright in 2 inches of cold water, and refrigerate, covered with a plastic bag, for 2 hours.

1 pound asparagus
1½ cups Sherry-Hazelnut Marinade (page 223)

Trim the asparagus, breaking off any rough ends, and scrape the rough outer
stalks with a vegetable peeler. Blanch in boiling water to cover until the
asparagus is cooked but still crisp, 2 to 3 minutes. Immediately plunge the
asparagus into a bowl of ice water to stop the cooking, and then drain. Place
the asparagus in a long, shallow glass baking dish, add the marinade, and
refrigerate for at least 4 hours. The asparagus will keep, refrigerated, for a
little over 1 week.

MARINATED WHITE ASPARAGUS. Replace the green asparagus with white
asparagus. Replace the Sherry-Hazelnut Marinade with Greek-Style Lemon-
Mint Marinade (page 222).

MEDITERRANEAN MARINATED OLIVES

MAKES 2 CUPS EACH

Mention olives, and I automatically think of Mediterranean food. In the following recipes, I've tried to keep the flavor of each marinade regionally correct by suggesting regional olives and their corresponding olive oils. Substitutions are perfectly acceptable; however, there's one rule that should be followed when purchasing olives. Keep the pits in! I've never had an olive that tasted good without the pit.

Marinating olives takes the brining process of olives one step further and infuses the olives with even more flavor. Marinated olives last indefinitely, and they'll provide you with a constant source of garnish, as well as praise. With marinated olives, the longer they sit, the better they taste. Use them to accompany tapas, meze-style appetizers, or antipasto, or for just plain snacking.

ITALIAN MARINATED BLACK OLIVES

⅔ cup extra virgin olive oil
2 or 3 cloves garlic, pressed
3 or 4 anchovy fillets, deboned
1 tablespoon capers
1 teaspoon dried oregano
1 pound black olives (preferably the brown-black Liguria type)

Combine the oil, garlic, anchovies, capers, and oregano in a ceramic baking dish or glass jar. Add the olives and toss to coat. Refrigerate for 2 to 3 days before ready to use, then bring to room temperature before serving. These will keep for up to 3 weeks in the refrigerator.

GREEK MARINATED OLIVES

⅔ cup Greek olive oil or extra virgin olive oil
Grated zest and juice of 1 lemon (about ¼ cup)
2 cloves garlic, pressed or minced
2 teaspoons dried oregano
1 teaspoon anise seeds
1 teaspoon cracked black peppercorns
1 pound Kalamata olives

Combine the oil, lemon zest and juice, garlic, oregano, anise seeds, and peppercorns in a ceramic baking dish or glass jar. Add the olives and toss to coat. Refrigerate for 2 to 3 days before ready to use, then bring to room temperature before serving. These will keep for up to 3 weeks in the refrigerator.

ROSEMARY MARINATED OLIVES

. . . .

½ teaspoon herbes de Provence (page 228)
2 tablespoons chopped fresh rosemary
½ cup extra virgin olive oil
1 tablespoon balsamic vinegar
½ teaspoon cracked black peppercorns
1 teaspoon grated lemon zest
1 pound Niçoise olives

Combine the herbs, rosemary, oil, vinegar, peppercorns, and lemon zest in a
ceramic baking dish or glass jar. Add the olives and toss to coat. Refrigerate
for 2 to 3 days before ready to use, then bring to room temperature before
serving. These will keep for up to 3 weeks in the refrigerator.

MARINATED SPANISH OLIVES

. . . .

⅔ cup Spanish olive oil
2 bay leaves
3 or 4 cloves garlic, pressed
1 teaspoon brandy
⅓ cup sherry vinegar
1 teaspoon cumin seeds
1 teaspoon dried oregano
2 to 3 tablespoons diced pimento
3 anchovy fillets, deboned and chopped
1 pound green Spanish olives

Combine the oil, bay leaves, garlic, brandy, vinegar, cumin seeds, oregano,
pimento, and anchovies in a ceramic baking dish or glass jar. Add the olives
and toss to coat. Refrigerate for 2 to 3 days before ready to use, then bring
to room temperature before serving. These will keep for up to 3 weeks in the
refrigerator.

TIP: To clean squid, separate the tentacles from the body by holding the sack in one hand and the tentacles in the other hand, and pulling. Squeeze out the bony beak from the sack and remove the bone from the body tube. Peel off the dark skin and discard. Rinse the squid with water.

SUBSTITUTION: Replace the marinade with Grapefruit Seviche Marinade (page 195).

MARINATED CALAMARI TAPAS SERVES 4 TO 6

Seafood marinades play an important role in Spanish tapas. This recipe combines tender calamari (squid) in sherry, citrus, and olive oil. To achieve perfectly tender calamari, there is no middle ground in cooking time. Squid sautéed longer than 2 to 3 minutes or less than 20 minutes will have the consistency of rubber bands. After 20 minutes, the squid begins to soften again, but it will have lost some of its initial flavor. The trick is to blanch the squid briefly, then let it marinate. No further cooking is required. Serve the squid on a small bed of greens.

2 tablespoons salt
2 pounds fresh squid, cleaned and cut into 1-inch rings
1½ cups Sherry Marinade (page 224)

In a large saucepan, bring about 3 quarts of water and the salt to a rolling boil. Blanch the squid for 60 seconds and immediately plunge the squid into a bowl of ice water to stop the cooking process. Drain the squid, place in a nonreactive bowl or resealable plastic bag, add the marinade, toss to coat, and marinate in the refrigerator for at least 12 hours.

TAPAS-STYLE MARINATED MUSSELS MONTADITOS OR PINXOS SERVES 4 TO 6

TIP: Although mussels are great at the end of a toothpick (you can call them *pinxos*), you also can serve them *montadito* style as a type of Spanish bruschetta. Slice a loaf of baguette into 1-inch-thick slices. Rub each slice with garlic, then toast each side in the oven or on the grill until lightly brown. Place the mussels on the toast and serve with a slice of pimento, spicy mayonnaise, or crumbled hard-boiled egg.

In this tapas-style marinade, mussels pick up the flavors of Spain's Iberian Peninsula—brandy, almonds, and oranges, amplified by a burst of sweetness from sherry vinegar. The recipe calls for 1 cup cooked mussels (24 to 25 count), which nets out from 2 to 2½ bags of mussels in the shell. But my favorite way of preparing this dish is using smoked mussels (available at seafood departments in grocery stores). The work of cooking mussels is already done, and the smoke flavor works well with the orange in the recipe.

1 cup steamed or smoked mussels
1½ cups Orange-Brandy Marinade (page 225)

Place the mussels in a small ceramic or glass baking dish or in a 1-quart resealable plastic bag. Add the marinade and toss. Refrigerate for 6 to 12 hours. Remove the marinated mussels from the refrigerator and strain over an open bowl. Add back some of the marinade solids to give some texture and color to the dish.

TAPAS-STYLE MARINATED SHRIMP. Replace the cooked mussels with cooked medium shrimp (35 to 45 count).

SICILIAN-STYLE WHITEFISH OR SMELTS
(PESCE BIANCO ALLA SICILIANA) SERVES 8 TO 10

I first had this traditional Sicilian antipasto in the home of Italian cooking instructor Dorothy Marcucci on New Year's Day, and I spent the rest of the day raving about it. Like Spanish escabèche fish, the whitefish is cooked first and then marinated, which hearkens back to the day when marinades were used as a preservative. Unlike the marinades with escabèche fish, this marinade uses raisins, and their sweetness undercuts the sourness of the lemon and vinegar. Serve the fish on a bed of greens or radicchio. If whitefish are unavailable, use small (51 to 60 count) shrimp instead.

2 cups warm Sicilian Marinade (page 221)
1 pound smelts or whitefish, cleaned
½ cup unbleached flour
2 to 3 tablespoons extra virgin olive oil

Prepare the Sicilian Marinade up to the point where it's still warm, before it cools to room temperature and 1 cup dry Italian white wine and grated zest and juice of 1 lemon are added. Reserve the wine and lemon.

Dust the fish with flour. Heat the olive oil in a skillet over medium heat, and brown the fish in the hot oil. With a slotted spoon, remove the fish to a glass or ceramic baking dish. Pour the warm marinade over the fish and cool to room temperature. Add the wine and lemon juice and zest from the Sicilian Marinade recipe. Cover and refrigerate for 2 to 3 days. Bring to room temperature before serving.

FRESH MARINATED SARDINES (SARDI A LINGUATI). Replace the smelts with 1 pound fresh sardines, heads removed and filleted. Replace the Sicilian Marinade with Ligurian Marinade (page 220).

GRILLED MEDITERRANEAN TUNA STEAKS WITH TOMATO COULIS SERVES 4

This recipe not only combines the flavors of Italy, but it combines the colors as well: red tomato coulis and green basil butter on a field of tuna. The colors of my friend Lisa Frank's tuna steaks deliver intense flavor to match. Serve with Asparagus with Sherry-Hazelnut Marinade (page 233), Italian Marinated Mixed Vegetables (page 232), and Mozzarella with Sun-Dried Tomato Marinade (page 219).

SUBSTITUTION: Replace the marinade with Tomato-Basil Marinade (page 218).

4 (6 ounces each) tuna steaks
1½ cups Basic Mediterranean Marinade (page 217)
½ lemon, thinly sliced, for garnishing

BASIL BUTTER MAKES ⅓ CUP

2 cloves garlic
Pinch salt
½ cup fresh basil leaves
4 tablespoons sweet (unsalted) butter, softened

TOMATO COULIS MAKES 1 CUP

3 ripe tomatoes, peeled, seeded, and diced
2 tablespoons balsamic vinegar
2 tablespoons tarragon vinegar
1 tablespoon dried parsley

Place the tuna in a nonreactive container or a 1-gallon resealable plastic bag. Pour the marinade over the tuna and refrigerate for 3 to 4 hours.

To prepare the Basil Butter, place the garlic and salt in a food processor and process into a paste. With the motor running, add the basil leaves and process until finely chopped. Add the butter and process until well blended. Refrigerate until ready to serve.

To prepare the coulis, in a heavy nonreactive saucepan, combine the tomatoes, both vinegars, and parsley. Cook over medium heat for about 20 minutes, until most of the liquid has evaporated and the coulis is quite thick. Keep warm until ready to serve.

To cook the tuna, remove it from the marinade and bring the marinade to a low boil; use for basting

To grill: Lightly brush the grill with vegetable oil. Grill the tuna steaks for 5 to 6 minutes. Turn and grill for 3 to 4 minutes more, until the tuna flakes with a knife. Baste often with the warm marinade.

To cook indoors: Preheat the broiler to its hottest setting and line a baking sheet with foil. Arrange the tuna on the baking sheet and broil for 8 to 10 minutes, until the tuna flakes with a knife. Baste often with the warm marinade.

To serve, top each tuna steak with a dollop of Basil Butter and a thin slice of lemon. Garnish each plate with 2 to 3 tablespoons of warm Tomato Coulis.

LIGURIAN POACHED SEA BASS IN PARCHMENT
SERVES 4

I love opening packages, especially ones that are steaming with flavor. The sea bass is steamed in its own marinade, along with fresh tomatoes and lemon. It's a surprise package bursting with color and Mediterranean aromas.

4 (6 ounces each) sea bass fillets
1 cup Ligurian Marinade (page 220)
4 (12 by 18-inch) pieces parchment paper
2 tablespoons extra virgin olive oil
4 bay leaves
2 large tomatoes, peeled, seeded, and sliced ¼ inch thick
4 thin lemon slices
¼ cup sambuca or anise-flavored liqueur, or ⅓ cup diced fresh fennel

Place the fillets in a nonreactive container or a 1-gallon resealable plastic bag. Pour the marinade over the fillets, and refrigerate for 2 hours.

Preheat the oven to 400°F. Remove the fillets from the container and reserve the marinade. Brush each parchment sheet with the olive oil and place a fillet at the center of each sheet lengthwise. Place a bay leaf on top of each fillet. Place the tomato and lemon slices on top. In a glass measuring cup, combine the reserved marinade and sambuca and drizzle about ¼ cup over each fillet.

Bring the top and bottom edges of the parchment together, folding them down together to enclose the fish tightly. Twist both ends of the packets and tuck the ends under. Place the packets in a ceramic or an ovenproof glass baking dish and bake for 25 minutes.

To serve, place each packet on a plate, and open the packets halfway with a sharp knife that is long enough to avoid any sudden burst of steam. This packet can also be done on the grill with the parchment packets wrapped in aluminum foil.

SAUTÉED TUNA WITH ALMOND-PEPPERCORN CRUST SERVES 4

The almond oil and sherry are perfect complements to the tarragon and chives in the paste, and the sautéed almond coating stops dinner conversation as your guests devour each morsel. Serve with Marinated White Asparagus (page 233).

4 (1-inch-thick, 6 to 8 ounces each) tuna steaks
1½ cups Sherry-Almond Marinade (page 223)
1 tablespoon coarsely cracked black peppercorns
1 tablespoon coarsely cracked white peppercorns
½ cup blanched almonds, toasted and coarsely chopped
2 to 3 tablespoons extra virgin olive oil

Place the tuna in a nonreactive container or 1-gallon resealable plastic bag. Pour the marinade over the tuna and refrigerate for 1 hour.

Combine the black and white peppercorns and almonds in a flat baking dish. Remove the fish from the marinade, discarding the marinade, and coat each fillet evenly in the peppercorn and nut mixture.

Heat the oil in a sauté pan over medium heat, add the tuna, and sauté on both sides until the crust is golden brown, 1 to 2 minutes per side. The tuna should have a ¼-inch gray rim with a red interior.

Serve immediately.

GRILLED IBERIAN PORK TENDERLOIN WITH BLOOD ORANGE–SHERRY SAUCE SERVES 6

This recipe can be shuttled indoors and out. It can be the centerpiece of a formal Spanish dinner party, or served on the deck as it's just pulled off the grill. Serve it cold over toasted baguettes for tapas. It's perfumed with sherry and orange, with a slight hint of saffron, and the color just glows.

I've tried this recipe with the Basic Brine for Pork and Poultry (page 47) for an extra flavor burst, but I'm leaving that option up to you, depending on your timing. Serve with Stir-Fried Carrots in Orange-Cinnamon Marinade (page 127), Asparagus with Sherry-Hazelnut Marinade (page 233), or Citrus Slaw (page 125). Garnish with Caramelized Onions (recipe follows) or Cassis–Red Onion Glaze (page 84) and toasted almond slivers.

2 to 2½ pounds lean boneless pork loin
2 cups Blood Orange–Sherry Marinade (page 224)
1 to 2 cups orange juice (if cooking indoors)
2 tablespoons peanut or canola oil
¼ cup toasted almond slivers, for garnish

CARAMELIZED ONIONS MAKES 1 CUP

2 tablespoons canola oil
2 red or sweet Vidalia onions, thinly sliced
2 tablespoons sugar
½ cup white wine, or ¼ cup white balsamic vinegar

Place the tenderloin in a nonreactive container or a 1-gallon resealable plastic bag, pour the marinade over the tenderloin, and refrigerate for 8 hours.

To caramelize the onions, in a small sauté pan, heat the oil and add the onions and sugar. Sauté the onions for about 10 minutes, until they are translucent. Add the wine and cook for about 30 minutes, until the liquid is reduced and the onions have a syrupy coating.

Remove the tenderloin from the marinade and reserve the marinade. Bring the marinade to a boil in a nonreactive saucepan and reduce to 1 cup, 10 to 15 minutes. Decrease the heat and keep warm.

To grill: Sear the tenderloin on a high-heat gas or charcoal grill on all sides for 4 to 5 minutes total. Move the tenderloin to an unheated part of the grill, cover, and roast for 10 to 15 minutes, until the internal temperature reaches 140° to 150°F. Remove the tenderloin from the grill and let it rest for 10 minutes before slicing.

To cook indoors: Preheat the oven to 450°F. Place a nonreactive baking pan with 1 to 2 cups orange juice on the floor of the oven for flavorful steam. Heat the oil in a large skillet (that can fit into your oven) over medium-high heat. Add the tenderloin and sear on all sides for 4 to 5 minutes total. Place the skillet in the center of the oven, decrease the heat to 375°F, and roast for 10 to 15 minutes, until the internal temperature reaches 150°F. Remove the tenderloin from the oven and let it rest for 10 minutes before slicing. Deglaze the skillet with the reserved marinade before serving.

To serve, spoon 3 to 4 tablespoons of the warm marinade onto 6 individual serving plates. Slice the tenderloin into ½-inch-thick slices and overlap 3 or 4 slices on top of the sauce. Top with the Caramelized Onions and toasted almond slivers. Serve immediately.

GRILLED CHICKEN KABOBS WITH PROVENÇAL COGNAC MARINADE SERVES 4

This recipe is from my friend and master butcher Marc Pauvert, who once operated a French butcher shop that immediately transported you to the Provence region of France. His marinade for chicken kabobs is your port of entry.

4 boneless, skinless chicken breast halves
3½ cups Provençal Cognac Marinade (page 228)
16 red pearl onions
16 white pearl onions
8 pita breads (optional)

Cut each chicken breast into 4 strips, 3 to 4 inches long. Place the chicken in a nonreactive container or a 1-gallon resealable plastic bag. Pour the marinade over the chicken, toss to coat, and refrigerate for 3 to 4 hours.

Blanch the red and white pearl onions in boiling water for 1 minute and plunge into cold water. Trim the tops and root ends and slip off the skins. Remove the chicken from the marinade and bring the marinade to a low boil in a nonreactive saucepan or microwave the marinade for 3 minutes on high; use for basting. Using presoaked bamboo skewers, thread 2 strips of chicken in an S shape, alternating with red and white onions within the loop. Each skewer should contain 2 strips of chicken with 2 red and 2 white onions.

To grill: Lightly brush the grill with vegetable oil and grill the chicken kabobs over medium-high heat for 9 to 10 minutes, turning often and basting with the warm marinade. The chicken is done when the juices run clear when pricked with a knife.

To cook indoors: Preheat the broiler to its hottest setting and line a baking sheet with foil. Arrange the chicken kabobs on the baking sheet and broil for 12 minutes, turning and basting often with the warm marinade after the first 6 minutes. The chicken is done when the juices run clear when pricked with a knife. To serve, transfer the kabobs to a warm serving plate and serve with the pita breads.

GRILLED COGNAC-MARINATED VEAL CHOPS
SERVES 4

• •

The Provençal Cognac Marinade, with its hint of mustard, pairs nicely with the subtle flavor of veal. Serve the dish with some crusty French bread, garlic-roasted potatoes, and a bottle of Côte du Rhône or Pinot Noir. Serve with Marinated Cremini Mushrooms (page 232), Stir-Fried Snow Peas with Balsamic-Ginger Marinade (page 337), or Marinated White Asparagus (page 233).

4 (1-inch-thick, 8 ounces each) boneless veal chops
3¼ cups Provençal Cognac Marinade (page 228)
2 to 3 tablespoons extra virgin olive oil (if cooking indoors)

Lay the veal between two sheets of waxed paper, and pound the meat with a kitchen mallet as thin as possible. Place the veal in a nonreactive container or a 1-gallon resealable bag. Pour the marinade over the veal and refrigerate for 12 hours.

Remove the veal from the marinade. Reserve half the marinade for the sauce. If grilling, bring the remaining marinade to a low boil in a nonreactive saucepan or microwave the marinade for 3 minutes on high; use for basting.

To grill: Lightly brush the grill with vegetable oil and grill the veal chops for 8 to 10 minutes per side over a medium-hot fire, basting often with the warm marinade. Remove the veal from the grill and let it rest for about 10 minutes before serving.

To cook indoors: Heat the olive oil in a sauté pan and sauté the veal chops over medium-high heat for about 10 minutes per side. Remove the veal from the pan and let it rest for about 10 minutes before serving. Deglaze the pan with the reserved marinade and cook over high heat for about 10 minutes, until reduced by one half.

To serve, spoon the sauce from the sauté pan over 4 heated serving plates and top each with a veal chop. If grilling, bring the reserved marinade to a low boil in a nonreactive saucepan or microwave the marinade for 3 minutes on high; drizzle over the plated veal chops. Serve hot.

PROVENÇAL GRILLED BEEF TENDERLOINS
SERVES 4

• •

Here is an easy one. There is no more perfect match than red wine and steak, and this recipe takes full advantage of this coupling.

4 (1½-inch-thick, 6 to 8 ounces each) beef filets
2½ cups Provençal Red Wine Marinade (page 227)

Place the beef in a nonreactive container or a 1-gallon resealable plastic bag. Pour the marinade over the beef and refrigerate for 6 to 8 hours.

Remove the container from the refrigerator and let it stand, covered, for 1 hour at room temperature. Remove the beef from the marinade.

To grill: Lightly brush the grill with vegetable oil and sear the beef for 1 minute on each side. Continue grilling the beef for 5 to 6 minutes for rare, or 7 to 8 minutes for medium rare, turning often. Remove the beef from the grill and let rest 3 to 4 minutes before serving.

To cook indoors: Preheat the broiler to its hottest setting. Place the beef on a broiler rack about 3 inches from the heat source, and sear the beef for 1 minute on each side. Continue broiling for 5 to 6 minutes for rare, or 7 to 8 minutes for medium rare, turning often. Remove the beef from the broiler and let rest 3 to 4 minutes before serving.

GRILLED BEEF TENDERLOINS AU POIVRE WITH GORGONZOLA. After marinating, remove the tenderloins and coat with Basic Mixed Peppercorn Rub for Beef (page 65). During the last few minutes of cooking, place 1 ounce crumbled Gorgonzola cheese on each tenderloin, cover if grilling, and let the cheese melt before serving.

BRAISED BEEF WITH PROVENÇAL RED WINE MARINADE SERVES 6

This elegant one-pot meal is perfect for Sunday dinner in winter. The house is filled with the aromas of herbs and vegetables—the kind of cooking I like. You can easily put together the ingredients, walk away from it for a while, and then come back to an incredibly tasty meal that tastes even better the day after it's made. Steamed carrots are an excellent accompaniment.

6 whole cloves
4 or 5 bay leaves
1 (3-pound) beef eye roast
½ cup chopped carrots
¼ cup chopped parsnips
½ cup chopped celery
½ cup chopped onions or leeks, white part only
¼ cup chopped shallots
5 cups Provençal Red Wine Marinade (page 227)
4 tablespoons extra virgin olive oil
Flour, for dusting

Wrap the cloves and bay leaves in cheesecloth. Combine the cheesecloth, beef, carrots, parsnips, celery, onions, shallots, and marinade in a large ovenproof roasting bag or a deep ceramic casserole. Cover, if using a casserole dish, and marinate in the refrigerator for 12 to 24 hours. Drain the meat and strain the vegetables and cheesecloth sack from the marinade, reserving the marinade.

In a heavy nonreactive saucepan, bring the marinade to a boil and cook for about 30 to 40 minutes, until reduced by one third. Reserve the marinade.

Preheat the oven to 325°F. In a large, heavy casserole or a Dutch oven, heat the olive oil over high heat. Dust the meat with flour. Brown the meat on all sides, then remove from the pan. Add the vegetables and brown for about 10 minutes, until caramelized. Remove the vegetables from the pan. Deglaze the pan with the reduced marinade, scraping the bottom of the pot. Add the cheesecloth sack, the beef, and the vegetables. The marinade should come no more than halfway up the beef. Cover the meat with an inverted sheet of aluminum foil. Cover the pot, place in the oven, and braise for 3 to 4 hours, until tender.

Remove the meat and the cheesecloth from the pot. Purée the marinade with the vegetables in a food processor and strain through a fine-mesh sieve. Return the purée to the pot and simmer for 15 minutes to reduce slightly for a rich sauce while the beef rests for carving.

To serve, place 2 slices of beef on each plate with a generous helping of the sauce.

MARINATED ROAST RACK OF LAMB SERVES 4

Marinated spring lamb need not wait for the season of its namesake. This elegant recipe from Marc Pervout, formerly of Charcuterie Pour Vous in Philadelphia, can be the centerpiece of a dazzling dinner party any time of the year. The preparation is easy, the cooking time is short, and the flavor is magnificent. Serve with Marinated White Asparagus (page 233), Braised Chanterelles (page 249), or Grilled Shiitake Mushrooms (page 92).

2 (1½ to 1¾ pounds each) lamb racks (7 or 8 ribs each)
5 cups Provençal Red Wine Marinade (page 227)

Trim the fat from between the ribs and trim the excess covering of fat from the meat. Place the lamb in a nonreactive container or a large plastic roasting bag, pour the marinade over the lamb, and refrigerate overnight.

Remove the lamb from the marinade and let it sit for 30 minutes at room temperature before roasting. Bring the marinade to a low boil in a nonreactive saucepan, or microwave the marinade for 3 minutes on high; use for basting.

Preheat the oven to 450°F. In a heavy sauté pan over high heat, sear the lamb for 1 to 2 minutes on both sides. Place the lamb on a rack in a roasting pan, place in the oven, and reduce the temperature to 400°F. Roast for 20 minutes for rare, 25 minutes for medium, or to an internal temperature of 125° to 130°F.

ROAST LAMB LOIN WITH FINES HERBES PESTO RUB SERVES 6

What's particularly nice about Jon Jividen's recipe is that the herb pesto infuses the lamb throughout. Serve warm with Marinated White Asparagus (page 233), Asparagus with Sherry-Hazelnut Marinade (page 233), or Stir-Fried Snow Peas with Balsamic-Ginger Marinade (page 337).

You can even serve this cold at a picnic with a Quick Orange Aioli (page 247), Mint-Cilantro Chutney (page 332), or Mustard-Horseradish Sauce (page 122).

2 to 3 pounds lamb loin, boned
2 cups Fines Herbes Pesto Rub (page 69)

Lay the lamb loin flat, fat side down. Rub ¼ cup of the herb pesto into the lamb. Roll the loin and tie securely. Rub the remaining pesto over the surface of the lamb loin. Place the lamb in a heavy-duty roasting bag and marinate in the refrigerator for up to 8 hours.

Preheat the oven to 425°F. Remove the lamb from the roasting bag and place in a shallow roasting pan. Place the lamb in the oven and roast for 30 minutes (for rare) to 40 minutes (for medium rare). Remove the lamb from the oven and let it sit for 10 minutes before carving.

TIP: Jon suggests using a roasting bag, but it's not mandatory and it doesn't improve the flavor. But it is the conveniently right size. You can also wrap the loin in a couple of layers of plastic wrap and then refrigerate.

QUICK ORANGE AIOLI MAKES ¾ CUP

This is not aioli from scratch in the traditional sense, but it is an easy condiment for grilled beef or lamb. You can play with the recipe by swapping out the orange and replacing it with equal amounts of lemon or lime zest and juice. With the lime version, you can raise the heat level with 1 tablespoon fresh ginger or chipotle chile purée. Serve with Roast Lamb Loin with Fines Herbes Pesto Rub (page 246).

½ cup mayonnaise
4 cloves garlic, minced or pressed
Grated zest and juice of 1 orange (about ¼ cup)

Combine the mayonnaise, garlic, and orange zest and juice in a blender or a food processor and process until all the ingredients are blended. Stored in a clean, airtight container, this will keep in the refrigerator for 1 week.

PICKLED HARICOTS VERTS SERVES 6

. . . .

This is the ultimate in refreshing, savory snack foods. I also use this as an accompaniment to grilled seafood. The mustard oil, which carries hints of horseradish and mustard, provides a very pleasant bite to these pencil-thin, fresh string beans. The two levels of tang in this recipe are the result of the champagne vinegar and the lemon juice added at the last minute.

½ to ⅔ pound haricot verts
1 tablespoon mustard oil (available where Indian foods are sold)
1 teaspoon capers
⅓ cup champagne vinegar
⅓ cup water
Julienned zest and juice of 2 lemons (about ⅓ cup)
1 tablespoon black peppercorns
1 teaspoon herbes de Provence (page 228)
½ teaspoon coarse-grain salt
1 teaspoon sugar

Rinse and drain the haricots verts, then blanch them in boiling water to cover for about 3 minutes. Refresh the beans in a bowl of ice water. They should be crisp. Pack the beans upright in a sterile pint jar, and spoon the mustard oil and capers over the beans.

In a small nonreactive saucepan, bring the vinegar, water, lemon zest, peppercorns, herbes de Provence, salt, and sugar to a boil. Decrease the heat and simmer for 10 minutes. Pour the vinegar mixture over the beans, top with the lemon juice, and seal the jar immediately. Keep refrigerated. Let the beans rest at least 1 week before using. These will keep for 2 months if unopened and refrigerated.

BRAISED CHANTERELLES SERVES 4

When my green grocer, Mike Anastasio of Philadelphia's Italian Market, told me that the only chanterelles he had that day were the large tough ones, I took them anyway, telling Mike that I would think of something. In this recipe, the apricot flavor of chanterelles comes through with a gentle nudge from the Sauternes and diced dry apricot. It pairs nicely with Sautéed Breast of Goose with Cassis Marinade (page 111) or Grilled Duck Breast with Pomegranate-Cognac Glaze (page 110).

SAUTERNES-APRICOT MARINADE MAKES 1¼ CUPS

½ cup Sauternes
1 tablespoon diced dried apricot
1 tablespoon cognac
½ cup full-bodied poultry stock
1 teaspoon cracked black peppercorns

CHANTERELLES

1½ pounds fresh chanterelles
2 to 3 tablespoons unsweetened butter or canola oil
¼ cup julienned leeks, white part only
1 teaspoon coarse-grain salt
1 tablespoon cracked black peppercorns

To make the marinade, combine the Sauternes, apricot, cognac, poultry stock, and peppercorns in a nonreactive mixing bowl.

To make the chanterelles, clean and slice them in half, sideways. Place the chanterelles in a nonreactive container or a 1-gallon resealable plastic bag, pour the marinade over the chanterelles, and refrigerate for at least 6 hours and preferably up to 12 hours.

Heat the butter in a Dutch oven or a large saucepan with a lid and sauté the leeks until translucent. Drain the chanterelles from the marinade, reserving the marinade, and add them to the sautéed leeks. Continue sautéing for 5 minutes longer. Add the reserved marinade and reduce over medium heat until the liquid evaporates. Season with the salt and pepper and serve immediately.

EASTERN MEDITERRANEAN, THE MIDDLE EAST & NORTH AFRICA

These are the cuisines that pulled me into food, and they haven't let go since. Even though I grew up eating red-sauce Italian, I soon discovered that the Mediterranean was a big sea that lapped up against different shores of flavors.

When you start to make your way east through the menus, starting in Greece and heading into the Eastern Mediterranean, some of the same basic ingredient patterns start to appear: yogurt, olives, olive oil, lemon, and onions. Then the grains, including rice and bulgur wheat, start to surface on the plate. Next comes the final course of seafood, poultry, or lamb, with these ingredients wrapped around them. But that's where the similarities end. What give these regional cuisines their culinary DNA are the spices.

Regionally, the area is a culinary conduit. It was a commuter hub for spice traders, and the recipes show that. Historically, the region influenced the way people cooked, and Europe was anything but immune from these flavors. Instead, they couldn't get enough of the spices and routed their commerce around them.

The Moors absorbed the exotic range of Arabian ingredients, including spices, herbs, fruits, and vegetables, and formed their own classical repertoire. The Moors carried it across the Mediterranean to Spain and Italy and into the Ottoman Empire.

The only cuisine area that even comes remotely close to the intricacies of the Middle Eastern and North African spice rack is India. It stands to reason, because many of the spices overlap. Middle Eastern and North African spices are more about spice blends. The flavorful whole is truly greater than the sum of its parts. In this recipe collection, you'll come across spice blends like Baharat (page 256), Charmoula (page 258), Lemon-Sumac Rub (page 259), Moroccan-Style Shaslick Paste (page 258), and others that are really about core spice components that seem to repeat themselves across recipes.

THE EASTERN MEDITERRANEAN, MIDDLE EAST & NORTH AFRICAN PANTRY

CITRUS: Lemons, limes, oranges.

DAIRY: Yogurt.

FRUIT: Fresh and dried figs.

VEGETABLES: Garlic, sweet onions (Vidalia or Maui).

FRESH HERBS: Cilantro, flat-leaf parsley, spearmint.

CHILES (FRESH AND DRIED): Cayenne pepper, red pepper flakes.

SPICES: Allspice, black and white whole peppercorns, cinnamon, cloves, cardamom, ground ginger, nutmeg, dried thyme, dried oregano, hot paprika, sesame seeds. *Special ingredients:* Anise seed, caraway seed, coriander seed, cumin, fenugreek, malagueta pepper, saffron, sumac.

OILS, VINEGARS, AND CONDIMENTS: Canola oil, extra virgin olive oil, sherry vinegar, fig vinegar (substitute balsamic).

SWEETENERS: Honey. *Special ingredient:* Pomegranate molasses.

WINES AND LIQUORS: Red wine, dry white wine.

TIP

Soak your skewers; this is the section for traditional food on a stick. Grilling skewered meats is the world's oldest and most popular cooking method. The technique goes back to the dawn of time, when early chefs held a pointed stick with pieces of that day's hunt over an open fire. Today, we may be wrestling with rush hour traffic instead of a saber-toothed tiger, but kabobs are still one of the best ways of preparing fresh kill from the supermarket. In this chapter, you'll find regional food ideas to get your skewered point across.

SPECIAL INGREDIENTS

ANISE SEEDS: These have a sweet, warm licorice flavor and are actually considered a sweet spice. Anise seed is a nice counterpoint to cumin in a spice rub. Purchase whole, not ground, and toast right before use (see page 40). You can substitute ground star anise for anise seeds.

CARAWAY SEEDS: Caraway has a persistent flavor that is slightly bitter; it can be used to offset sweet and salty flavors; in fact, the seeds are used in baked goods. Caraway seeds benefit from toasting, which not only brings up their flavor but also softens them. Purchase whole, not ground, and toast right before use (see page 40).

continued on page 252

SPECIAL INGREDIENTS, CONTINUED

CORIANDER SEEDS: Coriander seeds are on the essential ingredient list of the cuisines of India, the Middle East, Latin America, North Africa, and Southeast Asia. This is the actual seed of the herb cilantro, but each is a poor stand-in for the other. Purchase whole, not ground, and toast right before use (see page 40).

CUMIN: Actually part dried fruit and part seed, cumin is ever present in North Africa, Middle Eastern, and Indian cuisines. It has a distinct aroma and is able to stand up to some chiles, and that could indicate why it finds its way into chili powders and spicy rubs. Cumin usually tag teams with coriander seeds. Purchase whole, not ground, and toast right before use (see page 40).

FENUGREEK: You could almost describe the flavor of this spice as whiffs of bitter maple, and the flavor can really dominate curry powder. Fenugreek is almost as universal as cumin on the spice trail showing up in the cuisines of North Africa, India, Central Asia, and Indonesia. Purchase whole, not ground, and toast right before use (see page 40).

MALAGUETA PEPPER: Also known as "grains of paradise" or Guinea pepper, malagueta is spicy with a little bitter on the back end. It is available in Middle Eastern and African groceries. Purchase whole, not ground, and toast right before use (see page 40). You can substitute equal parts black peppercorn and cardamom.

POMEGRANATE MOLASSES: Pomegranate molasses is a syruplike reduction of pomegranate juice that has a tart-sweet flavor. It has the consistency of maple syrup and adds great depth to brines, marinades, and glazes. Store it in the refrigerator, where it will keep almost indefinitely. Look for the Cortas brand in Middle Eastern and specialty grocery stores. For a substitute, if bottled pomegranate juice is available, you can reduce 3 cups to ½ cup and adjust it with a little sugar to taste.

SAFFRON: Saffron threads are actually the dried stigmas of the saffron flower, *Crocus sativus* Linneaus. Each flower contains only three stigmas. These threads must be picked by hand, and more than 75,000 of these flowers are needed to produce just 1 pound of saffron threads, making it the world's most precious spice. Saffron is used to add both color and flavor to dishes, and the first rule of thumb is less is more. Too much saffron in a dish will make it taste medicinal. Look for threads that are red with orange tips. Although there are substitutes for color, there are no substitutes for saffron's flavor. Properly stored, saffron will keep for a minimum of 2 to 3 years. The flavor will diminish as it ages.

SUMAC: This sour-flavored spice gives a burst of savory lemon to rubs and kabobs. It also acts as a reddish colorant. Purchase whole, not ground, and toast right before use (see page 40). You can substitute lemon zest and salt, or lemon juice, or vinegar (in salads).

MEDITERRANEAN-STYLE YOGURT MARINADE

MAKES 2½ CUPS

TIMETABLE:

Chicken breasts, chicken kabobs, or turkey breast: 3 to 4 hours

Beef kabobs or lamb kabobs: 4 to 6 hours

Lamb shoulder or leg: 6 to 8 hours

Greece, Turkey, and Lebanon . . . anywhere you find yogurt and lamb in the Mediterranean, a variation of this recipe is in full swing. The ingredient base is multiregional. Three activators are hitting the meat at the same time: the acidic lemon, the enzymatic onions, and the yogurt. The regional flavor stamps come by way of the mint, cumin, and oregano. This is a nice contrast to Indian-style yogurt marinades from the opposite end of the spice route.

1 cup plain yogurt or laban (available at Middle Eastern grocery stores)
Grated zest and juice of 1 lemon (about 3 tablespoons)
¼ cup chopped fresh mint leaves
½ teaspoon ground cumin
1 teaspoon ground coriander
1 teaspoon dried oregano
1 teaspoon hot paprika
3 or 4 cloves garlic, minced
¼ cup finely chopped onion
3 tablespoons extra virgin olive oil

Combine the yogurt, lemon zest and juice, mint, cumin, coriander, oregano, paprika, garlic, and onion in a blender or a food processor and process until all the ingredients are blended. While the motor is running, drizzle in the oil a little at a time. Stored in a clean, airtight container, this will keep in the refrigerator for 1 week.

TUNISIAN SPICE BLEND MAKES ¼ CUP

TIMETABLE:

Scallops, shrimp, chicken breasts or kabobs, lamb rack or rib chops, lamb kabobs, beef kabobs, or burgers: 1 to 2 hours

This started out as Tunisian Five-Spice Powder, but I was fiddling around with the idea of adding a bit of cumin to it to taste "what if." It worked so well that I've used it to dust Grilled Scallops with Carrot-Curry Caramel (page 320).

1 tablespoon whole cloves
1 tablespoon cracked black peppercorns
1½ teaspoons malagueta pepper (see page 252)
1½ teaspoons freshly grated nutmeg
1 teaspoon ground cinnamon
1 teaspoon cumin seeds, toasted

In a spice grinder or blender, grind together the cloves, peppercorns, and malagueta pepper. Add the nutmeg, cinnamon, and cumin and mix together. Store in a clean, airtight container in the freezer for up to 6 months.

TURKISH-STYLE MARINADE FOR BEEF OR LAMB KABOBS MAKES 2 CUPS

Onions in Turkish cuisine take on a dual role as both an aromatic and a "tenderizing" element when juiced. The trick is to start with sweet, not cured, onions that have some juice when sliced. Storage or cured (yellow) onions tend to be drier. You should try to liquefy the onion as much as you can. Here's where a juicer can come in very handy.

2 cups chopped sweet onion
4 to 6 cloves garlic
Juice of 1 lemon (about 3 tablespoons)
2 teaspoons ground cinnamon
1 teaspoon ground cumin
1 tablespoon hot paprika
1 tablespoon freshly cracked black peppercorns
¼ cup fresh flat-leaf parsley leaves, chopped
¾ cup olive oil

TIP: The leftover pulp freezes well, and you can use it in burgers or ground lamb kabobs.

In a blender, food processor, or juicer, purée the onion and garlic until you have a smooth paste. Place the onion-garlic purée into a fine sieve over a nonreactive mixing bowl and press the solids with the back of a rubber spatula or wooden spoon to extract the juice. Reserve the pulp for later use. You should have about 1 cup of juice. Combine the onion-garlic juice, lemon juice, cinnamon, cumin, paprika, peppercorns, and parsley in a blender or a food processor and process until all the ingredients are blended. While the motor is running, drizzle in the olive oil a little at a time. Stored in a clean, airtight container, this will keep in the refrigerator for 1 week.

TURKISH BATH OF ONION AND GARLIC FOR LAMB OR BEEF MAKES 1½ CUPS

I've used this simple recipe on grilled New York strip steaks. All you need to do is let them take a long, leisurely, onion-perfumed bath. I've kept the ingredient list relatively simple. The essential ingredient is sweet uncured or fresh onions that pack a fair amount of juice, and that's not to say you can't go gangbusters by adding rubs to it. You could add ¼ to ⅓ cup of any of your favorite rub recipes.

1½ pounds sweet (Vidalia or Maui) onions, roughly chopped
4 or 5 cloves garlic, minced
2 teaspoons hot paprika
¼ cup fresh flat-leaf parsley, chopped
2 teaspoons coarse-grain salt
1 tablespoon freshly cracked black peppercorns
1 teaspoon Baharat (page 256) (optional)

In a blender, food processor, or juicer, purée the onion and garlic until you have a smooth paste. Place the onion-garlic purée into a fine sieve over a nonreactive mixing bowl and press the solids with the back of a rubber spatula or wooden spoon to extract the juice. Reserve the pulp for later use. Add the paprika, parsley, salt, pepper, and Baharat spice mix, and stir to incorporate the ingredients. Stored in a clean, airtight container, this will keep in the refrigerator for 3 days.

TIP: As you remove the meat from the marinade, you can also roll it lightly in the Basic Mixed Peppercorn Rub for Beef (page 65). The combination is fit for a sultan's feast.

MOORISH-STYLE MARINADE MAKES ½ CUP

This marinade has patches of both sides of the Mediterranean in its flavor fabric. The ingredients in this marinade may look similar to those of the Spanish and Sicilian recipes in the previous section, as well they should. The Moors crossed the Mediterranean with a very sophisticated cuisine in place, and they scattered it along the coasts of Spain and Sicily.

TIMETABLE:
Swordfish steaks, red snapper, catfish, sea bass, halibut, or scallops:
2 to 3 hours

2 teaspoons cumin seeds, toasted
1 teaspoon coriander seeds, toasted
1 teaspoon black peppercorns
3 cloves garlic, minced
½ teaspoon ground cinnamon
⅓ cup red wine or sherry vinegar
⅛ teaspoon (pinch) saffron, infused in 2 tablespoons boiling water
1 tablespoon freshly grated orange zest
1 teaspoon sweet paprika
1 teaspoon dried oregano
2 tablespoons extra virgin olive oil

In a spice grinder, combine the cumin seeds, coriander seeds, and peppercorns and grind to a powder. Combine the spice mix, garlic, cinnamon, vinegar, saffron and infusing water, orange zest, paprika, and oregano in a blender or a food processor and process until all the ingredients are blended. While the motor is running, drizzle in the oil a little at a time. Stored in a clean, airtight jar, it will keep in the refrigerator for up to 1 week.

TIMETABLE:
Swordfish steaks, red
snapper, catfish, sea bass,
halibut, scallops, or shrimp:
2 to 3 hours

Chicken breasts, chicken
kabobs, or turkey breast:
3 to 4 hours

Beef kabobs or lamb
kabobs: 4 to 6 hours

MOROCCAN-STYLE LEMON MARINADE

MAKES 1½ CUPS

Morocco's flavor points come brimming to the surface of this marinade.
Fenugreek and cumin give the marinade its bouquet, the peppers add some
spike, and the lemon and olive oil bring a Mediterranean current to the flavor.
Use it to marinate red snapper fillets or lamb kabobs, and then serve over
couscous.

2 teaspoons fenugreek seeds
1 tablespoon sesame seeds
Grated zest and juice of 3 lemons (about ½ cup)
1 teaspoon ground cumin
¼ teaspoon red pepper flakes
1 teaspoon coarse-grain salt
1 teaspoon coarsely cracked white peppercorns
3 cloves garlic, minced
¼ cup fresh flat-leaf parsley, chopped
⅔ cup olive oil

Toast the fenugreek seeds in a nonstick frying pan with a lid until they pop.
Shake the frying pan constantly to avoid burning. Grind the toasted seeds in
a blender or a spice mill.

In a nonstick frying pan, toast the sesame seeds until they turn golden
brown, shaking the pan constantly to avoid burning. Combine the fenugreek
seeds, sesame seeds, lemon zest and juice, cumin, red pepper flakes, salt,
white peppercorns, garlic, and parsley in a blender or a food processor and
process until all the ingredients are blended. While the motor is running,
drizzle in the oil a little at a time. Stored in the refrigerator, this will keep for
3 days.

TIMETABLE:
Tuna steaks, shrimp,
chicken breasts or kabobs,
beef kabobs, or lamb
kabobs: 1 to 2 hours

BAHARAT MAKES 1¼ CUPS

Bahar means pepper in Arabic, and at one time, every ingredient in this
pepper spice mix was considered currency along the trade routes. The
peppers and chiles, along with fragrant, sweet spices, are sometimes fried
briefly to open up the aromatics before adding the mixture to lamb or
chicken. Baharat can work as a stand-alone rub, or it can be rolled into a
yogurt-style marinade.

2 tablespoons coriander seeds
¼ cup cumin seeds, toasted
1 tablespoon cardamom seeds
¼ cup black peppercorns
2 tablespoons ground cinnamon
2 tablespoons whole cloves
2 tablespoons ground nutmeg
¼ cup hot paprika
½ teaspoon red pepper flakes (optional)

In a small frying pan, place the coriander, cumin, and cardamom seeds, and heat them over medium heat, shaking the pan or stirring the spices with a wooden spoon, for about 5 minutes, until they become fragrant. Remove them from the pan quickly to avoid burning, because they will continue to cook.

In a spice mill or blender, grind together the peppercorns, coriander seeds, cinnamon, cloves, cumin seeds, cardamom seeds, nutmeg, paprika, and red pepper flakes. Store in a clean, airtight container in the freezer for up to 6 months.

TIP: See Basic Syrian Spice Mix (below) for directions on toasting spices.

BASIC SYRIAN SPICE MIX MAKES ⅔ CUP

This cinnamon-driven spice rub was developed by my friend Barbara Boswell. It's neither sweet nor cloying when it finds its way into a savory context. This is a nice counterpoint to add to the regional yogurt-style marinades for lamb kabobs and kibbeh.

1 tablespoon coriander seeds
1 tablespoon cumin seeds
1 tablespoon cardamom seeds
2 tablespoons ground cinnamon
1 tablespoon allspice
1 tablespoon ground ginger
1½ teaspoons whole cloves

In a small frying pan, place the coriander, cumin, and cardamom seeds, and heat them over medium heat, shaking the pan or stirring the spices with a wooden spoon, for about 5 minutes, until they become fragrant. Remove them from the pan quickly to avoid burning, because they will continue to cook.

Combine the coriander, cumin, cardamom, cinnamon, allspice, ginger, and cloves in a spice mill or a blender and grind to a coarse powder. Stored in a clean, airtight container, this will keep in the freezer for 3 to 4 months.

TIMETABLE:
Salmon steaks or fillets, tuna steaks, swordfish steaks, scallops, or shrimp: 1 hour

Chicken breasts or kabobs, turkey breast, quail, beef kabobs, lamb kabobs, or lamb shoulder or leg: 1 to 2 hours

TIMETABLE:
Shrimp, fish, chicken
breasts, or quail:
2 to 4 hours

CHARMOULA MAKES 1½ CUPS

Charmoula or (chermoulla) can best be described as Moroccan pesto. What pulls this away from its Italian cousin, pesto, is the sweet heat combination of spices and peppers. Olive oil or fresh lemon juice can be added, should you want a lighter consistency.

½ cup chopped fresh parsley
½ cup chopped fresh cilantro or mint leaves
1 tablespoon ground cinnamon
1 tablespoon ground ginger
1 tablespoon hot paprika
1 teaspoon freshly ground black pepper
1 teaspoon coarse-grain salt
½ teaspoon ground cumin
½ teaspoon ground thyme
½ teaspoon cayenne pepper

Combine the parsley, cilantro, cinnamon, ginger, paprika, pepper, salt, cumin, thyme, and cayenne in a blender or a food processor and purée to a smooth paste. The paste will keep for about 1 week in the refrigerator.

TIMETABLE:
Beef kabobs, lamb kabobs,
lamb shoulder, or leg of
lamb: 3 to 4 hours

MOROCCAN-STYLE SHASLICK PASTE

MAKES ABOUT ¾ CUP

Shaslick paste is a cross between a rub and a pesto. This is a milder version, but the paprika can be replaced with red pepper flakes. The marinating paste can also be used on cubes of chicken breast and on jumbo shrimp.

Grated zest and juice of 1 lime (about 2 tablespoons)
¼ cup finely chopped fresh parsley
1 small onion, finely chopped (⅓ to ½ cup)
2 cloves garlic, pressed
1 tablespoon coarse-grain salt
1 tablespoon freshly ground black pepper
1 tablespoon hot paprika
1 tablespoon ground cumin
1 tablespoon ground coriander
¼ cup light olive oil

Combine the lime zest and juice, parsley, onion, garlic, salt, pepper, paprika, cumin, and coriander in a blender or a food processor and process until all the ingredients are blended. While the motor is running, drizzle in the oil a little at a time. Stored in a clean, airtight container, this will keep in the refrigerator for 1 week.

LEMON-CUMIN PASTE MAKES ²/₃ CUP

TIMETABLE:
Shrimp and scallops:
3 to 4 hours

Beef kabobs or lamb
kabobs: 4 to 6 hours

The lemon acts as a refreshing coolant against the spicy cumin and cayenne in this savory North African paste. The paste is perfect for flavoring grilled shrimp with a zest of spice and mild heat.

1 tablespoon lightly crushed cumin seeds
Grated zest and juice of 1 lemon (about 3 tablespoons)
1 teaspoon cracked white peppercorns
3 tablespoons fresh flat-leaf parsley
¼ cup olive oil
¼ cup chopped onion
1 teaspoon sugar
½ teaspoon coarse-grain salt
½ teaspoon cayenne pepper

Heat the cumin seeds in a nonstick frying pan until roasted, but do not burn. Combine the cumin seeds, lemon zest and juice, peppercorns, parsley, olive oil, onion, sugar, salt, and cayenne in a blender or a food processor and process until all the ingredients are blended. Stored in a clean, airtight container, this will keep in the refrigerator for 1 week.

LEMON-SUMAC RUB MAKES ABOUT ¼ CUP

TIMETABLE:
Swordfish steaks, shrimp,
chicken breasts or kabobs,
beef kabobs, or lamb
kabobs: 1 to 2 hours

This Casbah-style rub is a double dose of pucker. The lemon zest and sumac provide a nice complement to the fennel. You can also use this as a spice mix in some of the ground meat kabobs in this chapter.

2 teaspoons dried lemon zest (see page 60 for drying instructions)
1 teaspoon hot paprika
2 teaspoons fennel seeds, toasted
1½ tablespoons sumac
1 teaspoon dried mint
1 teaspoon freshly cracked black peppercorns
½ teaspoon salt

Combine the lemon zest, paprika, fennel seeds, sumac, mint, peppercorns, and salt in a spice mill or a blender and grind to a coarse powder. Stored in a clean, airtight container, this will keep in the freezer for 3 to 4 months.

TIMETABLE:
Shrimp, chicken breasts or kabobs, beef kabobs, or lamb kabobs: 1 to 2 hours

NORTH AFRICAN CUMIN SPICE RUB

MAKES ABOUT 1 CUP

While some of the spotlight on culinary heat waves seems to shine on Southeast Asia and the American Southwest, North African spices are just as complex, maybe even more so. The emphasis is primarily on sweet spices that once were traded throughout Asia, with a bit of heat added. A little bit of this rub goes a long way. One tablespoon per chicken breast is all you need, or dust 1 pound of shrimp with about ¼ cup and get ready to grill.

¼ **cup ground cumin**
2 **tablespoons hot paprika**
2 **tablespoons ground cardamom**
1 **tablespoon dark brown sugar**
1 **tablespoon freshly cracked black peppercorns**
1 **tablespoon cayenne pepper**
1 **teaspoon coarse-grain salt**
2 **tablespoons dried oregano**
1 **tablespoon ground cinnamon, or**
    1 **(3-inch) cinnamon stick, ground**

Combine the cumin, paprika, cardamom, sugar, black pepper, cayenne, salt, oregano, and cinnamon in a spice mill or a blender and grind to a coarse powder. Stored in a clean, airtight container, this will keep in the freezer for 3 to 4 months.

TIMETABLE:
Chicken breasts or kabobs, turkey breast, beef kabobs, lamb kabobs, or goat (baby kid) kabobs: 1 to 2 hours

TSIRE RUB MAKES ⅔ CUP

Tsire is a West African rub that finds its way onto chicken and goat kabobs. The recipe is easy to prep and great to improvise with. You can swap out the ground peanuts for almonds, cashews, or hazelnuts, and you can pull in another spice mix, such as Garam Masala (page 299) or North African Cumin Spice Rub (page 260). The spice mix, without the peanuts, is a rub in its own right and can even roll into a honey-based glaze.

8 whole cloves
1 teaspoon coriander seeds
1 teaspoon cumin seeds
¼ teaspoon allspice
1½ teaspoons ground cinnamon
1 teaspoon red chile flakes
¼ teaspoon cayenne pepper
½ teaspoon ground ginger
¼ teaspoon ground nutmeg
½ teaspoon salt
½ cup roasted peanuts, ground to a powder (avoid over-
    grinding, unless you like unusual-tasting peanut butter)

Toast the cloves, coriander seeds, and cumin seeds in a small frying pan over medium heat until fragrant, shaking the pan constantly. Remove from the pan immediately.

Combine the cloves, coriander seeds, cumin seeds, allspice, cinnamon, red chile flakes, cayenne, ginger, nutmeg, and salt in a spice mill or a blender and grind to a coarse powder. In a small bowl, combine the peanuts and the spices. Stored in a clean, airtight container, this will keep for 2 weeks.

SYRIAN HONEY-POMEGRANATE GLAZE MAKES 1 CUP

The first time I had this recipe was in the role of a glaze that my friend Barbara Boswell used on her Grilled Lamb Kabobs (page 267). The recipe can easily work as a marinade. There are just enough sassy, sweet, and sour flavors to balnce any spiced kabob that it pairs itself with.

2 cloves garlic
1 teaspoon ground cardamom
2 tablespoons pomegranate molasses
½ cup bottled pomegranate juice
1 teaspoon honey
1 teaspoon coarse-grain salt
1 teaspoon freshly cracked black peppercorns
⅓ cup canola oil

Combine the garlic, cardamom, pomegranate molasses, pomegranate juice, honey, salt, and peppercorns in a blender or a food processor and process until all the ingredients are blended. While the motor is running, drizzle in the oil a little at a time. This marinade freezes well with food for up to 3 months.

TIMETABLE:
Chicken breasts or kabobs; chicken wings, thighs, or legs; Cornish hen; turkey breast; quail; lamb rack or rib chops; or lamb kabobs: baste during the last 5 minutes of cooking

Chicken breasts or kabobs,
quail, beef kabobs, lamb
rack or rib chops, lamb
kabobs, or ground lamb:
baste during the last
5 minutes of cooking

MOROCCAN-STYLE FIG GLAZE MAKES 1½ CUPS

Some glazes take to certain cuts of food better than others. But the
Moroccan-Style Fig Glaze is pretty flexible for all cuts. It's particularly good
with grilled lamb medallions.

1 teaspoon coriander seeds
1 teaspoon cumin seeds
1 teaspoon caraway seeds
1 teaspoon cardamom seeds
1 teaspoon anise seeds
1 cup dried Calimyrna or Smyrna figs, chopped fine
½ cup dry white wine, or ¼ cup cider vinegar
1 cup water
¼ cup honey
1 teaspoon coarse-grain salt
2 tablespoons fig vinegar or balsamic vinegar

In a small frying pan, place the coriander, cumin, caraway, cardamom, and
anise seeds and heat them over medium heat, shaking or stirring the pan, for
about 5 minutes, until they become fragrant. Do not let the spices burn. Place
the toasted spices in a spice mill or a blender and grind to a coarse powder.

In a heavy-bottom nonreactive pot, add the toasted spices, figs, wine, water,
honey, salt, and vinegar. Simmer over medium heat for 20 minutes, or until
the figs break up and lose their shape. Stored in a clean, airtight container,
this will keep in the refrigerator for 2 to 3 months.

MOROCCAN-STYLE APRICOT GLAZE. Substitute an equal amount of dried
apricots for the figs and an optional ¼ cup apricot jelly for the honey and
simmer the mixture until the apricots are soft.

GRILLED MOORISH SWORDFISH KABOBS

SERVES 4

The Moorish-Style Marinade works more like paste on the swordfish. The flavor has a delicate intensity about it because the spices expose themselves one by one. You can definitely taste multiple degrees of spice separation. Serve with Cashew-Ginger Chutney (page 331), Mediterranean Yogurt-Cucumber Salad (page 268), and Coconut-Cucumber Slaw (page 335).

4 (6 ounces each) swordfish steaks
1 cup Moorish-Style Marinade (page 255)
Salt and cracked black peppercorns

Cut the swordfish into 1-inch squares and place in a nonreactive container or a 1-gallon resealable plastic bag. Pour the marinade over the swordfish and refrigerate for no longer than 1 hour.

Remove the swordfish from the marinade. Prepare the marinade for basting by bringing it to a boil before you are ready to baste. Thread the fish onto skewers.

To grill: Lightly brush the grill with vegetable oil and grill the swordfish for 5 to 6 minutes, turning after 4 minutes and basting often with the warm marinade.

To cook indoors: Preheat the broiler to its hottest setting and line a baking sheet with foil. Arrange the swordfish on the baking sheet and broil for 6 to 8 minutes on each side, basting often with the warm marinade.

Season with salt and pepper to taste, and serve.

GRILLED LEBANESE CHICKEN KABOBS
(SHISH TAOUK) SERVES 4

Lebanese Chicken Kabobs, or Shish Taouk, are very similar to tandoori chicken. The thick homemade yogurt called laban found at Middle Eastern grocery stores is tart and tasty, and the spices can be varied to your palate. You can replace the cumin with cayenne, and the coriander with cardamom or cinnamon. They all work in this yogurt-based marinade.

2 boneless, skinless chicken breasts
1¼ cups Mediterranean-Style Yogurt Marinade (page 253)
1 red onion, sliced into ¼-inch-thick slices
3 to 4 tablespoons olive oil
4 pita breads
2 to 3 tablespoons toasted pine nuts or sesame seeds, for garnish
Chopped fresh mint leaves, for garnish

Halve the chicken breasts and then cut into 4 strips, 3 to 4 inches long. Place the chicken in a nonreactive container or a 1-gallon resealable plastic bag. Pour the marinade over the chicken and refrigerate for 3 to 4 hours.

Remove the chicken from the marinade. Reserve the marinade and heat gently in a double boiler for basting. Using presoaked bamboo skewers, thread 2 strips of chicken onto each pair of skewers, to keep the chicken pieces from moving around when you turn them.

To grill: Lightly brush the grill with vegetable oil and grill the chicken kabobs for 9 to 10 minutes, turning often and basting with the warm marinade. Brush the onions with the olive oil and grill for 2 to 3 minutes on each side. Warm the pita bread on the grill for about 1 minute on each side.

To cook indoors: Preheat the broiler to its hottest setting and line a baking sheet with foil. Arrange the chicken kabobs on the baking sheet and broil the kabobs for 12 minutes, turning and basting often after the first 6 minutes. Preheat the oven to its lowest setting. Pan-fry the onions in the olive oil for a light glaze. Do not overcook; the onion should still be firm. Warm the pita bread in the oven.

To serve, half-fill each pita with chicken, add the grilled or sautéed onion, top with warm marinade, and garnish with pine nuts and mint.

GRILLED CORNISH HENS WITH MOROCCAN-STYLE FIG GLAZE SERVES 4

This recipe is pure Moroccan comfort food. I've seen guests bypass silverware and tear into these flavorful hens with their fingers. Serve with a rice pilaf studded with dried apricots.

2 quarts Basic Citrus Brine (page 46)
4 (1½ pounds each) Cornish hens, halved lengthwise through the breast
1 cup North African Cumin Spice Rub (page 260)
2½ cups Moroccan-Style Fig Glaze (page 262)
Salt and pepper

Pour the cold brine into a large nonreactive container, add the hens to the brine, and refrigerate for 8 hours. Remove the hens from the brine and pat dry with paper towels. Season with the North African Cumin Spice Rub and let sit at room temperature for 30 minutes.

To grill: Oil the grill with vegetable oil. Place the hens, skin side down, on the grill. Grill for about 10 minutes, until lightly browned on the underside. Use a metal spatula to loosen the hens and turn. Continue grilling, basting with the glaze, and turning and moving as necessary, until no longer pink in the thickest part, 20 to 25 minutes longer.

To cook indoors: Preheat the oven to 450°F. Pat the hens dry and sprinkle with salt and pepper. Roast, cut sides down, in a large heavy shallow baking pan (1 inch deep) for about 30 minutes, until just cooked through. Brush the glaze onto the hens and roast 5 minutes more. The hens are done when the juices run clear when pricked with a knife.

To serve, transfer the hens to a serving plate. Bring the remaining glaze to a boil and brush over the hens before serving.

GRILLED MIDDLE EASTERN BEEF OR LAMB KABOBS SERVES 6

Although nothing looks prettier than skewers of cherry tomatoes interspersed with pearl onions, garlic, and glistening nuggets of marinated beef or lamb, nothing is more demanding on the cook. Not one of those ingredients cooks the same way, or in the same amount of time. Use separate skewers for separate ingredients. Thread each kabob with 2 skewers to avoid having the food roll when it is turned. As for the bamboo skewers, they need not soak in just plain water. They can be soaked in white or red wine, apple cider, or fruit juice for extra penetrating flavor.

The following is a simple and flavorful Middle Eastern–style marinade for either beef or lamb.

2 pounds beef, from the eye round, or 2 pounds lean lamb, from the leg,
 cut into 1-inch chunks
2 cups Turkish-Style Marinade for Beef or Lamb Kabobs (page 254)
6 pieces pita bread, warmed

Place the meat in a nonreactive container or a 1-gallon resealable plastic bag. Pour the marinade over the meat, toss, and refrigerate for 6 hours. Remove the meat from the marinade and thread it onto presoaked bamboo skewers.

To grill: Lightly brush the grill with vegetable oil. Grill the meat over medium-high heat for 3 to 4 minutes per side.

To cook indoors: Preheat the broiler to its hottest setting and line a baking sheet with foil. Arrange the skewers on the baking sheet and grill for 3 to 4 minutes per side.

Slide the meat from the skewers into the warm pita breads and serve.

GRILLED LAMB KABOBS WITH SYRIAN HONEY-POMEGRANATE GLAZE SERVES 6

We were doing a marathon recipe testing for ground kabobs when my friend Barbara Boswell walked in with these Syrian lamb kabobs. They had a smooth texture with hints of toasted pistachio and a sweet spicing. But it was the Syrian Honey-Pomegranate Glaze that finished it that gave the dish its focus. The kabobs can be portioned in half for an appetizer version. Serve with Mediterranean Yogurt-Cucumber Salad (page 268), Marinated Moroccan Olives (page 269), and Stir-Fried Carrots in Orange-Cinnamon Marinade (page 127).

1½ pounds finely ground lamb (see Tip)
1 small sweet onion, peeled and chopped (about ⅔ cup)
3 cloves garlic, minced
2 tablespoons Basic Syrian Spice Mix (page 257)
¼ cup ground pistachio nuts, or 1 tablespoon chickpea flour
2 tablespoons freshly squeezed lemon juice
1 teaspoon honey
⅓ cup fresh flat-leaf parsley, minced
1 cup Syrian Honey-Pomegranate Glaze (page 261)

In a nonreactive mixing bowl, combine the lamb with the onion and garlic until well combined. Add the spice mix, pistachios, lemon juice, honey, and parsley and mix well.

Refrigerate the mixture for at least 6 hours or overnight to meld the flavors. Remove the lamb from the refrigerator and press the mixture around skewers, forming kabobs ¾ inch around and 3 to 4 inches long. Dip the lamb skewers into the Syrian Honey-Pomegranate Glaze. Grill over medium heat on a gas or charcoal grill for 5 to 8 minutes while basting with the remaining glaze.

Remove from the heat and serve immediately.

TIP: Barbara mentioned that after the first grind from the butcher she minced the lamb again in a food processor to form a smooth paste.

MOROCCAN LAMB KABOBS (SHASLICK) SERVES 6

At sidewalk stands on the street of Morocco, vendors slide tangy seasoned lamb kabobs from skewers into warm pitas. My friend chef Jon Jividen suggests serving these kabobs in mini pitas for hors d'oeuvres. If you like, you can alternate various firm vegetables, such as mushrooms, pearl onions, or even whole cloves of garlic, on the skewers with the lamb. Or use different skewers for grilling the lamb and the vegetables, so that the vegetables don't overcook before the meat is done.

2 pounds lean lamb, from leg or shoulder, cut into 1-inch cubes
¾ cup Moroccan-Style Shaslick Paste (page 258)
6 pita breads, warmed

Place the lamb in a nonreactive container or a 1-gallon resealable plastic bag. Add the paste, toss, and refrigerate for at least 4 hours, preferably overnight.

To grill: Lightly brush the grill with vegetable oil. Remove the lamb from the container, and thread the lamb onto presoaked bamboo skewers. Grill for 3 to 4 minutes per side.

To cook indoors: Preheat the broiler to its hottest setting and line a baking sheet with foil. Remove the lamb from the marinade, and thread the lamb onto presoaked bamboo skewers. Arrange the skewers on the baking sheet and grill for 3 to 4 minutes per side.

To serve, slide the meat from the skewers into the warm pita breads and serve.

MEDITERRANEAN YOGURT-CUCUMBER SALAD

SERVES 4

When I think of grilled lamb, I think of three things: yogurt, mint, and cucumber, and I'm not alone in my thinking. There are as many combinations of these ingredients as there are countries lining the Mediterranean. Tzatziki from Greece, cacik from Turkey, and khyar bil-laban from Lebanon all are basic variations on the same theme.

1¼ cups Middle Eastern Yogurt Dipping Sauce,
   cumin is optional (page 269)
1½ cups diced (¼-inch pieces) seedless cucumber

Combine the yogurt sauce and cucumber in a medium-size bowl and mix thoroughly. Cover and refrigerate. This salad will keep, refrigerated, for up to 1 week.

MIDDLE EASTERN YOGURT DIPPING SAUCE

MAKES 1¼ CUPS

This lemon-scented yogurt sauce is perfect spooned over kabobs of marinated lamb or chicken. For a quick, light dinner, combine grilled vegetables and marinated lamb in toasted pita bread and top with salad greens. Serve along with Grilled Middle Eastern Beef or Lamb Kabobs (page 266) or Moroccan Lamb Kabobs (page 268), or in combination with Greek-Style Lemon-Mint Marinade (page 222) or Tahini Marinade (page 295) on chicken.

1 cup plain yogurt or laban
2 cloves garlic, pressed
1 to 2 tablespoons chopped fresh mint
Grated zest and juice of 1 lemon (about 3 tablespoons)
½ teaspoon ground cumin
½ teaspoon coarse-grain salt
1 tablespoon freshly cracked black pepper

Combine the yogurt, garlic, mint, lemon zest and juice, cumin, salt, and pepper in a blender or a food processor. Pour into a glass jar and refrigerate until ready to use. This will keep for 1 to 2 weeks in the refrigerator.

MARINATED MOROCCAN OLIVES MAKES 2 CUPS

You'll find olives on both sides of the Mediterranean, and I put out a bowl of these Moroccan gems to begin any North African–themed dinner.

1 teaspoon whole cumin seeds
1 tablespoon cracked coriander seeds
1 tablespoon red pepper flakes
½ cup olive oil (preferably Greek or Tunisian)
Grated zest and juice of 1 lemon (about ¼ cup)
½ teaspoon cracked black peppercorns
1 pound black or Moroccan olives

Combine the cumin seeds, coriander seeds, red pepper flakes, oil, lemon zest and juice, and peppercorns in a ceramic baking dish or a glass jar. Add the olives and toss to coat. Refrigerate for 2 to 3 days before ready to use, then bring to room temperature before serving. These will keep for up to 3 weeks in the refrigerator.

ASIA

When globe-trotting through

cooking styles and cuisines, I look for foundation flavorings that act as edible postage stamps from the countries that sent them. The foundations in Asian cuisines are anchored by their shelf-staple condiments. These complex spice structures were born out of the need to flavor scarce ingredients for large populations. Maintaining a pantry of stock Asian condiments is like having a complete toolbox for brines, cures, marinades, rubs, and, especially, glazes.

Marinating styles and base ingredient proportions can be remarkably similar. But there are certain thumbprint ingredients that distinguish Thai from Indonesian, Burmese from Malaysian, Japanese from Korean, and Chinese from Vietnamese. There are overlapping ingredients used in all these cuisines, but what pulls them away from one another is how they're combined with other ingredients. Let's step back for a moment and visualize Asia as a large food market with lots of regional aisles. That's how Europe saw it during

the Middle Ages, and Europeans used ships and overland caravans instead of shopping carts. But before we start pulling items off the shelves, let's see whether we can get a profile of some regional styles that line the aisles.

Ever since the travels of Marco Polo, Europe has been enamored with Chinese takeout. China, with its highly developed cuisine, was one of the most important stops along the spice routes. China traded with the Spice Islands in the Indonesian archipelago and passed ingredients back to Europe. When I think of Asian cooking, I think of high-heat cooking that quickly sears meat and seafood, which are then glazed with prepared sauces such as oyster, plum, or hoisin, and then topped off with the heat of Szechuan peppers.

If there's anything one can learn about cooking from Japanese cuisine, it is that less is more. There is a wide range of dishes that can be created with a harmonious blend of just a few ingredients. Japanese cuisine is the lightest of the Asian recipe repertoire. It doesn't mean that it lacks impact. The fresh, clean, and focused flavors are more individually pronounced, with very little palate blearing.

Southeast Asia was one of the most important whistle stops along the spice routes. This is the area where Columbus was heading before another landmass got in the way, and he discovered chiles and tomatoes instead. The three basic cuisines that this pantry is all about are Thai, Vietnamese, and Indonesian (which also includes Malaysia and Singapore). Although they are regionally close, their cuisines are almost worlds apart.

Thai cuisine is not just about heat; it is about flavor over flame. Although chiles and Thai curries have their roles, they're not the only things pushing flavor. Thai food plays off a meld of aromatics, including ginger, garlic, shallots, and herbs like fresh mint and cilantro. Other flavorings are right off the spice routes, and they include peppercorns and cumin, as well as sweet spices like cinnamon, coriander, and cardamom. Binding them all together are coconut milk, fragrant kaffir lime leaves, lemongrass, and fish sauce (nam pla).

Vietnam is separated from Thailand by Cambodia and Laos, and the cuisines couldn't be more different. As part of China for ten centuries and under French rule from the sixteenth to the middle of the twentieth century, Vietnam developed a highly sophisticated cuisine that shares some of the same ingredients as other Southeast Asian countries but with Chinese and French overtones. By scanning the Vietnamese recipes in this chapter, you'll notice that there is more emphasis on fresh ingredients and less focus on the spices, chiles, and curries that characterize Thai and Indonesian cuisines. I think that Vietnamese cuisine is the most accessible by way of gathering ingredients. With a few exceptions, there are not a lot of exotics on the pantry list, and you'll find the food to be highly flavored and breezy in its lightness.

Leaving the Asian land mass puts us into the mother lode of ancient seasonings. The South Indian Ocean contains an archipelago of almost eighteen thousand volcanic-formed islands stretching from the bottom of the Philippines to the equator. It looks like a wide basket of islands catching flavor influences from China, India, Southeast Asia, and Africa. But I would like to think

it's the other way around. It's the other countries that draw from Indonesian flavors. It is the largest spice pocket in the world, and the brightly seasoned food reflects that. Most of the items we have in our spice rack today originated from this region.

Understanding the influence of Indian cuisine has a lot to do with understanding historical food geography. Regionally, Indian food is as varied as regional North American food. It can be as simple or as complex as you like. India is the first major stop on the spice routes, outside of the Middle East and North Africa. Although individual spices from different regions of India are exported to Europe and the New World, India exports refined spice mixes and condiments as well. You'll find curries and chutneys wrapping around Africa, moving up to Europe, and then looping over to the Caribbean. Some of the Indian condiments that have assimilated into our pantries, thanks to the British who thought they discovered them, are Worcestershire sauce, ketchup, and chutney

Some folks see Indian cuisine as long ingredient lists that are out of their reach, but the recipes here are pretty easy and forgiving if you're missing an item or two. There are a few traditional citrus marinades included in this series of recipes, but the ones containing real power have yogurt as their base. Yogurt by itself, with its active lactic enzymes, has a juicier effect on food than a citrus-based marinade does.

Asian ingredients really lend themselves to cross-continental creativity in the kitchen, and some of the recipes in this chapter are about combining Asian and Western flavors for a harmonious blend of both worlds. Asian ingredients are now becoming more and more available to the point where they're as common as balsamic vinegar and extra virgin olive oil. Ginger, cilantro, soy sauce, and even bok choy were once considered Asian exotics, but they have since been assimilated into Western pantries. Some of the following ingredients are pretty basic stuff, while others may require more work to get your hands on. The bulk of these ingredients can be found in most Asian grocery stores and online. Another source for fresh ingredients is Asian restaurants. They'll be able to point you to some of their suppliers and maybe put in an order for you.

THE ASIAN PANTRY

CITRUS: Limes, oranges.

DAIRY: Yogurt, whole milk (if making coconut milk).

FRUIT: Lychees, mangoes, pineapples.

VEGETABLES: Garlic, ginger, green onions.

FRESH HERBS: Basil, mint, cilantro. *Special ingredients:* Galangal, kaffir lime leaves, lemongrass.

CHILES (FRESH AND DRIED): Jalapeños, serranos. *Special ingredients:* Dried Asian chiles, bird (Thai) chiles.

SPICES: *Special ingredients:* Chinese five-spice powder, star anise, Szechuan peppercorns, togarashi chile powder, wasabi powder.

OILS, VINEGARS, CONDIMENTS, AND DRY INGREDIENTS: Peanut butter, roasted peanuts, cashews, unsweetened coconut, sesame seeds. *Special ingredients:* Asian chile oil; Asian fish sauce; coconut milk and toasted coconut; hoisin, oyster, and plum sauces; kecap manis; miso; peanut oil; rice wine vinegar; sesame oil; shrimp paste; soy sauce.

SWEETENERS: Light and dark brown sugar, turbinado sugar, granulated sugar, sherry (used as a sweetener), honey, molasses. *Special ingredients:* Crystallized ginger.

WINES AND LIQUORS: *Special ingredients:* Mirin, sake.

CANNED OR BOTTLED INGREDIENTS: Beef broth, low-sodium chicken broth, tamarind juice.

SPECIAL INGREDIENTS

ASIAN CHILE OIL: Essentially, this is made by steeping chiles in oil. Throughout Asia, the technique is the same; what differs is the regional choice of chile, which can run from hot to volcanic. You can substitute 2 parts peanut oil and 1 part Tabasco or hot sauce. For an upscale variation, see the recipe for Orange-Chipotle Oil (page 172), but replace the oranges zest with lime zest, replace the chipotles with dried Asian chiles (or any dried chile with some heat), and replace the canola oil with peanut oil. Proceed with the recipe as written.

ASIAN FISH SAUCE: Called nam pla in Thailand and nuoc nam in Vietnam, this sauce of fermented anchovies is an essential ingredient in Thai and Vietnamese cuisines. It's less salty than soy sauce and has a more savory depth. You can't always taste its presence in a dish, but when it's missing you know it. It's used in lieu of soy sauce in Southeast Asia. Once opened, you can leave it to your heirs; it'll last a generation or two in the refrigerator. For a substitute, in a saucepan, combine ½ cup water, ½ cup soy sauce, ¼ cup anchovy paste or 12 anchovy fillets (rinsed), 2 cloves garlic, minced, and ½ teaspoon brown sugar. Simmer for 15 minutes, cool to room temperature, and purée in a blender. Strain the sauce into a clean, airtight container.

CHINESE FIVE-SPICE POWDER: Five-spice powder can contain more than five different spices. Basically, it's made up of star anise, cloves, peppercorns, ground ginger, and cinnamon. Although it has some kick to it, five-spice powder is a sweet spice mix. For a substitute, you can get by with at least three of the above ingredients, one of them being black peppercorns.

COCONUT MILK AND TOASTED COCONUT: My choice for canned coconut milk is a Thai brand called Chaokoh. For a substitute, in a saucepan, combine 1 cup whole milk, ¼ cup toasted coconut, and 1 teaspoon sugar; simmer for 15 minutes. Strain and discard the toasted coconut.

CRYSTALLIZED GINGER: Crystallized ginger is generally made by boiling fresh ginger in simple syrup (1 cup water and 1 cup sugar). It's then dried and tossed with granulated sugar. You can substitute a mixture of 6 or 7 parts grated fresh ginger and 1 part sugar.

DRIED ASIAN CHILES AND BIRD (THAI) CHILES: These hot chiles are generally dried but can be found fresh. They're used in Szechuan, Indian, and even Caribbean cuisines. They are about 1½ to 2 inches long and should be seeded before using. The smaller the dried chile, the hotter its flame. Bird (Thai) chiles are so called because birds actually feed on them and help spread the seeds by their migratory habits. You can substitute any dried red chiles, such as whole cayenne or a pinch of dried red pepper flakes (about half the portion).

GALANGAL: Also known as ka or Laos, galangal is Thailand's hot ginger substitute. It can be purchased fresh or frozen in Asian grocery stores. It looks like a pinkish gold ginger root with rings. It combines well with lemongrass in spicy dishes. You can substitute fresh ginger.

HOISIN, OYSTER, AND PLUM SAUCES: When used in marinades, these table condiments give a distinctive Chinese signature to dishes. These sauces are generally thicker and more concentrated than other Asian condiments.

Slightly spicier than the other two, hoisin sauce is a sweet, reddish brown sauce, containing garlic, soybean, five-spice powder, and ground Asian chiles, among other ingredients. Once opened, it stores indefinitely in the refrigerator. Oyster sauce is the more savory of the Asian sauces. Thicker and richer than Asian fish sauce, it serves to introduce a rich, dark, slightly sweet flavor into Asian stir-fries. Oyster sauce should not be used as a substitute for Asian fish sauce. Once opened, it stores indefinitely in the refrigerator. Plum sauce, or duck sauce, is the sweetest of the three Chinese condiments. For marinating or glazing purposes, plum sauce needs to be thinned and balanced with other Chinese ingredients. You can substitute 1 part dry sherry and 1 part flat beer or dry vermouth for plum sauce.

KAFFIR LIME LEAVES: Kaffir lime leaves are extremely fragrant, and they perfume Thai, Vietnamese, and Indonesian recipes. I've found them fresh in urban Asian markets, and they freeze well. Dried ones can be found over the Internet. The flavor of kaffir lime leaves is irreplaceable, but you can substitute 1 tablespoon lime zest for 4 or 5 leaves.

KECAP MANIS: Kecap (pronounced "kechap") manis is one of the most common condiments in Southeast Asian cuisine. It's sometimes referred to as Indonesian sweet soya sauce and is usually found close to soy sauces in Asian grocery stores. The word *ketchup* is derived from it. For a quick substitute, use 1 part molasses and 2 parts Chinese soy sauce. For a really good worth-your-time version, combine ½ cup firmly packed dark brown sugar or ⅓ cup molasses, and 1 cup soy sauce in a saucepan. Heat until the sugar

continued on page 274

SPECIAL INGREDIENTS, CONTINUED

has dissolved. Add 1 clove garlic, chopped; ¼ teaspoon ground star anise or 1 whole star-anise pod; and 2 tablespoons freshly grated ginger. Simmer for 15 minutes. This substitutes for 1 cup kecap manis. The sauce can be stored in a clean, airtight container in the refrigerator for 3 to 4 months. For a creative substitute, use 2 parts pomegranate molasses and 1 part soy sauce.

LEMONGRASS: Lemongrass, which looks like a stalk of petrified green onion, is found in most Asian groceries. Lemongrass is to Southeast Asian marinades as garlic is to Mediterranean ones. It's a signature aromatic that gives a lemony, perfumelike flavor to Thai cuisine. Store the base in a glass of water to keep it from going too dry. Only the bulb, that is, the first 6 inches, is used (remove the stiff outer leaves). Lemongrass freezes well and is softer to chop after it has been frozen and thawed. The flavor of lemongrass is irreplaceable, but you can substitute ¼ cup chopped fresh lemon balm or lemon verbena, and the grated zest and juice of 1 lemon, for 1 stalk of lemongrass.

MIRIN: A slightly syrupy rice wine, mirin is indispensable to Japanese cooking. It acts as a balancing factor for the saltiness of soy sauce and the acidity of rice wine vinegar. Mirin has a low acid content and shouldn't be used on its own as an acidic element. Because it is sweeter, mirin should not be substituted for rice wine. You can substitute 4 parts dry vermouth, vodka, or sherry and 1 part sugar.

MISO: A soybean paste used in broths and soups, miso gives a sweet-salty-savory depth to dressings and marinades. You can substitute

2 parts hoisin sauce and 1 part light, unsalted chicken broth.

PEANUT OIL: Toasted, or dark, Asian peanut oil is found in Asian food markets; Loriva peanut oil, a domestic brand, is cold-pressed and actually tastes like roasted peanuts, whereas most domestic brands are great for deep-frying but lack a peanut flavor. Store peanut oil in the fridge after opening.

RICE WINE VINEGAR: Rice vinegar, or rice wine vinegar, is fermented from rice and is used in Asian marinades to counteract soy sauce and sesame oils. It cuts some of the oil's nuttiness, which can easily overpower a dish. Rice wine vinegar is ideal for marinating delicate fish and doesn't have the same acetic strength as white vinegar.

SAKE: Sake is brewed from rice. It's one of the pillars of Japanese cuisine, and it is also used as an acidic element in marinades. Sake counteracts and balances the saltiness of soy sauce. I use sake as a replacement for white wine and rice wine vinegar to give a recipe an interesting tweak. You can substitute 1 part dry sherry and 1 part flat beer or dry vermouth.

SESAME OIL: Sesame oil plays a strong, aromatic role. It's used in small portions in conjunction with other oils in Asian-style marinades. Dark brown and fragrant, sesame oil is pressed from roasted sesame seeds. As with its Italian cousin, olive oil, the better premium grades are cold-pressed. Because of its low smoking point, it shouldn't be used for sautéing or frying. For a substitute, combine 1 part toasted sesame seeds and 3 parts peanut oil in a blender. Purée it, and then store in a clean, airtight container. Let it seep for at least 6 hours. This will keep in the refrigerator for at least 1 week.

SHRIMP PASTE: Also called balachan or *kapi,* shrimp paste is used throughout Southeast Asia and Malaysia. It's sold in jars and in 8-ounce brick forms. It's pretty pungent, but the intensity cooks off. You can substitute anchovy paste (not as pungent), or 2 parts mashed anchovy fillets, 1 part soy sauce, and 1 part grated fresh ginger.

SOY SAUCES, LIGHT AND DARK: Light and dark refer to both flavor and color, not necessarily to sodium content. Japanese soy sauces are lighter in color, less salty, and a bit sweeter than the Chinese versions. To confuse matters even more, "light" Japanese soy sauce is saltier than "dark" Japanese soy sauce, "light" Chinese soy sauce is less salty than "dark" Chinese soy sauce, and Thai soy sauces are dark and sweet. If the marinade is Japanese, you can substitute a dark Chinese soy sauce, but use about one third less. I like using light Japanese soy sauce as a basis for Asian dipping sauces and light Japanese marinades for vegetables, fish, shellfish, and white-meat poultry. Dark soy sauce tends to stand up better to duck and beef. Buy soy sauce in the smallest glass bottles you can find. Once opened, refrigerate, covered, for 2 to 3 months; the flavor dips and the saltiness becomes more concentrated over time. The recipes in this book were tested with Chinese dark soy sauce and tamari.

STAR ANISE: The dried, eight-pointed star-shaped seedpod, in spite of its intense licorice flavor, has no relation to aniseed. Star anise is best bought whole. An average "star," when ground, produces more than 1 teaspoon of powder. Kept in a clean, airtight container in a cool environment, star anise can last for years. You can substitute Chinese five-spice powder, or crushed anise seeds and a pinch of allspice.

SZECHUAN PEPPERCORNS: Also known as Sichuan pepper, anise pepper, Chinese pepper, fagara, wild pepper, and sansho, Szechuan peppercorns have a peppery taste with some citrus flavors, and it is one of the ingredients in five-spice powder. In reality, this is not a true pepper, in spite of its many names that include the word *pepper.* Szechuan peppercorns are small, reddish brown berries that grow on a shrubby tree, not on a vine as pepper does. In China, the tree is native to the Szechuan province. Buy the peppercorns whole, not ground, because they lose flavor rapidly when ground. Dry roasting in a pan brings out the flavor and makes them easier to grind. Although it is not a close substitute, you could replace it with 2 parts cracked black peppercorns and 1 part grated orange or lemon zest.

TOGARASHI CHILE POWDER: Use this Japanese dried chile powder sparingly as part of a spice mix. You can substitute 3 parts ground Szechuan peppercorns and 1 part red pepper flakes.

WASABI POWDER: Also known as Japanese horseradish powder, wasabi powder is mixed with liquid to produce a paste that accompanies most Japanese dishes. Use the powder directly in marinades to give a floral or an herbal heat, as opposed to the more vegetal-tasting heat of chiles. The powder does have a short shelf life, and the quality deteriorates over time. Avoid wasabi in a tube; it has less flavor and no heat. You can substitute freshly grated horseradish.

TIMETABLE:
Chicken breasts or turkey breast: 8 to 12 hours

Duck breast or pork tenderloin: 24 hours

ASIAN TEA BRINE MAKES ABOUT 2½ QUARTS

The brine is a pure Asian infusion with the added bronzing of a light glaze. There is a pastiche of flavors that hits light licorice hints of star anise against molasses and Earl Grey tea.

1 tablespoon freshly ground black pepper
2 cups teriyaki sauce
1 cup dark molasses
½ cup crushed star anise
½ cup peeled and minced fresh ginger
2 quarts water
5 Earl Grey tea bags, or ¼ ounce loose tea

Combine the pepper, teriyaki, molasses, star anise, ginger, and water in a nonreactive saucepan and bring to a boil. Add the tea. Let the mixture steep until completely cool, then strain the brine. Refrigerate to 40°F before adding food. The brine can be made up to 3 days ahead.

TIMETABLE (GINGER-SZECHUAN BRINE):
Salmon steaks or fillets, tuna steaks, or shrimp:
1 to 2 hours

Chicken breasts or kabobs, Cornish hen, or quail:
6 hours

Whole chicken, or chicken wings, thighs, or legs:
8 to 12 hours

Pork tenderloin, pork chops, or pork kabobs:
6 to 8 hours

Pork shoulder, baby back ribs, or spareribs:
8 to 12 hours

Turkey breast:
12 to 24 hours

Whole turkey, 12 to 16 pounds: 12 to 24 hours

Whole turkey, 17 pounds and over: 12 to 48 hours

GINGER-SZECHUAN BRINE MAKES 2½ QUARTS

This Asian-infused brine gives seafood, poultry, and pork an added flavor spike. It's especially great for brining Asian-style baby back ribs.

2 quarts water
½ cup honey
¼ cup soy or tamari sauce
⅓ cup kosher salt
¼ cup Szechuan peppercorns
¼ cup peeled and minced fresh ginger
1 or 2 whole star-anise pods, crushed
2 tablespoons five-spice powder

In a large saucepan over medium-high heat, add the water, honey, soy sauce, and salt. Bring to a boil, and stir to dissolve. Add the peppercorns, ginger, star anise, and five-spice powder.

Decrease the heat and simmer for 30 minutes to brew the ingredients. Remove from the heat, let the brine cool to room temperature, then refrigerate to 40°F before adding food. The brine can be made up to 3 days ahead.

HONEY-SHERRY BRINE. Add 2 cups dry sherry, and omit the Szechuan peppercons and the star-anise pod.

SAKE-MIRIN BRINE MAKES ABOUT 6 CUPS

This clean-tasting seafood brine follows a Japanese style of ingredients that doesn't overwhelm fish. Seafood comes out of the brine and hits the grill or broiler, maintaining its natural color; its flavor will hit the upper levels.

2 cups sake
½ cup mirin
¼ cup soy or tamari sauce
2 cups water
2 tablespoons turbinado sugar
1 tablespoon honey
3 tablespoons peeled and minced fresh ginger
1 teaspoon coarse-grain salt
Grated zest of 1 lemon (about 1 tablespoon)
¼ cup cilantro leaves, minced

In a medium saucepan, combine the sake, mirin, soy sauce, water, sugar, honey, ginger, salt, and lemon zest. Bring to a boil, decrease the heat, and simmer for 10 minutes. Remove from the heat and add the cilantro, then refrigerate to 40°F before adding food. The brine can be made up to 3 days ahead.

TIMETABLE:
Shrimp, salmon steaks or fillets, or tuna steaks: 2 to 3 hours

THAI PICKLING BRINE FOR VEGETABLES

MAKES 4¾ CUPS

This brine can leap regions fairly easily. Although it locks into traditional Asian veggies, the brine does justice to Mediterranean vegetables as well.

4 or 5 cloves garlic, minced or pressed
6 dried red or Thai bird chiles, seeded, stemmed, and crumbled
4 tablespoons finely diced shallots
1 tablespoon peeled and grated fresh ginger
2 to 3 tablespoons Asian or domestic cold-pressed peanut oil
3½ cups rice wine vinegar
1 tablespoon sugar
¼ cup chopped lemongrass, outer leaves removed

Combine the garlic, chiles, shallots, and ginger in a blender or a food processor and blend to a smooth paste. Heat the oil in a wok and stir-fry the paste for 5 minutes. Cool the paste to room temperature. In a saucepan over high heat, bring the vinegar to a boil, add the sugar and lemongrass, decrease the heat, and simmer for 20 minutes. Add the paste, stir, then cool to room temperature. The brine can be made up to 3 days ahead.

TIMETABLE:
Salmon steaks or fillets:
1 hour

Chicken breasts, turkey
breast, or pork tenderloin:
4 to 6 hours

THAI-INFUSED BRINE MAKES 2 QUARTS

This brine will leave chicken and pork tenderloin infused with light hints of Thai ingredients, and it can be combined with some of the recipes that follow. You need to brew these ingredients for the brine to pick up their flavors. Any of the Thai marinades can be a source for brining by backing out the citrus juices, vinegars, nuts, and oils.

Pair the brine with Thai Red-Curry Marinade (page 289), Thai Coconut Marinade (page 287), or Grilled Thai-Marinated Chicken Kabobs with Cashew Sauce (page 328).

¼ cup coarse-grain salt
½ cup turbinado or light brown sugar
3 tablespoons chopped galangal or fresh ginger
5 or 6 kaffir lime leaves, bruised and thinly sliced
2 tablespoons Asian fish sauce (nam pla)
2 bird chiles, chopped (about 1½ tablespoons), or
    2 teaspoons red pepper flakes
2 stalks lemongrass, tough outer leaves removed,
    smashed and chopped (¾ to 1 cup)
3 shallots, chopped (¼ to ⅓ cup)
2 quarts of water

Combine the salt, sugar, galangal, kaffir leaves, fish sauce, chiles, lemongrass, shallots, and 1 cup of the water in a blender or a food processor and process until all the ingredients are well blended.

In a stockpot or large saucepan, add the brine mix and bring to a boil. Boil for 10 minutes on high, decrease the heat to low, and simmer for 45 minutes. Remove from the heat, let the mixture cool to room temperature, then add the remaining 7 cups water to bring the volume up to 2 quarts. Refrigerate to 40°F before adding food. The brine can be made up to 3 days ahead.

TIMETABLE:
Chicken breasts:
3 to 4 hours

Beef or pork tenderloin,
beef kabobs, or pork
kabobs: 6 to 8 hours

London broil, skirt steak,
flank steak, or beef short
ribs: 8 to 12 hours

BASIC ASIAN-STYLE MARINADE MAKES 1½ TO 2 CUPS

This is a basic all-purpose Asian starter kit that's brimming with classic Chinese flavors for chicken or beef. Basic Asian shelf staples assemble a great wall of flavor with the spicy-sweet foundation of hoisin sauce. The build continues with a spicy layer of licorice hints from star anise and five-spice powder. Binding the soak are the nutty flavors of sesame and peanut oil. Truly grill- and wok-friendly!

2 tablespoons peeled and grated fresh ginger

3 cloves garlic, chopped

4 tablespoons chopped fresh cilantro

¼ cup chopped green onions, green part only

Grated zest and juice of 4 limes (about ½ cup)

¼ cup soy or tamari sauce

2 tablespoons hoisin sauce

1 tablespoon honey

2 star-anise pods, crushed

1 teaspoon five-spice powder

⅓ cup Asian or cold-pressed domestic peanut oil

2 tablespoons sesame oil

Combine the ginger, garlic, cilantro, green onions, lime zest and juice, soy sauce, hoisin sauce, honey, star anise, and five-spice powder in a blender or a food processor. Process until all the ingredients are well blended. While the motor is running, drizzle in the oils a little at a time. Stored in a clean, airtight container, this will keep in the refrigerator for 1 week.

BALSAMIC-GINGER MARINADE MAKES ABOUT 2 CUPS

This East-meets-West marinade combines the Mediterranean flavors of balsamic vinegar, olive oil, and Dijon-style mustard with Asian soy sauce and ginger. Tastewise, it hits the sweet and sour buttons in your mouth. The combination works so well that I occasionally stir-fry shrimp in this marinade.

5 or 6 cloves garlic, chopped

¼ cup peeled and lightly chopped fresh ginger

2 to 3 tablespoons lightly chopped shallot or sweet onion

2 tablespoons dark soy sauce

1 cup balsamic vinegar

1 tablespoon Dijon-style mustard

1 teaspoon coarse-grain salt

1 tablespoon cracked black peppercorns

¼ cup extra virgin olive, hazelnut, or walnut oil

Combine the garlic, ginger, shallot, soy sauce, balsamic vinegar, mustard, salt, and pepper in a blender or a food processor and process until all the ingredients are well blended. Drizzle in the oil a little at a time. Stored in a clean, airtight container, this will keep in the refrigerator for 1 week.

TIMETABLE:

Salmon steaks, salmon fillets, or shrimp:
2 to 4 hours

Chicken breasts or kabobs, quail, veal loin, or veal paillards: 3 to 4 hours

Beef kabobs, lamb rack, or lamb rib chops:
4 to 6 hours

TIMETABLE:

Salmon steaks or fillets, tuna steaks, red snapper, catfish, sea bass, halibut, scallops, or shrimp:
2 to 3 hours

Chicken breasts or kabobs:
3 to 4 hours

SESAME MARINADE MAKES 1⅓ CUPS

This light Asian marinade has more taste than calories and uses minimum ingredients for maxing out the flavors of marinated tuna, monkfish, mahi mahi, or chicken breasts. This is one of my easy midweek soaks when I need something simple that works. The addition of toasted sesame seeds gives the marinade another level of crunch and flavor.

¼ cup Chinese black rice vinegar, rice wine vinegar, or balsamic vinegar
Grated zest and juice of 3 limes (about ⅓ cup)
1 tablespoon peeled and minced fresh ginger
⅔ cup safflower oil
1 tablespoon sesame oil
½ teaspoon sesame seeds, toasted

Combine the vinegar, lime zest and juice, and ginger in a blender or a food processor. Process until all the ingredients are well blended. While the motor is running, drizzle in the safflower and sesame oils a little at a time. Add the sesame seeds and pulse just to mix. Stored in a clean, airtight container, this will keep in the refrigerator for 1 week. This marinade freezes well with chicken for up to 3 months.

TIMETABLE:

Beef filets, rib eye, or beef kabobs: 4 to 6 hours

Chicken wings: 6 to 8 hours

London broil, skirt steak, flank steak, or baby back ribs: 8 hours to 12 hours

SPICY GARLIC MARINADE MAKES 1½ CUPS

Fair warning! This is one of those in-your-face garlic marinades that also packs a heated punch from cayenne pepper. If you happen to like garlic, you can ramp up the count and add more cloves. This recipe can easily be doubled to soak a London broil.

½ cup rice wine vinegar
½ cup low-sodium soy sauce
8 or 9 cloves garlic, chopped
2 teaspoons ground cayenne pepper
1 tablespoon ground ginger
2 tablespoons dark brown sugar
¼ cup Asian or domestic cold-pressed peanut oil

Combine the vinegar, soy sauce, garlic, cayenne pepper to taste, ginger, and sugar in a blender or a food processor. Process until all the ingredients are well blended. While the motor is running, drizzle in the oil a little at a time. Stored in a clean, airtight container, this will keep in the refrigerator for 1 week. This marinade freezes well with food for up to 3 months.

SZECHUAN SESAME MARINADE

MAKES 1½ CUPS

. . . .

This marinade is China's nutty-flavored answer to Thai peanut sauce, and it can work as a dipping sauce as well. You can use this as a base for Szechuan Sesame Chicken Salad (page 321). This marinade is wok- and grill-friendly for grilled chicken, shrimp, or pork tenderloin.

3 tablespoons sherry wine vinegar
3 tablespoons rice vinegar
¼ cup Asian sesame paste (not tahini;
    available where Asian foods are sold)
¼ cup chopped fresh cilantro
3 cloves garlic, minced
1 inch fresh ginger, peeled and minced
1 teaspoon Szechuan peppercorns
½ cup sesame oil
1 teaspoon Asian chile oil (see page 272)

Combine the vinegars, sesame paste, cilantro, garlic, ginger, and peppercorns in a blender or a food processor. Process until all the ingredients are well blended. While the motor is running, dizzle in the sesame and chile oils a little at a time. Stored in a clean, airtight container, this will keep in the refrigerator for 1 week. This marinade freezes well with food for up to 3 months.

TIMETABLE:
Scallops or shrimp:
3 to 4 hours

Chicken breasts or kabobs, turkey breast, quail, pork tenderloin, pork chops, or pork kabobs: 4 to 6 hours

Sirloin, porterhouse, New York strip, tri tips, or beef kabobs: 6 to 8 hours

Chicken wings, thighs, or legs; baby back ribs; spareribs; or beef short ribs: 8 to 12 hours

ORANGE SESAME MARINADE MAKES 1½ CUPS

Hot chile oil gives a Szechuan bite to this marinade, and the orange provides contrast to the nutty flavor of the oils. The marinade seems to be begging for a pound of diver scallops and a hot grill. Needless to say, I was happy to provide both.

¼ cup soy or tamari sauce
3 tablespoons red wine vinegar
1 tablespoon honey
Grated zest and juice of 3 juice oranges (about 1 cup)
1 tablespoon Asian chile oil (see page 272)
2 cloves garlic, minced
1 tablespoon peeled and minced fresh ginger
¼ cup Asian or domestic cold-pressed peanut oil
3 tablespoons sesame oil
1 teaspoon sesame seeds, toasted

Combine the soy sauce, vinegar, honey, orange zest and juice, chile oil, garlic, and ginger in a blender or a food processor. Process until all the ingredients are well blended. While the motor is running, drizzle in the peanut and sesame oils a little at a time. Add the sesame seeds and pulse to just mix. This marinade freezes well with food for up to 3 months.

TIMETABLE:

Salmon steaks or fillets, scallops, or shrimp: 2 to 3 hours

Chicken breasts or kabobs, turkey breast, quail, beef filets, or rib eye: 3 to 4 hours

Pork tenderloin, pork chops, or pork kabobs: 4 to 6 hours

SIMPLE SAKE MARINADE MAKES 1½ CUPS

Kitchen Zen! Simple, balanced, and too easy to make.

⅔ cup sake
⅓ cup soy or tamari sauce
½ cup mirin

Combine the sake, soy sauce, and mirin in a nonreactive mixing bowl. Stored in a clean, airtight container, this will keep in the refrigerator for 2 to 3 months.

BASIC JAPANESE-STYLE MARINADE. Add 1 tablespoon wasabi powder. Pulse in ¼ cup finely diced chives.

TIMETABLE:

Salmon steaks or fillets, tuna steaks, red snapper, catfish, sea bass, halibut, scallops, or shrimp: 2 to 3 hours

Chicken breasts or kabobs: 3 to 4 hours

Beef filets, rib eye, beef kabobs, London broil, skirt steak, or flank steak: 4 to 6 hours

SIMPLE SAKE GLAZE. Bring the sake and ¼ cup tightly packed dark brown sugar to a boil in a nonreactive saucepan. When the sugar is dissolved, add the mirin and soy sauce, decrease the heat, and simmer for about 20 minutes, until reduced to ¾ cup. Remove the glaze from the heat and cool to room temperature. The glaze will keep in a container in the refrigerator for up to 2 weeks.

SAKE-HONEY GLAZE. Follow the instructions for Simple Sake Glaze, but replace the brown sugar with ¼ cup honey.

WASABI MARINADE MAKES 1³/₄ CUPS

The wasabi packs a fair amount of firepower and depth in this Japanese-style marinade. Scale the wasabi up or down, depending on the heat button on your palate. Not only is the marinade flexible enough to handle poultry and seafood, but I also particularly like it for stir-frying vegetables. This is one of my favorite tuna soaks because of its fast-acting flavor.

3 tablespoons wasabi powder
3 tablespoons boiling water
⅓ cup sake
3 tablespoons rice vinegar
2 tablespoons mirin
1 tablespoon minced shallots
2 or 3 cloves garlic, chopped
1 tablespoon brown sugar
⅓ cup Asian or domestic cold-pressed peanut oil

In a ramekin or small bowl, stir together the wasabi and the water to form a paste. Combine the wasabi paste, sake, rice wine vinegar, mirin, shallots, garlic, and sugar in a blender or a food processor. Process until all the ingredients are well blended. While the motor is running, drizzle in the oil a little at a time. This marinade will keep in a clean, airtight container in the refrigerator for 1 week.

SAKE-MUSTARD MARINADE. Substitute 1 tablespoon Dijon-style mustard for the wasabi paste and proceed with the recipe above.

TIMETABLE:

Tuna steaks: 2 to 3 hours

Broccoli or cauliflower:
3 to 4 hours

Shrimp or scallops:
3 to 4 hours

Chicken breasts:
2 to 4 hours

Chicken wings: 6 to 8 hours

TIMETABLE:
Beef tenderloin:
2 to 4 hours

Shrimp: 1 to 2 hours

Beef kabobs, scallops,
or pork tenderloin:
3 to 4 hours

Chicken breasts:
2 to 3 hours

TIP: For quick marinating,
cut chicken into 1-inch
pieces and marinate for 30
minutes to 1 hour. This can
do double duty as a baste,
but bring it to a boil for 3
minutes before brushing
onto food.

YAKITORI MARINADE MAKES 1 CUP

The ingredients in this recipe are the same as Teriyaki Glaze (page 304),
but they are used to make a marinade this time. Japanese marinating
styles are perfect for our busy Western lifestyles because these marinades
need only an hour or so to work their flavor magic on chicken breasts and
skewered fish.

1 cup sake
½ cup mirin
1 cup soy or tamari sauce
2 tablespoons light miso (available at Asian groceries)
¼ cup rock or turbinado sugar
2 tablespoons crystallized ginger

Combine sake, mirin, soy sauce, miso, sugar, and ginger in a small saucepan.
Bring to a boil, then decrease the heat and simmer for about 30 minutes,
until the sauce is reduced to 1 cup. Remove from the heat and cool to
room temperature, then pour into a clean, airtight container and refrigerate
until ready to use. This marinade will keep in a clean, airtight container,
refrigerated, for 2 to 3 weeks.

TIMETABLE:
Chicken breasts:
3 to 4 hours

Beef or pork tenderloin,
beef or pork kabobs, or
buffalo steak: 6 to 8 hours

London broil, skirt steak, or
flank steak: 8 to 12 hours

KOREAN-STYLE MARINADE MAKES 2 CUPS

What pulls Korean flavors away from other Asian cuisines is their play on
sweet, sour, hot, spicy, bitter, and nutty. They're strong harmonic flavors for
marinating beef, pork loin, or even chicken for the grill.

¼ cup sesame seeds, toasted
1 tablespoon sesame oil
¼ cup rice wine vinegar
3 tablespoons soy or tamari sauce
2 tablespoons brown sugar
2 or 3 cloves garlic, chopped
2 to 3 tablespoons chopped green onions, white part only
1 teaspoon freshly ground black pepper
2 Asian dried red chiles, crumbled (remove seeds for less heat)
½ cup Asian or domestic cold-pressed peanut oil

In a spice mill or a blender, grind the toasted sesame seeds to a fine powder.
Combine the sesame powder, sesame oil, rice wine vinegar, soy sauce, sugar,
garlic, green onions, pepper, and chiles in a blender or a food processor.
Process until all the ingredients are well blended. While the motor is running,
drizzle in the oil a little at a time. Stored in a clean, airtight container, this will
keep in the refrigerator for 1 week.

BASIC SOUTHEAST ASIAN MARINADE MAKES 2 CUPS

Whether you marinate vegetables for a stir-fry, shrimp for the grill, or chicken breasts for the broiler, this versatile marinade is a catalog of Southeast Asian flavors. It's a play on shelf staples and fresh aromatics. The Asian fish sauce (nam pla), basil, and mint are typically Vietnamese; the sweet soy sauce is a Malaysian staple. Ginger, garlic, shallots, and lemongrass are traditional Asian essentials that give this soak added depth.

2 tablespoons vegetable oil
3 or 4 cloves garlic, minced or pressed
2 tablespoons chopped fresh lemongrass
2 tablespoons peeled and grated fresh ginger
3 shallots, chopped (about ¼ cup)
3 tablespoons Asian fish sauce (nam pla)
1 tablespoon kecap manis (see page 273)
¼ cup chopped fresh basil
2 to 3 tablespoons chopped fresh mint
1 teaspoon ground coriander
½ cup Asian rice wine vinegar
¼ cup Asian or domestic cold-pressed peanut oil

Lightly coat a nonreactive saucepan pan with the oil over medium heat. Sauté the garlic, lemongrass, ginger, and shallots for 5 to 10 minutes, until soft. Cool to room temperature. Combine the cooled mixture with the fish sauce, kecap manis, basil, mint, coriander, and vinegar in a blender or a food processor and process until all the ingredients are well blended. While the motor is running, drizzle in the oil a little at a time. This marinade will keep in a clean, airtight container in the refrigerator for 4 to 5 days.

TIMETABLE:
Vegetables, shrimp, chicken breasts, turkey breast, or pork tenderloin: 3 to 4 hours

Beef kabobs, lamb rack, or lamb rib chops: 4 to 6 hours

TIMETABLE:
Shrimp or soft-shell crabs:
3 to 4 hours

LEMONGRASS MARINADE MAKES 1½ CUPS

Chef Lynn Buono, of Feast Your Eyes Catering in Philadelphia, says that this is her stock Southeast Asian–style marinade for grilled soft-shell crabs as a main course and shrimp in the shell as an appetizer. The flavor centers on the lemony spice of lemongrass, with tangy Asian overtones. This makes enough to marinate 1 pound of unpeeled shrimp or 8 soft-shell crabs. Do not marinate the shellfish longer than 3 to 6 hours, or it will become too salty.

1 cup olive oil
2 stalks lemongrass, tough outer leaves removed, smashed and chopped
2 cloves garlic, minced or pressed
¼ cup soy or tamari sauce
1 tablespoon Asian fish sauce (nam pla)
Grated zest and juice of 1 lime (about 2 tablespoons)
1 jalapeño chile, stemmed, seeded, deveined, and chopped
2 tablespoons chopped fresh cilantro

In a skillet, heat the olive oil over medium heat, add the lemongrass and garlic, and cook for about 30 seconds. Cool to room temperature. Combine the lemongrass-garlic mixture, soy sauce, Asian fish sauce, lime zest and juice, jalapeño, and cilantro in a blender or a food processor and process until all the ingredients are well blended. Stored in a clean, airtight container, this will keep in the refrigerator for 1 week.

HOMEGROWN LEMONGRASS

Although lemongrass occasionally shows up in urban supermarkets, I asked Asian fusion cookbook author Hugh Carpenter about its quality. Hugh says, "It's such poor quality. It's dried out and dehydrated by the time it gets to the market. Unless you buy it at an Asian supermarket with a high turnover, it has lost its entire flavor. You might as well be grinding up a pencil into your dish. Fresh lemongrass has leafy fronds that are still green. The moment the leafy ends turn brown and brittle it's not worth buying." Well, this may not help with impulse Thai dinner planning, but I've brought supermarket lemongrass back from the dead by plopping the stalks in a vase of water and waiting for them to sprout in a few weeks. They are bulbs, after all. At that point, the choice is either to cook them or to plant them (sprouted lemongrass stalks begin to develop some thin purple rings that will get thicker if you plant them). Lemongrass is a pretty resilient plant that can be grown on balconies and decks and brought in during the winter.

THAI COCONUT MARINADE MAKES 2 CUPS

This marinade is a starter kit for Thai ingredients—lemongrass, coconut milk, fish sauce, basil, and chile. You'll find these mainstay ingredients in satays, soups, and sauces. These are not overpowering flavors, yet they taste different depending on what has been soaking in them.

3 tablespoons peanut oil
2 cloves garlic, minced
1 stalk lemongrass, tough outer leaves removed, smashed and chopped (about ¼ cup)
2 tablespoons peeled and grated fresh ginger
3 tablespoons finely diced shallots
1 (12-ounce) can Asian coconut milk
1 teaspoon Asian chile oil (see page 272)
Grated zest and juice of 2 limes (about ¼ cup)
3 tablespoons chopped fresh Thai basil or regular basil
1 teaspoon ground coriander
2 tablespoons Asian fish sauce (nam pla)
1 tablespoon dark brown sugar

In a nonreactive saucepan over medium heat, lightly coat the pan with the oil and sauté the garlic, lemongrass, ginger, and shallots until soft, 5 to 10 minutes. Add the coconut milk and chile oil and simmer for 20 minutes. Cool to room temperature and add the lime zest and juice, basil, coriander, fish sauce, and brown sugar in a blender or a food processor and process until all the ingredients are well blended. Stored in a clean, airtight container, this will keep in the refrigerator for 1 week. This marinade freezes well with food for up to 3 months.

TIMETABLE:
Salmon steaks or fillets:
2 to 3 hours

Shrimp or soft-shell crabs:
3 to 4 hours

Chicken breasts, pork tenderloin, pork chops, or pork kabobs: 4 to 6 hours

Chicken wings, chicken thighs, chicken legs, beef kabobs, London broil, skirt steak, flank steak, beef short ribs, baby back ribs, or spareribs: 8 to 12 hours

THAI CURRY PASTES

Don't confuse Thai curry pastes with Indian curries. Thai curries are quite complex and are made from a combination of fresh and dried chiles, lemongrass, shallots, and shrimp paste, to name a few ingredients. They are color-coded according to their heat, with green being the hottest, red in the middle, and yellow (which contains turmeric) the mildest. The curry pastes freeze well and can keep in the refrigerator under a coating of peanut oil. Several Thai cookbooks have recipes for making your own, but if you're in an Asian market shopping for those ingredients, the real things are readily available.

Shrimp or scallops:
2 to 4 hours

Chicken breasts or quail:
3 to 4 hours

Beef kabobs, lamb
kabobs, or pork tenderloin:
4 to 6 hours

THAI-STYLE TAMARIND MARINADE MAKES 2 CUPS

This has all the flavor complexity of a Thai marinade without the heat. The sour flavors of the tamarind and kaffir lime leaves make a great combination with the roasted coconut and fresh cilantro. This is one of my all-time favorite Thai seafood marinades. I never seem to run out of things to use it on.

6 to 8 ounces tamarind pulp (available at Asian and Latin groceries)
2 cups boiling water
4 large kaffir lime leaves, cut into narrow strips
¼ cup shredded coconut, toasted
Grated zest and juice of 3 limes (about ⅓ cup)
1 tablespoon soy or tamari sauce
1 shallot, finely chopped (about 3 tablespoons)
4 cloves garlic, chopped
1 tablespoon peeled and diced fresh ginger
1 tablespoon brown sugar
½ cup chopped fresh cilantro

Place the tamarind pulp in a small nonreactive bowl and pour the boiling water over the pulp. Soak the pulp in the water until soft, from 10 to 15 minutes. With your fingers, rub the pulp until it is dissolved and the seeds are free of the pulp. Strain and discard the seeds and fibers.

Combine the tamarind water, kaffir leaves, and coconut in a nonreactive saucepan and simmer over low heat until the kaffir leaves and coconut have softened. Remove from the heat and cool to room temperature. This will infuse the tamarind mix. Combine the tamarind infusion, lime zest and juice, soy sauce, shallot, garlic, ginger, brown sugar, and cilantro in a blender or a food processor. Process until all the ingredients are well blended. Stored in a clean, airtight container, it will keep in the refrigerator for 3 days.

Shrimp: 3 to 4 hours

Chicken breasts or
kabobs, turkey breast,
pork tenderloin, or pork
kabobs: 4 to 6 hours

THAI PEANUT MARINADE MAKES 2½ CUPS

This marinade is more of a coating than a soak. The twist is to take a standard Thai satay recipe and run it in reverse with flavors hitting the food before grilling, as opposed to after. But there's no reason not to get the flavor coming and going. Although grill-friendly, this marinade is begging to soak shrimp, calamari, or chicken strips. Then coat the food in panko crumbs and deep-fry.

½ cup rice wine vinegar
Grated zest and juice of 3 limes (about ⅓ cup)
2 tablespoons dark brown sugar
¼ cup smashed and chopped fresh lemongrass (about 1 stalk)

2 cloves garlic, minced

2 tablespoons chopped shallots or green onions, white parts only

1 tablespoon peeled and grated fresh ginger

1 tablespoon curry powder or garam masala (page 299)

1 cup unsalted peanut butter (preferably fresh ground)

½ cup Asian or roasted peanut oil

1 tablespoon sesame oil

Combine the vinegar, lime zest and juice, brown sugar, lemongrass, garlic, shallots, ginger, and curry powder in a blender or a food processor and process until all the ingredients are well blended. Add the peanut butter in batches and pulse until incorporated. While the motor is running, drizzle in the oils a little at a time. Stored in a clean, airtight container, this will keep in the refrigerator for 1 week.

TIP: If you're going to make the marinade ahead, keep in mind that it will thicken. Don't add the vinegar and lime juice until the time you're going to use the marinade, then combine these ingredients along with the marinade in a blender or a food processor and reprocess the mixture.

THAI RED-CURRY MARINADE MAKES 2½ CUPS

Kaffir lime leaves throw off a very aromatic perfume along with fresh galangal, ginger's spicier cousin, the two signature ingredients in this recipe. Tying it all together are the flavors of coconut and Thai red-curry paste. Great on beef, the marinade works equally well on shrimp. All of the ingredients can be found in most Asian grocery stores, and kaffir lime leaves and galangal can be frozen.

1 (12-ounce) can Asian coconut milk (preferably Chaokoh brand)

1 (4-ounce) can Thai red-curry paste

1 stalk lemongrass, tough outer leaves removed,
      smashed and finely chopped (about ¼ cup)

6 kaffir lime leaves, chopped into very thin shreds

1-inch square fresh galangal, peeled and grated

¼ cup chopped fresh cilantro

Grated zest and juice of 3 limes (about ⅓ cup)

2 tablespoons Asian fish sauce (nam pla)

1 tablespoon kecap manis (see page 273)

¼ cup Asian or roasted peanut oil

TIMETABLE:

Salmon steaks or fillets:
2 to 3 hours

Shrimp or soft-shell crabs:
3 to 4 hours

Chicken breasts, pork tenderloin, pork chops, or pork kabobs: 4 to 6 hours

Chicken wings, chicken thighs, chicken legs, beef kabobs, London broil, skirt steak, flank steak, beef short ribs, baby back ribs, or spareribs: 6 to 8 hours

Combine the coconut milk, curry paste, lemongrass, and kaffir leaves in a small saucepan, and simmer over low heat for 20 minutes. Cool to room temperature. Combine the coconut-curry mixture along with the galangal, cilantro, lime zest and juice, fish sauce, and kecap manis in a blender or a food processor. Process until all the ingredients are well blended. While the motor is running, drizzle in the oil a little at a time. Stored in a clean, airtight container, this will keep in the refrigerator for 1 week. This marinade freezes well with food for up to 3 months.

TIMETABLE:

Salmon steaks or fillest:
2 to 3 hours

Shrimp or soft-shell crabs:
3 to 4 hours

Chicken breasts, pork
tenderloin, pork chops, or
pork kabobs: 4 to 6 hours

Chicken wings, chicken
thighs, chicken legs, beef
kabobs, London broil, skirt
steak, flank steak, beef
short ribs, baby back ribs,
or spareribs: 6 to 8 hours

BASIC VIETNAMESE MARINADE (NUOC CHAM)
MAKES 1²/₃ CUP

This marinade is a variation on a Vietnamese table condiment called nuoc cham. When used as a marinade, I put a little aside to use as a light basting sauce for the grill. I also like to scale up the batch by three and steam shrimp or mussels in it. Splash a little bit over some freshly shucked oysters for an easy Asian appetizer.

2 cloves garlic, minced
1 serrano chile, stemmed, seeded, deveined, and diced
2 tablespoons turbinado or light brown sugar
¼ cup rice vinegar
¼ cup Asian fish sauce (nam pla)

Combine the garlic, chile, sugar, vinegar, and fish sauce in a blender or a food processor and process until all the ingredients are well blended. Pour into a clean, airtight container and refrigerate until ready to use. This will keep for 1 week in the refrigerator.

TIMETABLE:

Shrimp: 3 to 4 hours

Chicken breasts or quail:
4 to 6 hours

Tofu, beef kabobs, lamb
kabobs, or pork kabobs:
6 to 8 hours

VIETNAMESE PEANUT-TAMARIND MARINADE
MAKES 1¹/₂ CUPS

Vietnamese cuisine can take the same herbs and spices of piquant Thai marinades and turn the heat into a delicate, savory fragrance. To make a delectable dipping sauce, warm the leftover marinade to a gentle simmer and serve.

1 cup canned tamarind nectar
⅓ cup rice wine vinegar
3 tablespoons peanut butter
1 stalk lemongrass, tough outer leaves removed,
    smashed and finely chopped (about ¼ cup)
2 or 3 cloves garlic, minced or pressed
¼ cup chopped fresh mint
1 tablespoon Asian fish sauce (nam pla)
1 tablespoon dark brown sugar
½ teaspoon ground turmeric

Combine the tamarind nectar, vinegar, peanut butter, lemongrass, garlic, mint, fish sauce, sugar, and turmeric in a blender or a food processor. Purée until all the ingredients are well blended. Stored in a clean, airtight container, this will keep in the refrigerator for 1 week. This marinade freezes well with food for up to 3 months.

INDONESIAN MARINADE MAKES 1¾ CUPS

Indonesian Marinade is a tropical Asian mix of sweet coconut, fragrant lemongrass, tart lime, and tangy chile, all playing off the nutty flavor of sesame oil. Part of the appeal of this marinade is its three-way heat. There's a bit of bite to the fresh ginger, with the dried bird and serrano chiles adding another row of teeth.

Grated zest and juice of 4 limes (about ½ cup)
2 tablespoons Asian fish sauce (nam pla)
¼ cup shredded unsweetened coconut
3 tablespoons peeled and grated fresh ginger
1 stalk lemongrass, tough outer leaves removed,
    smashed and finely chopped (about ¼ cup)
3 dried bird chiles, stemmed, seeded, and crumbled
1 serrano chile, stemmed, seeded, and diced
3 cloves garlic
3 green onions, white part only, chopped
¼ cup sesame oil

Combine the lime zest and juice, fish sauce, coconut, ginger, lemongrass, red chiles, serrano, garlic, and green onions in a blender or a food processor and process until all the ingredients are well blended. While the motor is running, drizzle in the oil a little at a time. Stored in a clean, airtight container, this marinade will keep in the refrigerator for 1 week. It freezes well with food for up to 3 months.

TIMETABLE:

Shrimp, chicken breasts or kabobs; chicken wings, thighs, or legs; or quail: 3 to 4 hours

Pork tenderloin, baby back ribs, or spareribs: 4 to 6 hours

TIMETABLE:
Shrimp, chicken breasts
or kabobs, duck breast, or
quail: 3 to 4 hours

Beef, lamb, or pork kabobs;
pork tenderloin; or pork
chops: 4 to 6 hours

Chicken wings, chicken
thighs, chicken legs,
beef filets, rib eye, sirloin,
porterhouse, New York
strip, or tri tips: 6 to 8 hours

Baby back ribs or
spareribs: 8 to 12 hours

SINGAPORE-STYLE MARINADE MAKES 1 CUP

The flavors of this South Sea–style marinade let loose with a typhoon
intensity. Its sweet, sour, and savory heat typifies the full-bodied aromas of
skewered Malaysian street food.

½ cup canned tamarind nectar
1 tablespoon soy sauce
¼ cup rice wine vinegar
1 tablespoon sambal oelek (chile paste), or
    2 to 3 tablespoons hot sauce and 2 cloves garlic, minced
1 tablespoon shrimp paste
3 tablespoons chopped fresh cilantro
3 to 4 tablespoons chopped fresh mint
1 tablespoon brown sugar

Combine the tamarind nectar, soy sauce, vinegar, sambal oelek, shrimp
paste, cilantro, mint, and brown sugar in a blender or a food processor and
process until all the ingredients are well blended. Stored in a clean, airtight
container, this will keep in the refrigerator for 1 week.

CURRYING FLAVOR

Indian curries are quite different from the curries found in the West
Indies, which vary in spice and heat. Commercial curry powders
contain anywhere from six to eight ingredients, as opposed to
rempahs and garam masala, which can contain up to twenty-five
ingredients. Use curries sparingly in marinades, because they can
easily overpower a dish. Over time, the flavor of curry spices can
age and break down unevenly. Some will taste more assertive,
while others will taste flat. Date and store curry powders in tightly
covered glass jars in the refrigerator or in a cool, dark place. They
will hold on to flavor for at least 3 months.

BASIC CURRY MARINADE MAKES 1¼ CUPS
. . . .

The Indian sweet-heat flavor of curry comes rolling across your mouth, hitting every corner of your taste buds. Every time I make this I find something new to put it on—shrimp, chicken wings, spareribs, tofu, anything.

¼ cup curry powder or garam masala (page 299)
1 teaspoon ground cinnamon
2 tablespoons dry sherry
Grated zest and juice of 3 limes (about ⅓ cup)
Grated zest and juice of 2 lemons (about ⅓ cup)
2 to 3 tablespoons chopped shallots
¼ cup chopped fresh cilantro
2 dry red chiles, crumbled (seeded for less heat)
1 tablespoon dark brown sugar
⅓ cup Asian or domestic cold-pressed peanut oil

In a blender or a food processor, combine the curry, cinnamon, sherry, lime zest and juice, lemon zest and juice, shallots, cilantro, chiles, and brown sugar. Process until all the ingredients are well blended. With the motor running, drizzle in the oil a little at a time. Stored in a clean, airtight container, this will keep in the refrigerator for 1 week.

COCONUT CURRY MARINADE. Add ½ cup toasted shredded coconut and replace the peanut oil with 1 (12-ounce) can Asian or Thai unsweetened coconut milk.

TIMETABLE:
Tofu or shrimp: 2 to 4 hours

Chicken breasts:
3 to 4 hours

Lamb kabobs: 4 to 6 hours

Chicken wings or spareribs:
6 to 8 hours

TIMETABLE:
Salmon steaks or fillets,
shrimp, chicken breasts,
or chicken kabobs:
4 to 6 hours

Lamb kabobs: 6 to 8 hours

TANDOORI YOGURT MARINADE MAKES 2 CUPS

This Indian-style marinade gives lamb kabobs a tart and spicy taste. Savory yogurt marinades don't require oil and are able to keep lamb and chicken kabobs moist and fragrant, whether the meat is grilled or broiled. Also try the equally flavorful Mediterranean-Style Yogurt Marinade (page 253).

¼ cup finely chopped fresh mint
2 tablespoons peeled grated fresh ginger
½ cup chopped onion
2 cloves garlic, chopped
1½ teaspoons garam masala (page 299) or curry powder
2 tablespoons hot paprika
½ teaspoon ground coriander
½ teaspoon ground cardamom
Pinch cayenne pepper
½ teaspoon coarse-grain salt
1½ cups plain yogurt

Combine the mint, ginger, onion, garlic, garam masala, paprika, coriander, cardamom, cayenne, salt, and yogurt in a food processor or a blender and process until all the ingredients are well blended. The marinade will keep refrigerated in a clean, airtight container for up to 1 week.

TIMETABLE:
Salmon steaks or fillets,
tuna steaks, or scallops:
2 to 3 hours

Chicken breasts, chicken
kabobs, or pork tenderloin:
3 to 4 hours

Beef filets; rib eye; or beef,
lamb, or pork kabobs:
4 to 6 hours

MANGO CHUTNEY MARINADE MAKES 1 CUP

This marinade is so good that you can eat it right out of the jar. Many chutneys work well in this recipe, so experiment and be creative.

½ cup Major Grey's mango chutney
1 tablespoon tomato paste concentrate
Grated zest and juice of 2 lemons (about ⅓ cup)
1 serrano chile, stemmed, seeded, deveined, and diced
2 cloves garlic, minced or pressed
1 teaspoon coarsely cracked black peppercorns
1 teaspoon coarse-grain salt
⅓ cup olive or peanut oil

Combine the chutney, tomato paste, lemon zest and juice, serrano, garlic, pepper, and salt in a food processor or a blender and purée. With the motor running, drizzle in the oil a little at a time. Stored in a clean, airtight container, this marinade will keep in the refrigerator for 1 week. It freezes well with food for up to 3 months.

TAHINI MARINADE MAKES 1½ CUPS

The flavors of this marinade are best described as Middle East meets Far East. Sesame ties the regional ingredients together. Tahini, the sesame-seed paste of the Middle East, complements the toasted flavor of sesame oil from the Orient, as they combine ingredients of the Mediterranean Sea and the South China Sea. This is a savory seafood soak for tuna, red snapper, swordfish, and pretty much any cut of meat.

3 tablespoons tahini paste
1 tablespoon Asian sesame oil
Grated zest and juice of 2 lemons (about ⅓ cup)
1 tablespoon light soy sauce
2 tablespoons honey
3 tablespoons peeled and chopped fresh ginger
4 cloves garlic, chopped
¼ cup chopped fresh cilantro
1 teaspoon Chinese five-spice powder
¼ cup extra virgin olive oil

Combine the tahini, sesame oil, lemon zest and juice, soy sauce, honey, ginger, garlic, cilantro, and spice mix in a blender or a food processor and process until all the ingredients are well blended. While the motor is running, drizzle in the oil a little at a time. Stored in a clean, airtight container, this marinade will keep in the refrigerator for 1 week. It freezes well with food for up to 3 months.

TIMETABLE:

Tuna steaks, swordfish steaks, red snapper, catfish, sea bass, halibut, or scallops: 2 to 3 hours

Shrimp: 3 to 4 hours

Chicken breasts or kabobs, turkey breast, duck breast, beef filets, rib eye, beef kabobs, lamb kabobs, pork tenderloin, or pork chops: 4 to 6 hours

London broil, skirt steak, flank steak, beef brisket, prime rib, or rib roast: 8 to 12 hours

TIMETABLE:

Scallops or shrimp: 1 hour

Chicken breasts or kabobs,
quail, or pork tenderloin:
2 to 4 hours

Beef or lamb kabobs:
4 to 6 hours

Baby back ribs or
spareribs: 6 to 8 hours

ASIAN SAUTERNES MARINADE MAKES 1½ CUPS

My favorite marinades combine Eastern and Western flavors. Asian lemongrass and ginger are a delight with French Sauternes and Calvados. Because of their high sugar content, Sauternes and other late-harvest wines have a higher acidity that may cut down on your marinating time.

¾ cup Sauternes or comparable late-harvest wine
3 tablespoons Calvados, brandy, or cognac
Grated zest and juice of 1 lemon (about 3 tablespoons)
1 tablespoon soy sauce
¼ teaspoon ground nutmeg
2 to 3 tablespoons peeled and diced fresh ginger
¼ cup chopped fresh lemongrass, tough outer leaves removed
3 to 4 tablespoons chopped fresh cilantro
1 teaspoon coarse-grain salt
1 tablespoon cracked black peppercorns
⅓ cup canola oil

Combine the Sauternes, Calvados, lemon zest and juice, soy sauce, nutmeg, ginger, lemongrass, cilantro, salt, and pepper in a food processor or a blender and process until all the ingredients are well blended. While the motor is running, drizzle in the oil a little at a time. Stored in a clean, airtight container, this marinade will keep in the refrigerator for 1 week.

TIMETABLE:

Tuna steaks, scallops,
shrimp, chicken breasts or
kabobs, beef filets, rib eye,
sirloin, porterhouse, New
York strip, tri tips, lamb rack
or rib chops, lamb kabobs,
pork tenderloin, pork
chops, or pork kabobs:
1 to 2 hours

JAPANESE SEVEN-SPICE POWDER

(SHICHIMI TOGARASHI) MAKES ⅓ CUP

This is a Japanese table spice that makes an excellent rub for grilled tuna. It's equally good on grilled chicken and beef. There is a fair amount of heat that will give your mouth some ting, but you'll still taste the other flavors. Balance this rub by serving food with Japanese Dipping Sauce (page 339).

2 teaspoons white sesame seeds
1 teaspoon black sesame seeds
1 tablespoon sansho or Szechuan pepper (available at Asian grocery stores)
1 teaspoon crumbled nori
1 tablespoon dried tangerine, lemon, or orange zest
1 tablespoon togarashi chile powder
1 teaspoon poppy seeds

Combine the white and black sesame seeds, sansho, nori, tangerine zest, togarashi chile powder, and poppy seeds in a spice mill or a blender and grind to a coarse powder. Stored in a clean, airtight container, this will keep in the freezer for 3 to 4 months.

WASABI RUB MAKES 1 CUP

More of a paste than a rub, this recipe is the perfect match for grilled flank steak. The heat in this concoction comes from the Japanese horseradish powder called wasabi. The spices are Chinese, with mustard seeds thrown in. Serve with Japanese Dipping Sauce (page 339).

1 tablespoon white peppercorns
1 tablespoon black peppercorns
1 tablespoon yellow mustard seeds
1 tablespoon Chinese five-spice powder
1 teaspoon crushed star-anise pods
3 to 4 teaspoons warm water
2 tablespoons wasabi powder
¼ cup sake
¼ cup soy or tamari sauce
¼ cup mirin

Combine the white peppercorns, black peppercorns, mustard seeds, five-spice powder, and star anise in a spice mill or a blender. Grind to a coarse powder.

In a small bowl, stir 3 teaspoons of the warm water into the wasabi powder until smooth, adding more water (½ teaspoon at a time) if necessary. Let the wasabi stand uncovered for 15 minutes to let the flavor develop. In a small bowl, combine the spice mix, wasabi paste, sake, soy sauce, and mirin. Stored in a clean, airtight container in the refrigerator, the rub will keep for 1 week.

TIMETABLE:

Tuna steaks, scallops, or shrimp: 1 to 2 hours

Beef filets, rib eye, sirloin, porterhouse, New York strip, tri tips, beef kabobs, beef steak: 2 to 3 hours

Brisket or flank steak: 8 to 12 hours

FAUX WASABI VERSUS THE REAL DEAL

That wad of green paste sitting next to your sushi may not be wasabi. It could be green food coloring mixed with horseradish and Chinese mustard. Real wasabi is expensive and rare because it's one of the most difficult vegetables in the world to grow. If you have the chance to taste the real thing at an ultra high-end sushi bar, you'll know it immediately. It has a sweet, pungent flavor that dies off in a short period of time. It needs to be constantly refreshed.

If you're buying wasabi paste or powder, look for the words *100 percent grated hon-wasabi* on the label. Barring that, you might as well substitute freshly grated farmers' market horseradish that still has its bite. I'll leave the optional green food coloring up to you.

TIMETABLE:
Shrimp: 3 to 4 hours

Chicken breasts or kabobs, pork tenderloin, or pork chops: 4 to 6 hours

Baby back ribs or spareribs: 8 to 12 hours

SAMBAL MINT PASTE MAKES 1 CUP

Indonesian sambals are incendiary blends that can be added sparingly to perk up the flavor of blander dishes and sauces. Texture-wise, this should remind you of a pesto, and you can use it the same way. This particular version is a little gentler on the tongue due to the mint and cilantro. The paste is great for grilled shrimp.

½ cup (1 bunch) tightly packed mint leaves
½ cup (1 bunch) tightly packed cilantro leaves
¼ cup unsalted cashew pieces
½ cup canned tamarind nectar
4 or 5 bird chiles, or 3 or 4 dried red chiles, seeded

Combine the mint, cilantro, cashews, tamarind nectar, and chiles in a food processor or a blender and blend to a paste. Stored in a clean, airtight container, this will keep in the refrigerator for 1 week.

TIMETABLE:
Salmon steaks, salmon fillets, or shrimp:
2 to 4 hours

Chicken breasts or kabobs, duck breast, or quail: 3 to 4 hours

SINGAPORE SESAME PASTE MAKES 1 CUP

This sweet and spicy paste wraps chicken, pork tenderloin, and even shrimp in a shiny glaze that simply sparkles with flavor. The combination of sweet and savory spices, along with the chiles, is a nice foil for the sweetness supplied by the hoisin sauce and kecap manis. The sesame seeds provide an added nutty crunch.

⅓ cup sesame seeds, toasted
1 tablespoon sesame oil
4 tablespoons hoisin sauce
3 tablespoons kecap manis (see page 273)
2 tablespoons soy sauce
2 or 3 dried red chiles, stemmed, seeded, and crushed
2 tablespoons freshly grated orange zest
1 teaspoon ground coriander
½ teaspoon ground cumin
1 tablespoon shrimp paste
2 or 3 cloves garlic, minced or pressed

Combine the sesame seeds, sesame oil, hoisin sauce, kecap manis, soy sauce, chiles, orange zest, coriander, cumin, shrimp paste, and garlic in a blender or a food processor and process until all the ingredients are well blended. Stored in a clean, airtight container, the paste will keep for about 1 week in the refrigerator.

GARAM MASALA MAKES ⅓ CUP

Garam masala is a sweet Indian spice that's added to curries and marinades and gives India its culinary thumbprint. When it's cooking, it fills the kitchen with a bouquet of sweet, exotic fragrance. One teaspoon of homemade garam masala does wonders when added to store-bought curry powders or when stirred into plain yogurt for a marinade.

3 tablespoons cardamom pods
1 (3-inch) cinnamon stick
2 teaspoons fenugreek seeds
1 tablespoon whole cumin seeds
1 tablespoon whole coriander seeds
2 teaspoons ground turmeric
1 tablespoon freshly ground black pepper
½ teaspoon whole cloves

Break open the cardamom pods, discard the skins, and reserve the seeds. Break the cinnamon stick into small pieces between two sheets of waxed paper, using a rolling pin or a kitchen mallet.

Heat a dry skillet for about 2 minutes over medium heat. Combine the cardamom, cinnamon, fenugreek, cumin seeds, and coriander seeds, and toast in the hot skillet until the seeds turn golden brown. Cool the toasted spices and combine with the turmeric, pepper, and cloves in a spice mill or a blender, and grind to a fine powder. Store the mix in a jar and remember to date it. This will keep in the refrigerator, tightly covered, for up to 3 months.

TIMETABLE:
Shrimp or scallops:
3 to 4 hours

Chicken breasts or lamb
kabobs: 4 to 6 hours

BENGAL SPICE PASTE MAKES 1½ CUPS

You'd be surprised how much flavor this paste packs when it's pressed into chicken or tossed with shrimp. The cilantro acts as a coolant for the spicy curry and cayenne, and the cashews give the right amount of savory density when roasted along with whatever you're grilling.

½ cup tightly packed cilantro leaves
Grated zest and juice of 2 lemons (about ⅓ cup)
2 tablespoons curry powder
1 tablespoon garam masala (page 299) or curry powder
½ teaspoon cayenne pepper
4 cloves garlic, minced or pressed
¼ cup cashew pieces, roasted
¼ cup cold-pressed peanut oil

Combine the cilantro, lemon zest and juice, curry powder, garam masala, cayenne, garlic, cashews, and peanut oil in a food processor or a blender and purée to a smooth paste. Tightly covered, this will keep for up to 1 week in the refrigerator.

TIMETABLE:
Salmon steaks or fillets,
scallops, shrimp, chicken
breasts or kabobs, chicken
wings, chicken thighs,
chicken legs, quail, turkey,
Cornish hen, beef kabobs,
pork tenderloin, pork
chops, pork kabobs, baby
back ribs, or spareribs:
baste during the last
5 minutes of cooking

CARAMELIZED GINGER GLAZE MAKES 1¼ CUPS

The problem with this glaze is trying to think of what it won't go with. It's easy to prepare and can lie in wait, ready to pounce on anything you may bring in from the market that day, including carrots.

¼ cup peeled and julienned fresh ginger
2½ tablespoons sugar
¼ cup water
1 cup kecap manis (see page 273)
2 tablespoons freshly cracked black peppercorns
Grated zest and juice of 1 lemon about 3 tablespoons)
1 teaspoon coarse-grain salt

In a heavy nonreactive pot, combine the ginger, sugar, and water, and lightly simmer until the ginger is soft and translucent. Add the kecap manis and peppercorns and simmer for 10 minutes more. Remove the glaze from the heat and stir in the lemon zest and juice, to brighten, and the salt, to balance the flavors. Store in a clean, airtight container and refrigerate until ready to use. The glaze will keep in the refrigerator for 4 weeks. Brighten with additional lemon juice after the first week of storage before using again.

GINGER POMEGRANATE GLAZE. Replace the kecap manis with pomegranate molasses. Proceed with the recipe as written above.

CILANTRO-GINGER PESTO MAKES 1½ CUPS

Here is ginger at its piquant best. What separate this Pacific Rim pesto from its Med-rim cousins are its bite and spicy depth. For openers, place the paste under the skin of a whole chicken breast bound for the grill or the broiler. Got shrimp? Grab a resealable plastic bag and a pound of crustaceans and toss; serve as a main course or as an appetizer brimming with Asian seasonings.

½ cup peeled and chopped fresh ginger
6 to 8 cloves garlic
1½ cups chopped fresh cilantro
1 teaspoon ground nutmeg
1 teaspoon five-spice powder
1 tablespoon dark brown sugar
3 tablespoons soy or tamari sauce
Grated zest and juice of 2 limes (about ¼ cup)
2 tablespoons sherry vinegar
¼ cup peanut oil

Combine the ginger, garlic, cilantro, nutmeg, five-spice powder, sugar, soy sauce, lime zest and juice, and vinegar in a blender or a food processor and purée to a smooth paste. While the motor is running, add the oil a little at a time. Store in the refrigerator and use the marinade within 3 days, because cilantro's flavor will fade.

LIME-CILANTRO PESTO. This is a lighter and breezier version of the above recipe. Omit the ginger and nutmeg, and reduce the garlic to 2 cloves, chopped. Add the grated zest and juice of 3 limes (about ⅓ cup).

TIMETABLE:
Swordfish steaks, halibut, or shrimp: 2 to 3 hours

Chicken breasts or kabobs: 3 to 4 hours

Turkey breast: 4 to 6 hours

Beef kabobs, lamb kabobs, veal rib eye, veal chops, or buffalo steak: 6 to 8 hours

PLUM SAUCE GLAZE MAKES 2 CUPS

This is becoming a stock item in my refrigerator, especially during warm-weather grilling months. The spicy yet fragrant Asian glaze clings to spareribs and chicken wings and creates a brilliant red hue.

⅔ cup plum sauce
2 tablespoons hoisin sauce
2 tablespoons dry sherry
1 tablespoon soy or tamari sauce
1 tablespoon peeled and grated fresh ginger
2 cloves garlic, minced or pressed
¼ cup chopped fresh cilantro
½ teaspoon crushed dried red chile

Combine the plum sauce, hoisin, sherry, soy sauce, ginger, garlic, cilantro, and chile in a blender or a food processor. Process until all the ingredients are well blended. Stored in a clean, airtight container, this will keep in the refrigerator for 2 weeks or in the freezer for up to 3 months.

ORANGE–STAR ANISE GLAZE MAKES 1½ CUPS

The ingredient that triggers the flavor of this glaze is star anise. I've used this glaze piped from a squirt bottle to accent plates as a sauce.

2 tablespoons peanut oil
1 tablespoon minced garlic
2 tablespoons peeled and minced fresh ginger
½ cup sugar
½ cup rice wine vinegar
4 cups freshly squeezed orange juice
6 whole star anise
2 tablespoons soy sauce
2 tablespoons Asian fish sauce (nam pla)
1 tablespoon freshly grated orange zest

In a heavy nonreactive pot, heat the peanut oil; add the garlic and ginger and sauté over medium-high heat for about 10 minutes, until translucent. Add the sugar, vinegar, orange juice, star anise, soy sauce, and fish sauce to the saucepan. Bring to a simmer and simmer for about 30 minutes, until reduced to 1½ cups. Cool to room temperature and strain. Add the orange zest to brighten the flavor. Store in a clean, airtight container and refrigerate until ready to use. The glaze will keep in the refrigerator for 2 to 3 months.

CARROT–STAR ANISE GLAZE. Replace the orange juice with carrot juice. Proceed with the recipe as written above.

CANTONESE GLAZE MAKES 2½ CUPS

If you have a hankering for take-out Chinese ribs, brush your racks with this classic Asian sweet-and-sour glaze. This is a glaze that you may want to make in batches and freeze in 1-cup deli containers to keep your cravings at bay.

2 tablespoons peanut oil
¼ cup minced green onions, white part only
6 cloves garlic, minced
1 cup hoisin sauce
½ cup plum sauce
⅓ cup oyster sauce
⅓ cup Chinese black vinegar, or ¼ cup rice wine vinegar
    and 2 tablespoons balsamic vinegar
⅓ cup sherry
¼ cup honey
1 tablespoon sesame oil

In a heavy nonreactive pot, heat the peanut oil and sauté the green onions and garlic over medium-high heat for about 10 minutes, until translucent. Add the hoisin sauce, plum sauce, oyster sauce, black vinegar, sherry, honey, and sesame oil. Bring to a simmer and simmer for about 30 minutes, until reduced to 2½ cups. Stored in a clean, airtight container, this will keep in the refrigerator for 4 to 6 weeks or in the freezer for up to 3 to 4 months.

TIMETABLE:
Shrimp, chicken breasts or kabobs, chicken wings, chicken thighs, chicken legs, quail, pork tenderloin, pork chops, pork kabobs, baby back ribs, or spareribs: baste during the last 5 minutes of cooking

MIRIN-RAISIN GLAZE MAKES 1 CUP

This simple glaze beams with Japanese ingredients. The golden raisins add a Madeira-like flavor, which complements the honey. The fresh lemon on the back end brightens the glaze with a light pucker.

1 cup mirin
¼ cup soy or tamari sauce
½ cup rice wine vinegar
¼ cup golden raisins
½ cup honey
1 teaspoon togarashi chile powder (see page 275)
Grated zest and juice of 1 lemon (about 3 tablespoons)

In a heavy nonreactive pot, combine the mirin, soy sauce, vinegar, raisins, honey, and togarashi. Bring to a simmer, and simmer for about 30 minutes, until reduced to 1 cup. Cool to room temperature, strain, and stir in the lemon zest and juice.

TIMETABLE:
Salmon steaks or fillets, scallops, shrimp, chicken breasts or kabobs, chicken wings, chicken thighs, chicken legs, quail, pork tenderloin, pork kabobs, baby back ribs, or spareribs: baste during the last 5 minutes of cooking

TERIYAKI GLAZE MAKES 1 CUP

The basic difference between teriyaki and yakitori is that yakitori uses the ingredients as a marinade (see page 284), while teriyaki works as a glaze.

1 cup sake
½ cup mirin
1 cup soy or tamari sauce
2 tablespoons light miso (available at Asian grocery stores)
¼ cup rock or turbinado sugar
2 tablespoons crystallized ginger

Combine the sake, mirin, soy sauce, miso, sugar, and ginger in a small saucepan. Bring to a boil, then decrease the heat and simmer until the sauce is reduced to 1 cup, 10 to 15 minutes. Remove from the heat and cool to room temperature, then pour into a clean, airtight jar and refrigerate until ready to use. The glaze will keep in the refrigerator for 4 weeks.

PINEAPPLE-TERIYAKI GLAZE. Omit the turbinado sugar. When the mixture has reduced to 1 cup, add 1 (12-ounce) jar pineapple marmalade or preserves and simmer for an additional 5 to 10 minutes, until the marmalade has dissolved.

RASPBERRY-TERIYAKI GLAZE. Omit the turbinado sugar. When the mixture has reduced to 1 cup, add 1 (12-ounce) jar seedless raspberry (or blackberry) jam and simmer for an additional 5 to 10 minutes, until the jam has dissolved.

RASPBERRY PONZU GLAZE MAKES 1⅓ CUPS

This Pacific Rim–style glaze will taunt you with its initial burst of sweetness. But it's nicely balanced with an air of citrus and contains a gentle spike of heat from the togarashi.

¾ cup seedless raspberry or blackberry jam
½ cup sake
¼ cup light soy sauce
Grated zest and juice of 1 orange (about ⅓ cup)
¼ teaspoon togarashi spice or dried crushed red chile

Combine the jam, sake, soy sauce, orange zest, and togarashi in a small heavy saucepan. Bring to a light boil over medium-high heat, stirring until the jam dissolves. Simmer until the mixture is reduced to 1 cup, 15 to 20 minutes. Cool the glaze to room temperature and add the orange juice. Cover and refrigerate. The sauce can be prepared up to 1 day ahead. Stored in a clean, airtight container, it will keep in the refrigerator for 3 weeks.

ORANGE PONZU GLAZE. Substitute ¾ cup orange marmalade for the raspberry jam.

WASABI CARAMEL MAKES ¾ CUP

This is a great starting point for Japanese and Pacific Rim glazes, and it can be doubled and used in a brine as a savory sweetener. As is, you can gently glaze grilled or broiled scallops, shrimp, or salmon.

3 tablespoons wasabi powder
3 tablespoons boiling water
¼ cup white wine vinegar
2 teaspoons black peppercorns
½ cup sugar
2 tablespoons water
1 tablespoon light corn syrup
1 tablespoon soy or tamari sauce
1 teaspoon fresh lime juice

In a small bowl, combine the wasabi and boiling water and stir to form a paste. Combine the wasabi paste, vinegar, and pepper in a blender or a food processor and process until all the ingredients are well blended.

In a medium-size heavy saucepan, stir the sugar, water, corn syrup, and soy sauce together. Bring to a boil over medium-high heat and cook until the sugar starts to color, brushing down the sides with a wet pastry brush to avoid crystals. Gently stir the pan with a long wooden spoon for about 10 minutes, until the mixture turns a medium amber color. Immediately remove the pan from the heat.

Gradually stir in the wasabi vinegar. It will get annoyed and bubble up. Cool to room temperature and stir in the soy sauce and lime juice. Stored in a clean, airtight container in the refrigerator, this will keep for up to 1 month.

TIMETABLE:
Salmon steaks or fillets, scallops, shrimp, chicken breasts or kabobs, chicken wings, chicken thighs, chicken legs, quail, pork tenderloin, baby back ribs, or spareribs: baste during the last 5 minutes of cooking

TIP: To increase the natural heat of this marinade, juice or purée 2 to 3 tablespoons peeled and pressed fresh ginger. Ginger juice has a piquant flavor when juiced or squeezed through a garlic press.

305

Shrimp, chicken breasts or kabobs, chicken wings, chicken thighs, chicken legs, quail, pork tenderloin, pork chops, pork kabobs, baby back ribs, or spareribs: baste during the last 5 minutes of cooking

VIETNAMESE GLAZE MAKES 1 CUP

One of the base ingredients of Vietnamese cuisine is a caramel called nuoc mau, and it's used to contrast the nam pla, or fish sauce. Rice vinegar is added at the end to give the glaze a slight bite.

NUOC MAU (VIETNAMESE CARAMEL)
MAKES ABOUT 1 CUP

½ cup sugar
1 tablespoon water
⅓ cup Asian fish sauce (nam pla)
1 tablespoon freshly cracked black peppercorns

GLAZE

2 to 3 tablespoons peanut oil
2 stalks lemongrass, tough outer leaves removed, smashed and finely chopped (about ½ cup)
2 shallots, diced (about ¼ cup)
½ cup hoisin sauce
1 tablespoon Asian fish sauce (nam pla)
2 tablespoons honey
⅓ cup nuoc mau or caramel
3 tablespoons rice wine vinegar

To make the nuoc mau, in a heavy stainless-steel saucepan, combine the sugar and water over medium-high heat and cook for about 10 minutes, until the caramel turns a medium amber color. Immediately remove the pan from the heat. Add the fish sauce. The sauce will boil vigorously. Return to medium heat and cook until slightly thickened, 30 seconds to 1 minute. Stir in the pepper. Stored in a clean, airtight container, it will keep in the refrigerator for 3 weeks.

To make the glaze, in a saucepan over medium heat, heat the oil and sauté the lemongrass and shallots for about 5 minutes, until translucent. Cool the mixture to room temperature. Combine the lemongrass-shallot mixture, hoisin sauce, fish sauce, honey, and nuoc mau in a blender or a food processor and process until all the ingredients are well blended. Return the purée to the saucepan and simmer for 20 minutes, or until the glaze thickens. Remove from the heat and cool to room temperature. Stir in the vinegar. Stored in a clean, airtight container, this will keep in the refrigerator for up to 1 month.

INDONESIAN CURRY GLAZE MAKES 1 CUP

Not as incendiary as the sambals from this region, this glaze is just as flavorful when it hits shrimp, chicken, pork tenderloin, or lamb. Its introductory-level sweet heat with a ponzu-like balance plays the teriyaki and citrus against the garam masala and dried red chile. Hitting your flavor buttons next are the sweet underpinnings of the sherry and honey.

¼ cup good-quality teriyaki sauce
Grated zest and juice of 3 juice oranges (about 1 cup)
⅓ cup honey
⅓ cup dry sherry
2 tablespoons finely chopped garlic
1 tablespoons garam masala (page 299) or curry powder
½ teaspoon crumbled dried red chile

Combine the teriyaki, orange zest and juice, honey, sherry, garlic, garam masala, and chile in a small nonreactive saucepan. Bring to a boil and decrease the heat. Simmer for about 20 minutes, until reduced to 1 cup,. If grilling or roasting seafood, meat, or poultry, turn and baste with the glaze during the last 5 minutes of cooking. Stored in a clean, airtight container, this will keep in the refrigerator for 1 month.

TIMETABLE:
Salmon steaks or fillets, tuna steaks, shrimp, chicken breasts or kabobs, quail, lamb kabobs, pork tenderloin, pork chops, pork kabobs, baby back ribs, or spareribs: baste during the last 5 minutes of cooking

INDONESIAN HONEY-CHILE GLAZE MAKES 1½ CUPS

The sweet, spicy flavors of Indonesia combine nicely in this glaze for chicken wings, quail, and baby back ribs.

¼ cup honey
3 to 4 tablespoons kecap manis (see page 273)
Grated zest and juice of 2 limes (about ¼ cup)
1 tablespoon rice wine vinegar
2 tablespoons canned tamarind nectar
3 or 4 bird chiles, seeded and diced
2 tablespoons peeled and chopped fresh ginger

Combine the honey, kecap manis, lime zest and juice, vinegar, tamarind nectar, chiles, and ginger in a blender or a food processor. Process until all the ingredients are well blended. The glaze will keep in the refrigerator for 2 to 3 months.

TIMETABLE:
Chicken wings, quail, or baby back ribs: baste during the last 5 minutes of cooking

TIMETABLE:

Salmon steaks or fillets, chicken breasts or kabobs, chicken wings, chicken thighs, chicken legs, beef filets, rib eye, beef kabobs, lamb kabobs, pork tenderloin, pork chops, baby back ribs, or spareribs: baste during the last 5 minutes of cooking

INDONESIAN-STYLE BARBECUE SAUCE

MAKES 2½ CUPS

A lot of American condiments, such as Worcestershire sauce, have their roots in Southeast Asia. This sweet and spicy sauce, when made with fresh tomatoes, is a forerunner of ketchup. You can put it into a red squeeze bottle for ketchup with a kick, and it's excellent on burgers.

2 tablespoons peanut or canola oil
1 tablespoon peeled and minced fresh ginger
2 tablespoons smashed and chopped fresh lemongrass,
    tough outer leaves removed
3 cloves garlic, minced
2 bird or serrano chiles, stemmed and seeded
1 small dried Asian red chile, or ¼ teaspoon cayenne
½ cup kecap manis (see page 273)
1½ cups tomato ketchup
¼ teaspoon nutmeg
¼ teaspoon ground cardamom
½ teaspoon ground cinnamon
Grated zest and juice of 2 limes (about ¼ cup)

In a heavy-bottom saucepan over medium heat, heat the oil, add the ginger, lemongrass, garlic, and bird chiles, and sauté for 4 to 5 minutes, or until the vegetables soften. Add the dried chile, kecap manis, ketchup, nutmeg, cardamom, and cinnamon to the saucepan and simmer for 20 minutes. Remove the glaze from the heat and cool to room temperature. Stir in the lime zest and juice. The glaze will keep in the refrigerator for 2 weeks.

GRILLED PINEAPPLE–COCONUT GLAZE

MAKES 2½ CUPS

• •

Grilling pineapple slices lightly caramelizes the fruit and gives it a real flavor spike. I like working with pineapple rings because they're easy to flip under fire.

2 tablespoons peanut or canola oil
1 stalk lemongrass, tough outer leaves removed,
    chopped (2 to 3 tablespoons)
1 tablespoon peeled and minced fresh ginger
2 tablespoons chopped shallots
3 cloves garlic, minced
6 (1-inch-thick) grilled pineapple rings, chopped into
    1-inch segments (about 2 cups)
1 (12-ounce) can Asian coconut milk
¼ cup firmly packed light brown sugar
¼ cup soy or tamari sauce
1 teaspoon garam masala (page 299) or curry powder
¼ teaspoon allspice
¼ cup shredded coconut, toasted

In a 2-quart (or larger) heavy-bottom saucepan over medium heat, heat the oil, add the lemongrass, ginger, shallots, and garlic, and sauté for 4 to 5 minutes, or until the vegetables soften. Add the pineapple, coconut milk, brown sugar, soy sauce, curry, and allspice to the saucepan and simmer for 30 minutes to reduce it slightly.

Remove from the heat and cool to room temperature. Pour the glaze into a blender or a food processor and process for 20 seconds, or until all the ingredients are well blended. Strain the glaze over a bowl and discard the solids. Stir in the toasted coconut. Store in a clean, airtight container and refrigerate until ready to use. The glaze will keep in the refrigerator for 2 to 3 weeks.

TIMETABLE:
Salmon steaks or fillets, chicken wings, chicken thighs, chicken legs, pork tenderloin, pork kabobs, baby back ribs, or spareribs: baste during the last 5 minutes of cooking

TIP: Although you may not get that outdoor grill flavor, you can broil the pineapple rings indoors. Arrange the rings on a lightly oiled baking sheet, sprinkle with brown sugar, and broil 6 inches from the heat for 5 to 6 minutes.

TIP: Available in Spanish grocery stores and the Latin section of many supermarkets.

EAST–WEST INDIES TAMARIND GLAZE
MAKES 1½ CUPS

This tasty glaze borrows ingredients from both ends of the spice route, Asia and the Caribbean. It's a grill feast waiting to happen.

4 ounces tamarind pulp (see Tip), broken into pieces
1 cup boiling water
2 tablespoons peeled and chopped fresh ginger
¾ cup plum wine
1 tablespoon soy or tamari sauce
¼ cup kecap manis (see page 273)
2 tablespoons dark rum
¼ cup mango or guava jelly (see Tip) or apricot jelly
1 star-anise pod, crumbled
1 teaspoon vanilla extract

Place the tamarind pulp in a small nonreactive bowl and pour the boiling water over the pulp. Soak the pulp in the water until soft, 5 to 15 minutes. With your fingers, rub the pulp until dissolved and the seeds are free of pulp. Strain and discard the seeds and fibers. Combine the tamarind, ginger, and plum wine in a 2-quart pot. Bring to a boil, then decrease the heat and simmer for about 20 minutes, until reduced to 1 cup. Add the soy sauce, kecap manis, rum, jelly, star anise, and vanilla and cook gently for 15 minutes. Strain through a sieve into a small bowl. Store in a clean, airtight container and refrigerate until ready to use. The glaze will keep in the refrigerator for 2 to 3 weeks or in the freezer for up to 3 to 4 months.

LYCHEE GLAZE MAKES 1 CUP

This Pacific Rim glaze builds its flavor by using puréed fruit with reduced Asian syrup. This technique will also work with frozen peaches or pears.

1 (20-ounce) can lychees, with syrup
2 cloves garlic, minced
1 piece ginger, 1 inch long by ¼ inch thick, peeled and diced
½ cup dry white wine
2 tablespoons dark soy sauce
1 tablespoon sesame oil
¼ cup honey
1 teaspoon Chinese five-spice powder
2 star-anise pods, ground
1 (3-inch) cinnamon stick, ground, or 1 tablespoon ground cinnamon
¼ teaspoon red pepper flakes (optional)

Drain the lychees over a nonreactive bowl and set aside, reserving the lychee syrup. Combine the lychee syrup, garlic, ginger, wine, soy sauce, sesame oil, honey, five-spice powder, star anise, cinnamon, and red pepper flakes in a blender or a food processor and process until all the ingredients are well blended.

Add the mixture to a heavy nonreactive pot and bring to a low boil. Simmer for about 30 minutes, until reduced to ½ cup. When the mixture has reduced, purée the reserved lychees in a food processor or a blender and add them to the saucepan, decrease the heat, and simmer for an additional 5 minutes. Remove from the heat and cool to room temperature. Store in a clean, airtight container and refrigerate until ready to use. The glaze will keep in the refrigerator for 2 to 3 months.

GRILLED TOFU WITH MANGO CHUTNEY MARINADE SERVES 6 TO 8 AS AN APPETIZER

This has always been a grill staple for my veggie friends, but now the "carnivies" have caught on to it, too.

1 block tofu (14 to 18 ounces)
1 cup Mango Chutney Marinade (page 294)

Cut the tofu into 1-inch squares and lightly score them with a paring knife. Place the tofu squares into a nonreactive container or a 1-gallon resealable plastic bag. Pour the marinade over the tofu and refrigerate for at least 6 hours. Remove the tofu from the marinade, and warm the reserve marinade for basting. Thread the tofu onto a pair of presoaked bamboo skewers for each serving.

To grill the tofu, lightly brush the grill with vegetable oil and grill the tofu over medium-high heat for 12 to 15 minutes, turning often and basting with the warm marinade. Serve hot.

SALMON STEAMED IN A JAPANESE MARINADE
SERVES 4

· ·

Japanese foods are marinated for only a short period of time and with only a few ingredients so that one flavor doesn't overpower another. This exquisite dish can be assembled in no time at all and has the shortest marinating time in the book. Its presentation is a beautiful play of rosy pink salmon on a bed of clear bean thread noodles. The Japanese marinade can also work with chicken breasts or shrimp.

4 (6 ounces each) salmon fillets
1½ cups Basic Japanese-Style Marinade (page 282)
1 (2-ounce) package bean thread noodles
¼ cup minced preserved ginger, or ¼ cup peeled and
    minced fresh ginger and 1 teaspoon light brown sugar

Rinse the fish under cold water and pat dry with paper towels. Place the salmon fillets in a nonreactive container or a 1-gallon resealable plastic bag. Pour the marinade over the salmon and refrigerate for no longer than 1 hour.

While the salmon is marinating, soak the noodles in very warm water for about 30 minutes or until they are translucent. Plunge the noodles into a large pot of boiling water and boil them until they are clear (about 5 minutes). Remove the noodles and drain.

Remove the salmon from the marinade and bring the marinade to a high boil in a covered nonreactive saucepan with a vegetable steamer. Place the salmon fillets on the steamer, cover, and steam for 15 to 20 minutes. Remove the lid and, with a fork or the tip of a sharp knife, gently separate the flesh at its thickest point. If the interior of the fillet is opaque and just beginning to flake, the salmon is done.

Preheat the oven to 300°F. Remove the salmon with a slotted spoon, place on a warm plate, cover with a bowl, and place in the oven. Add the ginger to the remaining marinade, and cook for about 10 minutes, until the marinade is reduced by about half.

To serve, place the noodles on the center of a plate, add the salmon fillets, and cover the fillets with the remaining marinade.

TAMARIND-MARINATED POMPANO STEAMED IN BANANA LEAVES SERVES 4

Steamed fish parcels know no borders. The pompano is marinated in light Asian flavors primarily to highlight the fish and its savory companions. Green (unripe) mango is used in the recipe to provide a fruity yet tart counterpart to the julienned carrots. If you like this style of wrapped cuisine, check out its traditional Mexican counterpart, Yucatecan Grilled Fish (page 200).

TIP: To prepare the banana leaves, defrost them in the refrigerator overnight. Heat each whole leaf section over a flame or in a dry skillet until it changes texture and becomes more pliable. Do not overheat or it will become brittle. Trim into 12-inch by 18-inch sections.

4 (6 ounces each) pompano fillets
2 cups Thai-Style Tamarind Marinade (page 288)
4 (12 by 18-inch) pieces banana leaves (see Tip)
2 small unripe green mangoes, peeled and julienned
1½ cups julienned carrots, blanched
2 limes, sliced ⅛ inch thick
½ to ⅔ cup cashew pieces, toasted
½ cup chopped fresh mint or cilantro, or a combination of the two

Rinse the fish under cold water and pat dry with paper towels. Place the fish in a nonreactive container or a 1-gallon resealable plastic bag. Pour the marinade over the pompano and refrigerate for 2 to 4 hours. Remove the pompano from the marinade, reserving about 1½ cups of the marinade.

Lay out each banana leaf, shiny side up. Divide the mangoes and carrots into 4 portions and place a portion in the center (middle third) of each banana leaf. Top with the fish and spoon about ¼ cup of the reserved marinade over each portion. Garnish with the lime slices, cashews, and mint. Fold the flaps of the banana leaves over like an envelope and secure each side with a presoaked bamboo skewer. If your banana leaves begin to split, make a foil boat under them before you place them in the oven. You'll still get the flavor of the leaves without losing the juices.

To grill: Heat the grill to medium-high heat. Place the parcels on the grill and cover. Allow 10 minutes per inch of thickness of each parcel, 20 to 25 minutes total.

To cook indoors: Preheat the oven to 450°F. Place the parcels on a baking sheet and bake for 20 to 25 minutes (or 10 to 12 minutes per inch of thickness).

To serve, remove the parcels from the heat and slide them onto a serving plate. At the table, cut an X in the banana leaves with a sharp pointed knife and peel back the leaves.

GRILLED SALMON WITH RASPBERRY PONZU GLAZE AND MANGO-JICAMA SALSA SERVES 4

This is a dish that's constantly shifting flavor gears. The centerpiece salmon gets a dose of a savory raspberry lacquer, then shifts to a citrusy mango to balance the plate.

SUBSTITUTIONS: Replace the Mango-Jicama Salsa with Lime-Cilantro Jicama Slaw (page 213).

4 (6 ounces each) salmon fillets
1¼ cups Raspberry Ponzu Glaze (page 304)
4 cups Mango-Jicama Salsa (page 166)
1 tablespoon black sesame seeds or toasted white sesame seeds
6 lemon wedges, for garnish

Rinse the fish under cold water and pat dry with paper towels. Brush the grill with vegetable oil. Brush each salmon fillet with the glaze. Grill the salmon, skin side up, for 3 minutes. Turn the salmon fillets and brush each again with the glaze. Grill for about 5 minutes, until the salmon is just cooked through. Salmon is done when you can almost flake it, but it's still somewhat orange in the middle.

To serve, transfer 1 salmon fillet to each of 4 plates. Top with the salsa, dividing equally. Sprinkle with sesame seeds, garnish with lemon wedges, and serve.

GRILLED SAKE-GLAZED SHRIMP SERVES 4

You can use this recipe as a main course serving or as single portion shrimp appetizers. The brine is optional, but I find that it pumps up the shrimp with a little bit of added juiciness.

SUBSTITUTIONS: Replace the dipping sauce with Ponzu Sauce (page 339) or Japanese Dipping Sauce (page 339).

1 pound large shrimp (12 to 16 count to the pound), peeled and deveined
6 cups Sake-Mirin Brine (page 277) (optional)
¾ cup Sake-Honey Glaze (page 282)
½ cup Sesame Ginger Dipping Sauce (page 338)

To brine (optional): Rinse the shrimp under cold water and pat dry with paper towels. In a 1-gallon resealable plastic bag, add the shrimp, pour the brine over the shrimp, toss to coat, and refrigerate for 2 hours. Remove the shrimp from the bag and discard the brine.

Divide the shrimp into 4 portions and run 2 presoaked wooden skewers through the shrimp so that each one is skewered in two places. There should be 3 or 4 shrimp per pair of skewers.

To grill: Lightly brush the grill with vegetable oil and grill the shrimp for 3 to 4 minutes, turning often and basting with the Sake-Honey Glaze, until the flesh becomes opaque.

To cook indoors: Preheat the broiler and line a baking sheet with foil. Arrange the shrimp skewers on the baking sheet and broil about 6 inches from the heat source. Broil for 6 to 8 minutes, turning the skewers every few minutes and basting with the Sake-Honey Glaze, until the flesh becomes opaque.

To serve, divide the dipping sauce into 4 individual ramekins and serve with the shrimp.

INDONESIAN SHRIMP SERVES 8 AS AN APPETIZER

The only problem with this recipe is the eventual shrimp shortage as guests clamor for more. This recipe can be doubled, and often is the next time you serve it. Serve with Marinated Indonesian Carrot Sticks (page 336).

1½ to 2 pounds large shrimp (16 to 20 count to the pound),
    shelled and deveined
1½ cups Indonesian Marinade (page 291)
2 mangoes, peeled and chopped into 1-inch chunks
1½ cups Indonesian Honey-Chile Glaze (page 307)

Rinse the shrimp under cold water and pat dry with paper towels. Place the shrimp in a nonreactive container or a 1-gallon resealable plastic bag, pour the marinade over the shrimp, and refrigerate for 3 to 4 hours.

Remove the shrimp from the marinade. Run 2 presoaked wooden skewers through each shrimp, alternating with a chunk of mango. There should be 2 or 3 shrimp per pair of skewers.

To grill: Lightly brush the grill with vegetable oil and grill the shrimp for 4 to 5 minutes, turning often and basting with the glaze, until the flesh becomes opaque and the shells turn red.

To cook indoors: Preheat the broiler to its hottest setting and line a baking sheet with foil. Arrange the shrimp skewers on the baking sheet and broil about 6 inches from the flame for 6 to 8 minutes. Turn and baste with the glaze while cooking. The shrimp is done when the flesh becomes opaque and the shell turns red.

Serve hot.

SOFT-SHELL CRABS WITH THAI COCONUT MARINADE SERVES 4

It's not flowers that I think of come spring, but "softies." I could think of a dozen ways to prep these molted crustaceans. The Thai Coconut Marinade infuses the crabs with coconut and spicy lemongrass, with accents of curry and chile oil. Try tossing them in a breading of panko flakes and crushed hazelnuts, then fry them. The Lemon-Sorrel Marinade substitute brings a nice citusy soak if you want to sauté them. Either way, soft-shell crabs taste best when they are cooked within a few hours of being cleaned.

SUBSTITUTIONS: Replace the marinade with Tandoori Yogurt Marinade (page 294) or Lemon-Sorrel Marinade (page 51).

4 jumbo soft-shell crabs, or 8 "hotel" size
2 cups Thai Coconut Marinade (page 287)
2 tablespoons Asian or domestic cold-pressed peanut oil (for cooking indoors)
1½ tablespoons sesame oil (for cooking indoors)

To clean soft-shell crabs, place the crabs on a clean cutting surface and cut off the face section (about ¼ inch). Lift up the sides of the back, and scrape away the featherlike gills with a knife. Turn the crabs onto their backs and remove the apron flap. Wash the crabs and pat dry.

Place the soft-shell crabs in a nonreactive container or a 1-gallon resealable plastic bag. Pour the marinade over the crabs and refrigerate for 3 to 4 hours. Remove the crabs from the marinade and bring the marinade to a boil for 3 minutes. Reserve half for basting and half for saucing.

To grill: Lightly brush the grill with vegetable oil and grill the crabs for 5 to 8 minutes, turning often and basting with the warm marinade.

To cook indoors: Preheat the oven to 300°F. Heat the peanut and sesame oils in a large skillet, add the crabs, and sauté over medium-high heat for 4 to 5 minutes on each side until brown, adding more oil if needed. Place the crabs in the oven to keep warm. Deglaze the pan with the reserved marinade. Bring the marinade to a boil and reduce to a simmer for 5 minutes.

To serve, cover the surface of each plate with the reduced marinade. Place a crab on top and serve immediately.

GRILLED TANDOORI LOBSTER KABOBS
SERVES 4 AS AN APPETIZER

The spices in the Tandoori Yogurt Marinade perfume the lobster meat without dominating it. You can do the bulk of this recipe a day ahead and let it sit in the marinade overnight until you're ready to grill it. Serve with Marinated Indonesian Carrot Sticks (page 336) or Lime-Cilantro Jicama Slaw (page 213).

2 (1½ pounds each) lobsters, alive and kicking
1½ cups Tandoori Yogurt Marinade (page 294)
1 cup Mint-Cilantro Chutney (page 332)

Bring a large pot of salted water to a rapid boil. Place a lobster on its stomach, protect your hands with a towel, and with a very sharp, strong knife, make a quick incision between the lobster's eyes and twist. Repeat for second lobster. If you would rather not kill the lobsters yourself, have the seafood market steam them for 2 to 3 minutes only.

Place the lobsters into the boiling water, cover tightly, and let cook for 4 or 5 minutes, until the lobster tails are curled and the shells have turned bright red. With tongs, remove from the water and place in an ice-water bath to stop the cooking. Break off the claws. Separate the head from the tail. Remove the meat from the tail in one piece by cutting along the soft underside shell to expose the meat. With the back of a knife, lightly crack the shells of the large claws and carefully remove the meat in one piece.

Place the lobster tail and claw meat in a bowl, pour in the marinade, cover, and refrigerate for 4 to 6 hours.

Remove the lobster meat from the marinade and cut the tail down the center. Arrange 1 claw and 1 tail section on presoaked wooden skewers.

To grill: Lightly brush the grill with vegetable oil. Grill the kabobs over medium-high heat for 2 to 3 minutes on each side, or until the lobster meat is opaque and the marinade is slightly browned.

To cook indoors: Preheat the oven to 500°F and line a baking sheet with foil. Place the marinated lobster meat on the baking sheet and cook for about 4 minutes, or until the meat is opaque white and the marinade is slightly browned.

To serve, place one skewer each on four serving plates garnished with ¼ cup of mint chutney.

TANDOORI JHINGA (PRAWNS) KABOBS. Substitute 1 pound (16- to 20-count) large shrimp, shelled and butterflied, and thread onto skewers as you would the lobster meat.

VIETNAMESE GRILLED LOBSTER SALAD SERVES 4

This recipe works on a number of levels. Although I like to grill lobsters, you can also use the marinade below and steam them in it. Either way you do it, the recipe is true lobster elegance.

DRESSING MAKES 1¼ CUPS

3 small cloves garlic, minced
2 tablespoons sugar
½ cup rice wine vinegar
1 tablespoon freshly squeezed lemon juice
1 tablespoon freshly squeezed lime juice
¼ cup Asian fish sauce (nam pla)
3 tablespoons sesame oil
2 kaffir lime leaves, chopped (see Tip) (optional)
¼ cup fresh mint, finely chopped
3 tablespoons good-quality peanut oil

LOBSTER SALAD

SUBSTITUTIONS: Replace the marinade with Vietnamese Mint Dipping Sauce (page 341).

2 (1½ to 2 pounds each) lobsters, alive and kicking
1 cup Basic Vietnamese Marinade (page 290)
2 seedless cucumbers, peeled, halved, and sliced on the diagonal
1 large (about 1 pound) jicama, peeled and julienned
½ small red onion, thinly sliced
1 red bell pepper, seeded and diced

To prepare the dressing, combine the garlic, sugar, vinegar, lemon juice, lime juice, fish sauce, sesame oil, lime leaves, and mint in a blender or food processor. Process until all the ingredients are blended. While the motor is running, drizzle in the oil a little at a time.

To prepare the lobsters if grilling, place a lobster on its stomach, protect your hands with a towel, and with a very sharp, strong knife, make a quick incision between the lobster's eyes and twist. With a sharp chef's knife, split the lobster in half. Repeat for the second lobster. If you would rather not kill the lobsters yourself, have the seafood market steam them for 2 to 3 minutes only.

Brush the lobsters with the marinade and refrigerate for 4 to 6 hours. Reserve the remaining marinade.

To grill: Lightly brush the grill with vegetable oil. Over medium heat, grill the lobsters, flesh side down, for 6 to 8 minutes for 1½-pound lobsters, or 8 to 10 minutes for 2-pounders. Flip often to baste the meat often with the reserved marinade.

To cook indoors: In a large pot bring 2 cups of water to a boil. Add the lobsters, cover, and steam for 15 minutes, or until the lobsters are bright red. Let the lobsters cool to room temperature. Remove the meat from the tail in one piece by cutting along the soft underside shell to expose the meat. With the back of a knife, lightly crack the shells of the large claws and carefully remove the meat in one piece. Combine the lobster meat and the marinade in a nonreactive container or plastic resealable bag and refrigerate for 4 hours. Remove the lobster meat from the marinade before serving.

To prepare the salad, toss the cucumbers, jicama, onion, and pepper in a bowl with ½ of the dressing.

To serve, place a lobster cavity on each serving plate. Garnish each cavity with the salad, arrange the lobster meat around the salad, and drizzle the remaining dressing over the lobster meat. If using steamed marinated lobster meat, prepare a mound of salad on four serving plates, add the lobster meat, and drizzle with remaining dressing.

ASIAN-STYLE TEA-BRINED DUCK

SERVES 8 AS AN APPETIZER OR 4 AS A MAIN COURSE

Chef Jon Jividen's recipe glazes the duck with a lacquer of Asian spices, molasses, and Earl Grey tea. The duck is best when slowly smoked in an outdoor water smoker, but you can also roast it in the oven. Either way, you will have a sure-fire winner.

4- to 5-pound whole duck
2½ quarts Asian Tea Brine (page 276)

In a large plastic roasting bag or deep nonreactive pot, cover the duck with the brine and refrigerate for a minimum of 24 hours; 2 to 3 days is best.

To smoke outdoors: Remove the duck from the brine. Add the brine to the water pan in an outdoor smoker and smoke over charcoal coals for 4 to 6 hours. The duck is done when the joints move freely. The internal temperature should read about 170°F on a meat thermometer. Remove the duck from the smoker and let it rest for 10 minutes.

To roast indoors: Preheat the oven to 325°F. Remove the duck from the brine and place the duck on a rack in a roasting pan. Add the brine to the roasting pan to a depth of 1 inch. Place the pan in the oven and roast for 1½ hours. Remove the duck from the oven and let it rest for 10 minutes.

Cut the duck into thin slices and serve.

ORANGE–STAR ANISE GLAZED SCALLOPS WITH SMOKED PEPPER POWDER SERVES 4

TIP: Dry-packed scallops, because they haven't been treated with chemicals to extend shelf life, may be a bit more expensive, but they are worth it. They are sweeter and fuller tasting.

SUBSTITUTIONS: Replace the glaze with Carrot-Curry Caramel (page 82) and make the powder with yellow peppers instead of red.

Grilled scallops with either the Orange–Star Anise Glaze or dusted with the Smoked Pepper Powder would fly off the plate. But the two together put a rocket of flavor under them. The speed of this recipe lies in the planning. The glaze and the pepper powder can be made-ahead pantry items. The recipe can then be assembled and cooked in minutes. Serve with Southwestern Tabbouleh (page 146), Thai Pickled Vegetables (page 333), or Mango-Jicama Salsa (page 166).

1½ pounds large dry-packed sea scallops (about 16 scallops) (see Tip)
2 tablespoons canola or extra virgin olive oil
3 tablespoons Smoked Pepper Powder using red peppers (page 68)
Salt and cracked black peppercorns
¾ cup Orange–Star Anise Glaze (page 302)

Toss the scallops and the oil together in a medium-size bowl. Add the pepper powder and the salt and pepper to taste, and toss again. Thread the scallops onto doubled skewers with the flat sides facing out.

To grill: Lightly brush the grill with vegetable oil. Grill the scallops over medium heat for 2 minutes on each side. Brush with the glaze one side at a time. Cook an additional 3 to 4 minutes, or longer depending on the thickness of the scallops, until the scallops begin to caramelize.

To cook indoors: Preheat the oven to 425°F. In a shallow baking pan, place the scallops in a single layer. Roast, uncovered, for 5 minutes. Flip the scallops, brush on the glaze, and cook an additional 3 to 4 minutes, or longer depending on the thickness of the scallops, until the scallops begin to caramelize.

To serve, warm the remaining glaze over low heat, pour into a squeeze bottle, and paint it in a spiral on each of 4 plates. Arrange 4 scallops in a row on each plate and serve immediately.

SZECHUAN SESAME CHICKEN SALAD
SERVES 8 AS AN APPETIZER OR 4 AS A MAIN COURSE

. . . .

Hacked chicken, or chicken bonbon, is traditionally served as a cold appetizer on noodles, but you can expand it into a chicken salad with some additional ingredients.

POACHED CHICKEN

. . . .

2 whole chicken breasts (about 2 pounds), halved
3 cups white wine or unsalted chicken broth
1 tablespoon peeled and slivered fresh ginger
¼ teaspoon Szechuan or whole black peppercorns
1½ cups Szechuan Sesame Marinade (page 281)

SALAD

. . . .

1 cup snow peas, blanched
1 (2-ounce) package bean thread noodles, soaked in boiling
    water until soft, drained, and cooled
¼ cup chopped green onions, white part only
½ cucumber, peeled, seeded, and thinly sliced (about 1 cup)
2 tablespoons sesame seeds, toasted

To poach the chicken, in a large nonreactive saucepan, combine the wine, ginger, and peppercorns and bring to a boil. Add the chicken breasts, decrease the heat to low, cover, and poach for 8 to 10 minutes. Remove the pan from the heat, remove the chicken from the poaching liquid, and cool to room temperature. When cooled, remove and discard the skin and the bones, cut the meat into bite-size pieces, and refrigerate until cold.

When cold, place the chicken in a large nonreactive bowl, pour the marinade over the chicken, cover, and refrigerate for at least 8 hours.

To prepare the salad, toss the snow peas, noodles, and green onions with the chicken and the marinade in a large nonreactive bowl.

To serve, line the circumference of individual serving plates with the cucumber, add the salad, and garnish with sesame seeds.

ORANGE-SESAME CHICKEN STIR-FRY SERVES 4

Marinades are perfect for Asian stir-fries. Any of the Asian-style marinades will work on chicken, shrimp, and vegetables. For an all-vegetarian variation of this dish, omit the chicken and marinate the vegetables for 3 to 4 hours.

**2 whole skinless, boneless chicken breasts (about ⅔ to ¾ pounds),
    cut lengthwise into ½-inch-wide strips**
1½ cups Orange-Sesame Marinade (page 282)
½ cup Asian or domestic cold-pressed peanut oil
1 tablespoon sesame oil
2 carrots, julienned
1 red bell pepper, seeded and julienned
1 cup broccoli florets
2 to 2½ cups hot cooked rice
Coarsely crushed toasted peanuts, for garnish

Place the chicken in a nonreactive container or a 1-gallon resealable plastic bag. Pour the marinade over the chicken and refrigerate for 4 to 5 hours.

Remove the chicken from the marinade, reserving the marinade. In a nonreactive saucepan, bring the marinade to a quick boil, decrease the heat to a simmer, and keep warm. Heat ¼ cup of the peanut oil in a large skillet or wok. When the oil is hot, add the chicken strips in batches and sauté until they're tender. Remove from the heat and keep warm.

Preheat the oven to 250°F. Heat the remaining ¼ cup peanut oil along with the sesame oil in the wok. When the oil is hot, add the carrots, and stir-fry for 1 minute. Then add the bell pepper and cook for 1 minute more. Add the broccoli and cook for 1 minute more. Remove the vegetables with a slotted spoon, transfer to a roasting pan, and keep warm in the oven. Return the reserved marinade to the wok and cook for 1 minute over low heat.

To serve, spoon the rice onto 4 plates, place the chicken on top, top with vegetables, spoon the remaining marinade over all, and sprinkle with crushed peanuts.

THE ASIAN RIB CAGE SERVES 6

This is a quick anatomy lesson on one of the more savory parts of the Asian hog—its rib cage. The Chinese have been breeding pigs for more than 7,000 years, and it's considered a sign of wealth to have a pig in one's household. Asian ribs differ from their traditional American counterparts because they tend to be slightly sweeter and less smoky.

Serve with Thai Pickled Vegetables (page 333), Marinated Black Bean Salad (page 334), or Coconut-Cucumber Slaw (page 335).

2 (2½ pounds each) full racks St. Louis–style spareribs,
    or 3 (1½ pounds each) racks baby back ribs
2½ quarts Ginger-Szechuan Brine (page 276; if brining)
2 cups Yakitori Marinade (page 284; if marinating)
1 cup Plum Sauce Glaze (page 302)

If brining: In large nonreactive container, add ribs, pour the brine over the ribs, and refrigerate for 8 hours. Remove the ribs from the brine and pat dry with paper towels.

If marinating: Place the ribs in a 1-gallon resealable plastic bag, pour in the marinade, and marinate in the refrigerator for 6 to 8 hours. Remove the ribs from the bag and let stand for 20 to 30 minutes before cooking.

To cook outdoors: Follow the grill's instructions for using wood chunks or chips and cook the ribs over indirect medium heat (at about 220°F) for about 3 hours. While the ribs are cooking, preheat your oven to 375°F and line a baking sheet with foil. Remove the ribs from the grill/smoker, transfer to the baking sheet, and generously baste with the glaze. Finish the ribs in the oven for 30 minutes.

To cook indoors: Preheat the oven to 450°F and line a baking sheet with foil. Transfer the ribs to the baking sheet and brown the ribs for 20 to 30 minutes. Decrease the heat to 300°F and roast the ribs for about 90 minutes.

Apply the glaze during the last 5 minutes of cooking. Remove the ribs from the oven and let stand for 10 minutes before serving.

TIP: If you are going for a trio of a brine, marinade, and glaze, try to keep your flavors focused. Asian fusion can be tasty, but *confusion* of clashing flavors is not.

SUBSTITUTIONS: Replace the brine with Asian Tea Brine (page 276), Sake-Mirin Brine (page 277), or Thai-Infused Brine (page 278).

Replace the marinade with Balsamic-Ginger Marinade (page 270), Orange-Sesame Marinade (page 282), Korean-Style Marinade (page 284), or Thai Red-Curry Marinade (page 289).

Replace the glaze with Teriyaki Glaze (page 304), Cantonese Glaze (page 303), East–West Indies Tamarind Glaze (page 310), or any of the glazes in this chapter.

CHINESE-STYLE BEEF AND BROCCOLI STIR-FRY
SERVES 4

• •

Marinades lend themselves to stir-fries. Not only do they initially coat the meat with flavor, but they also finish the dish with a sauce as well. Needless to say, any of the Asian marinades will work in the following recipe, but this is my favorite with beef.

SUBSTITUTIONS: Replace the marinade with Basic Southeast Asian Marinade (page 285), Thai Red-Curry Marinade (page 289), or Indonesian Marinade (page 291).

1 (½- to ¾-pound) eye round or flank steak,
   sliced ¼ inch thick against the grain
2 cups Basic Asian-Style Marinade (page 278)
1 pound broccoli
4 to 6 tablespoons Asian or domestic cold-pressed peanut oil
2 to 3 teaspoons Asian chile oil (page 272)
2 tablespoons peeled and minced fresh ginger
2 tablespoons minced garlic
½ cup chopped green onions, white part only
¼ cup water
2 to 2½ cups cooked rice
Toasted sesame seeds, for garnish

Place the beef in a nonreactive container or a 1-gallon resealable plastic bag, pour the marinade over the beef, and refrigerate for at least 6 hours, preferably overnight.

Cut the broccoli florets from the main stem, and split the florets in half. With a vegetable peeler, remove the rough outer husk from the stems, and slice the stems into ¼-inch-thick slices.

Preheat the oven to 350°F. Heat 2 tablespoons of the peanut oil along with the chile oil in a wok. When the oil is hot, add the ginger and garlic, and cook briefly. Add the broccoli and stir-fry for 1 minute. Then add the green onions and stir-fry for 1 additional minute. Add the water, cover the wok, and let the broccoli steam for 3 to 4 minutes. Remove the vegetables with a slotted spoon, transfer to an ovenproof dish, and keep warm in the oven.

Cook the wok liquid over high heat for about 10 minutes, until reduced to a glaze. Add the remaining 2 to 4 tablespoons of peanut oil.

Remove the meat from the marinade and add the meat to the wok, reserving ¼ cup of the marinade. Stir-fry until slightly firm. Add the vegetables and ¼ cup reserved marinade. Toss with the meat for 5 minutes.

To serve, spoon the rice onto 4 plates, place the beef and broccoli on top of the rice, and garnish with sesame seeds.

GRILLED JAPANESE BEEF ROLLS (NEGIMAKI)

SERVES 8 AS AN APPETIZER OR 4 AS A MAIN COURSE

. . . .

In this version of negimaki, we have two distinctly flavored marinades working independently from one another, resulting in a whole that's truly greater in flavor than the sum of its parts. Because the beef is rolled, we can incorporate one marinade in the center, and the second marinade on the completed beef roll. Both marinades come together when you take your first of many bites.

8 large green onions
1 cup Yakitori Marinade (page 284)
1 pound eye round, cut into ½-inch-thick slices
1½ cups Simple Sake Marinade (page 282)

Blanch the green onions in a pot of boiling salted water for 45 seconds, then transfer them with a slotted spoon to a bowl of ice cold water to stop the cooking process. Transfer the green onions to paper towels to drain and pat dry. Combine the green onions and the marinade in a resealable plastic bag and refrigerate for 2 hours.

Place the beef slices between two pieces of waxed paper and pound with a kitchen mallet to ¼-inch thickness. Remove the green onions from the marinade and reserve the marinade. Lay about one-fourth of the meat slices side by side, with the edges slightly overlapping, along the length of the green onions. Lay 2 green onions along the edge closest to you and brush the meat with 1 to 2 tablespoons of the reserved Yakatori Marinade. Roll the beef up around the green onions and secure each roll with 2 presoaked bamboo skewers. Repeat with the rest of the beef slices to form 3 additional beef rolls.

Place the beef rolls in a nonreactive container or a 1-gallon resealable plastic bag. Pour the Simple Sake Marinade over the beef rolls and refrigerate for 1 hour. Remove the beef from the marinade, reserving the marinade, and cut the rolls in half to give you 2 skewered beef rolls. Bring the marinade to a boil for 3 minutes and keep warm for basting.

To grill: Lightly brush the grill with vegetable oil and grill the rolls for 5 to 6 minutes, turning often and basting with the warm marinade.

To cook indoors: Preheat the broiler and line a baking sheet with foil. Arrange the beef rolls on the baking sheet and broil for 5 to 6 minutes, turning and basting with the warm marinade.

To serve, transfer the beef rolls to a cutting board and let them rest for 10 minutes. Slice the beef into ½-inch-thick slices and serve on warm plates.

KOREAN BARBECUE BEEF (BULGOGI)
SERVES 10 AS AN APPETIZER

Bulgogi is Korean barbecue at its best. It's usually served wrapped in lettuce and garnished with sesame seeds, limes, and kimchee, which is like fiery hot, cold sauerkraut. Traditional Korean barbecue sometimes uses beef or pork short ribs, thinly sliced across the bone. I'm using beef sirloin in its place. You can also adapt this recipe for pork tenderloin or chicken kabobs.

2 pounds beef sirloin
2 cups Korean-Style Marinade (page 284)
10 to 12 romaine lettuce leaves
1 lime, thinly sliced
10 to 12 green onions
Toasted sesame seeds, for garnish
1½ cups kimchee (optional; available at Asian grocery stores)

Place the sirloin in the freezer for 30 minutes to firm it up for slicing. Slice the beef diagonally across the grain into long, thin slices about ¼ inch thick. Place the beef and the marinade in a resealable plastic bag and refrigerate for 8 hours.

Remove the meat from the bag and bring the marinade to a boil for 3 minutes; keep warm for basting.

Thread the beef strips lengthwise on 10 to 12 metal or presoaked bamboo skewers.

To grill: Brush the grill with vegetable oil and lay the skewers on the grill over medium-high heat. Grill the beef, basting with the reserved marinade, until medium rare, 3 to 4 minutes.

To cook indoors: Preheat the broiler and line a baking sheet with foil. Arrange the beef skewers on the baking sheet and broil for 5 to 6 minutes, turning and basting with the warm marinade.

To serve, transfer the beef to a serving platter and remove the skewers. Serve with the lettuce leaves, lime slices, green onions, sesame seeds, and kimchee. Invite your guests to wrap and roll.

INDONESIAN GRILLED QUAIL WITH NUTMEG SAUCE SERVES 4

This particular dish typifies some of the sweet-heat flavors of Malaysia. What the brothlike nutmeg sauce lacks in consistency it makes up for in intensity. Serve this with a simple rice dish to mop up the sauce.

NUTMEG SAUCE MAKES 2 CUPS

1 quart homemade chicken stock or low-salt canned chicken broth
1 stalk lemongrass, tough outer leaves removed,
    smashed and chopped (about ½ cup)
1 teaspoon ground cardamom
1 tablespoon peeled and grated fresh ginger
3 tablespoons diced shallots
¼ cup kecap manis (see page 273)
1 teaspoon freshly grated nutmeg
1 bay leaf, crumbled
2 tablespoons peanuts or hazelnuts, ground to a powder
    in a blender or spice mill

QUAIL

8 quail, boned
1½ cups Indonesian Honey Chile Glaze (page 307)

To make the sauce, combine the chicken stock, lemongrass, cardamom, ginger, shallots, kecap manis, nutmeg, and bay leaf in a heavy nonreactive saucepan. Bring to a boil, decrease the heat, and simmer for 40 to 45 minutes. Strain the sauce and blend in the peanut powder to thicken; keep the sauce warm until serving.

To prepare the quail, place the quail in a nonreactive container or a 1-gallon resealable plastic bag. Pour the glaze over the quail and refrigerate for at least 2 hours.

Remove the quail from the glaze and bring the glaze to a boil for basting. Keep warm.

To grill: Lightly brush the grill with vegetable oil and grill the quail for 3 to 4 minutes on each side, basting with the warm marinade.

To cook indoors: Preheat the broiler to its hottest setting and line a baking sheet with foil. Arrange the quail on the baking sheet and broil for 3 to 4 minutes on each side, basting with the warm marinade.

To serve, remove the quail from the heat and spoon the warm Nutmeg Sauce over it.

GRILLED THAI-MARINATED CHICKEN KABOBS WITH CASHEW SAUCE SERVES 8 AS AN APPETIZER

This is a satay with a different spin on the sauce. Replacing the traditional peanut sauce is a cashew sauce that winks at other parts of the spice trail.

SUBSTITUTIONS: Replace the marinade with Thai Coconut Marinade (page 287) or Thai Red-Curry Marinade (page 289).

3 whole boneless chicken breasts, cut into 1-inch-wide strips
2 cups Lemongrass Marinade (page 286)
2 cups Cashew Satay Dipping Sauce (page 340)

Place the chicken in a nonreactive container or a 1-gallon resealable plastic bag, pour the marinade over the chicken, and refrigerate for 4 to 6 hours.

Remove the chicken from the marinade and bring the marinade to a low boil in a nonreactive saucepan or microwave on high for 3 minutes. Keep warm and use for basting. Thread the chicken onto 12 presoaked bamboo skewers.

To grill: Lightly brush the grill with vegetable oil and grill the chicken for 15 to 20 minutes, turning often and basting with the warm marinade.

To cook indoors: Preheat the broiler and line a baking sheet with foil. Arrange the skewers on the baking sheet and broil about 6 inches from the flame for about 10 minutes, turning the skewers every few minutes after basting with the warm marinade.

Serve hot with the cashew sauce.

THAI FRIED CHICKEN

SERVES 8 AS AN APPETIZER OR 4 AS A MAIN COURSE

The marinade in this recipe does double duty. First and foremost, it flavors the chicken with a wonderful spicy Thai peanut sauce (served with satays), and second, it acts as a batter for a curry peanut coating, which locks in the flavors. For a main course, cook chicken breast halves; for an hors d'oeuvre, cut the chicken breasts into strips.

2 chicken breasts, boned, skinned, and quartered
2½ cups Thai Peanut Marinade (page 288)
1 cup all-purpose flour
1 cup coarsely chopped peanuts, roasted
1 tablespoon curry powder or garam masala (page 299)
4 to 6 tablespoons peanut oil, for pan-frying

Place the chicken in a nonreactive container or a 1-gallon resealable plastic bag, pour the marinade over the chicken, and refrigerate for at least 6 hours.

Combine the flour, peanuts, and curry powder in a brown paper bag. Remove the chicken from the marinade (the marinade will be thick), place each piece in the bag, and gently shake to coat the chicken evenly.

In a skillet, pour the peanut oil to a depth of ½ inch and heat over medium-high heat to 365°F on a candy thermometer (a bread cube dropped into the hot oil will brown in 60 seconds). Pan-fry the chicken for about 10 minutes on each side. Drain on paper towels before serving.

TIP: Should you want to cut down on oil, broil the chicken instead. Preheat the oven to 500°F, coat the bottom of cast-iron or ovenproof frying pan with a little oil, transfer the chicken to the pan, and broil for 8 to 10 minutes per side. The chicken will be as crisp as if it were pan-fried.

THAI RED-CURRY BEEF SERVES 8 AS AN APPETIZER

The raves received for these skewered appetizers are due largely to the savory and spicy signature of the Thai Red-Curry Marinade. The marinade has great flavor penetration with small slices of meat. The dipping sauce is light and tart, with a little sweetness to contrast the curried marinade. To take the flavors to a higher level, serve the appetizers around a portion of Thai Pickled Vegetables (page 333).

2½ pounds flank steak, sliced ⅛ inch thick across the grain
2½ cups Thai Red-Curry Marinade (page 289)
1 cup Spicy Thai Dipping Sauce (page 341)

Place the steak in a nonreactive container or 1-gallon resealable plastic bag. Pour the marinade over the steak and refrigerate for 8 to 12 hours.

Remove the steak from the marinade, reserving the marinade, and skewer the strips onto presoaked bamboo skewers. Bring the marinade to a low boil in a nonreactive saucepan and simmer for 10 minutes, or microwave the marinade on high for 3 minutes. Use for basting.

To grill: Lightly brush the grill with vegetable oil and grill the steak strips for 2 to 3 minutes over a hot fire, turning often and basting with the warm marinade.

To cook indoors: Preheat the broiler to its hottest setting and line a baking sheet with foil. Place the skewers on the baking sheet and broil for 2 to 3 minutes per side, basting with the warm marinade.

Serve immediately with the Thai Dipping Sauce.

TANDOORI CHICKEN BREASTS SERVES 4

The trick to really succulent Tandoori chicken is to sear the meat at high heat to seal in the juices, then decrease the heat and baste with the marinade. The paprika gives the chicken its characteristic red color. Serve with Marinated Indonesian Carrot Sticks (page 336), Mint-Cilantro Chutney (page 332), chilled Coconut Curried Cauliflower (page 336), or grilled red onion rings.

3 whole chicken breasts, halved
2 cups Tandoori Yogurt Marinade (page 294)
Lime wedges, for garnish

Place the chicken in a nonreactive container or a 1-gallon resealable plastic bag. Pour the marinade over the chicken and refrigerate for 8 hours. Remove the chicken from the marinade, and bring the marinade to a boil for basting. Keep warm.

To grill: Lightly brush the grill with vegetable oil and grill the chicken for about 10 minutes, then baste with the warm marinade, turn, and grill for an additional 10 minutes. To cut down on grilling time, you can sear the chicken under the broiler first, and then finish the chicken on the grill.

To cook indoors: Preheat the oven to 375°F and line a baking sheet with foil. Arrange the chicken on the baking sheet and bake for 20 to 25 minutes, until the juices run clear when pricked with a fork. Baste with the warm marinade after 15 minutes.

To serve, transfer the chicken to serving plates and garnish with lime wedges.

INDONESIAN GRILLED LAMB WITH CASHEW-GINGER CHUTNEY SERVES 6

Chef Jon Jividen's marinated lamb and chutney are a medley of sweet-heat taste sensations. Your palate spins around the combination of lemongrass and chile, with the surprise match of ginger and cashews.

CASHEW-GINGER CHUTNEY MAKES 1½ CUPS

1 cup raw cashews
2 jalapeño chiles, stemmed, seeded, and diced
¼ cup peeled and chopped fresh ginger
½ cup fresh cilantro or mint leaves (or both)
1 tablespoon coarse-grain salt

LAMB

3 pounds loin of lamb, boned
1¾ cups Indonesian Marinade (page 291)

To make the chutney, finely chop the nuts in a food processor, then add the jalapeños, ginger, cilantro, and salt and process again until the chutney is well blended. You may want to thin it with water or yogurt to use it on pasta or as a dressing.

To prepare the lamb, place the lamb in a shallow glass baking dish, fat side up. Pour the marinade over the lamb, cover, and refrigerate overnight. Remove the lamb from the marinade and bring the marinade to a boil for basting. Roll the lamb and tie with presoaked butcher's twine.

To grill: Lightly brush the grill with vegetable oil. Place the loin about 6 inches above the heat source and cook, turning frequently and basting with the warm marinade, for about 30 minutes, until the meat is medium rare. Remove the lamb from the grill and let the roast rest for 10 minutes before slicing.

To cook indoors: Preheat the oven to 425°F. Place the lamb in a shallow baking dish and roast in the top portion of the oven for 30 to 40 minutes. Baste the lamb frequently with the warm marinade and pan juices. Remove the lamb from the oven and let the roast rest for 10 minutes before slicing.

To serve, slice the lamb loin into ¼-inch-thick slices and serve each portion with ⅓ to ½ cup of the Cashew-Ginger Chutney.

GRILLED INDIAN LAMB KABOBS WITH MINT-CILANTRO CHUTNEY

SERVES 8 AS AN APPETIZER OR 4 AS A MAIN COURSE

I've had my eye on Indian marinades for quite some time. Besides flavorful and exhilarating spice mixes, the cuisine relies on enzymatic reactions from green papaya or yogurt. In this recipe, the marinade is part of the kabob.

LAMB

TIP: Green papaya is usually found in Indian grocery stores. Don't substitute a ripe yellow one.

TIP: To make the papaya, garlic, and ginger purées, process each separately in a food processor. Do not overprocess. Squeeze the juice from the pulp through a cheesecloth or fine-mesh strainer.

1 pound ground lean lamb
2½ tablespoons raw green papaya purée or ripe fresh
    pineapple purée (about ¼ cup fresh fruit) (see Tip)
1 tablespoon garlic purée (see Tip)
1½ tablespoons ginger purée (see Tip)
⅛ teaspoon mace powder
¼ teaspoon cardamom powder
¼ teaspoon cinnamon
⅛ teaspoon cayenne pepper
¼ cup finely ground roasted unsalted cashews
1 teaspoon coarse-grain salt
1 teaspoon freshly cracked black peppercorns
8 warm rotis or pita breads

MINT-CILANTRO CHUTNEY MAKES ABOUT ½ CUP

1 cup tightly packed cilantro leaves
½ cup tightly packed mint leaves
1 clove garlic, minced
2 Thai green chiles or serrano chiles, seeded, deveined, and chopped
½ teaspoon cumin powder, roasted
Grated zest and juice of 1 lime (about 2 tablespoons)
Salt

Freeze the ground lamb for about 15 minutes. In a small bowl, combine the papaya, garlic, and ginger purées; mace; cardamom; cinnamon; cayenne to taste; cashew powder; salt to taste; and peppercorns, then combine with the lamb. Divide the mixture into 8 portions. Roll each portion into a cigar shape and thread onto 2 metal or presoaked wooden skewers. Refrigerate for 6 to 8 hours.

To make the chutney, in a blender, combine the cilantro, mint, garlic, chiles, cumin, lime zest and juice, and salt to taste and grind to a smooth paste, adding a little water, if required. Stored in a clean, airtight container, this will keep in the refrigerator for 1 week.

To cook the lamb, remove the skewers from the refrigerator and let sit at room temperature for 30 minutes before cooking.

To grill: Brush the grill rack with vegetable oil. When the grill is ready, place the lamb skewers on the rack, cover, and cook, turning once, just until done, 5 to 6 minutes per side. During the last few minutes of grilling, place the rotis or the pitas on the outer side of the grill. Remove the lamb skewers from the grill.

To cook indoors: Preheat the broiler and line a baking sheet with foil. Arrange the lamb skewers on the baking sheet and broil for 10 to 12 minutes.

To serve, place the lamb on the roti, remove the skewers, and add the chutney. Roll the bread, slice on the diagonal, and serve.

THAI PICKLED VEGETABLES SERVES 8 TO 12

. . . .

This is my favorite Thai condiment. This Thai version of Italian giardiniera makes an excellent cooling contrast to the hot flavors of traditional Thai marinades.

1 cup baby corn
1 cup broccoli florets, rough stems removed
1 cup ¼-inch-thick diagonal carrot rounds
½ cup sliced bok choy, white part only
1 cup (3 by ¼-inch) strips seeded cucumber
4¾ cups Thai Pickling Brine for Vegetables (page 277)
⅓ cup minced fresh cilantro, for garnish
2 to 3 tablespoons toasted sesame seeds, for garnish

To prepare the vegetables, bring 4 quarts water to a rolling boil in a large pot. Place the corn, broccoli, carrots, bok choy, and cucumber strips in a colander or large strainer, set them in the boiling water, and blanch for 2 to 3 minutes. Refresh the vegetables in a bowl of cold water to stop the cooking process, and then drain. Place the vegetables in a nonreactive mixing bowl. Pour the brine over the vegetables. Cool to room temperature. Stir in the cilantro and sesame seeds. Stored in a clean, airtight container, this will keep in the refrigerator for 1 week.

MARINATED BLACK BEAN SALAD SERVES 6

I asked my good friend Nina Hardenbergh to work on a black bean recipe. Half expecting something like a Southwestern black bean relish, I was absolutely delighted with this Asian tour de force. The marinated black beans taste as good as they look. By the way, the method for cooking black beans is foolproof for holding their shape.

ASIAN VINAIGRETTE MAKES ½ CUP

4 tablespoons peanut oil, divided
1 teaspoon peeled and finely diced fresh ginger
1 teaspoon minced garlic
½ teaspoon hot chile oil
1 teaspoon sesame oil
¼ cup rice wine vinegar
1½ tablespoons soy or tamari sauce
1 tablespoon sherry

BEAN SALAD

1 quart water
1 cup uncooked black beans
½ cup diced red bell pepper
⅓ cup minced green onions, white part only
½ cup diced canned water chestnuts or jicama
1 cucumber (preferably seedless), peeled, for garnish
Radicchio leaves, for garnish
1 red bell pepper, sliced into ¼-inch-thick rings, for garnish

To make the vinaigrette, heat 1 tablespoon of the peanut oil in a sauté pan. Add the ginger and garlic and sauté for 1 to 2 minutes. Remove from the heat and let cool. Combine the garlic-ginger mixture, peanut oil, chile oil, sesame oil, vinegar, soy sauce, and sherry in a blender or a food processor and pulse until all the ingredients are well blended. Stored in a clean, airtight container, this will keep in the refrigerator for 1 week.

To prepare the bean salad, bring the water to a boil. Preheat the oven to 550°F. Place the black beans in a deep 2-quart casserole or a Dutch oven, and cover with the boiling water. Place the beans in the oven and cook for 20 minutes. Decrease the heat to 200°F and cook for 1 hour more. Remove the beans from the oven, drain in a colander, and cool to room temperature. You should have about 3 cups.

Combine the cooled black beans with the diced red pepper, green onions, and water chestnuts. Toss with the dressing and refrigerate for 3 to 4 hours.

To serve, use a vegetable peeler to shave the cucumber into long, flat strips working around its core. Line 6 salad plates with radicchio. Form a nest with the shaved cucumber strips and top with about ⅔ cup of black beans. Garnish with red pepper rings.

COCONUT-CUCUMBER SLAW SERVES 4

This salad combines crunch with cool—coconut with lime and chiles. The slaw picks up flavors from Southeast Asia, but the ingredients can be just as much at home in the Caribbean. Slaws can balance almost any smoked or grilled dish. This particular slaw is a nice accompaniment to grilled Indonesian Shrimp (page 315) and Soft-Shell Crabs with Thai Coconut Marinade (page 316).

COCONUT-CHILE DRESSING MAKES 1 CUP

3 tablespoons rice wine vinegar
2 tablespoons shredded unsweetened coconut
1 tablespoon peeled and shredded fresh ginger
3 tablespoons fresh lime juice
1 tablespoon grated lime zest
4 or 5 fresh bird chiles, or 1 habanero chile, seeded and diced
2 teaspoons sugar
⅛ teaspoon ground cumin

SLAW

1 cup matchstick-julienned jicama
1 cucumber, peeled, seeded, and julienned into matchsticks
2 to 3 tablespoons chopped fresh basil

SUBSTITUTION: Replace the dressing with Citrus-Cilantro Dressing (page 212).

To make the dressing, warm the vinegar in a nonreactive saucepan over low heat. Add the coconut and ginger to soften. Cool to room temperature, and combine the coconut-ginger mixture with the lime juice and zest, chiles, sugar, and cumin. Stored in a clean, airtight container, it will keep in the refrigerator for 1 week.

To make the slaw, combine the jicama, cucumber, and basil in a nonreactive mixing bowl. Pour the dressing over, toss to combine, and marinate in the refrigerator for 2 hours before serving.

MARINATED INDONESIAN CARROT STICKS
SERVES 8 AS AN APPETIZER

Served cold, this makes a great summertime snack food, or stir-fry the marinated carrots and serve hot for an Indonesian rijsttafel (buffet). This makes an excellent accompaniment for grilled Indonesian Shrimp (page 315).

SUBSTITUTIONS: Replace the marinade with Thai-Infused Brine (page 278), Balsamic-Ginger Marinade (page 279), or Orange-Cinnamon Marinade (page 53).

1 pound carrots, julienned into 2-inch-long pieces
1 cup Singapore-Style Marinade (page 292)
2 to 3 tablespoons peanut oil (if stir-frying)

Bring a pot of salted water to a boil and blanch the carrots for 1 to 2 minutes. Refresh the carrots in a bowl of cold water to stop the cooking process. In a nonreactive bowl, combine the carrots with the marinade and refrigerate for 4 hours. Bring to room temperature before serving. The carrots will keep for at least 1 week refrigerated.

To stir-fry, marinate the carrot sticks for at least 4 hours. Heat the peanut oil over high heat. Drain the carrots, reserving the marinade, and stir-fry in 2 to 3 tablespoons marinade for 3 to 4 minutes, or until firm (not crisp). The remaining marinade can be warmed separately and served as a sauce.

ORANGE-CINNAMON STIR-FRIED CARROTS. Slice the carrots into ¼-inch-thick rounds. Marinate the carrots in Orange-Cinnamon Marinade (page 53). Drain the carrots and reserve the marinade. In a wok or deep-sided sauté pan over high heat, cook the marinade for about 15 minutes, until reduced to one third its original volume. Add the carrots to the pan and stir-fry for 2 to 3 minutes. Stir in ¼ cup golden raisins and cook until heated through, 3 to 4 minutes.

COCONUT CURRIED CAULIFLOWER SERVES 4

To be honest, as a kid when I would see cauliflower I would run for cover; now when I see it I run for a wok. Cauliflower is one of my favorite vegetables to work with because it can absorb marinades like a sponge. Locked in the florets will be wonderful bursts of curry, coconut, and zesty lime waiting to be released by the steam of your wok. The Coconut Curry Marinade can also be used on grilled chicken or shrimp kabobs. Stylistically, the recipe follows an Indian track. Any of the Indian marinades can be interchanged.

1 head cauliflower
1¼ cups Coconut Curry Marinade (page 293)
2 tablespoons Asian or cold-pressed domestic peanut oil

Rinse and trim the cauliflower and break the florets into individual pieces. Slice the florets in half lengthwise and place in a nonreactive container or a 1-gallon resealable plastic bag. Pour the marinade over the cauliflower and refrigerate for 4 to 6 hours.

Bring the marinated cauliflower to room temperature. Heat the peanut oil in a wok. Add the cauliflower and the marinade and toss for 3 to 4 minutes over high heat. Serve immediately.

SUBSTITUTIONS: Replace the marinade with Tandoori Yogurt Marinade (page 294).

STIR-FRIED SNOW PEAS WITH BALSAMIC-GINGER MARINADE SERVES 4

This East-meets-West marinade combines the Mediterranean flavors of balsamic vinegar, olive oil, and Dijon-style mustard with the Orient's soy sauce and ginger into glazing perfection. The combination works so well that I occasionally stir-fry shrimp in the marinade.

1 pound snow peas, ends trimmed
1 cup Balsamic-Ginger Marinade (page 279)
1 tablespoon toasted sesame seeds, or 2 tablespoons toasted pine nuts

Place the snow peas in a nonreactive container or a 1-gallon resealable plastic bag, pour the marinade over, and refrigerate for at least 4 hours. Remove the snow peas from the marinade and reserve the marinade.

In a wok or deep-sided sauté pan over high heat, cook the marinade for about 10 minutes, until reduced to one third its original volume. Add the snow peas and stir-fry for 3 to 4 minutes. Stir in the sesame seeds and cook for 3 to 4 minutes more. Serve immediately.

SUBSTITUTIONS: Replace the marinade with Orange-Cinnamon Marinade (page 53), Lemon-Soy Marinade (page 52), or Sherry-Hazelnut Marinade (page 223).

SESAME-GINGER DIPPING SAUCE MAKES ½ CUP

This dipping sauce is the perfect accompaniment for chicken wings or spareribs. Serve with food marinated in Szechuan Sesame Marinade (page 281), Spicy Garlic Marinade (page 280), Orange-Sesame Marinade (page 282), or Orange-Ginger Marinade (page 54).

¼ cup soy or tamari sauce
1 tablespoon Asian or domestic cold-pressed peanut oil
1 tablespoon sesame oil
2 tablespoons dry sherry
2 tablespoons peeled and diced fresh ginger

Combine the soy sauce, peanut oil, sesame oil, sherry, and ginger in a blender or a food processor. Pour into a glass jar and refrigerate until ready to use. This will keep for 1 to 2 weeks in the refrigerator.

WASABI-GINGER AIOLI MAKES ⅔ CUP

I first made this versatile sauce as a topping for Grilled Japanese Beef Rolls (page 325), but the leftover aioli hit my sandwiches throughout the rest of the week. Although the recipe calls for wasabi powder, you can use wasabi paste from any sushi counter as well.

2 tablespoons wasabi powder, or 1 tablespoon wasabi paste
2 tablespoons boiling water
½ cup mayonnaise
2 tablespoons sour cream
2 cloves garlic, finely chopped
2 teaspoons peeled and minced fresh ginger
Grated zest and juice of 1 lime (about 2 tablespoons)

If using wasabi powder, in a small bowl, stir together the wasabi powder and boiling water until smooth, adding additional water (½ teaspoon at a time) if necessary. Let the wasabi stand, uncovered, for 15 minutes to let the flavor develop. Combine the wasabi paste, mayonnaise, sour cream, garlic, ginger, and lime zest and juice in a blender or a food processor and process until all the ingredients are well blended. Stored in a clean, airtight container, this will keep in the refrigerator for 1 week.

JAPANESE DIPPING SAUCE MAKES ABOUT 1 CUP

This dipping sauce is simple to prepare and intensely flavored. It can also be used as a baste for grilled salmon, swordfish, or shrimp. Serve with Grilled Japanese Beef Rolls (page 325) and in combination with Simple Sake Marinade (page 282).

½ cup soy or tamari sauce
2 tablespoons rice wine vinegar
2 tablespoons mirin
1 tablespoon chopped pickled ginger (available at Asian grocery stores)

Combine the soy sauce, vinegar, mirin, and ginger in a blender or a food processor and process until all the ingredients are well blended. Pour into a glass jar and refrigerate until ready to use. This will keep for 2 to 3 weeks in the refrigerator.

PONZU SAUCE MAKES 1½ CUPS

Not all Asian condiments need to come from a bottle. This easy-to-make citrusy Japanese dipping sauce can be splashed over grilling scallops or shrimp. The citrus is interchangeable. You can swap out the lemon with individual doses or combinations of orange, grapefruit, and, of course, lime.

⅓ cup soy or tamari sauce
Juice of 2 lemons (about ⅓ cup)
¼ cup mirin
¼ cup rice wine vinegar
1 tablespoon dried bonito flakes (available at Asian grocery stores)

Combine the soy sauce, lemon juice, mirin, vinegar, and bonito flakes in a nonreactive bowl. Cover and steep for at least 2 to 3 hours to allow the flavors to blend; strain before using. Stored in a clean, airtight container, this will keep in the refrigerator for up to 2 weeks. This recipe freezes well with food.

CASHEW SATAY DIPPING SAUCE MAKES 2 CUPS

By substituting cashew butter for peanut butter and adding garam masala, I've given an Indian tang to traditional Thai peanut sauce. And that's just the beginning. Any nut butter, such as almond or hazelnut, can be substituted and will work flavor wonders.

1 cup cashew butter (available at health food stores) or
    peanut butter (for traditional satay sauce)
1 (12-ounce) can Asian coconut milk
¼ cup chicken stock or low-salt canned chicken broth
¼ teaspoon garam masala (page 299) or curry powder
¼ teaspoon ground cardamom
2 tablespoons unsulphured molasses
2 tablespoons low-sodium soy sauce
Juice of 2 limes (about ¼ cup)
¼ cup plain yogurt
1 clove garlic, minced or pressed

Combine the cashew butter, coconut milk, chicken stock, garam masala, cardamom, molasses, and soy sauce in a heavy nonreactive saucepan, bring to a boil, decrease the heat, and simmer for 20 minutes. Remove from the heat and stir in the lime juice, yogurt, and garlic. Warm the cashew sauce slightly before serving. Stored in a clean, airtight container, it will keep in the refrigerator for 1 week.

ALMOND OR HAZELNUT SATAY SAUCE. Replace the cashew butter with 1 cup blanched almonds or hazelnuts, toasted and then ground to a paste in a food processor.

SPICY THAI DIPPING SAUCE MAKES ½ CUP

There are as many Thai dipping sauces as there are Thai marinades. Any of the Thai marinade recipes in the book can double as a dipping sauce. Here's a simple one that's infallible with almost all variations of Thai grilled meat and fish. Feel free to add diced ginger or chopped lemongrass for flavor variations. Serve with Grilled Thai-Marinated Chicken Kabobs with Cashew Sauce (page 328) or Thai Red-Curry Beef (page 329), and in combination with Thai Coconut Marinade (page 287), Basil Marinade (page 217), or Thai Red-Curry Marinade (page 289).

¼ cup soy or tamari sauce
3 tablespoons rice wine vinegar
1 tablespoon kecap manis (see page 273)
3 cloves garlic, crushed
2 to 3 tablespoons chopped fresh basil
2 bird chiles, stemmed, seeded, and chopped

Combine the soy sauce, vinegar, kecap manis, garlic, basil, and chiles in a blender or a food processor. Pulse the ingredients to a coarse paste. Transfer to a glass jar and refrigerate until ready to use. This will keep for 2 to 3 weeks in the refrigerator.

VIETNAMESE MINT DIPPING SAUCE MAKES ½ CUP

This lively dipping sauce, flavored with mint and serrano chiles, picks up its regional signature from nuoc nam, Vietnamese fish sauce. Serve with grilled Indonesian Shrimp (page 315) and in combination with Vietnamese Peanut-Tamarind Marinade (page 290), Citrus-Cilantro Marinade (page 213), Thai-Style Tamarind Marinade (page 288), Indonesian Honey-Chile Glaze (page 307), or Singapore-Style Marinade (page 292).

¼ cup fresh mint leaves
1 serrano chile, stemmed, seeded, and diced
2 cloves garlic, pressed
Grated zest and juice of 2 limes (about ¼ cup)
2 tablespoons Asian fish sauce (nam pla)

Combine the mint, chile, garlic, lime zest and juice, and fish sauce in a blender or a food processor and process until well blended. Pour into a glass jar and refrigerate until ready to use. This will keep for 2 to 3 weeks in the refrigerator.

SELECTED BIBLIOGRAPHY & ONLINE REFERENCES

Aidells, Bruce, and Denis Kelley. *The Complete Meat Cookbook.* New York: Houghton Mifflin, 1998.

Arndt, Alice. *Seasoning Savvy.* Binghamton: Haworth Herbal Press, 1999.

BBQ FAQ Online Version, version 2.0. Edited by William W. Wright. http://www.eaglesquest.com/~bbq/faq2.

BBQ Forum. http://www.rbjb.com/rbjbboard.

Bladholm, Linda. *Latin & Caribbean Grocery Stores Demystified.* Los Angeles: Renaissance Books, 2001.

Carpenter, Hugh, and Teri Sandison. *Pacific Flavors.* New York: Stewart, Tabori, and Chang, 1988.

Civitello, Linda. *Cuisine and Culture: A History of Food and People.* Hoboken: John Wiley & Sons, 2004.

Cook's Thesaurus. http://www.foodsubs.com.

Cost, Bruce. *Asian Ingredients.* New York: Quill, 2000.

DeWitt, Dave, and Nancy Gerlach. *The Whole Chile Pepper Book.* Boston: Little, Brown and Company, 1990.

eGullet Society for Culinary Arts and Letters. http://www.egullet.org.

Fiery Foods. http://www.fiery-foods.com.

Haroutunian, Arto der. *A Turkish Cookbook.* London: Ebury Press, 1987.

————. *North African Cookery.* London: Century Publishing, 1985.

Harris, Dunstan A. *Island Cooking: Recipes from the Caribbean.* Berkeley: Crossing Press, 1988.

Hom, Ken. *Ken Hom's Asian Ingredients.* Berkeley: Ten Speed Press, 1996.

Joachhim, David. *The Food Substitutions Bible.* Toronto: Robert Rose, 2005.

Johns, Pamela Sheldon. *Balsamico!* Berkeley: Ten Speed Press, 1999.

Kendall, Pat. *New Recommendations for Jerky Preparation.* Colorado State University Cooperative Extension (Oct. 2000). http://www.ext.colostate.edu/pubs/columnnn/nn001003.html.

Kennedy, Diana. *The Cuisines of Mexico.* New York: Harper & Row, 1972.

Livingston, A. D. *Cold-Smoking & Salt-Curing Meat, Fish, & Game.* New York: Lyons & Burford Publishers, 1995.

McGee, Harold. *On Food and Cooking,* revised edition. New York: Scribner, 2004.

Parsons, Russ. *How to Read a French Fry.* New York: Houghton Mifflin, 2001.

Peterson, James. *The Duck Cookbook.* New York: Stewart, Tabori, & Chang, 2003.

Rojas-Lombardi, Felipe. *The Art of South American Cooking.* New York: HarperCollins, 1991.

Rozin, Elisabeth. *Blue Corn and Chocolate.* New York: Alfred A. Knopf, 1992.

Tarantino, Jim. "Cooking with Hugh Carpenter." *On the Grill* (Oct. 1997): 20.

Wolfert, Paula. *The Cooking of the Eastern Mediterranean.* New York: HarperCollins, 1994.

INDEX

O

Oils
Annatto Oil, 172
chile, 272
Lime-Habanero Oil, 172
olive, 216
Orange-Chipotle Oil, 172
peanut, 274
sesame, 274
Olives, 216
Greek Marinated Olives, 234
Italian Marinated Black Olives, 234
Marinated Moroccan Olives, 269
Marinated Spanish Olives, 235
oil, 216
Provençal Cognac Marinade, 228
Rosemary Marinated Olives, 235
Tapenade Marinade, 226–27
Onions, 39–40
Caramelized Onion–Fig Glaze, 229
Caramelized Onions, 241
Cassis–Red Onion Glaze, 84
Pickled Red Onions (Escabèche de Cebolla), 211
powder, 40
Red Onion–Marmalade Glaze, 84
Red Onion Powder, 67
Savory Onion Wet Rub, 206
Turkish Bath of Onion and Garlic for Lamb or Beef, 254–55
Turkish-Style Marinade for Beef or Lamb Kabobs, 254
Oranges, 38
Bitter Orange Marinade, 176
Blood Orange–Sherry Marinade, 224–25
Citrus Slaw, 125
Cranberry Marinade, 58
Cranberry-Orange Chutney, 127
Cranberry-Orange Chutney Salad, 108–9
Grilled Iberian Pork Tenderloin with Blood Orange–Sherry Sauce, 240–41
Grilled Orange-Ginger Marinated Tuna, 104–5
Indonesian Curry Glaze, 307
Juniper and Orange Cured Venison with Herb Salad, 126
Orange and Juniper Cure, 44
Orange-Beet Glaze, 83
Orange-Brandy Marinade, 225
Orange–Chile Powder Rub, 142
Orange-Chipotle Marinade, 174–75
Orange-Chipotle Oil, 172
Orange-Chipotle Powder, 181
Orange-Chipotle Vinegar, 171
Orange-Cinnamon Marinades, 53
Orange-Cinnamon Stir-Fried Carrots, 336
Orange-Cumin Powder, 66
Orange Duck Pastrami, 107
Orange-Ginger Glaze, 55
Orange-Ginger Marinade, 54–55
Orange Marinade, 53

Orange Pastrami Spice Mix, 67
Orange Ponzu Glaze, 305
Orange-Saffron Marinade, 53
Orange-Saffron Marinated Tilapia in Parchment, 101
Orange-Sesame Chicken Stir-Fry, 322
Orange Sesame Marinade, 282
Orange–Star Anise Glaze, 302
Orange–Star Anise Glazed Scallops with Smoked Pepper Powder, 320
Orange-Tarragon Marinade, 54
Passion-Fruit Glaze, 190
Quick Orange Aioli, 247
Red Currant Marinade, 58
Savory Orange Glaze, 72
Stir-Fried Carrots in Orange-Cinnamon Marinade, 127
Yucatecan-Style Brine, 171
Oyster sauce, 273

P

Pantry items
American South and Southwest, 130
Asian, 272–75
basic, 43
Eastern Mediterranean, Middle East, and North African, 251–52
Latin American and Caribbean, 169–70
liquor, 41–42
Mediterranean, 215–16
Papayas
Island Caramel, 188–89
Passion-Fruit Glaze, 190
Pastes
Bengal Spice Paste, 300
Charmoula, 258
curry, 287
flavor management and, 17–18
Lemon-Cumin Paste, 259
Moroccan-Style Shaslick Paste, 258
Roasted Garlic and Jalapeño Paste, 70
Sambal Mint Paste, 298
shrimp, 275
Singapore Sesame Paste, 298
Southwest Chile Paste, 142
Pastrami
Orange Duck Pastrami, 107
Orange Pastrami Spice Mix, 67
Salmon Pastrami, 93
Peach Salsa, 165
Peanuts
oil, 274
Southwestern Peanut Sauce, 162
Thai Fried Chicken, 328–29
Thai Peanut Marinade, 288–89
Tsire Rub, 260–61
Vietnamese Peanut-Tamarind Marinade, 290
Pears
Poire William Glaze, 85
Poire William Marinade, 85
Poire William Sauce, 85

Peas
Stir-Fried Snow Peas with Balsamic-Ginger Marinade, 337
Szechuan Sesame Chicken Salad, 321
Yellow Split Pea Soup with Maple Turkey Jerky, 118
Pebre, 210
Pecan-Breaded Catfish with Mustard-Buttermilk Marinade, 145
Peppercorns. See also Szechuan peppercorns
Baharat, 256–57
Basic Mixed Peppercorn Rub for Beef, 65
Basic Southern Barbecue Rub, 140
Cajun Rub, 140–41
Cognac-Peppercorn Cured Salmon or Salmon Pastrami, 93
Grilled Beef Tenderloins au Poivre with Gorgonzola, 244
Sautéed Tuna with Almond-Peppercorn Crust, 240
Smoked Salmon with Tangerine–Pink Peppercorn Marinade, 94
Sour Mash–Pink Peppercorn Rub, 70–71
Tangerine–Pink Peppercorn Marinade, 55
Pescado Tikin Xic, 200–201
Pesce Bianco alla Siciliana, 237
Pestos
Chimichurri Pesto, 185
Cilantro-Ginger Pesto, 301
Fines Herbes Pesto Rub, 69
flavor management and, 17–18
Lime-Cilantro Pesto, 301
Rosemary-Mint Pesto, 69
Pineapple
Grilled Pineapple–Coconut Glaze, 309
Grilled Turkey Kabobs with Pineapple Glaze, 204
Island Caramel, 188–89
New Mexican Pineapple Marinade, 135
Pineapple-Jalapeño Salsa, 164
Pineapple-Teriyaki Glaze, 304
Swordfish and Pineapple Seviche, 194
Piri-Piri Marinade, 174
Plums
Plum-Cassis Glazed Pork Tenderloin, 120
Plum-Cassis Glaze or Baste, 86
Plum sauce, 273
The Asian Rib Cage, 323
Cantonese Glaze, 303
Plum Sauce Glaze, 302
Poire William
Poire William Glaze, 85
Poire William Marinade, 85
Poire William Sauce, 85
Pomegranate molasses and juice, 43, 252
Ginger Pomegranate Glaze, 300
Grilled Duck Breast with Pomegranate-Cognac Glaze, 110
Grilled Lamb Kabobs with Syrian Honey-Pomegranate Glaze, 267
Maple-Pomegranate Glaze, 87